AMERICAN FASCISM

Brynn Tannehill

AMERICAN FASCISM

How the GOP is Subverting Democracy

Brynn Tannehill

TRANSGRESS·PRESS

Dedication

To Paul Lowes: You put up with me all the way through high school and mentored me through my capstone paper on late-stage politics in the Weimar Republic. This book, almost 30 years later, wouldn't have been possible without you. It's one of the great regrets in my life that you didn't have the opportunity to read what you inspired.

To Monica Roberts: You were never afraid to say it like it is, call a fool for what he was, or speak truth to power. I hope this carries on the tradition in a way you would have found pleasing.

Table of Contents

Figures

Tables

Preface

"We cannot get out. The end comes soon. We hear drums, drums in the deep. They are coming."

— J.R.R. Tolkien

I've always had an interest in how democracies collapse. In high school and college, I wrote my capstone papers on how the political infighting between center, left, and communist parties in the Weimar Republic paved the way for its downfall. I spent the middle part of my military career desperately trying to prop up weak democracies in Iraq and Afghanistan against theocratic, totalitarian insurgencies. My post-graduate work used econometrics to build models to predict which countries in Africa were most likely to descend into civil war and genocide. I wanted to be able to allow people to see the very earliest quantitative signs of things going sideways.

Then, in 2015, Trump ran for office. Like most Americans I initially treated it like a joke. I thought that the Republican Party (GOP) was committing suicide, and that this was the last gasp of the Tea Party. But then, something he said during his speeches pricked up my ears. Trump kept repeating the phrase, "One people, under one God, saluting one flag."[1] I had heard this phrase before, but it wasn't in English.

This was way too close to the mottoes of both the Second and Third Reich for my comfort: *"Ein Reich. Ein Volk. Ein Gott."* (One nation. One people. One God.), and *"Ein Volk, Ein Reich. Ein Führer!"* (One people. One Nation. One Leader!), respectively.

This is when I began to hit the panic button, when few others were. I had seen this before, and it didn't end well. Everyone could see that this was a right-wing populist candidacy, but there was always the assumption that things would be fine, because this is America. There were so many excuses: Trump can't win. We're not that stupid, as a country and as a people. The system will prevent him from doing too much harm even if he is elected. The courts. The federal bureaucracy. The Republican establishment. The norms of our institutions and our democracy. The constitution itself.

Just days before the 2016 election on Halloween, I had one of the most memorable and eye-opening conversations of my life. I was attending a behind-the-scenes meeting for LGBTQ leaders, and the topic of discussion was what we were going to focus on going forward and how we were going to do it. Most of the folks were leaders of grassroots movements; I was brought on board as a futurist and opposition analyst who mostly hung out in the back with the senior legal analyst to temper people's enthusiasm with unpleasant realities.

As the day went by, I realized something; everything we discussed was predicated on Hillary Clinton winning the White House. During a break, I took one of the conference organizers aside. "So… what are we going to do if Trump wins?" I asked.

"He's not gonna win," he replied confidently.

"Yeah, but suppose he does? There's a chance. What are we going to do then? We're in deep trouble, and all this…" I gestured around the room, "…doesn't happen. What's the plan?"

"I don't know. I guess we'll figure it out when it happens," my friend replied.

This answer wasn't reassuring and, as someone who had studied military history, it was a poor strategy. The late-19th century French military philosophy of *debrouillez-vous* ("we'll muddle through somehow") is generally looked back upon as precisely how not to plan for conflict. And, in fact, neither the LGBTQ community nor Democratic leadership ever came up with an effective answer for how to deal with Trump and the GOP's autocratic attempt.

As the initial shock in the days after the 2016 election wore off, I was filled with a cold dread. I knew this was going to be bad. The only thing limiting how bad it would be over the next four to eight years was how far into authoritarianism the GOP would be willing to go and how fast. A few people who studied democratic decline understood precisely how dangerous right-wing, theocratic, nationalist populist movements are. As a member of one of the groups this movement actively despises, the danger was far more than academic. I wrote this in the week following the election:

> "People want to know why the hell I'm so scared as a transgender person after the election of Donald Trump. Why the hell I'm updating my passport. Why my wife is renewing her Canadian passport and getting citizenship papers lined up for our three kids. We're consolidating 401k's, and establishing lists using his-

torical analogies on what events trigger our departure, and how quickly those contingency plans would have to be implemented to get out of Dodge on a moment's notice...

In case you hadn't noticed, we are now a nation with one political party controlling virtually everything. The White House. The U.S. Senate. The Supreme Court (especially after Trump's nominees are confirmed). The U.S. House of Representatives. Thirty-three of the fifty Governors' Mansions, and 67 of 98 State Legislative Chambers.

The system is rigged, but not the way Donald Trump claimed. Due to gerrymandering, most state legislatures are unwinnable to Democrats. And in most of these states where Republicans control the legislature, the demise of the Voting Rights Act (VRA) means that voter suppression laws will skew gubernatorial, Presidential, and Senatorial races further to the right.

It won't get better either. A Supreme Court full of little Scalias will not strike down gerrymandered districts, voter suppression, or any of the million legalistic or bean-counting ways Republicans can use to ensure that they never leave power. In 2018, 25 seats held by Democrats will be up for election, and only eight are held by Republicans. In 2020 when they conduct the census, and districts are drawn up for the 2022 election, two-thirds of the states will still likely have Republican majorities across all three branches, and the gerrymandering situation is likely to get even worse.

It is no coincidence that Clinton underperformed in the polls so badly in the first election since the VRA was struck down. It's also part of the Democratic death spiral we have entered. As demographics get worse and worse for Republicans, the more they will suppress the vote and rig districts. In turn, elected officials will look less and less like the people in their states and represent their interests less and less. For elected Republicans, as a result of gerrymandering, there is also a perverse incentive to ignore people in your state who aren't just like you: white, Christian and straight.

Which is why I look at the protests and realize just how little they really mean: not only is there zero reason for these Republican legislators to give a damn, but they would be actively punished by their constituents if they did.

If transgender people and leadership are expecting things to get better in the legislatures, or preparing for "a better day," they need to think again. By 2040, we're looking at a brown majority nation that has been completely disenfranchised, impoverished, and demonized by an aging white aristocracy, while police forces have been given carte blanche to keep their Republican masters in power. There's only one ending to a situation like this, and when those police forces decide it's not worth protecting the autocracy anymore, the end looks a whole hell of a lot like what happened to Nicolae Ceaușescu.

The cavalry ain't coming until most everyone reading this is dead..."

Masha Gessen also identified the gravity of the situation at the same time I wrote my thoughts on why I believed we were in deep trouble. In their famous essay on surviving autocracy, written days after the election, they articulated the basic rules:

Rule #1: Believe the autocrat. He means what he says. Whenever you find yourself thinking, or hear others claiming, that he is exaggerating, that is our innate tendency to reach for a rationalization.

Rule #2: Do not be taken in by small signs of normality.

Rule #3: Institutions will not save you. It took Putin a year to take over the Russian media and four years to dismantle its electoral system; the judiciary collapsed unnoticed.

Rule #4: Be outraged. If you follow Rule #1 and believe what the autocrat-elect is saying, you will not be surprised.[2]

As a nation, we failed to follow most of these. Most people did not want to believe the truth about Donald Trump, even when he carried through with nearly every anti-democratic promise he made, such as refusing to acknowledge election results. The press constantly showered him with praise as having finally grown into the presidency whenever he delivered a speech that wasn't nationalistic gibberish. We kept counting on institutions like the FBI, Department of Justice, and Senate to save us. Democrats spent four years pretending all of this was normal, definitely not fascist, and definitely not a soft coup. By the end, we had simply lost the capacity for outrage, even as Trump and much of the GOP launched a naked attempt to overthrow the American government.

By the end of Trump's four years, it was clear to most outside subject matter experts that American democracy wasn't just in steep decline, but that we were in the middle of an autocratic attempt. It required a black swan event in the form of COVID-19 to prevent an autocratic breakthrough of a second Trump term, which would almost certainly have guaranteed a fall into permanent minoritarian single-party rule.

The U.S. was one of the world's oldest and most stable democracies. Theoretically, what we just saw happen shouldn't be possible. The founding fathers foresaw the possibility of demagogues and populists and believed they had devised a system to prevent it. Alexander Hamilton wrote in the *Federalist Papers*: "The process of election affords a moral certainty, that the office of President will never fall to the lot of any man who is not in an eminent degree endowed with the requisite qualifications."

Throughout all of this, I kept asking the question: how could this happen? How did we end up with a radicalized, reality-challenged, right-wing populist movement in charge of most of the government? Is this ascendant movement fascist, and what does that mean for us?

I went back to my training as an analyst and crash scene investigator to understand how we had bypassed all the safety mechanisms that had been intended to prevent demagogues and autocrats. During my final year in the Naval Reserves, I trained to investigate when aircraft go down to help determine if they had been shot down, or if it was an accident. This process looked much like a National Transportation Safety Board (NTSB) mishap report: we mapped out the sequence of events that led to the crash in detail, investigated all the key contributing factors that led to that moment in time, combined the two to determine how and why the aircraft ended up making an unscheduled landing that left a crater, and determined what would need to change to prevent similar results in the future.

The worst possible outcome to these investigations is that future fatalities are inevitable due to inherent flaws in the aircraft. At that point, there's often nothing that can be done other than ground the fleet and start over. It doesn't work that way for a country, though; there is no pause button to redesign a government that must function continuously.

NTSB reports tend to be comprehensive and holistic in their approach to what causes mishaps: from the design history of the aircraft to what the pilots had for lunch. This book is meant to provide a similar approach to understanding what has happened to the U.S., and what will likely continue to occur. Factors include U.S. history, the role of modern media, religion in America, economics, political science, law, the historical characteristics of right-wing populism and fascism, and academic theories on democratic decline. There are many great books by Pulitzer Prize-winning journalists and Nobel Prize-winning economists that touch on these, but none on all of them.

After years of literature review, this book is the first that I am aware of that attempts to pull all of these elements together to paint a complete picture of how and why the U.S. seemed to fall so fast and so far. It's meant for political junkies and academics alike; both can hopefully learn something new given the broad-spectrum approach.

However, this book also serves as a warning. The U.S. never seriously confronted the fact that a fascist movement attempted a coup, even if it was stupid and ill-conceived. So was the Beer Hall Putsch of 1923. Moderates and progressives fail to reckon with the difficulty of addressing the underlying issues that facilitated an autocratic attempt, and that the next would-be autocrat has a massive highly motivated base just waiting to embrace them. Until that day, media sources with an unreality-based agenda will keep this base at a frothing boil, waiting for the next strong man savior.

Thus, I say this as a helicopter pilot who never flew with a parachute after basic flight training: given how polarized we are, and how hard it is to make structural changes to our government, I am forced to conclude that more likely than not we're riding this one all the way in until the next, more successful autocratic attempt and breakthrough.

One

The Original Sin

"It did not start with Donald Trump; he is the symptom, not the cause."
Barak Obama

As a pilot, one of the first things that they teach is that catastrophic mishaps do not occur in a vacuum. There is almost always a long chain of human failures leading up to the moment where everything goes horribly, catastrophically wrong, and everyone dies on impact. The disaster could have been avoided by changing any one of the many bad decisions responsible for it. There can be a host of contributing factors, such as poor maintenance practices, cutting corners on costs, engineering flaws, manufacturing issues that go undetected, lack of training for pilots, or pilots using non-standard procedures.

This is an apt metaphor for where the American political system was during much of the Trump Administration. We were in what appeared to be an unrecoverable, uncontrolled 500 knot vertical dive. The people up front knew how screwed we were; everyone in back was terrified and helpless; and the preventable factors that led up to the situation started long before we hit the point of no return.

But instead of poor maintenance practices, bad training, tired pilots, or task-saturated air traffic controllers, the root cause of where we are at today can be traced to the two original sins of our nation: racism and slavery.

Slavery and the Genesis of Modern American Politics

"Any general acceptance of disenfranchisement requires a show of democracy."
Richard M. Valelly

People easily forget that the U.S. has only been a democracy for about 55 years. Before that, the right to vote was forbidden, or insufficiently guaranteed for vast swathes of the population. Race, religion and geography are the great divisions in America since its inception. Thirty-four of the 47 people depicted in John Trumbull's painting commemorating the signing of the Declaration of Independence

13

were slave owners.[1] The original U.S. Constitution also made it clear that the union was something of a shotgun marriage, where slavery and racism were the biggest sticking points. The "Three-Fifths Compromise" counted Blacks as a fraction of a person. The Second Amendment was put in place at the insistence of slave states, particularly Virginia. The primary purpose of militias in the south at that time was to put down slave rebellions, like the one in 1739 in Stono, South Carolina.[2] The 1820 Missouri Compromise was little more than a band-aid that was eventually ripped off by the Taney Supreme Court.

After the fractious 1856 elections, the political landscape became drawn along fairly clear boundaries based on attitudes toward slavery. The issue was unavoidable, once the Taney Supreme Court's 1857 Dred Scott decision negated the Missouri Compromise, enshrined discrimination against Blacks in the constitution, and allowed slavery to spread to every territory of the U.S.[3] Democratic President James Buchanan's ineptitude helped drive the U.S. further down the path to Civil War as well.[4] Finally, the election of 1860 was the breaking point, leading to the Civil War, which killed between 620,000 and 750,000 people and wounded another 419,000.[5]

During this time, Southerners viewed a future without slavery in apocalyptic terms that went far beyond their fear of losing cheap labor. South Carolina Senator John C. Calhoun, one of slavery's most ardent defenders, described his vision of what a post-emancipation South would look like. In his mind, Blacks would be:

> "Raised above whites… in the political and social scale. We would, in a word, change the condition with them—a degradation greater than has ever yet fallen to the lot of a free and enlightened people, and one from which we could not escape… but by fleeing the homes of ourselves and our ancestors, and by abandoning our country to our former slaves, to become the permanent abode of disorder, anarchy, poverty, misery, and wretchedness."

One of the most important splits over slavery was within the Baptist Church. In 1845, Southern Baptists split from the church over its prohibition on slave owners serving as missionaries. Southern Baptists believed this prohibition meant the church thought that "slaveholding brethren were less than followers of Jesus."[6] They devoted themselves to the task of finding apologetics such as the "Curse of Ham," which claimed black skin was a curse on a son of Noah from the Old Testament, to prove that the King James Bible not only justified slavery, but encouraged it.[7]

This led the Southern Baptist Convention (SBC) and its theological seminary to become two of the dominant political and religious organizations defending first slavery, and then segregation. It was not until 1995 that the SBC acknowledged their role in both, and even a 2018 report by the organization glossed over many of the details of their active role in these institutions.[8] This is crucial, given that by the mid-twentieth century it was the largest denomination in the U.S.[9] However, Catholicism doesn't get a pass either. Census data showed that one-fifth of all the Catholics in Maryland in 1785 were slaves.[10]

The debate over slavery produced division within the parties as well. At the Democratic Convention of 1860, Northern Democrats put forward the (relatively) moderate Stephen Douglass (D-IL), who believed that each state should be allowed to decide whether slavery was legal. This was essentially an extension of the status quo created by the Kansas-Nebraska Act of 1854, which allowed those two states entering the Union to organically decide the issue of slavery. The resulting rush to "pack" the states, and allegations of election fraud, resulted in several rounds of elections, competing legislatures and bloodshed.

The hardline Southern Democrats walked out of the 1860 convention when it failed to adopt a resolution to support extending slavery into territories whose voters did not want it. While this sounds extreme, there was a calculus behind the decision: Southern Democrats were well aware of how demographics and public opinion were shifting in the country. They could clearly see that in the long run they were nearly certain to lose influence, as a smaller and smaller percentage of Americans supported slavery. With much of the territory of the Western United States waiting for statehood, it was only a matter of time before a constitutional amendment abolishing slavery would be passed. They knew that time, demographics, and the tide of history were going to end the institution upon which their entire political, religious, and economic system depended.

The Constitutional Union Party was formed by remnants of the Know Nothing and the Whig parties to avoid secession and ignored the issue of slavery altogether. They carried most of the slave-states that separated the North from the South: Tennessee, Kentucky, and Virginia. They almost carried Maryland as well, losing by 722 votes out of 92,000 cast.[11] There was perhaps a certain pragmatism to these states' positions: a large number of the bloodiest battles fought in the Civil War were fought in Tennessee, Maryland, and Virginia.

Republicans were the party of the North and the far western states of California and Oregon. The party's positions on slavery in 1860 ranged from staunchly abolitionist to a willingness to let demographics and time take care of the issue. Abraham Lincoln was selected as the nominee because he was seen as the moderate choice, and he had alienated fewer constituencies than some of his rivals at the convention.

Figure 1. Results of 1860 Presidential Election

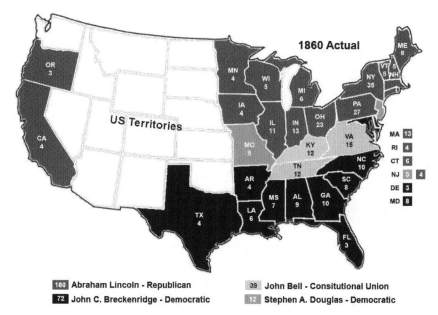

Source: Data from 270towin.com

Southern politicians liked to couch their claims in words like "freedom" and "equal rights," but clearly it did not extend beyond white men. Basil Manly, Sr., chaplain at the Alabama Secession Convention, prayed that representatives might "promote the maintenance of equal rights, of civil freedom, and good government, and promote the welfare of man, and the glory of Thy name!"[12]

From a modern standpoint it is hard to square this with the words of Alexander Stephens, future Vice President of the Confederacy, who gave his infamous "Cornerstone Speech" a few weeks later. He stated that the Confederacy's "cornerstone rests upon the great truth, that the Negro is not equal to the white man; that slavery—subordination to the superior race—is his natural and normal condition. This, our new government, is the first, in the history of the world, based upon this great physical, philosophical, and moral truth."

Blacks who lived in this system of divinely ordained chattel slavery took a rather dim view of the hypocrisy of their Christian masters endorsing freedom and equal rights exclusively for white people. Frederick Douglass recalled of his former slave masters:

"The man who wields the blood-clotted cowskin during the
week fills the pulpit on Sunday, and claims to be a minister of
the meek and lowly Jesus... He who sells my sister for purposes
of prostitution, stands forth as the pious advocate of purity... I
have seen him tie up a lame young woman, and whip her with
a heavy cowskin upon her naked shoulders, causing the warm
red blood to drip; and in justification of the bloody deed,
he would quote this passage of scripture—"He that knoweth
his master's will, and doeth it not, shall be beaten with many
stripes."""[13]

After the Civil War, there was a brief period where Blacks were able to vote
and held office. This was due to the passing of the 13th, 14th and 15th Amendments, which freed the slaves, guaranteed equal protection under the law and
(theoretically) guaranteed the right to vote. It also helped that Union troops oc-
cupied the south to help ensure the enforcement of U.S. law. Between 1870 occupying and 1900, 22 Blacks served as Representatives in Congress, two as Senators.
This situation was intolerable to white Southerners. It was seen as a humiliation
to be represented by a Black man.

The Colfax Massacre may have been the most important instigating event in
the failure of Reconstruction and was a direct result of Black men holding elected office in the South. After the disputed Louisiana election of 1872, the Klan
and other local whites trapped approximately 100-150 Black freedmen and state
militia members at the Grant Parish courthouse in Colfax, Louisiana. They shot
at it with a cannon and set fire to the building, forcing those inside to surrender.
The mob took them prisoner and executed all the survivors several hours later.
President Ulysses S. Grant was enraged by this slaughter, calling it a "butchery"
that "in bloodthirstiness and barbarity is hardly surpassed by any acts of savage
warfare."[14]

Today, two monuments mark the site. Both were erected by whites. They por-
tray the Blacks as "rioters," rather than as people making a desperate last stand
against white terrorists bent on mass murder. One plaque mourns the three white
men killed in the attack on the courthouse. The other celebrates how the killings
"marked the end of carpetbag misrule in the south."[15]

Seventy-two men were charged with these murders under the Enforcement
Acts of 1870, which had been passed to allow the federal government to take
legal action against the Klan. Many of those charged admitted freely to having
participated. However, their convictions were overturned by the Supreme Court
in the 1876 case of *United States v. Cruikshank*. The court found that the federal

government only had authority to enforce the Fourteenth Amendment (equal protection) against governments, not individuals. This effectively ended the authority of the Enforcement Acts.

The final nail in the coffin of Reconstruction came in 1877. The 1876 election was intensely contested, and the Democratic (southern controlled) House of Representatives refused to count the electors. The stalemate was broken when the House offered a deal: They would allow Republican Rutherford B. Hayes to take office if sitting President Ulysses S. Grant removed all remaining Northern troops from the south and granted southern states the right to deal with Blacks without interference. Republicans took the deal, called the Compromise of 1877. It effectively destroyed Republican influence in the South, Reconstruction and any hope for Black Americans.[16]

With the failure of Reconstruction, the white Baptist South gleefully fell back into its antebellum ways of corruption, racism, segregation, disenfranchisement, and single-party rule by Democrats. Republicans had attempted to address the ongoing racial discrimination in the South with the Civil Rights Act of 1875, which was intended to guarantee that everyone in the United States was "entitled to the full and equal enjoyment of public accommodations and facilities regardless of race or skin color." The Supreme Court, however, found the Civil Rights Act of 1875 unconstitutional in 1883. It ruled 8-1, based in part on *Cruikshank*, that the 14th Amendment did not give Congress the right to prevent discrimination by businesses or individuals.

Similarly, in 1879 the Supreme Court ruled in *Virginia v. Rives* that all-white juries trying a Black person were constitutional, since an all-white jury was not proof of discrimination. The Civil Rights Act of 1875 had been intended to prevent all-white juries, but after it was overturned, Southern states easily found ways to exclude Blacks. The most notorious post-Reconstruction civil rights case was *Plessy v. Ferguson*. In 1896 it enshrined the legality of segregation under the concept that came to be known as separate but equal. This marked the end of any chance for civil rights for another 58 years. It was not overturned until *Brown v. Board of Education* in 1954.

Few attempts were made to address racial discrimination after 1876. In the North, the Republican Party came to be dominated by financial and industrial elites with no interest or appetite for civil rights for Blacks. Henry Cabot Lodge's 1890 Federal Elections Bill would have allowed federal oversight of elections and helped ensure Blacks could vote; but it failed. The North abandoned Blacks to their fate and left the South in the hands of illiberal democracy, where a toxic brew of racism, religious justification, corruption, single-party rule, and Supreme Court decisions turned into almost 80 years of Jim Crow.

Systematic disenfranchisement was the cornerstone of putting white, evangelical Democrats back in power in the South. In 1893 Alabama state Senator Anthony D. Sayre introduced legislation explicitly meant to prevent Blacks from voting, declaring that it, "eliminates the Negro from politics, and in a perfectly legal way." He went on to become Chief Justice of the Alabama Supreme Court in 1901, where he spent the next 22 years systematically suppressing Black civil rights.[17]

Black election turnout in the South dropped from 96 percent in 1876 to 61 percent in 1880, to 11 percent in 1898, to two percent in 1912. By 1896 in Tennessee it was close to zero. The entirety of the American South was back in the hands of the very men who had fought for slavery.[18] Similar trends were seen elsewhere in the South, such as Louisiana. Laws that were neutral on their face (such as the grandfather clause, poll tax, and understanding clause) were used to systematically disenfranchise Blacks after the collapse of Reconstruction and throughout Jim Crow.

Figure 2. Voter Registration Rates by Race in Louisiana, 1878 - 2010

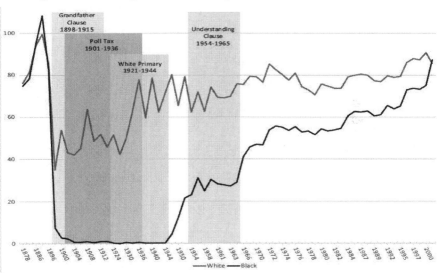

Source: Keel, Cubbison, and White[19]

Any efforts to end this disenfranchisement were swiftly met with overwhelming force. The worst election day violence in the history of the U.S. happened on November 2, 1920 in Ocoee, Florida. Moses Norman, a Black man, tried to vote, but was turned away. That evening a white mob surrounded the house where he was believed to be hiding. Gunfire broke out, and in the end at least seven were lynched, with the true total more likely in the range of 30 to 60. Their bodies were likely cast into a mass grave or dumped in a nearby alligator infested lake. Many homes and the local Black church were burned. The rest of the Black citizens in the town fled or were forced out, and their land effectively stolen. No one was ever prosecuted for this mass murder. The leader of the mob became mayor.[20]

White Northerners had ceased to care about the issue of civil rights because Blacks now had theoretical equality, resulting in a period of relative political unity and stability that lasted until the late 1960's. Thus, the blame for this tragedy of American history falls not only upon the racism of the white South, but also on Northerners and the courts. Both thwarted efforts to prevent horrors at every turn, agreeing with the arguments put forth by those committing atrocities. Adam Serwer of *The Atlantic* summarized this period in history:

> "The justices did not resurrect *Dred Scott v. Sandford's* antebellum declaration that a black man had no rights that a white man was bound to respect. Rather, they carefully framed their arguments in terms of limited government and individual liberty, writing opinion after opinion that allowed the white South to create an oppressive society in which black Americans had almost no rights at all. Their commitment to freedom in the abstract, and only in the abstract, allowed a brutal despotism to take root in Southern soil."[21]

This should sound familiar: the Roberts Court is accepting similar arguments to undermine civil rights today, not just for Black people, but also for LGBTQ people, women, the disabled, people over 40, immigrants, Muslims, union workers, and anyone that white Southern evangelicals have deemed a threat to the existing moral order. We are already seeing results in cases today that will likely be remembered in the same breath as *Cruikshank, Rives,* and *Plessy.*

The Beginnings of a Demographic Shift

> *"The evils in the North are not easy to understand and fight against, or at least not as easy as Jim Crow... There are few specific injustices, such as a segregated lunch counter, that offer both a clear object of protest and a good chance of victory. Indeed, the problem in the North is not one of social injustice so much as the results of institutional pathology."*
>
> Bayard Rustin

Prior to World War I, geography generally dictated demographics. But, as the centers of Black population moved, so did parties and politics. Broadly speaking, the political patterns of the states did not change much between the end of the Civil War and 1932. Republicans carried western and northern states, though the western states were more often in play than others.[22] Democrats carried the south. It was not until 1884 that Democrats again took the White House in a closely fought election. Grover Cleveland won by winning the tipping point state of New York by only 1,200 votes out of over a million cast.[23]

In 1928, Republican Herbert Hoover ran on a platform of continuing the peace and "prosperity" seen during the Harding and Coolidge administrations in the 1920's. The prosperity was something of an illusion. Business-friendly policies resulted in the highest levels of wealth inequality seen in the United States up until that time.[24] Simultaneously, a demographic shift was occurring. Blacks in the American south had been migrating northwards since 1916, seeking work in Northern factories and an escape from the omnipresent oppression of the south. Between 1916 and 1940 approximately 1.6 million rural Blacks moved to northern cities. The military build-up of World War I, the roaring twenties economy, and the increased availability of transport (rail and automobile) facilitated what became known as "The Great Migration."

The Blacks coming north were Republicans both out of tradition, and because the Democratic Party was still the Southern party of discrimination, Jim Crow, and racism.[25] By one estimate, somewhere between two-thirds and three-quarters of Blacks living in northern urban wards voted for Republican Herbert Hoover in 1932.[26] However, Hoover's failed economic policies and his efforts to cozy up to southern segregationists began to sour Black voters on the Republican Party. Black voters had also been hit harder than most by the Great Depression, and Hoover had failed to address a staggering Black unemployment rate of 38 percent.[27]

Franklin D. Roosevelt (FDR) also initially did little to court Black voters. His evasive positions on civil rights and his segregationist Texan of a running mate, John Garner, held little appeal for them. However, by 1936 he had taken some limited steps to address the economic concerns of Blacks via New Deal programs. Predictably, Blacks ended up excluded from many of these programs in the South, a casualty of Roosevelt's deal to gain Southern Democrats' support for the legislation. Nevertheless, the 1936 Black vote swung dramatically towards Democrats—over 70 percent voted for FDR.[28]

Their hopes in FDR were somewhat rewarded in 1937, when the Supreme Court partially overturned *United States v. Cruikshank* along with *De Jonge v. Oregon*, which found that the 14th Amendment applies to individuals in some circumstances—in this case, limitations on the freedom of assembly.

Post WWII and the Civil Rights Movement

"These are not bad people. All they are concerned about is to see that their sweet little girls are not required to sit in school alongside some big black bucks."

President Dwight D. Eisenhower

During World War II and continuing through the 1970's, a second phase of the Great Migration of Black Americans occurred. It was over three times larger than the first. These two phases transformed the political landscape. They were a big reason why Northerners were finally willing to tackle the issue of civil rights again, and also set in motion the cataclysmic changes in the Republican Party that would transform it into the party of white evangelical southerners.

President Harry Truman, a Democrat who hailed from the southern state of Missouri, was infuriated by reports of Black veterans returning to their homes in the South and facing further violence and persecution after making tremendous contributions in World War II. Such tales motivated him to desegregate the military via Executive Order 9981. This antagonized much of the Democratic southern base, and Truman was forced to fire Secretary of the Army Kenneth Claiborne Royall in 1949 for deliberately failing to implement his desegregation orders. President Truman also signed executive orders forbidding discrimination on the basis of race in civil service and forming a committee to ensure defense contractors did not discriminate either. Truman also supported the elimination of poll taxes and federal anti-lynching laws (which were not actually passed until 2019).

These civil rights actions by Truman caused a major fracture in the Democratic Party and led to South Carolina Governor Strom Thurmond running as a third-party candidate in the 1948 Presidential Election. Thurmond's platform focused on defending segregation. He deemed the civil rights movement a stepping-stone to "communism," and declared that electing Truman would lead to "totalitarianism."[29] When Thurmond and his States Rights Democratic Party tried to sound more moderate, they made appeals to states' rights, individual liberty, and limited government, just as the Confederacy did in 1861. They also made appeals to "secure and maintain Southern tradition, civilization and ideals." They denounced evidence that "Negroes" weren't inferior to white people as "pseudo-science." They attacked the civil rights movement as unconstitutional, and civil rights laws as a violation of their own personal freedoms.[30] In the end, Thurmond won Louisiana, Mississippi, Alabama, and South Carolina, and earned 39 Electoral College votes. It was not enough to deprive Truman of a win and did not change the ultimate outcome of the election.

Figure 3. States Requiring Segregation Before *Brown v. Board of Education*

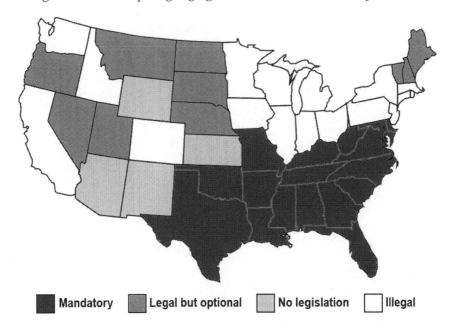

| **Mandatory** | **Legal but optional** | **No legislation** | **Illegal** |

The last segregated military unit was disbanded under the Eisenhower administration in 1954. More important, however, was the *Brown v. Board of Education* decision which overturned *Plessy v. Ferguson*, and segregation with it.

Eisenhower's status as a war hero won him an overwhelming majority of Electoral College votes in 1952, carrying all nine southern states. He even managed to take Florida and Texas as a Republican, the first time the GOP managed that in 24 years. Still, his support for desegregation was tepid at best. While the Eisenhower Department of Justice filed an amicus brief in support of Brown, Eisenhower himself pulled Chief Justice Earl Warren aside and admonished him. "These are not bad people," he said, referring to Southerners supporting segregation. "All they are concerned about is to see that their sweet little girls are not required to sit in school alongside some big Black bucks."[31] Warren was appalled by the encounter.

Eisenhower's response to the decision itself was exactly what you would expect of a military man forced to follow an order he didn't particularly agree with: "The Supreme Court has spoken, and I am sworn to uphold the constitutional process in the country. And I will obey." During the 1956 Presidential campaign, the Republican Party platform stated that it "accepted" the ruling, rather than "concurring" with it. As a result, Eisenhower neither hindered nor led on civil rights issues, reflecting the continuing Republican indifference to civil rights. Eisenhower explained his lack of support for civil rights legislation with: "You cannot change people's hearts merely by laws."[32]

The 1960 Presidential Election deepened the schism between northern and southern Democrats. While civil rights were not one of the top overall issues in the elections, they were extremely important to two opposing groups: southern segregationists and Black Americans. The Democratic national platform affirmed the party's desire to "create an affirmative new atmosphere in which to deal with racial divisions and inequalities which threaten both the integrity of our democratic faith and the proposition on which our nation was founded—that all men are created equal."[33] The platform supported government efforts to desegregate schools and ensure voting rights. These positions did not sit well with southern Democrats, and would be a major factor in their Electoral College votes.

Despite most voters' disinterest in civil rights, Martin Luther King, Jr. may have decided the 1960 presidential election. Dr. King was arrested and imprisoned in Georgia on trumped up charges from a peaceful Atlanta protest in which he participated. Vice President Richard Nixon, who previously had a warm relationship with Dr. King, quietly asked Eisenhower to pardon him. After this was rejected, Nixon let the matter drop, apparently deciding that he needed white southern votes more than he needed Black votes in a decision that presaged—and possibly precipitated—his Southern Strategy.[34]

Senator John F. Kennedy (D-MA), however, was convinced by campaign advisors and ardent civil rights proponents to take a much more active role in supporting Dr. King.[35] Kennedy ended up calling Coretta Scott King and Dr. King's father. He also called Governor Vandiver of Georgia to secure his release, cajoling him with a mixture of thinly veiled carrots and sticks.[36]

This cleared Kennedy's reputation as a vacillator on civil rights, and the election of 1960 ended up being one of the closest in modern American history by vote count. Kennedy won with 49.72 percent to Nixon's 49.55 percent. Black voters were at least partially responsible, as Nixon got 7 percent less of the Black vote than Eisenhower had in 1956. Some Republicans believed Kennedy's actions swung crucial states with large Black populations into the Democratic column.[37]

There was a price to be paid for this, however. All eight of Mississippi's electors refused to follow the popular vote. Instead of casting their ballots for Kennedy, they did so for Harry Byrd (D-VA), a segregationist senator from Virginia. Six of Alabama's 11 did the same, and so did one of Oklahoma's. This presaged the wider split that was coming, which would become permanent after 1976.

Two

The Rise of the Religious Right

"The Democratic Party has abandoned the people. It has repudiated the Constitution of the United States; it is leading the evolution of our nation to a socialistic dictatorship."

Senator Strom Thurmond, on leaving the Democratic Party and becoming a Republican because of the Civil Rights Act

If one event could be said to be the watershed event that guaranteed the exodus of southern evangelical segregationists into the Republican Party, and made Blacks a core Democratic demographic, it was the Civil Rights Act of 1964. The Civil Rights Act (CRA) finally codified into federal law bans on racial discrimination in employment and public accommodations, while also providing the means to enforce this law. President Kennedy had proposed this legislation in 1963, and President Johnson pushed it forward after Kennedy's assassination.

The federal government made the novel argument that the CRA was constitutional under the Commerce Clause of the Constitution. It also had the advantage of a more liberal Supreme Court that, with the precedent of *Cruikshank* weakened, had upheld *Brown v. Board of Education* and mandated its implementation. Thus, the Civil Rights Act of 1964 was far more likely to survive challenges than similar acts proposed during Reconstruction.

Modern Republicans try to cast the Civil Rights Act as a fight between Democrats and Republicans, and like to claim credit for its passage. However, it is far more accurate to describe the debate as between former slave-holding segregationist states and the rest of the U.S. While there were far more Democrats in Congress from the old South than Republicans, southern Republicans were just as likely (if not more so) to oppose the CRA as their democratic counterparts. Conversely, northern Democrats were more likely to support the CRA than their Republican counterparts. Indeed, not a single southern Republican voted for the CRA.

Table 1. Votes for the Civil Rights Act of 1964

House of Representatives

	Yea	Nay	Percent in Favor
Southern Democrats	7	87	7 percent
Southern Republicans	0	10	0 percent
Northern Democrats	145	9	94 percent
Northern Republicans	138	24	85 percent
Total	290	130	69 percent

Senate

	Yea	Nay	Percent in Favor
Southern Democrats	1	20	5 percent
Southern Republicans	0	1	0 percent
Northern Democrats	45	1	98 percent
Northern Republicans	27	5	84 percent
Total	73	27	73 percent

The Guardian[1]

After the CRA passed, legend has it that President Johnson turned to his press secretary and remarked, "I fear we have lost the South for a generation."[2] Whether or not this is true, events since then have essentially eliminated white southern Democrats from Congress, and there is little reason to believe this will change anytime soon. Strom Thurmond,[3] who ran as a segregationist in 1948, switched parties to become a Republican in 1964 as a result of the CRA, claiming Democratic civil rights efforts would pave the way for America to become a "socialist dictatorship."[4]

The 1964 Presidential Election solidified the migration of blacks to the Democratic Party. Senator Barry Goldwater (R-AZ), known as "Mr. Conservative," courted southern states with talk of limited government and states' rights—music to segregationist ears. Additionally, Goldwater had voted against the CRA because he claimed it was government overreach. As a result, Goldwater carried less than 6 percent of the Black vote, compared to Nixon's 32 percent in the previous election.[5] This sort of rapid, radical demographic shift is almost unheard of in modern politics. On the other hand, Goldwater carried the states of Louisiana, Mississippi, Alabama, Georgia, and South Carolina. No Republican had carried them all before and none since 1876. The 1964 election also represented something of a high-water mark for radicals within the GOP, at least until the Tea Party came along.

During the 1950's, Republicans had been caught up in Wisconsin Senator Joseph McCarthy's witch hunt for communists. After this flamed out, the staunchly anti-communist and paranoid John Birch Society (JBS) rose in 1958. It was initially spearheaded by some conservative heavyweights like William F. Buckley Jr., who soured on the organization quickly and urged Goldwater to distance himself from it in 1962.[6] Buckley had reached the conclusion that the Society was "nuts" after they alleged that over half the U.S. government was controlled by the Reds, and that President Eisenhower was a "dedicated, conscious agent of the communist conspiracy."

At the time, the GOP had the good sense to try to expel the craziest aspects of its base. Richard Nixon repeatedly stated that, "members of the John Birch Society should either get out of the Republican Party or get out of the Birch Society."[7] Goldwater, who also took a hard line on relations with the Soviet Union, once stated that, "extremism in defense of liberty is no vice," and was popular with JBS members. Goldwater denounced some of the JBS leadership's comments but refused to distance himself from the base. As a result, he was seen in the 1964 election as extremist, radical, and unhinged. He lost by a landslide.

As part of the McCarthy, JBS and Goldwater dynamic, historian Richard Hofstadter identified what he called the "paranoid style in American politics" in 1964. He found that in the history of American politics paranoia offered an outlet and tool for politicians to identify and harness "the sense of heated exaggeration, suspiciousness, and conspiratorial fantasy" as a political weapon.[8] His observation remains true nearly six decades later.

However bad the loss was, the post-1964 ideological and electoral shift towards Southern states represented an opportunity for the Republican Party. There is considerable debate over whether the party's "Southern Shift" in 1968 was a top-down Nixonian strategy, or a bottom-up grass roots effort led by southern churches. Regardless, Nixon courted states on the border between the North and the South (e.g. Kentucky, Tennessee, Missouri) by running on a "law and order" and "states' rights" platform, which served as dog whistles for existing opposition to the civil rights movement.

White House Chief of Staff Harry R. Haldeman noted that Nixon "emphasized that you have to face the fact that the whole problem is really the blacks. The key is to devise a system that recognized this while not appearing to."[9] By the 1970 mid-term elections, there appears to have been a clearer focus on picking off Dixiecrats like Albert Gore, Sr. of Tennessee. Nixon campaign advisor Kevin Phillips observed in 1969, "White Democrats will desert their party in droves the minute it becomes a black party."[10]

Kevin Phillips, author of *The Emerging Republican Majority* in 1969 and inspiration for Nixon's Southern Strategy, homed in on exploiting polarization, animosity towards Lyndon Johnson, and fear of Blacks and the Civil Rights movement as the way to bring the South into the Republican fold. "Republicans would be short-sighted if they weakened the Voting Rights Act. The more Negroes who register as Democrats in the South, the sooner the Negrophobe whites will quit the Democrats and become Republicans," he wrote at the time.[11]

In April 1970, Nixon's Department of Labor produced a memo titled, "The Problem of the Blue-Collar Worker." It, too, identified a divide-and-conquer strategy for the White House to pursue:

> "Recent reports have identified the economic insecurity and alienation which whites in this group have felt... The blue-collar worker is more prone to transfer his economic and social frustrations to racial and ethnic prejudices... They are overripe for a political response to the pressing needs they feel so keenly... they feel like 'forgotten people'–those for whom the government and society have limited, if any, direct concern and little visible action."[12]

If this appeal to "the forgotten" white people sounds familiar, it should be. The Trump campaign was populated with "Dirty Tricksters" like Roger Stone who cut their political teeth in the Nixon administration in which the catchphrase "forgotten people" was used repeatedly to refer to non-college educated whites throughout his campaign and administration.[13]

By the Presidential elections of 1972, Republicans had swept the South. In 1976, Jimmy Carter, an evangelical governor from Georgia, became the last Democratic presidential candidate to carry most of the region. Arkansas governor Bill Clinton carried about half of southern states in 1992 and 1996. Since 1996, however, the South has remained solidly Republican, excepting swing states Virginia, and Florida.[14] Republican dominance of the South today is comparable to Democratic dominance pre-1965, but the demographic driving this control is the same: namely, white evangelicals. This deliberate exodus of whites from the Democratic Party to the GOP became known by political scientists as "the great white switch."[15]

Their Origins as Segregationists

"Mark my word, if and when these preachers get control of the [Republican] Party, and they're sure trying to do so, it's going to be a terrible damn problem. Frankly, these people frighten me. Politics and governing demand compromise. But these Christians believe they are acting in the name of God, so they can't and won't compromise. I know, I've tried to deal with them."

Senator Barry Goldwater (R-AZ)

There is a certain irony to the fact that Goldwater, who wasn't that alarmed by the beliefs of the John Birch Society's members, eventually found the prospects of southern preachers controlling the GOP terrifying. He said this in 1994, after decades of watching how the religious right tore down democracy and institutional norms. At heart, Goldwater was more of a libertarian than anything else, and the prospect of theocracy was appalling.

Religious conservatives had stopped believing that religion was primarily a private function and concluded that it was part of one's public political identity instead in great part due to the Civil Rights Movement.[16] Their potent cultural force drove the political shifts of the South during the 1950's, 1960's, and 1970's, even before they became a distinct political entity. They led the intellectual charge away from Democrats and into the arms of whomever was willing to entertain their ideals and goals regarding civil rights and segregation. It was an open secret that the Klan drew its strength from evangelical churches in the South and worked hand in glove (or head in hood) with them. According to The Journal of Southern History in 1956:

> "A number of students investigating the Klan noted a close tie-up between it and Protestantism. These writers generally agree that the Klan worked hand and glove with the more Fundamentalist denominations, that it received the open or tacit support of countless clergy-men, and that many of its officers were Protestant ministers. Moreover, both the secular and church press occasionally carried news items telling of the Klan visiting a church."[17]

Generations of children in the U.S., and particularly in the South, were taught that southerners had been the victims of vengeful federal occupying forces, had black politicians forced upon them, and were victims of "carpetbaggers" stealing their political and economic power. The "Lost Cause" had become a part of their religion. They grew up surrounded by statues to Robert E. Lee, Stonewall Jackson and Jefferson Davis erected everywhere in the south between 1900 and 1930 in response to this belief.

Churches erected after the Civil War frequently featured stained glass with the Confederate battle flag ("stars and bars"), General Robert E. Lee, and General "Stonewall" Jackson. Not limited to Southern Baptists, white Methodist churches also "promoted white supremacy during the civil rights era."[18] These symbols were even in the National Cathedral in Washington, D.C. until 2016 and 2017, respectively.[19]

Whites-only Churches themselves were used as meeting places to plan and assemble for many of the over 2,000 lynchings of Black Americans between 1865 and 1950. This includes the infamous case of Samuel Thomas Wilkes in 1899 in Georgia, who killed a white man in self-defense.[20] Whites went directly from their churches on an Easter Sunday to storm the courthouse, drag Wilkes out and burn him alive. One of the people in the crowd reportedly yelled out, "Glory! Glory be to God!" as Wilkes screamed and thrashed in agony to escape the flames. Afterwards, the churchgoers took his charred bones as souvenirs.

Thus, it should come as no surprise that opposition to integration was centered on white, southern churches and religious leaders. Robert P. Jones, in his book *White Too Long*, discusses the integral role churches and religion played in America's racist history, our present, and our reluctance to acknowledge the link:

> "Much of the recorded history of slavery, segregation, and racism gives scant treatment to the integral, active role that white, Christian leaders, institutions, and laypeople played in constructing, maintaining, and protecting white supremacy in their local communities... white churches served as connective tissue that brought together leaders from other social realms to coordinate a campaign of massive resistance to black equality. But at a deeper level, white churches were the institutions of ultimate legitimization, where white supremacy was divinely justified via a carefully cultivated Christian theology."[21]

In 1956, shortly after the ruling in *Brown v. Board of Education*, there was perhaps no more influential Southern Baptist figure in the nation than W.A. Criswell, the pastor of the First Baptist Church in Dallas. In a speech to the Southern Baptist Convention in 1956 he outlined what would become the "religious freedom" argument for decades to come:

"Don't force me by law, by statute, by Supreme Court decision...to cross over in those intimate things where I don't want to go. Let me build my life. Let me have my church. Let me have my school. Let me have my friends. Let me have my home. Let me have my family. And what you give to me, give to every man in America and keep it like our glorious forefathers made–a land of the free and the home of the brave."[22]

This 60-year-old rhetoric has been a prescient guide to understanding the longstanding efforts to establish a seemingly libertarian religious right to discriminate and segregate, based on the First Amendment. Indeed, Criswell's arguments that discrimination is natural and good is still used today by libertarian-sounding right-wing outlets such as The Federalist.

Dyed-in-the-wool segregationists like Bob Jones, Jr. (for whom the university is named) formulated the religious arguments for segregation and racism. In 1960 he gave a sermon, later turned into a 32-page pamphlet, titled "Is Segregation Scriptural?" His answer was, unsurprisingly, yes. Based on a single verse (Acts 17:26, *ESV*), he concluded:

And he [God] made from one man every nation of mankind to live on all the face of the earth, having determined allotted periods and the boundaries of their dwelling place... Now, what does that say? That says God Almighty fixed the bounds of their habitation... God Almighty did not make of the human race one race in the sense that He did not fix the bounds of their habitation. That is perfectly clear. It is no accident that most Chinese are in China."[23]

He implied that God put different people in different places because he didn't want them together, which made desegregation a violation of God's plan, and therefore a sin.

Jones' argument was born from the same "Curse of Ham" rationale used to justify slavery: that black people are the descendants of Ham who had been cursed by God to live in subordination to whites (i.e., those without "the mark"). Throughout the Civil Rights movement, Southern Baptist preachers and congregations were among the most reliable defenders of segregation. The Southern Baptist Convention did not formally renounce teaching the Curse of Ham until 2018.[24] Historian (and former Baptist) Wayne Flynt described the SBC as "the last bastion of segregation."[25]

It almost goes without saying that Southern Baptist churches were segregated, or *de facto* so. When a liberal theologian invited Martin Luther King, Jr. to speak at his church in 1961, the backlash nearly cost him his job. On Sunday June 9, 1963, NAACP field secretary Medgar Evers led a group of white and black civil rights activists to attend services at segregated Baptist and Methodist churches in Galloway Mississippi. These were, at the time, the two largest in the state. They were also the home congregations of the governor of Mississippi and mayor of Galloway, respectively. Evers and his fellows were turned away and threatened with arrest.[26] Three days later, Evers was assassinated by a local white supremacist. This was suspected to be retaliation (at least in part) for Evers attempting to enter a white church.

In 1968, the First Baptist Church of Oxford, Mississippi voted to ban blacks from services. This was one of the last attempts by the SBC and other white southern evangelicals to overtly impose segregation before the Supreme Court essentially made it illegal.[27] This same year, the SBC convention voted to endorse desegregation, while at the same time electing Criswell president of the organization.[28]

Fights over efforts to desegregate schools continued in the later 1960's and into the 1970's. Evangelicals created segregated private schools funded by tax-free donations, but they were denied tax-exempt status by the Supreme Court.[29] In 1970, the IRS began sending letters to evangelical Christian schools to verify compliance with the CRA. This included schools run by Jerry Falwell, Sr. and Bob Jones, Sr., which they considered a valuable source of revenue, recruiting, and indoctrination. Falwell was not happy. "In some states," he complained, "It's easier to open a massage parlor than a Christian school."[30]

Rise of the Moral Majority

Until the 1970's, there had been a certain reticence among white evangelical leaders to meddle directly in politics. Jerry Falwell, Sr. maintained that, "Preachers are not called to be politicians, but to be soul winners."[31] Unsurprisingly, his opinion changed once the IRS began targeting the tax-exempt status of segregated Christian private schools like his.

While Bob Jones, Sr. decided to fight the IRS in court (losing in the process), Falwell decided to try to turn the tide culturally and politically. For this, he turned to an up-and-coming young Catholic Conservative politico named Paul Weyrich, founder of the conservative think tank The Heritage Foundation and the American Legislative Exchange Council (ALEC) to help him start a political movement.[32] While Weyrich had bigger designs (particularly on abortion), fighting back against integration was the *entrée* he needed to leverage conservative religion into politics.

He had Falwell quickly pivot away from Bob Jones' arguments and instead encouraged rallying around the argument of "religious freedom." He argued that since Falwell's schools didn't take federal money, the government couldn't tell them how to run their schools. They re-framed the issue of segregated schooling as one of a big, intrusive federal government agency attacking good, honest Christians who just want to send their children to schools reflecting their values. Not only did this stave off charges of racism, but it also tapped into the indignation of aggrieved southern evangelical whites who were losing the battle to keep their schools segregated.

Thus, in the mid-70's, Weyrich crafted a messaging playbook that is still used today:

> "The new political philosophy must be defined by us [conservatives] in moral terms, packaged in non-religious language, and propagated throughout the country by our new coalition... When political power is achieved, the moral majority will have the opportunity to re-create this great nation."

Weyrich recognized that coded language appealing to racism had succeeded in wooing white evangelicals into politics where other issues had failed. He latched onto these racial dog-whistles to help keep evangelical religious schools segregated, as it was the issue that evangelicals cared most about at the time. But, he also recognized that couching religious beliefs in secular sounding apologetics were more likely to be successful in swaying a larger audience.

It is important to note that this embryonic religious right, and its affiliated connections within the Republican Party, had little anchorage in abortion and LGBTQ issues. Weyrich knew that these issues had failed to hook evangelicals in the early 1970's and did not focus on them. The Southern Baptist Convention expressed support for laws liberalizing abortion access in 1971.[33] Criswell himself expressed support for the Supreme Court's decision in *Roe v. Wade*, taking the traditional theological position that life began at birth, not conception.[34]

Weyrich wasn't the only one to realize that white evangelicals were an untapped source of political power. Gary Jarmin, a lobbyist for the Christian Voice organization, noted at the time that, "The beauty of it is that we don't have to organize these voters. They already have their own television networks, publications, schools, meeting places and respected leaders who are sympathetic to our goals."[35]

When Jimmy Carter, a self-described born again Christian ran for president in 1976, it raised hopes among some white southern evangelicals that they would find a sympathetic ear in the White House. He carried about half of their vote, which was a significant increase. However, evangelicals quickly turned against him as he failed to halt the IRS' removal of tax-exempt status from segregationist religious schools.[36]

Ronald Reagan challenged incumbent President Gerald Ford in the 1976 Republican primaries, and his strategy revolved around trying to win southern states as a continuation of Nixon's Southern Strategy. Reagan shared much of Nixon's world views on communism and race.[37] One theme of Reagan's campaign against Ford was "welfare queens" cheating hard working, tax paying, real (read: white) Americans out of their money.[38] While Reagan did not succeed in unseating Ford for the party's nomination, he was exactly the sort of politician Weyrich and Falwell were looking for after Carter failed to deliver.

Weyrich credited inaction by Carter with the genesis of the white evangelical religious right as a political force: "What galvanized the Christian community was not abortion, school prayer, or the E.R.A. I am living witness to that because I was trying to get those people interested in those issues, and I utterly failed. What changed their mind was Jimmy Carter's intervention against the Christian schools."[39] They were also angered, to a lesser extent, by the perception that Carter did not actively fight against gay rights and the Equal Rights Amendment hard enough.[40] By the 1980 election, Carter was roundly denounced as an enemy of Christian family values by the evangelical community.[41] Paul Weyrich and Jerry Falwell were recognized, even then, as key figures influencing this shift.[42]

Weyrich and Falwell wanted to change the traditional Southern Baptist stance of avoiding direct participation in political debates. Falwell was furious with Carter, saying that "godless, spineless leaders have brought our nation floundering to the brink of death."[43] Thus, in June 1979, Weyrich and Falwell founded the Moral Majority, a Southern Baptist-dominated umbrella organization for political action committees dedicated to spreading conservative (white) Christian political influence. It became the model for other such organizations. During its heyday in the 1980's it was one of the largest political lobbying groups in the United States. The Moral Majority helped rebuild the electoral ground game of the moribund Republican Party in the South, and greatly aided Ronald Reagan's 1980 election.

It wasn't until 1979 that the issue of abortion took center stage. This was primarily the brain-child of Paul Weyrich.[44] Having succeeded in winning over evangelicals, he now worked to convince their leaders that this issue was now more palatable to the rest of America than that of keeping Black children out of white Christian schools. The "hook" issue for evangelical voters as late as 1980 remained the fight against integration. When presidential candidate Ronald Reagan spoke to the SBC in August of 1980, he never mentioned abortion. His did, however, explicitly support the SBC's position on private religious schools and vigorously denounced the "unconstitutional regulatory agenda" directed by the IRS "against independent schools."[45]

Thus, evangelicals swung hard to Ronald Reagan and away from Carter in 1980. This happened despite Carter trying to put policies in place reducing the number of abortions performed in the U.S., and Reagan signing the most liberal abortion law in the country as Governor of California in 1967.[46] While somewhat revisionist history credits popular concern for conservative social issues with the rise of the Moral Majority and the modern Republican Party, those inside the Reagan campaign knew differently.

Lee Atwater was a Republican strategist for Reagan, and later became the chairman of the Republican National Committee. After the 1980 election, he spoke candidly about what really swung the voters:

> "You start out in 1954 by saying, "N...r, n...r, n....r." By 1968 you
> can't say "n...r"—that hurts you, backfires. So you say stuff like,
> uh, forced busing, states' rights, and all that stuff, and you're get-
> ting so abstract. Now, you're talking about cutting taxes, and all
> these things you're talking about are totally economic things and
> a byproduct of them is, blacks get hurt worse than whites....
> "We want to cut this," is much more abstract than even the bus-
> ing thing, uh, and a hell of a lot more abstract than "N....r, n....r.
> So, any way you look at it, race is coming on the backbone."[47]

In other words, he acknowledged that using carefully coded racist language that appealed to erstwhile segregationists was the key to winning them over. Not abortion. Not gays. Not the ERA. From the top down, there were efforts to swing the South with racism. At the same time, evangelical leaders like Falwell helped create the grassroots movement that could effectively and willingly respond to these dog whistles.

The Moral Majority faded out by the late 1980's, but not before mapping out the path to political power for a host of other organizations that followed. Focus on the Family transformed from a radio show in the 1970's to a lobbying power-house by using these strategies. The Family Research Council (founded by James Dobson of Focus on the Family), the Heritage Foundation, and the Alliance Defending Freedom all worked closely with the Trump White House and Department of Justice to implement and legally defend social and tax policies favorable to the evangelical right and conservative Catholics. They influenced the Trump Administration into packing the courts with lawyers representing, or employed, by religious right organizations.

The Alliance Defending Freedom spends much of its efforts on enshrining the First Amendment right for religious conservatives to individually and collectively ignore civil rights laws. They argue that these rights allow adoption agencies (conservative and religious, of course) to exclude gays and lesbians, and even Jews and Catholics as potential parents. They also argue that these rights permit them to kick LGBTQ students out of schools.

Indeed, school segregation—as in keeping LGBTQ youth, youth with LGBTQ parents and LGBTQ teachers out of religious schools--remains one of the religious right's top priorities today. So, too, is ensuring that they won't lose federal funding or their tax-exempt status if they discriminate on the basis of sex, sexual orientation, or gender identity. Nor do they have to comply with labor laws, after the decision in *Our Lady of Guadalupe School v. Morrissey-Berru*, which extended the "ministerial exception" to employees like nurses, teachers, and even janitors. The fight for segregation and a religious right to ignore civil rights laws lives on, whether we recognize it or not.

Reagan Fails to Deliver

"It just isn't going to work, and it's very interesting that the man who invented this type of what I call a voodoo economic policy is Art Laffer, a California economist."

George H.W. Bush, April 1980

Republican racial hostility spread beyond the segregated schools' debates and bled over into economics. America had a long history of punishing Blacks with economic policies such as "red lining," and the Reagan administration carried these efforts on by other means.[48] Lee Atwater's vision for turning economic policy into a coded-language call to war on Blacks worked in the long run. It acted as a political wedge and damaged the economic prospects of Blacks in the United States. This quiet war of economic inequality outlasted the Reagan administration, surging all the way through Clinton's terms in office, and continues today. Economic warfare was not the religious right's first choice for carrying on their battle for segregation, but it is what they got. More than any other policy, it was perhaps the Reagan administration's most significant contribution to the democratic decline experienced during the 2010's.

White evangelicals entered the Reagan administration with high hopes for what they could accomplish. Two days after being inaugurated, Reagan hosted Falwell and other ministers at a White House meeting. Falwell was ecstatic. "We now have a government in Washington that will help us," he declared.[49] They believed Reagan and his Attorney General, William Smith, would help them to get a favorable Supreme Court ruling that allowed segregated Christian private schools to retain their tax-exempt status. Some, like Weyrich, were eager to begin reshaping the court in their own image.

The Family Protection Act proposed by the religious right was their marquee piece of legislation. This evangelical wish list contained 31 items, including limiting access to abortion by minors, taking funding from any school that limited school prayer, and extending tuition tax credits for private schools (and presumably for those that remained segregated). So ebullient was their mood in early 1981 that they believed it would pass. These dreams died quickly, however. Reagan's top priority was dealing with the country's terrible recession. Huge tax cuts for the wealthy, spending cuts to social programs, tight money policy at the Federal Reserve, and increasing defense spending were the focus of his administration, rather than social policies exclusively favoring the Christian right.

Thus, The Family Protection Act was dead on arrival due to lack of support from moderate Republicans. Stand-alone bills to eviscerate Roe v. Wade went nowhere. Reagan was forced to abandon his promise to protect the tax-exempt status of segregated private schools. The first Supreme Court vacancy that came up in July 1981 was filled by Associate Justice Sandra Day O'Connor, a libertarian-ish moderate from Arizona who had supported the ERA and abortion rights as a state senator. In 1983, after decades of legal wrangling, and without the support of Reagan's Attorney General, Bob Jones University finally lost its Supreme Court case to retain its tax-exempt status as a segregated institution by an 8 to 1 vote. O'Connor concurred with the majority. Only Justice William Rehnquist dissented.

The religious right's reaction to Reagan's abandonment of their agenda was mixed. Paul Weyrich was extremely dissatisfied, both with Reagan and with his fellow religious conservatives. He believed they were too happy with their "meaningless access" to the Reagan Administration. "What overshadowed all their concerns was simply the pleasure of being able to get in... They didn't want to do anything to jeopardize that."[50] When asked to give a grade to the Reagan Administration itself, he rated it as "barely passing."[51] Still, Weyrich had established one of the central grievance narratives of white evangelicals for decades to come: that the government would take away their freedoms, unless a strong leader who would thwart the judicial system came to power.

As a conservative Catholic primarily concerned with abortion, Weyrich was something of the outsider within his own movement. Catholic bishops had undercut themselves within the administration by opposing Reagan's social cuts and nuclear arms build-up. Falwell and the Moral Majority still had a better seat at Reagan's table than Weyrich.

Jerry Falwell, and other white evangelicals in the Southern Baptist Convention, however, embraced the Reagan administration's focus on cutting taxes, building defense, and slashing social spending. Falwell had always been a staunch anti-communist, and, like the modern Republican movement, branded anything that looked like government spending on the poor and any tax on the wealthy as a form of godless, creeping socialism. To his mind this was basically the same as communism. He had founded the Moral Majority in part to fight this, declaring that "young people have been reared under the influence of a government that has taught them socialism and welfarism."[52] Civil rights were a form of communism in Falwell's world, and he branded both Dr. King and Bishop Desmond Tutu as such.[53]

The Fall of the Moral Majority

Despite Falwell and Weyrich's claim that they registered 5 million voters for Reagan, won on free market issues, and were responsible for Reagan's landslide win in 1984 and Republican control of the Senate, the Moral Majority's influence on GOP social policy did not improve during Reagan's second term. The proposed School Prayer Amendment to the Constitution, supported mostly by Republicans and southern Democrats, failed by 11 votes in the Senate (56-44).[54] The anti-abortion amendment never even got a vote. When Republicans lost the Senate in 1987, it guaranteed that none of their legislation would move through Congress during Reagan's last two years in office.

Despite appointing the extremely conservative Antonin Scalia to the Supreme Court in 1986, the religious right's efforts to put another far right justice on the court the following year failed. The confirmation hearings of arch-conservative jurist Robert Bork (the Nixon hatchet-man responsible for pulling the trigger in the Saturday Night Massacre firing of Special Prosecutor Archibald Cox) denied Bork a seat on the bench and ended the Moral Majority's influence as a driving force in politics.

Conservative religious figures from James Dobson to Pat Robertson to Jerry Falwell, Sr., had gone all in on getting Bork confirmed. Weyrich's Free Congress Foundation was also on the front lines of the fight. Still, it wasn't enough. During Senate confirmation hearings, Bork responded to questions about *Brown v. Board of Education* with answers unacceptable to all but white southern evangelicals. Similarly, his views on women, civil rights, abortion, and even birth control were so far outside the mainstream that moderate Republicans couldn't find a way to justify voting for him.

38

After Bork went down in flames, Reagan nominated centrist Anthony Kennedy for the Supreme Court. He ended up becoming widely reviled by the religious right for his rulings on abortion (*Whole Women's Health v. Hellerstedt*) and gay rights (*Romer v. Evans, Lawrence v. Texas, Windsor v. United States*, and *Obergefell v. Hodges*). The Bork fiasco helped cement resentments surrounding the civil rights era and the conviction of religious conservatives (and particularly white southern evangelicals) that they were powerless to stop the cultural shift away from their values. It also planted a seed of hope: Perhaps the Republican Party needed evangelicals more than evangelicals needed Republicans.

Four Years in the Wilderness

"Your guilty conscience may force you to vote Democratic, but deep down inside, you secretly long for a cold-hearted Republican to lower taxes, brutalize criminals, and rule you like a king!"

Sideshow Bob, *The Simpsons*

As the disappointment over Reagan's eight years in office sank in, the Moral Majority collapsed. Falwell had struggled for years with an organization that was effectively a confederation, trying to rein in the most radical chapters' bizarre and extremist positions, including a group in Santa Clara California that called for the death penalty for gays.[55] Falwell excused these radical stances by claiming that he had no control over local leaders, although he himself had called AIDS "the wrath of God on homosexuals." When questioned about these sorts of stances, two of Falwell's aides sheepishly admitted, "We are kind of monarchists," meaning that they wanted someone to rule over the United States like an Old Testament king.[56]

Falwell, too, had become a target of both the left and right and was unpopular even in his home state of Virginia. His support of Apartheid in South Africa further marginalized him and his organization. With very little to show for his support of Reagan, funding began dropping in 1985. Finally, a shadow of what he had been earlier in the decade, Falwell resigned from the Moral Majority in 1987.

As a result, the Christian right shifted its strategy to running directly for office. Pat Robertson threw his hat into the ring during the Republican primaries for the 1988 Presidential election. On the surface, Robertson seemed like a decent candidate: an affable, mild-mannered, Ivy-League law school graduate, and well-known televangelist and media entrepreneur. At his 1985 peak, Nielsen ratings showed that 27 million viewers watched his *700 Club* broadcasts per month.[57]

Paul Weyrich and beer-baron Joseph Coors thought Robertson could win the primary. His campaign slogan was "Restore the Greatness of America Through Moral Strength," presaging the shorter and pithier "Make America Great Again" used by Trump to appeal to white evangelicals almost three decades later.

Pat Robertson came from the charismatic Christian school of evangelism which emphasizes miracles, spiritual gifts and the holy spirit. However, he was never able to unify other mainstream evangelicals, such as Southern Baptists, behind him. After running second in Iowa, he finished a distant third in New Hampshire and withdrew before the convention. The result convinced him that Christians faced a great deal of discrimination in society, which became a recurrent theme in his sermons. It also showed that a candidate relying on the evangelical vote would have to unify charismatics and others behind him like Trump, who brought prosperity gospel figures like Paula White and Creflo Dollar into the tent.[58]

Robertson's economic agenda was also far more populist than that of the Republican mainstream of the time. He tried to present himself as a fiscal conservative and business owner rather than as a preacher. However, as videos of Robertson performing faith healings and commanding hurricanes to change direction in God's name emerged, his campaign generally wasn't taken seriously.

In the 1988 general election, George H.W. Bush won 81 percent of the evangelical vote, a feat matched by Trump. They were dubious of a mainline Protestant from New England, but felt they had no choice given that they had burned all their bridges with Democrats during the Reagan Administration.[59] It could be argued that his campaign's infamous race-baiting Willie Horton advertisements, created by the equally infamous Lee Atwater, may have burnished Bush's credentials among racists somewhat.[60]

However, they were probably right to be dubious, because Bush put moderates and liberals in his cabinet and appointed David Souter, a reliably progressive vote, to the Supreme Court. Bush ignored calls for defunding the National Endowment for the Arts over the "Piss Christ" exhibit and pictures by (deceased) gay artist Robert Mapplethorpe. He also invited gay activists to the White House to discuss the AIDS crisis. Bush also raised taxes on the wealthy to deal with deficits and backed progressive civil rights and environmental laws. None of this made businesses, the wealthy, or evangelicals particularly happy. It came back to haunt him when he was held accountable in the 1992 election for breaking his "Read my lips, no new taxes" pledge.

Regardless, the Bush administration was never really in a position to focus on social policy issues. The collapse of communist Warsaw Pact states in Eastern

Europe, the fall of the Berlin Wall and German reunification, the First Gulf War in 1990-1991, the recession caused by the Gulf War, peace talks in the Middle East, and the fall of the Soviet Union in late 1991 meant that the first Bush administration was primarily focused on foreign policy, and then economic recovery. What domestic policy Bush did pursue was generally moderate or even progressive, including his signature Americans with Disabilities Act and the Clean Air Act.

Bush, a rather genteel old school Episcopalian who believed one's religion was primarily personal, was unenthusiastic at best, and deeply uncomfortable at worst, addressing social issues. When he did step into culture wars, the results were disastrous. He tried to make his 1992 campaign about "family values," using a phrase meant to appeal to the Christian right. He famously declared at the 1992 National Religious Broadcasters' convention that, "We are going to keep on trying to strengthen the American family, to make American families a lot more like the Waltons and a lot less like the Simpsons." On the very next episode of The Simpsons, Bart fired back: "Hey, we're just like the Waltons. We're praying for an end to the Depression, too."[61]

All that social conservatives could hang their hat on was the successful confirmation of Supreme Court Justice Clarence Thomas, whose bruising confirmation hearings included credible testimony that he had sexually harassed Anita Hill. Unsurprisingly, Pat Robertson's Christian Coalition had lobbied hard for Thomas. Evangelicals also lobbied for Brett Kavanaugh three decades later, the Trump Supreme Court nominee who was also credibly accused by several women of being a drunkard and a rapist.[62]

Deprived of any real influence in the White House, and amidst the world-shaking changes caused by the fall of communism, the Christian right began descending into the conspiracy theories that would haunt them, and the Republican Party, for decades to come. Pat Robertson's 1991 book, The New World Order, was a mishmash of paranoid theories claiming that a "cabal of internationalists was waging a sustained conspiracy to control the world economy and create a one-world government."[63] It also declared that former communists and the United Nations were working in conjunction with lenders to destroy American sovereignty, which echoed anti-Semitic propaganda from the early 20th century. These sorts of conspiracies emerged as one of the primary strains of unhinged agitprop that dominated right-wing talk radio during the Clinton Administration in the 1990's and presaged the post-truth politics that came to define the GOP after 2010.

The Republican Revolution of 1994

"You're fighting a war. It is a war for power."

Newt Gingrich, 1978

This paucity of successes during the Bush Administration did not go unnoticed by the Christian right. After his failed 1988 Presidential run, Pat Robertson and Ralph Reed founded the Christian Coalition as a successor to the Moral Majority. Unlike its predecessor, it was focused on the grass roots instead of pastors and attempted more centralized national control. GOP operatives Jack Abramoff (who went to prison for fraud) and Grover Norquist (who forced most Republicans to sign a pledge to never raise taxes regardless of any circumstances) had also been involved in standing the organization up.

Other Christian right organizations emerged in the 1980's and 1990's that focused almost exclusively on abortion and gay rights: The Family Research Council (FRC) in 1983 and the Alliance Defending Freedom (ADF, formerly the Alliance Defense Fund) in 1993. The FRC is primarily a lobbying organization in Washington, D.C., and ADF focuses on impact litigation in the courts. The ADF has brought nine cases to the Supreme Court in the past few decades and won them all.

Both were founded by Dr. James Dobson, who started as a religious radio show host. He also created the hugely influential organization Focus on the Family (FOF) in 1977. Though declaring itself a church to protect the anonymity of donors, Focus on the Family functions primarily as a lobbying organization. Dobson emerged in the 1990's as one of the more influential figures in Republican politics. The ADF, FRC and Focus on the Family remain among the most influential religious right organizations in politics today.

In many ways, President Clinton was the perfect foil for the Christian right. He embodied all the 1960's values they hated. He had smoked weed (but didn't inhale). He was a sexual libertine, notorious for being a womanizer, and (possibly) draft-dodger during Vietnam. He was well liked by Black Americans, and was (at the time) called "America's first Black President" by Toni Morrison.[64] Hillary Clinton was a feminist and a lawyer who scoffed at the idea she should have "stayed home and baked cookies," rather than pursue a legal career.[65] Worse: Bill Clinton was seen as a racial and religious traitor, as he was raised a white southern evangelical yet embodied none of the ideas they held dear.

The religious right, and conservative radio shock-jock Rush Limbaugh, were widely credited for helping to mobilize the right in the 1994 election that swept

Republicans into house leadership for the first time in 40 years. Democrats were not only the enemy; they were literally against God's plan. To religious conservatives, the Republic was dying, decaying from the inside. Newt Gingrich was the new avatar of their political movement and was there to kill off "the old order," and sweep in something new.[66] He epitomized the new Southern Republican: extreme, beyond compromise, and there to own the libs.

Gingrich had advised Republicans to stop using "Boy Scout words, which would be great around a camp-fire, but are lousy in politics." From his first day in office in 1979, he rejected norms of civility and bipartisan cooperation. He used over-the-top language on the floor of the House and questioned the patriotism of Democrats, comparing them to Mussolini. He handed out memos to other Republicans instructing them to use adjectives to describe Democrats like *pathetic, sick, bizarre, betraying, antifamily*, and *traitors*.

Some might be inclined to believe that American politics have always been this polarized and angry, but they haven't. Gingrich represented a turn in American political discourse. Former Georgia state Democratic Party leader Steve Anthony observed, "the things that came out of Gingrich's mouth… we had never heard that before from either side. Gingrich went so far over the top that the shock factor rendered the opposition frozen for a few years."[67] Gingrich established "politics of warfare" as the dominant Republican strategy, one that continues today. It rejects the concept of mutual tolerance and embraces actions that may be legal but are entirely damaging to the Republic and the established norms of a democratic society. Former congressman Barney Frank called him "a McCarthyite who succeeded."

Gingrich, and his scorched-earth politics of "victory at any cost," did not spring up in a vacuum. He was a reflection of the shifting demographics of the Republican Party. As the party's base had shifted towards the South (and by extension white evangelicals), it adopted the values of white evangelicals still immensely resentful of the social changes since World War II. The combination of over-heated rhetoric and demographic change resulted in the radicalization of the Republican Party, which became increasingly homogeneous when compared with the diversifying coalition of communities forming the Democratic base.

The emergence of right-wing radio personalities like Rush Limbaugh in the late 1980's and *Fox News* in the 1990's helped create an echo chamber that accelerated this process. As time went by and moderate Republicans began to disappear, the Republican Party became a party of the far right. One example of this endangered species, moderate Republican Senator Arlen Spectre of Pennsylvania, was well aware of the squeeze caused by the religious right. "If we let this thing continue to percolate without attacking it head-on, we will assure President Clinton's reelection," he noted in 1994.[68] He was right. Quantitative analysis showed that by 2015, Republican moderates in Congress were virtually extinct, and Clinton easily won a second term.[69]

Nineteen-ninety four was also the first time that Republicans controlled the majority of U.S. House seats in the South. By 1996, they controlled the majority of southern Senate seats as well.[70] The *Campaigns and Elections* study of 1994 showed that the religious right was the dominant influence in eighteen state parties, and all of the southern ones. It was also influential in thirteen others.[71]

During their 1994 campaign, the GOP pledged to pass a raft of eight reforms and ten bills if elected. This "Contract with America" was based on a 1985 speech by Ronald Reagan and focused on policies supported by at least 60 percent of the American public.[72] The bills focused on tax cuts for small businesses, term limits, welfare reform, a balanced budget requirement, tort reform, and social security reform. Most of all, though, it proposed to cut capital gains taxes in half, benefiting mostly those invested in real estate and stocks. Some credited the contract with helping sweep the GOP into power in 1994. Ultimately, very few of these largely impractical measures passed.

Gingrich had deliberately omitted contentious social issues in the contract, as few (if any) of them garnered the necessary 60 percent support and would have bogged down the more popular items. Ralph Reed and the Christian Coalition unveiled its own Contract with the American Family in May 1995.[73] It featured a mix of old items like curbs on abortion, cutting welfare in favor of religious charities, prayer in schools, and some new ones like tax credits for homemakers and children. It also proposed eliminating the Department of Education.[74] Oddly, homosexuality was hardly mentioned.

The Christian Coalition proposal was unpopular on both sides. The Pat Buchanan wing of the party called it "unduly modest," and the American Civil Liberties Union (ACLU) called it "dangerous and radical."[75] As a result, it went nowhere. Just as in 1992, when Robertson backed the incumbent Bush over Buchanan against the wishes of its base, Ralph Reed and the Christian Coalition backed the moderate Bob Dole in 1996 over Buchanan again. While Reed correctly understood that the policies and constitutional amendments the Christian right wanted would never pass, he failed to understand that these were central to the desires of the people he was representing, and that the new paradigm of the GOP base did not allow for any sort of compromise.

James Dobson took a more modern, Gingrich-like view of the 1996 election. There was no room for accomodation, and he didn't give Presidential endorsements at that time. (Later, he would endorse Trump). He had a three-hour meeting with Dole prior to the election, demanding that he take hard line positions on social issues. Dole ignored him, and Dobson voted for third party candidate Howard Phillips. Dole ended up carrying only 41 percent of the popular vote, while Clinton got 36 percent of the evangelical vote in a year when evangelical voting dropped by six percentage points.

After Clinton was re-elected in 1996, Weyrich openly despaired that the religious conservatives fueling the Republican Party were taken for granted. "The religious right saved the Republicans, but some in the GOP have already drawn the long knives to further disassociate the party from the issues of concern to social conservatives." Dobson, however, saw it as an opportunity to flex his movement's muscles. He threatened to blow the whole thing up by doing radio interviews calling for the faithful to boycott the 1998 election if the GOP refused to try to pass socially conservative bills that were effectively dead on arrival. This was the no-compromise, hardball, pointless politics of eternal warfare that Gingrich had introduced, now being turned against him.

Republicans didn't have the votes to override a Presidential veto, nor even get past a Senate filibuster. It was only a last-minute meeting with two dozen top members of the House begging Dobson not to nuke the Republican Party from orbit (or his radio booth) that got him to back down. He got his votes, which went nowhere. Still, he had enough leverage to force House Republicans to take social votes on unpopular issues they knew they could not win.[76]

Racially, white America continued its economic punishment of minorities. For all the accolades Bill Clinton received as the "first Black President," his two pieces of signature legislation disproportionately harmed Black people. Clinton used the strategy of "triangulation" when adopting popular positions, even if they aligned with the opposition. Thus, he supported the Violent Crime Control and Law Enforcement Act in 1994. This act included "three strikes" mandatory sentencing laws, money for 100,000 more police officers, $9.7 billion dollars for new prisons, and expansion of the death penalty.[77] The 1996 Personal Responsibility and Work Opportunity Reconciliation Act (PRWORA) was meant to "end welfare as we know it," but instead mostly just left lower income individuals more vulnerable to economic crises like the 2008-2009 Great Recession, where Black family median wealth was devastated and never recovered.[78]

It speaks volumes, however, that the only common grounds Democrats and Republicans could find in the 1990's were in laws that punished poor Blacks and

LGBTQ people (via the Defense of Marriage Act). They contributed to their lasting poverty and facilitated the age of mass incarceration. Still, the fact that the Clintons acted on racial dog whistles and anti-LGBTQ animus wasn't enough for the right to drop their vendetta against the couple.

The 1998 impeachment of President Clinton represented a high-water mark for the influence of Reed and Robertson's Christian Coalition. Their base had been fed a steady diet of conspiracy theories about Clinton since day one of his Administration, from rumors that Hillary had Vince Foster killed, to the New World Order using black UN helicopters to spy on the American public. When news of the Monica Lewinsky affair broke, Gingrich and other socially conservative members of the House thought there was an opportunity. Reed, and the Christian Coalition, enthusiastically supported the impeachment. However, public opposition to the impeachment hovered around 66 percent, and his impeachment failed in the Senate.[79]

This was an embarrassing defeat. Already weakened after the 1996 election and suffering from years of declining revenue, as well as IRS penalties and investigations, the Christian Coalition essentially ceased to function. Ralph Reed moved on to become a political consultant. The immovable Dobson, however, remained where he was. His organizations (ADF, FRC, FOF), along with The Heritage Foundation, went on to become the dominant entities in the culture wars to come. The only victories they achieved during the Clinton Administration were where their views overlapped with fiscal conservatives and Clinton's strategy of triangulation, such as welfare reform and the Defense of Marriage Act. For a block with such theoretical clout, they had little to show for it.

However, they had learned that they had some electoral clout, or at least enough to prevent insufficiently conservative Republicans from being elected President. Thus, they could function as king-makers after the 1996 election. They were no longer afraid to burn the party down in order to get their way. Which, in the end, is exactly what they did in 2016.

Three

Abandoning Democracy

"Remember, democracy never lasts long. It soon wastes, exhausts, and murders itself. There never was a democracy yet that did not commit suicide."

John Adams

Most Republicans in Congress had stopped playing the democracy game in the 1990's, preferring a scorched-earth, winner-takes-all approach to governance. The Christian right realized as early as Clinton's second term that there was precious little hope for constitutional amendments permitting school prayer or banning same-sex marriage or abortion. By the end of George W. Bush's (a.k.a "Dubya") second term, this had hardened into conventional Republican wisdom.

This is also when Republican presidents began to win despite losing the popular vote. Since 1988, a Republican has won the popular vote only once. Both their social stances and economic policies were drifting further and further away from the mainstream American public. The Great Recession of 2008 was fueled by greed and a lack of risk management by the government. It left average Americans reeling, while the people who caused the catastrophe received government bailouts. Tax cuts for the wealthy, *laissez faire* capitalism, and "let the market decide" weren't winning at the ballot box. Thus, the GOP establishment recognized that the only way to win in the long run was to rig the game permanently.

Decades of right-wing propaganda have taken its toll as well. Right-wing "news," politics, and entertainment melded into a singularity from which not even truth could escape. The GOP and its media arm had cultivated "crazies" as their base for years; inevitably they found a way to seize the levers of power that the GOP had tried to keep them away from, whereupon they promptly drove the world's oldest surviving democracy to attempt suicide.

Dubya

"Our enemies are innovative and resourceful, and so are we. They never stop thinking about new ways to harm our country and our people, and neither do we."

George W. Bush

During the 2000 Presidential election primaries, the Christian Right was faced with a relatively easy choice: John McCain, or George W. Bush?

Bush was somewhat problematic, as he was running on a platform of "compassionate conservatism," thereby signaling his unwillingness to embrace the culture-wars of Republicans like Pat Buchanan. Still, Bush had his own "born again" narrative and wasn't afraid to talk about his faith. But McCain? He was a hard "no" for religious conservatives. Much like his Arizona predecessor Barry Goldwater, McCain was disdainful of what he called the "whackadoodles" or "crazies" of the Republican Party, who had until then been kept (mostly) in check and at arm's length.[1]

In 2000, McCain showed little interest in wooing social conservatives. For their part, they already viewed his proposed campaign finance reforms with suspicion and hostility, due to the effects they would have on Christian non-profits.[2] It was their belief that if McCain won, Christian conservatives would have very little say in the White House.

Oligarchs and plutocrats weren't big fans of McCain either. His tax cut plan delivered less than 2 percent of its benefits to the top 1 percent, as opposed to Bush's plan, which gave them 40 percent of the benefit. McCain's tax cuts weren't central to his campaign, and in his opinion the GOP focused on them too much. Similarly, McCain relied on small donor contributions to finance his 2000 primary campaign and criticized the GOP's reliance on big money donors. Having been caught up in the Savings & Loan scandal of the late 1980's and early 1990's, McCain championed removing money and lobbyists from politics and regarded tax breaks for companies with large lobbies as unethical.[3]

After McCain won the New Hampshire primary by a landslide of 19 points, Christian conservatives rallied behind Bush. Jerry Falwell and James Dobson both went on the offensive against McCain: "I will certainly speak out when I see overt displays of hostility toward conservative people of faith, especially when it is emanating from the party that historically welcomed and encouraged our participation," wrote Falwell. McCain fired back, calling Falwell and Robertson "agents of intolerance."

48

Though not directly attributable to the religious right, a smear campaign against McCain in South Carolina ensued. Rumors and robocalls accused McCain's adopted Bangladeshi daughter, Bridget, of being the result of an illicit union. This tapped into latent racism, as well as longstanding white evangelical revulsion at the idea of miscegenation.[4] It was sufficient to propel Bush to a convincing win in South Carolina, and McCain rapidly faded into the rear-view mirror.

Evangelicals flexed their muscles in the general election, as well as the primaries. They constituted 40 percent of the votes for Bush on election day. Despite Al Gore being a life-long Southern Baptist, 84 percent of white church-going evangelicals voted for Bush. Bush narrowly won Florida by 537 votes, which decided the election. His religious base could reasonably claim credit for pushing Bush across the line. Even without a strong national organization acting as a political machine, the religious right was a demographic capable of determining who would be president, and they knew it. "Without us, I do not believe George Bush would be sitting in the White House," remarked Pat Robertson.

Before Bush ever took office, any hopes of being a "uniter," as he claimed during the campaign, were quickly dashed by Tom DeLay (R-TX). After Gingrich had left the House in disgrace in 1998, House Majority Whip Delay became the real Republican power in Congress. DeLay was known as "The Hammer" for the heavy-handed tactics he used to keep other Republicans in line with his beliefs, and for his no-holds-barred style of politics with his opponents, using any and all means available to get his way. He had no respect for tradition, and his K-Street Project was essentially a pay-to-play operation for lobbyists. One fellow Republican described DeLay's philosophy on governance as: "If it wasn't illegal, do it."[5] Tom reportedly told the incoming president: "We don't work with Democrats. There'll be none of that uniter-divider stuff."

Even with DeLay's encouragement, Bush failed to move his faith-based initiatives bill through the Senate. In the end, he simply issued an executive order establishing a faith-based initiative office in the White House. This office ended up being an unaccountable slush fund that kept no central records, but did provide millions of dollars to conservative pet projects like abstinence-only sex education. Bush also forbade discrimination against religious organizations seeking federal funding, which the Supreme Court later ensconced into Constitutional law in the case of *Trinity Lutheran v. Comer*.[6]

Bush delivered in other ways as well. He signed a "partial birth" abortion ban into federal law in 2003. He also placed social conservatives throughout his administration, such as Kay Coles James at the U.S. Office of Personnel Management. Previously, she had been a board member at Focus on the Family and the Senior Vice President at the Family Research Council. As of this writing, she is President of The Heritage Foundation.

The Bush White House maintained continuous communication with the religious right, holding frequent scheduled conversations. Paul Weyrich observed of Bush in 2001 that "I've been through five Republican administrations, and the effort to communicate with conservatives and to understand our concerns and address our concerns and involve us in the process is the best of any of the Republican administrations, including Ronald Reagan. In fact, far superior to Ronald Reagan."[7]

Like Reagan and Trump, Bush passed tax cuts in 2001 and 2003 that primarily benefited the ultra-wealthy and drove up the deficit. These enjoyed only modest public support, though in 2001 this could be excused by the fact that the budget was (at that time) not yet running a huge deficit. Like most economic policies, it also served to worsen wealth inequality, which is discussed in detail in Chapter 7.[8]

The attacks on September 11th, 2001 changed the American cultural narrative from a "melting pot" to a war of us vs. them, a fight against "evil" and battle with Muslims, which appealed to the religious-right base. Franklin Graham, who became one of Trump's staunchest and most influential supporters in 2016, declared Islam to be "wicked and evil" in the days following the attacks.[9] While Bush sometimes tried to push back against the most extreme pronouncements against Islam and Muslims, evangelicals were strongly supportive of U.S. military operations in both Afghanistan and Iraq: 80 percent of evangelicals supported the latter in 2003.[10] Even in 2007, after most Americans no longer supported the Iraq War, a majority of evangelicals continued to. Like his father, war and a recession sucked most of the oxygen out of the room for advancing conservative social issues during Bush's first two years. However, unlike Dubya's father, a culture war bigger than sacrilegious art or Bart Simpson was thrust upon him.

In 2003, the Supreme Court poured gasoline on the fire of conservative outrage with its 6-3 decision in *Lawrence v. Texas*, which ruled that sodomy laws (primarily targeting gay men) were unconstitutional. Antonin Scalia, in a blistering dissent, bemoaned the fact that religion could not be used to set moral law, and (correctly) predicted that this ruling would lead to legalization of same-sex marriage throughout the United States.[11] Worse, from the perspective of religious conservatives, four Republican-appointed Justices (Kennedy, O'Connor, Stevens, and Souter) voted with the majority.

The panic was immediate. In September 2003, James Dobson declared that "unless we act quickly, the family as we have known it for 5,000 years will be gone. With its demise will come chaos such as the world has never seen."[12] The right-wing rhetoric reached a fever pitch after the Massachusetts Supreme Judicial Court ruled on November 18th, 2003 that the state's ban on same-sex marriage was unconstitutional. While these pronouncements of doom if lesbians and gays were allowed to marry might seem odd today, in 2003 only 33 percent of the public supported same-sex marriage.[13] It was one of the few culture-war issues to exceed Gingrich's theoretical 60 percent threshold of public support for the GOP to embrace it as a platform, which is why such issues weren't part of the Contract with America in 1994. Thus, it represented one of the only times in recent memory where a socially conservative culture war issue was broadly popular.

Bush campaign strategist Karl Rove also recognized that he needed to mobilize evangelicals and the religious right to win reelection in 2004. The Federal Marriage Amendment (FMA) to the constitution had been introduced in 2002 as a means to prevent courts from allowing lesbians and gays to marry. Written by Robert Bork (among others), it failed to gain enough traction in Congress to make it out of committee while the country was reeling from the 9/11 attacks and fighting two simultaneous wars. Bush pivoted quickly from letting states decide to allow civil unions[14] to offering implicit support for the FMA during his State of the Union address in January 2004. "Activist judges," he said, "have begun redefining marriage by court order, without regard for the will of the people and their elected representatives... If judges insist on forcing their arbitrary will upon the people, the only alternative left to the people would be the constitutional process."[15]

When the FMA failed to make it through Congress in the summer of 2004, anti-marriage equality initiatives were placed on the ballots of 13 states. All would go on to pass and were considered to be instrumental in getting out the vote for Bush. This is particularly true in the swing state of Ohio, where Bush won by only 60,000 votes in 2004; however, the ballot initiative to amend the state constitution to forbid same sex marriage passed by a 62-38 margin. Bush's campaign had also gone to great lengths to ensure evangelicals came out to vote for him, some of which were only marginally better than *quid quo pro* kickbacks, such as the millions in unregulated, no strings attached grants to conservative Black church organizations in swing states.[16]

Breaking the Faith with Democracy

"I believe we have probably lost the culture war. That doesn't mean that the war is not going to continue... But in terms of society in general, we have lost."

Paul Weyrich

Despite winning the White House again in 2004, the Christian right remained pessimistic. They knew that, in the long run, they were losing the culture wars. Demographic and cultural trends were not moving in their favor on LGBTQ issues, abortion was a stalemate, and they had to reluctantly admit that there was no plausible path to passing the FMA. This left the door open to a future Supreme Court ruling mandating the legalization of same-sex marriage. They saw a society changing in ways that they could not control and once again were being left further behind. As a result, some within the Christian right and the GOP began to look to other non-democratic countries as potential models for achieving their aims. Thus, when the Christian right met Vladimir Putin, a seed was planted.

When the Soviet Union collapsed, many evangelicals (and the Mormon Church) saw it as an opportunity to spread their brand of religion. Communists were replaced by "cultural Marxists" as the Godless, socialist, secular fifth-column enemy of choice of the far right. In the 1990's, Paul Weyrich began regular trips to Russia to train activists in the culture wars there.[17] As early as 1995, members of the American Christian right began working on ways to formalize ties with fellow social conservatives in Russia. The result was the founding of the World Congress of Families (WCF) in 1997, which would come to serve as the conduit between the American religious right, the Catholic Church, the Russian Orthodox Church, and Russian Oligarchs looking to support a global Christian movement and spread Russian soft power.[18] Weyrich rapidly became a cheerleader for Vladimir Putin, as did others in his sphere of influence.

William Lind, a close associate of Weyrich, argued that Russia was a natural ally in the war between civilized Christianity and barbarous Muslims. "It is a war of Islam against everyone else. Russia is Christendom's most important barrier against Islam," he told a conference of American and Russian policy makers in May 2001, four months before the 9/11 attacks.[19] Lind thereafter pushed for a "spiritual alliance" as well. He predicted that the U.S. and Russia "will become real partners and what was once Christendom will again be united." He admitted that Putin wasn't perfect, but "I would much rather be dealing with a leader who proclaims that Russia should once again seek to be known as Holy Russia by returning to her Christian roots than some of the ugly alternatives waiting in the wing."[20]

Weyrich, and some Republican allies like Congressman Dana Rohrabacher (R-CA), embraced Russia's democratic decline so long as it served to bolster Christianity. "Their system may not end up looking the way we would prefer," wrote Weyrich in 2004, "but if we can count on Russia as an ally, why should we fret?"[21] American evangelical activist Scott Lively spent 2006-2007 lecturing and organizing in Russia and the Baltic states against LGBTQ civil rights. At the end of the tour, he concluded: "My purpose in writing this article is to contrast the positive developments in the former Soviet Union with recent anti-family developments in the west and to offer a better way forward. Victory is still theoretically possible for the pro-family movement in the west *if we are willing to pay the price.*"[22]

The implication was clear: it was better to abandon democracy and embrace autocracy, rather than to become something less than conservatively Christian. Though Weyrich died in 2008, his influence in the modern GOP through the Heritage Foundation and the Christian right movement cannot be overstated. Nor can his impact on strengthening the Christian right's willingness to engage in politics and tear down democracy in order to achieve Christian Nationalist goals.

It did not help that Bush implicitly endorsed Putin in 2001 when he remarked: "I looked the man in the eye. I found him to be very straightforward and trustworthy... I was able to get a sense of his soul."[23] This was an odd thing to say, given that former Secretary of State Madeleine Albright had described Putin as "small and pale, so cold as to be almost reptilian," after their first meeting.[24] Regardless, it gave right-wing Christian activists what they wanted: Bush's moral stamp of approval as they sought closer ties with Putin and his oligarchs. Putin's Russia was now a country to be emulated, not feared.

The Bush win in 2004 did not translate into the policy legislation social conservatives had hoped for. Bush quickly expended what political capital he had in his second term on the abortive attempt to partially privatize social security. In 2005, the Food and Drug Administration (FDA) approved the "morning after" pill, which made it possible for women to prevent pregnancy before the fertilized egg attaches to the uterine wall. Religious conservatives saw this as making abortion easier and done in the setting of a woman's own home, beyond the sphere of things they could regulate. (It is worth noting that if a fertilized egg doesn't attach it is neither a pregnancy nor an abortion.)[25]

Despite this panic, the FMA once again failed to achieve enough support to move forward in either side of Congress. Thus, instead of spending their own capital on achievable policy or legislation, cultural and religious conservatives instead blew it on the unwinnable, unpopular, and pointless fight to keep Terri Schiavo alive. Schiavo had been in a persistent vegetative state for 15 years (since 1990) with no meaningful brain activity, and no objective doctor saw a hope of recovery. Her husband wanted to remove life support, stating that she would not want to live that way. All attempts at rehabilitation had failed. Schiavo's parents sued to prevent this.

The religious right, goaded on by talk radio hosts like Rush Limbaugh and Sean Hannity, worked their base into a lather with deceptively-edited videos and wild (read: entirely false) claims by Terri's parents that she was responsive and could be rehabilitated. Republican leaders Tom DeLay (Speaker of the House as of January 2003) and Senate Majority Leader Bill Frist (R-TN) leaped on what their base was demanding and passed emergency legislation to transfer jurisdiction of the case to federal courts.[26] Ultimately, these courts declined to intervene, and Schiavo was allowed to die in March 2005.

The autopsy showed that her brain had suffered massive damage, atrophy, and 70 percent of the neurons were dead. In short: the opinions of doctors who stated that there was no significant brain function or hope of recovery were correct. Claims that she "sobbed in her mother's arms" when the order was made to remove the feeding tubes were pure fabrication, designed to whip up the base; the damage she had sustained rendered that a medical impossibility.[27] These sorts of outrageous, verifiably false, right-wing narratives came to dominate conservative "news" over the next decade, as it devolved into a form of interactive agitprop. This came to a head when "Stop the Steal" narratives pushed by right-wing outlets and social media incited their base into attempting a violent coup on January 6, 2021.

Polling showed that 80 percent of Americans supported a right to die in similar cases, and 60 percent supported Schiavo's husband over her parents.[28] Another 70 percent deemed Congress' actions in the matter inappropriate. The religious right was well aware of these numbers, which fed into their growing conviction that in order to save America they must be willing to destroy democracy and majority rule to get their way.

The religious right reacted in a way that was a preview of their behavior to come under Trump. Judge George Greer, who ordered the removal of the feeding tube, received numerous death threats. Senator John Cornyn (R-TX) opined that judges making these sorts of decisions naturally lead people to "engage in violence." James Dobson went further, suggesting that Congress should simply defund and bypass courts that don't bend to the will of the religious right. "All they have to do is say the 9th Circuit doesn't exist anymore, and it's gone."[29] Underneath it all was the constant refrain: Christians, like you, are the real victims in society, and democracy is the enemy of Christian governance.

With its political capital spent, Tom DeLay headed to prison for money laundering, and with the disastrous 2006 blue-wave mid-term election looming, the most meaningful part of Bush's second term settled into the now-familiar fight surrounding the appointment of federal judges. Historically, filibustering judicial nominations had been a rarity. Bush, however, had nominated more than a few unqualified ideologues (such as White House Counsel Harriet Miers), and between 2002 and 2006 Democrats filibustered several of these nominees. Seven Democrats and seven moderate Republicans (including John McCain) cut a deal to let some of the nominees through. This earned McCain further enmity from the right as a traitor and collaborator.

Thus, the one thing the Bush administration did deliver to the religious right was reliably conservative justices. While Chief Justice John Roberts may have angered them over the years with a few decisions (such as *Bostock v. Clayton County, Altitude Express v. Zarda,* and *Harris Funeral Homes v. E.E.O.C,* which protected LGBTQ employees from discrimination under Title VII of the Civil Rights Act), he had generally toed the line, particularly on tearing down voting rights. When he didn't, he also generally left clear instructions to the religious right on how to come back and win the next time, as he did in 2020 when striking down an anti-abortion law in Louisiana.[30] Samuel Alito, who replaced Sandra Day O'Connor, reliably provided scathing opinions in line with Scalia and Thomas on civil rights, voting rights, labor unions, religious freedom, and corporate power.

The 2006 elections handed the House and Senate to Democrats. This was the result of a backlash against an unpopular war and against an even more unpopular Congress. The religious right appeared to be adrift with no national leadership, no agenda, and no way to move policy or law forward. Popular opinion was shifting in favor of LGBTQ rights, and the religious right held unpopular positions on most social issues. But—and this is an important—they had shifted the Supreme Court just enough to the right to deliver the decisions they needed in order to begin subverting democracy in their favor.

Over the next decade, between 2006 and 2016, the Roberts' Court would deliver a series of devastating decisions that effectively hastened democratic decline and opened the door to autocracy. The 2008 decision in *Crawford v. Marion County Election Board* upheld voter ID laws that were meant to disenfranchise reliably Democratic voting groups.[31] In 2010's *Citizens United v. Federal Election Commission (F.E.C.),* the court opened the door to a flood of unlimited and virtually unregulated "dark" corporate money into elections. In 2013's *Shelby County v. Holder*, the Roberts Court gutted the Voting Rights Act by stripping its enforcement provisions, which freed the GOP to gerrymander Democrats out of existence in any states where they had a legislative majority.[32] In 2018's *Gill v. Whitford*, Roberts ruled that no matter how egregious the gerrymander is, no matter how thoroughly most people in an entire state are effectively disenfranchised, gerrymanders are constitutional because it is not the Supreme Court's responsibility to prevent political gerrymandering.[33] Finally, in 2018, federal courts lifted the injunction on the Republican Party from posting "poll watchers,"[33] which was originally put in place to prevent voter intimidation and challenges to ballots by minorities.[34]

To paraphrase Adam Serwer's assessment of the Court's role in creating the Jim Crow South: The Roberts Court's commitment to democracy is in the abstract—and only in the abstract—and is allowing a creeping despotism to take root in American soil. Which, as it has become increasingly clear, is exactly what the Republican base wants. They came away from the Bush administration in far better shape than they realized. They just needed time for the Roberts Court decisions to do their long-term damage.

Magic Mushrooms in the Tea

"It is useless to attempt to reason a man out of a thing he was never reasoned into."

Jonathan Swift

The 2008 elections were, in military parlance, a "shit sandwich" for conservatives within the GOP. While former Republican Governor of Arkansas Mike Huckabee was a perfectly serviceable candidate on paper for white evangelicals and the Christian right, he failed to earn their support. He was reliably anti-gay and anti-abortion…but on the other hand, he had also raised taxes and embraced environmental issues and anti-poverty measures for children. He preferred talking about these rather than railing against issues that got the white evangelical base riled up.[35] At the time, people were perplexed as to why the Christian right didn't flock to him, given the paucity of choices, and since, in those days, Huckabee also came across as a mild-mannered, reasonable politician. Huckabee won primaries in Alabama, Arkansas, Georgia, Louisiana, Tennessee, Kansas, and West Virginia, but he was unable to expand his appeal enough to win elsewhere.

The other leading Republican candidates all had huge strikes against them from the perspective of the religious right. McCain was a centrist, and willing to work with Democrats. Mitt Romney was also a centrist Mormon and former governor of deep-blue Massachusetts. Rudy Giuliani was a former mayor of New York City who had previously supported abortion and gay rights, making him a definitive "no." The Christian right was looking for someone far less mild-mannered and reasonable.

Nor were Barack Obama or Hilary Clinton going to pull in white evangelical votes. The decades of agitprop aimed at Clinton made her one of the most hated politicians in America. It didn't help that she lacked charisma and struggled to connect at an individual level. Barack Obama, a one-term Senator from Illinois, had a combination of charisma and poise unseen since John Kennedy; however, he was Black, and attended a church that taught Black liberation theology. Obama's church blended Martin Luther King, Jr. and Malcolm X, emphasizing "a theology that sees God as concerned with the poor and the weak," and "often portrays Jesus as a brown-skinned revolutionary."[36] This, combined with the "Goddamn America" sermon of his former pastor, Jeremiah Wright, brought racial resentment back to the surface of American politics.

After McCain secured the Republican nomination in the 2008 primaries, party apparatchiks prevailed upon him to pick former Alaska Governor Sarah Palin over centrist Senator Joe Lieberman, who was a Democrat-turned-independent. Palin was everything the base loved (and everything that McCain came to despise): someone who read little, spoke in slogans, and had no coherent policy ideas beyond "drill baby, drill!" She was, however, well suited for whipping the base into a froth. She was also desperately out of her league on the national stage, and McCain came to regret selecting her.[37] But, she was also a harbinger of candidates to come. Obama realized that though Palin hurt the Republican ticket, she represented a fundamental shift in the party. "The power of Palin's rallies compared with McCain's rallies—just contrast the excitement you would see in the Republican base. I think this hinted at the degree to which appeals around identity politics, around nativism, conspiracies, were gaining traction," he noted in an interview.[38]

McCain ended up losing the general election in a landslide. Republicans were unpopular due to the plunging economy and the endless, bloody, unwinnable war in Iraq. Obama's messages of "hope" and "change" played well in such times, and it looked like he might actually deliver on his bold promises with a democratically-controlled House and nearly filibuster-proof majority in the Senate. Unfortunately, despite the popular mandate, there was never a chance that Republicans would work with him. They felt that their backs were against the wall, and that this was war. In previous eras, leaders of both parties would talk about a president from the opposite party with phrases like, "We look forward to working with the president, and we'll see if he brings us things we can find common ground on."

But not so with Obama. He had pleaded for a unified nation just prior to the 2008 election: "There are no real and fake parts of this country. We are not separated by the pro-America and anti-America parts of this nation—we all love this country, no matter where we live or where we come from."[39] In response to this plea, Rush Limbaugh told his radio audience, "I hope he fails," four days after Obama was sworn in, and flogged his listeners to call their congressmen, urging them not to cooperate in any way, shape, or form with the new president.[40] Senate Minority Leader Mitch McConnell (R-KY) declared that "the single most important thing we want to achieve is for President Obama to be a one-term president."[41] According to Obama's memoir, when Joe Biden went to discuss the merits of a bill that was being blocked in the Senate, Mitch McConnell told Biden, "You must be under the mistaken impression that I care." In the end, Obama regarded McConnell as "shameless" in his "dispassionate pursuit of power."[42]

After the 2008 election, new developments happened at the state level that had grave consequences. Project REDMAP was a GOP plan to win back state legislatures in 2010, and to then use that victory to gerrymander their way into permanent power.[43] It went far better than they expected, and several swing or blue leaning states (such as Ohio, Wisconsin, and North Carolina) became Republican bastions. This paved the way for continuing Republican electoral advantages at the state and federal levels. Chapter 8 delves more deeply into REDMAP and its enduring consequences.

Legislative achievements during the Obama Administration were non-existent after the 2010 electoral wipeout for Democrats. His signature achievements were frequently unpopular or insufficient. The Affordable Care Act (ACA), dubbed "Obamacare" by the right, was a step in the right direction towards reducing the number of uninsured people in the U.S. However, health care remained expensive and out of reach to many, while Republicans fought tooth and nail against providing it to all Americans. They rallied the base against universal health care, using fantastical claims that the ACA would result in death panels, socialism, and the destruction of the American health care system.[44]

The American Recovery and Reinvestment Act of 2009 stimulus bill, though helpful, was woefully insufficient. The bailout of the auto industry saved General Motors and Chrysler, but less than half of the population approved of it initially, taking a "let them die" attitude towards American automakers they believed were producing inferior vehicles.[45] Most of the Dodd-Frank Wall Street Reform and Consumer Protection Act of 2010, which was intended to prevent a repeat of the events that led to the Great Recession of 2008, was torn down by conservative courts and the Trump administration within a decade.[46]

President Obama's sole foray into the culture wars during his first term was repealing "Don't Ask, Don't Tell." He did this during the congressional lame-duck session of 2010, allowing lesbians and gays to serve openly. This drew howls from the religious right and only strengthened their belief that he would destroy the American military and the Christian way of life by allowing LGBTQ people to exist openly in the military.[47] Ending DADT was supported by the majority of the public this time, and further reinforced the religious right's belief that they could not win the culture war through normal democratic means.

The TEA (Taxed Enough Already) Party emerged very shortly after Obama was inaugurated. Ostensibly a grassroots organization focused on fiscal responsibility, it was actually launched with funding from the billionaire Koch brothers.[48] The Koch's "Americans for Prosperity" organization primarily pushed for libertarian economic policy (e.g. anti-union, low taxes on the rich, etc.) and decried Keynesian spending during the Great Recession. The first Tea Party protest occurred on February 27, 2009 against the Bush-era Troubled Asset Relief Program (TARP) to bail out banks and the related Obama stimulus bill.

Fox News played a critical role in launching the Tea Party. It urged viewers to attend their rallies and provided coverage of them. At the same time, *Fox* advertised that their celebrity talking-head hosts, like Sean Hannity, would be attending the rallies as well. This incestuous relationship of generating the news and being the news at the same time likely convinced fence-sitters that the Tea Party movement would probably succeed.[49]

Fiscal issues alone would have been insufficient to sustain a movement. What the Kochs, GOP, and *Fox* created was something even more powerful: a Frankenstein's Monster spawned in a think-tank laboratory from parts they found lying around. It got loose and then ran amok. The rampage was fueled by its own bottomless well of rage, paranoia, and grievance, and continually fed more by *Fox* and talk radio. The decentralized Tea Party initially had little formal organization or leadership. They organized via the new tools of social media and were able to rally quickly and organically.

The Tea Party as a movement was increasingly dominated by white evangelicals. A 2010 polling found that 57 percent of Tea Partiers considered themselves part of the Christian Conservative movement. They weren't libertarian: 63 percent wanted abortion outlawed and only 18 percent supported legalizing same sex marriage. Eighty-three percent reported voting Republican.[50] (If this number sounds familiar, 81 percent of white evangelicals voted for Trump.) Polling data eventually showed the Tea Party moving further to the right and homogenizing. A 2012 poll showed that 89 percent of self-identified Tea Partiers were white and overwhelmingly male and middle-aged.[51] It was also geographically concentrated in the South: while only 31 percent of Americans live in the "old south," 56 percent of Tea Party supporters live there.[52]

The Tea Party was not about was economic insecurity. The Public Religion Research Institute (PRRI) found that working-class whites were no more likely to support the Tea Party than college-educated whites.[53] Tea Partiers also had higher incomes than the general population.[54] They had bought into conservative dogma about taxes as well. Sixty-two percent of Americans supported raising taxes on those making more than a million dollars per year, while only 33 percent of Tea Partiers did, despite skyrocketing wealth inequality and the massive bailouts for banks that they were protesting against in the first place.[55] Instead, Tea Partiers latched onto a racially-tinged fringe theory that blamed the housing market collapse on loan programs for minorities, rather than on the actual cause: unregulated trading of sub-prime mortgage commodities.[56] Which then begs the question: what was really at the heart of the Tea Party movement, if not economic insecurity? As with most socially conservative movements over the past 150 years, the answer is predictable: race and religion.

Two-thirds of Tea Partiers agreed with the statement: "The government has paid too much attention to the problems of blacks and other minorities."[57] Seventy-three percent agreed with the statement: "Today discrimination against whites has become as big a problem as discrimination against blacks and other minorities."[58] Social scientists who studied this found a much stronger quantitative correlation between racial resentment attitudes and Tea Party affiliation, than with economic stress, which was very weakly correlated at best.[59] Tea Partiers also were the staunchest opponents of immigration and the Deferred Action for Childhood Arrivals policy (DACA).[60]

A retrospective study of 2006 survey data found that the strongest predictor of who would join the Tea Party was the Christian Nationalist belief that religion should play a central role in politics.[61] Survey data from 2012 also found that most Tea Partiers believe the U.S. is a Christian nation, in the sense that they do not believe in the separation of church and state.[62] Unsurprisingly, in 2011 Pew Research found that white evangelicals were the demographic most likely to support the Tea Party.[63]

Tea Party rallies have included signs covered with racist slogans such as "A Village in Kenya Is Missing Its Idiot: Deport Obama!" "Congress = Slave Owner; Taxpayer = N**gar, [sic]" and "Imam Obama Wants to Ban Pork: Don't Let Him Steal Your Meat."[64] With all the demographic data pointing towards the conclusion that the Tea Party's core were the descendants of the very people who fought for slavery and against desegregation, and that racial animus was still their driving motivator, it is hard to reach any conclusion but that their seething hatred of Obama was born not out of his policies, but rather from his race and from what he represented in the White House. To Tea Partiers, he was the ultimate sign that they had lost the culture wars and that progressives, minorities, and people who believed in secular government had won. This may also have been part of the reason why many Tea Partiers also fell down the conspiracy hole and never emerged.

The Obama administration marked a point when disinformation became central to the social conservative movement. Polling during the Obama administration showed that 54 percent of Republicans believed Obama was secretly a Muslim.[65] Another 45 percent believed that he was born outside the U.S.[66] By the 2016 election, these conspiracy-based theories were endemic among Trump supporters. Two-thirds of Trump supporters believed Obama was a Muslim and only 13 percent believed he was a Christian (which he is).[67] In other words, belief in anti-Obama conspiracy theories increased throughout his two terms in office.

To them, it didn't matter that mainstream Republicans like McCain and Romney denounced this kind of conspiracy thinking. It didn't matter that Obama attended church or quoted scripture in his speeches. It didn't even register that there was a contradiction in attacking him for going to a Christian church that preached Black liberation while at the same time calling him a closeted Muslim.

Over time, the conspiracy theories grew more and more bizarre. "Obama is gay." "Michelle Obama was born male and is actually a transgender woman." "Sasha and Malia aren't really Barack and Michelle's biological children; they were secretly kidnapped from a family that is now looking for them."[68] Tea Partiers and the Republican base were going to believe whatever felt "right" to them. At the same time, *Fox News* figures like Glenn Beck and Sean Hannity peddled an endless series of increasingly outlandish ideas and gave airtime to their proponents like Donald Trump.[69]

Unlike the John Birch Society, the Tea Party was grudgingly allowed inside the GOP tent as their power grew. They rapidly gained veto power within the GOP over any efforts by mainstream Republicans in the House and Senate. At its peak, the House Tea Party Caucus had 60 members, and made it impossible for House Republicans to move legislation without their assent. Although the Tea Party Caucus faded out as an institution, it had effectively won the war for power within the GOP and paved the way for Trump.[70] It had driven the GOP to the right and forced out moderates.[71] It also produced a cadre of individuals that would become the core of the Trump Administration, including his Chiefs of Staff Mick Mulvaney and Mark Meadows.

The Tea Party was a product of the new school of politics: no compromise, not ever, and that now included rejecting insufficiently conservative Republicans. They were largely responsible for the lengthy government shut down in 2013.[72] They also claimed the scalps of three House Majority Leaders in less than a decade: Eric Cantor (R-VA) was unseated in a Republican primary, and John Boehner and Paul Ryan both quit in disgust over the prospect of continuing to try to wrangle a mob incapable of either compromise or rational thought. As political scientists Steven Levitsky and Daniel Ziblatt observed in their book, *How Democracies Die*: "Top Republican figures--including the one who would soon be president--had overtly abandoned norms of mutual toleration, goaded on by a fringe that was no longer fringe."[73]

Ironically, white evangelicals had finally achieved the control over the Republican Party they sought after they had lost cohesion as a political entity and their primary lobbying groups were at their lowest point since the 1970's. It was only when they became a force of pure inchoate rage in politics, unfettered by any sort of leadership, message or coherent policy, that they gained the level of control over the GOP that they had sought for decades.

It wasn't clear at the time, but it is now: by 2014, the Republican Party had effectively become a more-or-less willing hostage to a movement fueled by racial animus, grievance, and conspiracy theories. It had no use for politics or democratic norms, and no interest in maintaining a functional or democratic government. This group's goal was to win at all costs and to "Make America Great Again" by forcing the country to all live under their minority rule, while preventing any democratic or electoral means to contest it.

2016 Election

"We've had vicious kings and we've had idiot kings, but I don't know if we've ever been cursed with a vicious idiot for a king."

Tyrion Lannister

After Mitt Romney lost in 2012 to Barack Obama, the GOP attempted an "autopsy," which broadly concluded that if the GOP was going to stay relevant in the long run, they would need to do better with women and minorities.[74] "We need to campaign among Hispanic, black, Asian, and gay Americans and demonstrate we care about them, too," concluded the report. Louisiana Governor Bobby Jindal was blunt in his assessment in a 2013 speech to the Republican National Committee:

"We must stop being the stupid party. It's time for a new Republican party that talks like adults... We had a number of Republicans damage the brand this year with offensive and bizarre comments... We must stop insulting the intelligence of voters... We must quit "big." We are not the party of big business, big banks, big Wall Street bailouts, big corporate loopholes, or big anything. We must not be the party that simply protects the well off so they can keep their toys..."[75]

Jindal's speech was hailed at the time as "bold," "dynamite," and "visionary," and Senator Lindsey Graham (R-SC) agreed at the time, warning, "We're not generating enough angry white guys to stay in business in the long term."[76] He wasn't wrong. White protestants hadn't been a majority in the U.S. since 1993. In 2008, white Christians were 54 percent of the population, and dropped to 42 percent by 2018.[77] Unfortunately, it bore no resemblance to the GOP's actual response. They continued to embrace "trickle down" economic theory and culture war fringe elements. This rejection of change ultimately brought Donald J. Trump into power. Stuart Stevens, a campaign advisor to five Republican presidential candidates, described the mood of the GOP establishment when the party embraced Trump and abandoned the conclusions of the 2012 autopsy: "Then we got to Donald Trump, and we just threw it all out the window kind of like an audible sigh of relief, like thank God, we don't have to pretend we actually care about this stuff. We can still just win with white people."[78] By 2018, Jindal had also wholeheartedly embraced the "stupid," as had any remaining leadership within the Republican Party.[79]

To Trump's base, "we don't have to pretend" meant something slightly different. Whereas Republican leadership had been pretending to care about minorities and poor people, the base no longer felt they had to hide how hostile they were to minority groups. Trump was promising to reverse progress, end "political correctness," and let "his" people's antipathy towards an inclusive and pluralistic society become the permanent dominant force in America. Hannah Arendt, a Jewish woman who escaped Nazi Germany before the war and became a prominent scholar on fascism, described this phenomenon decades ago: part of the allure of fascism is its invitation to "throw off the mask of hypocrisy."[80]

Donald Trump had played around with the idea of running for president for decades. He openly pondered it in 1988, 2000, and 2012, while changing his party registration five times.[81] He had a long and nasty reputation, including taking out full page ads in 1989 accusing five innocent Black teens in New York of crimes, and demanding their arrest and execution.[82] He had a history of stiffing his contractors and then forcing them to take pennies on the dollar in court.[83] There were decades of shady deals with Russian mobsters and Putin-aligned oligarchs.[84] His infidelity was both legendary and part of his branding as a rich playboy with models for wives.[85]

Trump was an odd choice to lead a populist movement rooted in the American South as a billionaire from Manhattan. He had never spent a day in his life without wealth and privilege. But this is part of what attracted his base: They were the same audience as people watching *Lifestyles of the Rich and Famous* in the 1980's. He was what poor people believed the rich, famous, and successful look like, even if it was all a sham built on a house of cards.

Nor has Trump ever been pious in a conventional sense. He rarely if ever set foot inside a church, mispronounced Second Corinthians as "Two Corinthians," and didn't believe that he had anything he needed to ask God forgiveness for.[86] His "successful billionaire" persona was in great part an artifact of playing one on his reality TV show, *The Apprentice*, and not from his six bankruptcies between 1990 and 2009.[87] Trump was part mafia Don, part Borscht-belt insult comic, part P.T. Barnum, and part Archie Bunker. He was a carnival barker inviting everyone to come see the show—and he was the show.

He followed the proverb (attributed to Barnum) that there's no such thing as bad publicity. His outlandishness, and his schtick, helped him gain nearly 2 billion dollars worth of free media coverage during the 2016 election. He essentially found an exploit made possible by his wealth and reputation to break the game.[88] Thus, he was hardly the candidate most people would expect to appeal to white evangelicals, Christian nationalists and the religious right. However, Trump made the most direct and effective appeal to the actual desires of the GOP base that any politician had ever made, in a language and tone they trusted, through talk radio and *Fox News* commentators. Holocaust historian Christopher Browning summarized what made Trump so good at appealing to the Christian nationalist base:

> "Donald Trump has a political instinct for how to arouse grievance and resentment. Trump also knows how to frame issues in terms of making oneself into a victim. Trump may not know much of anything about the specifics of public policy or the issues, but he certainly does have an uncanny instinct for the jugular." [89]

During the Obama administration, Trump had been one of the biggest promoters of the claims that the president had been born in Kenya. Sean Hannity and *Fox News* spent the better part of a decade giving him plenty of space to run with those claims on the air.[90] Trump even went so far as to claim that he had hired private investigators in Hawaii, whom he said could find no evidence Obama was born there. Never mind the fact that the White House provided copies of Obama's original long-form Hawaiian birth certificate.[91] Or that a birth announcement for him had been published in the Honolulu Advertiser on August 13th, 1961. It was a show, and everyone was invited to gawp and suspend their disbelief.

This was the "jugular" to which Browning refers. Trump was willing to embrace narratives, ideas, convictions, biases, conspiracies, and impulses that are part of the GOP base's belief system, but which "normal" Republican politicians cringed away from supporting. He was willing to say out loud what the now whackadoodle-centric base was thinking and confirm their biases in a way that felt gratifying. Indeed, research suggests that people get a hit of dopamine (the pleasure inducing neurotransmitter released when people use drugs like cocaine) when they hear information that confirms their biases.[92]

When Trump said of Mexicans, "They're bringing drugs. They're bringing crime. They're rapists. And some, I assume, are good people," the right-wing Republican base got a thrill hearing a politician saying what they already believed but had—until now—felt uncomfortable expressing.[93] When Trump described "thugs who are so happily and openly destroying Baltimore," evoking images of criminal Black men, he was throwing kilos of Bolivian marching powder to the crowd. When Trump said he would enact "a total shutdown of Muslims entering the United States," his base was hearing what they had wanted for fifteen years, but no other politician would even hint at giving them. Thus, for the Tea Party base of the GOP, supporting Donald Trump was like chasing the dragon.[94] Melanie Austin, a Pennsylvania voter who believes Obama is a gay Kenyan Muslim and that Michelle Obama is transgender, summarized why she loves Trump: "Finally! Someone who thinks like me."[95]

Trump was willing to wallow in meaningless culture war fights, too. He protested against the lack of "Merry Christmas" and objected to Starbucks' non-denominational coffee cup decorations.[96] He hated who the religious right hated, mocking and ridiculing enemies both real and imagined, and threatening to arrest political enemies they both despised. Evangelicals saw someone who was finally going to do something, who saw the world the way they did. They saw him as someone who wasn't going to try to make the GOP a bigger tent. Someone who wasn't "politically correct." He was going to make the GOP look like the Tea Party: old, white, southern, Christian Nationalist, racist, aggrieved, vengeful, and bent on obtaining power regardless of its cost to democracy.

Trump was speaking to this group in a way that no other politician had done before—in their own language. There was no nuance. No nod to a "diverse America" that was unrecognizable to them. Instead, he provided unvarnished promises to wreak unholy vengeance on the elites and minorities that had usurped their white Christian nationalist place in the social order. For white evangelical Christians who believe that no one is discriminated against in America more than them, the promise to torture Muslim prisoners at Guantanamo Bay was music to their ears. They wanted police to crack down on Black Lives Matter. They wanted someone to hunt down and deport every undocumented immigrant in the U.S., including the dreamers brought here as children.

They wanted Trump to hurt the people they believed deserve it.[97] "Make liberals cry again" became the battle hymn of the Republican Party under Trump: a raw expression of dominance and sadism.[98] Filmmaker Michael Moore predicted Trump would win in October 2016, based on white voters sending a message to those they saw as elites: "Trump's election is going to be the biggest 'fuck you' ever recorded in human history—and it will feel good."[99]

Trump's Republican opponents at first tried to ignore him, hoping that his appalling outrageousness would sink his campaign. It didn't, because his racist, xenophobic, outrageous statements were a feature, not a bug. When his opponents tried calling him out as the ignorant buffoon that he was, he responded with the kind of insults one expects of a 7th grade bully, which his supporters loved. Finally comprehending Trump's dynamic, his opponents tried to stoop to his level; but their own taunts sounded forced and scripted, as if it physically hurt them to have to think like a 13-year-old.

White evangelicals turned out and voted for Donald Trump as much, or more, than they did for the most religiously conservative Republican in the primary race: Senator Ted Cruz (R-TX). While the most fervent and frequently church-going tended to swing for Cruz initially, Donald Trump managed to be more "everything" than him.[100] More anti-Muslim. More anti-immigrant. More racist. More misogynistic. Trump basically tore up the 2013 election post-mortem report and proved that you can still win with mostly angry white guys. He became part of their religious identity. By the end of his Presidency, there was a strong positive correlation between how often self-identified born-again Christians go to church, and how likely they were to vote for Trump.

Once Trump had captured most of the evangelical leaders' base, he courted these leaders themselves almost as an afterthought. Some were wary, given that Trump had previously supported LGBTQ people and abortion rights. Evangelical king-maker James Dobson declared, "I would never vote for a kingpin within that enterprise… I don't really believe Trump is a conservative."[101] This hesitancy didn't last long. First, Trump promised to only appoint Supreme Court justices who would ban abortion.[102] Then he went before an audience of about a thousand evangelical leaders and promised them what they had always wanted most: to revoke the IRS rules barring tax-exempt churches from directly supporting political campaigns.[103]

This was apparently enough for James Dobson, who did a 180 and declared that Trump was a born-again, saved, Christian man.[104] Dozens of other leading evangelical hold-outs who had previously lambasted Trump switched to singing his praises and leading the charge for Team Trump.[105] Others, such as Tony Perkins of the anti-LGBTQ Family Research Council,[106] were brought on board as advisors. Perkins ended up writing most of the social policy in the ultra-conservative 2016 (and by default 2020) Republican platforms.[107]

It's unclear whether religious-right leaders had much choice in embracing Trump, given that their base had already aligned behind him. Leaders like Southern Baptist Convention President Russell Moore, who never came around on Trump, were sidelined or forced out.[108] Though Trump had their base locked up, picking Mike Pence as vice president was an additional promise that evangelical concerns would not fall by the wayside during his administration.

Trump, for his part, reveled in the fawning and adoration. He is areligious. He doesn't really care about the issues important to the religious right. Transactional ("I do for you, you do for me") relationships are the only kinds he understands. According to Trump's former lawyer and "fixer" Michael Cohen, after evangelical leaders met with him at Trump Tower and laid their hands on him in prayer, Trump asked him, "Can you believe that bullshit?[109] Can you believe people believe that bullshit?" This revelation did nothing to reduce evangelical enthusiasm for his second term, however.

All of this explains why white Christian nationalists voted overwhelmingly for Trump. Eighty-one percent of white evangelicals voted for him. Sixty-four percent of white Catholics and fifty-seven percent of white mainline Protestants voted for him as well. The only white religious demographic that did not vote for Trump was those who do not identify with any religion, 62 percent of whom voted for Clinton.[110] This is in part why even most "moderate" Republicans quickly fell in line with Trump. Trump's approval rating with Republican voters remained in the high 80's to low 90's throughout his presidency, seemingly invulnerable to everything he did.[111] Very few Republicans in office were willing to repudiate Trump's outrages, and those who did usually left office afterwards.

Negative polarization has made voting for a Democrat unimaginable to the vast majority of Republicans. No matter what Trump does, they still imagine it would be worse if a Democrat was in office. Many knew Donald Trump is a terrible person and completely unqualified, but believed Hillary Clinton and Joe Biden would enact even more disastrous policies. This antipathy towards the other party and its members is known as "affective" or "negative" polarization, and it has come to be a dominant force in American electoral politics.[112] Some Trump voters were even convinced that Democrats would take their guns and put them in labor camps, where they would die of malnutrition, eating boiled lawn clippings and crickets like North Korean villagers in a famine.

Thus, by this delusional standard Trump looked good to many otherwise moderate Republicans. GOP voters knew that Trump was completely unfit for the job, but they could always imagine a worse outcome under a Democrat, thanks to the propaganda continuously churned out by *Fox News* and other sources of conservative disinformation. The data backs up these anecdotal observations: studies show that both Democratic and Republican voters believe the opposition is evil, likely to commit violence, and are influenced by malignant forces.[113] It also shows that ethnic antagonism is closely related to a Republican lack of commitment to democracy, just as it was 120 years ago in the Old South.[114]

This is how the Republican mainstream, already aligning behind Trump, sold the idea of President Trump to otherwise (reluctant) traditional Dwight Eisenhower and McCain Republicans. In the surprisingly successful essay, "The Flight 93 Election," an anonymous author tried to make the case that Trump is certainly a narcissistic, erratic, unreliable, authoritarian-leaning potential disaster… but Hillary Clinton was guaranteed to be worse. It implicitly acknowledged that social conservatives had lost the culture war and winning in 2016 was their last chance to try to hold back the tide. They foresaw permanent victory for the left if they did not win. Underpinning this acknowledgment was another: we must be willing to break our country, and democracy, to save the United States for God, Christianity and "our" white European heritage. It justifies electing an incompetent authoritarian and destroying our democracy, because we're saving America for the "real" Americans."[115] And if Hillary Clinton won? "Our back up strategy is to fuck her up so badly that she can't govern," responded Trump strategist and former *Breitbart* editor Steve Bannon.[116]

These sorts of responses are indicative of the extreme political polarization in the U.S., which continued even after the election. Republicans no longer see Democrats as the loyal opposition: they are instead a catastrophic evil to be defeated. This framing is entirely intentional, encouraged by GOP leaders, Trump, right-wing religious leaders, and the conservative media ecosystem. The data also shows that this polarization is asymmetric: Republicans had drifted much farther to the right than Democrats had to the left.[117] The result is the GOP becoming the most powerful far-right party in the Western world.[118]

Republican leaders, who knew exactly how inept and corrupt the Trump Administration was, were willing to go along with it because they had completely subscribed to the "war for power" interpretation of politics. All that mattered was power, and doing anything to contradict Trump hindered the political control that they sought. Stuart Stevens concurred: "[Trump] realized that this is a group of weak people who don't really believe in anything, except winning, except power. And if I can give them power, they will allow me to be whatever I want to be. And I think he was right." These same Republicans had seen the death threats and intimidation of judges and politicians who crossed the GOP base, and they simply didn't have the stomach for that sort of fight.[119] The fact that this base had already claimed the scalps of Eric Cantor and John Boehner did not help, either. The insurrection after the 2020 election confirmed that their fears of their own base were entirely justified. Republican leaders learned they could potentially be killed if they did not back Trump to the bitter end.

Populism, either left or right, can be damaging to democracy even under the best of circumstances. When one party, led by a single powerful leader who uses demagoguery and racial antipathy as rhetorical fertilizer, seizes permanent control of the party and the country, this is authoritarianism. When a right-wing populist and his movement seize permanent control of a country based on racial and ethnic grievances, *this is the basis for fascism.* If Trump hadn't come along and taken advantage of this environment of grievance and desperation, eventually someone else would have. Republicans were a party hungry for power at any cost, in possession of a reality-challenged angry base that felt they were losing power, and a right-wing media echo chamber eager to stoke the fires. President Obama was correct: Trump was a symptom of much larger problems. He just happened to be the first right-wing populist to exploit the situation fully, and with the intention of never losing an election again.

What has been described so far in this book is a brief synopsis of the long road that led the world's oldest republic to the brink of destruction, and the attempted establishment of an autocracy supported by a fascist movement. The rest of this book looks at the contributing factors and key enablers that led America to the only moment in its history where such a descent into autocracy was possible.

Chapters 4 and 5 examine the media and its evolutionary role in stoking populist appetite for authoritarianism and destroying faith in expertise and science.

Chapter 6 discusses the beliefs and psychology of the Christian nationalist movement. Chapter 7 focuses on how the democracy-destroying effects of runaway wealth inequality have fanned the flames of ideological entrenchment and animosity towards minorities in the Republican base. Chapter 8 describes how the GOP is rigging elections to establish permanent minority rule, and how the U.S. Constitution itself aids them in their effort. The following chapter examines the characteristics of fascism, how it applies to the current political situation in the U.S., and the dangers such movements pose. Chapter 10 explores how other democracies in the post-Cold War world have failed and how America is vulnerable to the same factors. It concludes with a look at the 2020 election and what it means for the nation, and makes some suggestions of what needs to be done going forward to stop the further descent into fascism and re-gain control over our democracy.

Four

Dazed and Confused

"In an ever-changing, incomprehensible world the masses had reached the point where they would, at the same time, believe everything and nothing, think that every-thing was possible and that nothing was true."

Hannah Arendt

It would be impossible to examine how democracy in America melted down without a discussion of the media's role in the debacle. Over time, an entire right-wing media ecosystem has developed specifically to ensure that its followers believe the absolute worst of the opposition and refuse to listen to information originating outside that system. It particularly demonizes experts and academics. The result is a toxic right-wing media monoculture that has blotted out daylight and prevented any ideas originating outside the monoculture from ever taking root.

Senator Daniel Patrick Moynihan (D-NY) observed in 1983 that, "Everyone is entitled to his own opinion, but not his own facts." This remark, which was self-evident in a previous age, now seems quaintly naive. In this brave new world of *Fox News, One America News (OAN), Breitbart,* and social media, everyone has a right to their own facts. There is no longer a single reality shared among people of different parties; rather, everyone has their own set of "facts" that confirm a predetermined ideological conclusion. In such an environment, consensus and rational discourse becomes impossible. Decisions are made via brute force by the most powerful people in the room, rather than through knowledge, study and reason. It promotes the ends-justify-the-means approach to politics that has become the hallmark of the Republican Party over the past three decades.

This divergence is mostly one-sided. The right wing has drifted much farther away from reality than the progressive left, or the center. Conservatives are now significantly less capable of telling fact from fiction.[1] As long as the fiction supports their preconceived notions and comes from within their media ecosystem, it rapidly becomes gospel and tribal knowledge. As a result, up to 56 percent of Republicans believed in bonkers conspiracy theories: that globalists, Democratic elites, and Tom Hanks steal children, sell them as sex slaves, and drink their blood for a magic substance they call "adrenochrome."[2]

The result is highly lethal to a democratic society. Experts are only listened to if they follow the party line and parrot things that the base thinks they already know. The politics of us vs. them has become the norm. Fewer and fewer people can discern the truth, and many simply give up in exhaustion. Access to power increasingly requires accepting lies. Even when hundreds of thousands of people die as a result of the lies, it changes nothing; Republican leaders either believe the lies, or go along with the status quo to preserve their careers and chances of upward mobility. Even media outlets that have not been "captured" feel obligated to present both sides in situations where truth has only one face.

The irony is that a free, uninhibited media market could end up producing a result that is nearly indistinguishable from the Soviet system that gave us the mishandling of the Chernobyl nuclear disaster in 1986.

De-Evolution of American Media

"The ideal subject of totalitarian rule is not the convinced Nazi or the convinced Communist, but people for whom the distinction between fact and fiction and the distinction between true and false no longer exist."

Hannah Arendt

If we had to choose a moment in the chain of failures in the media that led to where the U.S. is today, it would be August 4th, 1987. On that date, the Federal Communications Commission (FCC) voted unanimously to eliminate the Fairness Doctrine, which had required licensed broadcasters to give equal time to differing political views. Little did they know that this decision, which they believed unfairly infringed on the First Amendment rights of journalists and stifled debate, would lead to the President of the United States calling journalists enemies of the people and suing the *New York Times* for criticizing him.[3]

Within a year of the demise of the Fairness Doctrine, the first signs of trouble could be heard. On August 1st, 1988 Rush Limbaugh's radio show began nationwide syndication. Limbaugh was originally a college drop-out from Missouri who "flunked everything." He was a z-list disc jockey who bounced from gig to gig because his outsized personality seemed to inevitably lead to conflict with management. Once the Fairness Doctrine was gone, Limbaugh was free to become even

72

more uncompromising on the air, and his radio stations felt no need to balance his minimally-factual schtick. His listeners were presented with his warped and uneducated views as gospel truth, day after day, without hearing opposing views or a bit of fact checking.

And it was a huge hit. His radio program rapidly became the most popular in America. It was abrasive, mocking agitprop for white conservatives who wanted confirmation of the things they believed but couldn't get away with saying. He screened his callers to ensure they almost universally agreed with him. Indeed, his listeners began identifying as "dittoheads," a tacit nod to their agreement with everything he said, even when it was demonstrably false or an outright conspiracy theory.[4]

Part of what made Limbaugh different was that he set himself up as the sole source of truth amid the infinite lies, fallacies, and misdirections of the "lame-stream media." In great part because of Limbaugh, the Republican rank-and-file came to hate journalists more than most "non-dittoheads" could understand.[5] It was only when Trump began calling journalists "enemies of the people" to wild applause from his supporters, who proceeded to send death threats to *CNN* correspondents, that the extent of the antipathy for mainstream media was truly revealed.[6]

Limbaugh's early program was full of commie-baiting. He popularized the term "feminazi," and played directly to the racist undercurrents of the Reagan administration. He applauded the administration's "handling" of the HIV/AIDs crisis and was a staunch foe of climate science. He has consistently promoted a host of conspiracy theories, ranging from Hillary Clinton ordering the murder of Vince Foster, to Egypt legalizing necrophilia, to the New Zealand mosque shootings being a false flag operation.[7] Over the course of 30-plus years, he racked up an impressive tally of horrible, ignorant, and offensive quotes.[8]

It is hard to overstate the influence Limbaugh had over the GOP base since the early 1990's. By 1991, he had 14 million listeners. Within a few more years, it expanded to 20 million. When Republicans celebrated their stunning electoral gains in 1994 at Camden Yards baseball park in Baltimore, Limbaugh was the guest of honor and named an honorary member of the Freshman Congressional class. Gingrich's top advisor, Vin Weber, introduced him by saying: "Rush Limbaugh is really as responsible for what happened as any individual in America. Talk radio, with you in the lead, is what turned the tide." Limbaugh responded that Republicans might want to "leave some liberals alive" so "you will never forget what these people were like."[9]

However, Limbaugh was just the beginning of the de-evolution of American political discourse via electronic media. The U.S. had not seen such a combative, obnoxious, truth-twisting, right-wing populist on the air since the 1930's-era Nazi sympathizer Father Coughlin. Even Coughlin, though, once his Nazi sympathies were recognized, got yanked back to parish duties by the Church after Germany invaded Poland. He narrowly avoided sedition charges only because the Roman Catholic church promised he would never be heard from again.

When a movement is homegrown, it only further elevates voices like Limbaugh. Limbaugh was part of the "Gingrichization" of conservative politics in the 1990's: no-prisoners, no compromise, southern, believing that power is all that matters. This new media was disdainful of science, expertise, and "political correctness." Limbaugh also showed the way forward for other conservative political operatives. This included Roger Ailes, who produced Rush Limbaugh's syndicated TV show which ran from 1992 to 1996.[10]

As much as Limbaugh bashed the "lame-stream liberal media," until 1996 he didn't believe conservatives had any alternative to himself. That all changed in January 1996, when media magnate Rupert Murdoch announced that *Fox* would be creating its own news channel on cable to compete with *CNN*. He hired conservative political operative Roger Ailes to stand up the network. Ailes had worked for Richard Nixon during the 1972 elections as a TV media content manager, and had wanted another crack at creating a conservative news network since Television News Incorporated folded in 1975. Ailes was given free rein to shape the network in his own image. Thus, the fact that the resultant network is conservative in its slant and Nixonian in its ethics was intentional.

Fox News

> *"What is the cost of lies? It's not that we'll mistake them for the truth. The real danger is that if we hear enough lies, then we no longer recognize the truth at all."*
>
> Valery Legasov, *Chernobyl*

> *"You're saying it's a falsehood… Sean Spicer, our press secretary, gave alternative facts to that."*
>
> Kelly Anne Conway

The *Fox News* channel debuted on October 7th, 1996. From the start, it was slanted towards conservative viewpoints, despite its "fair and balanced," and "we report, you decide" mottoes. It was always light on actual reporting, having only a third of the staff of *CNN*, fewer of whom were actual journalists. Many of the news readers they hired had no qualifications other than basic literacy and being former beauty queens. *Fox* was notorious from the beginning for giving softball interviews to Republicans and using graphics and bullet points to reduce information to a bare minimum, while still hammering home the point they were trying to make.[11] Nevertheless, *Fox* quickly became the most watched cable news network in America.

If Ailes had not invented *Fox News*, someone else would have, for Limbaugh had already proved that there was a huge market for this sort of conservative-slanted "news lite" that encouraged similar misinformation and conspiracy thinking. As conservative Charles Krauthammer quipped, Ailes "discovered a niche audience, half the American people."[12]

The evening hosts were the stars of the network. Over time, their purpose became nothing more than the promotion of conspiracy theories and half-truths supporting the simplistic message of "Republicans good, Democrats bad," and inventing controversies like Obama's tan suit or his choice of condiments. Sean Hannity, Bill O'Reilly and Tucker Carlson all owe a debt to Rush Limbaugh, having embraced the basic style he developed in the late 1980's and early 1990's to create a similar rapid fire, simplistic, nakedly partisan, angry rhetoric that plays upon negative stereotypes and fears about women, gays, transgender people, Muslims, liberals, blacks, Hispanics, and anyone else who runs afoul of older white people. The median age of a *Fox News* viewer in 2015 was 68 years old, and 94 percent of them were white.[13]

Over time, *Fox News* has shifted further and further to the right, abandoning any pretense of being fair or balanced.[14] Research into *Fox News'* effect on popular opinion has not only shown that Republicans who watch *Fox News* are more conservative than those who don't, but that *Fox News* itself is responsible for that shift. Other studies found that people who watched *Fox News* had less knowledge of issues outside of what Republicans focus on, and a reduction in news obtained from other sources.[15] It also seems to have shifted legislators to the right as early as 2000.[16] By 2010, 69 percent of Republicans were *Fox News* viewers.[17]

Eventually, some top Republicans realized the error of letting the inmates (Limbaugh in particular) run the asylum. Vin Weber observed, 20 years after introducing Limbaugh at Camden Yards, that "conservative media has become... much more powerful than John Boehner or Mitch McConnell." Former Republican Senate Majority Leader Trent Lott (R-MS) bitterly complained, "If you stray the slightest from the far right... you get hit by the conservative media." John Boehner's (R-OH) chief of staff was even more blunt in his assessment of where the balance of power lay and to what effect after his boss was ousted: "We fed the beast and it ate us."[18]

Media outlet biases are demand-driven in that they produce what people want to hear.[19] The meteoric rise of Rush Limbaugh and *Fox News* suggests there is clearly a demand for what they were, and are, producing. Today, there is a powerful fraternity of conservative news outlets that dominate the market. *Breitbart, Daily Signal, Newsmax, One America News, The Federalist* and *PJ Media* churn out a steady stream of slanted articles designed more to provoke outrage at liberals than to provide actual information.[20] Obnoxious right-wing personalities like Ben Shapiro, Steven Crowder, Dan Bongino, Franklin Graham, and others consistently get far more shares and views on Facebook than stories by legitimate outlets.[21]

Consumption of conservative media degrades people's ability to participate in civic life by actively making them more ignorant. A 2012 study found that *Fox News* viewers were less knowledgeable of current events than people who watched nothing at all.[22] Another, more recent study found that older and more conservative people in the U.S. are significantly more likely to share fake news stories and hoaxes on social media, which is a pretty accurate description of the demographics of *Fox News* viewers.[23] Under the Trump Administration, *Fox News* coverage took on an even more bizarre and dangerous role—*official state media*. It was the network for Trump's base: white, older, rural, little college education, and less urban.[24] It's no surprise that 99 percent of Republicans who watch *Fox News* and 99 percent of Republican white evangelicals opposed the impeachment and removal of Trump.[25] Such high percentages of support are rarely seen outside of rigged third-world elections for dictators.

It also suggests that people who don't already agree ideologically with *Fox* don't watch it, and vice versa. *Fox News* is by far the news source most trusted by Republicans. (There is no equivalent organization among Democrats or Independents.) Thirty-six percent of *Fox* viewers are white evangelicals who constitute only ~15 percent of all Americans. *Fox* viewers are also disproportionately whiter and wealthier than the general public.[26] Despite roughly 26 percent of Americans having no religious affiliation, less than 5 percent of *Fox News* viewers are "nones"[27]

There are significant differences between Republicans who get their news from *Fox* and those who do not. *Fox News* Republicans (FNRs) are significantly more likely to be white evangelicals than other Republicans. *Fox* watchers also share the same skewed perceptions about whites and Christians being discriminated against more than any other groups in the U.S. It appears that the Venn diagram of *Fox News* Republicans, Trump supporters, and white Christian Nationalists, is nearly a perfect circle.[28]

People are predisposed to reject information that runs counter to what they think they know, or worse, runs counter to their belief system. This is known as confirmation bias. *Fox News* exploits this tendency of its viewers to its fullest, with stories about conspiracies, lobster-eating welfare queens, and transgender athletes dominating the evening opinion shows.[29] Confirmation bias also entails the tendency to believe misinformation as long as it validates what we already believe, which unveils another unsettling thought about the GOP base. The fact that 56 percent of Republicans believed, at least in part, the QAnon conspiracy theory that global elites and Democratic leaders (like Hillary Clinton) are child molesting cannibals suggests that the GOP base already believed that Democrats are child molesting cannibals, or wanted to believe so.[30] It also means that they're likely to reject any suggestion that Democrats are, in fact, none of these things.

The rule-of-thumb known as Occam's razor assumes that the most likely explanation is the one that requires the simplest assumptions or fewest leaps of logic. Right-wing conspiracy theories are essentially kryptonite to Occam's razor; sure, it's simpler to accept that Hillary Clinton wanted pepperoni toppings at Comet Ping Pong Pizza in D.C., and that Comet Ping Pong Pizza simply does not have a basement. However, many Republicans would much rather *believe* that she and John Podesta were keeping child sex slaves underground at the location.[31] It also appeals to their sense of heroism, which is why PizzaGate and QAnon supporters have been showing up at places with assault rifles looking to "liberate the children."[32]

Akin to this is the concept of *tribal epistemology*. This describes the process by which "Information is evaluated based not on conformity to common standards of evidence or correspondence to a common understanding of the world, but on whether it supports the tribe's values and goals and is vouchsafed by tribal leaders." "'Good for our side' and 'true' begin to blur into one," according to David Roberts at *Vox*.[33] This combination of sensationalized, imaginary threats, and tribalism are the hallmarks of American right-wing media, and also explains how they capture their audiences.[34]

Rush Limbaugh summarized this world outlook in 2008. "We live in two universes... Everything run, dominated, and controlled by the left here and around the world is a lie... And seldom do these two universes ever overlap." Thus, anyone who evaluates external information runs the risk of being branded a heretic. Republicans distrust even assiduously neutral news sources such as *NPR*, *ABC News*, *Reuters*, the *Associated Press*, *The New York Times, Washington Post* and *CBS News* that provide fact-based reporting with a low degree of bias.[35] Indeed, they trust outlets that spew nothing but conspiracy theories, like Alex Jones' *Infowars* more than they do the *New York Times*.[36] (To put the disparity in perspective, Jones is being sued into the ground for promoting the theory that the Sandy Hook Elementary School shooting never happened and was an Obama plot to seize people's guns.)

Conservatives also tend to receive their information from fewer sources than left-wing audiences, making them far more likely to fall into an echo chamber.[37] As a result, Republicans trust journalists less than any other ruling party demographic in a 2018 Pew survey of 20 large countries. The same survey revealed a gap between Democrats' and Republicans' trust in media that was also the largest in any country surveyed.[38] The same lack of trust in journalism cannot be said of Democrats, who tend to distrust sources that actually should quantitatively be distrusted (such as *Hannity*, *Limbaugh*, *Fox News*, and *Breitbart*), which all fare poorly on both bias and factuality.[39] At the same time, they tend to draw their information from a wider range of sources.

Conservative outlets are very effective at distorting reality, even for people who know better. Bobby Lewis of *The Guardian* watched *Fox News* every day for 44 days and noted that "opinion is king" over facts, and marveled at its ability to turn Trump's billion-dollar loss on investments into a glowing recommendation of his business acumen.[40] McKay Coppins of *The Atlantic* deliberately subscribed to conservative social media news outlets during the impeachment, and to his surprise it became harder and harder for him to discern truth from fiction. "I'd assumed that my skepticism and media literacy would inoculate me against such distortions. But I soon found myself reflexively questioning every headline…in this state of heightened suspicion, truth itself—about Ukraine, impeachment, or anything else—felt more and more difficult to locate."[41]

Trump's new favorite network, *One America News* (*OAN*), went a step further in currying favor with the administration. Virtually nothing negative about the President ever penetrated its coverage. *OAN* comes across as something of a dime-store knock-off of *Fox News*, with worse production values and the jingoism dialed to eleven. One journalist watched sixteen straight hours of *OAN* on the same day that news broke that Trump had told Bob Woodward he had deliberately downplayed the danger of the novel coronavirus in March of 2020. No mention of this shocking news was made on *OAN*, until the White House press secretary denied it during the daily press conference (despite Trump admitting on tape what Press Secretary McEnany denied.)[42]

It is little wonder that otherwise intelligent people were unable to discern reality when getting their information from *Fox News* and the conservative media ecosystem. One survey showed that less than half of all Republicans believed that Trump had asked Ukrainian President Zelensky to investigate former Vice

President Joe Biden, despite this request literally being in the rough transcript provided by the Trump White House itself.[43] Simply put, *Fox News* and other conservative media distort reality so badly that you cannot glean basic, crucial, facts about an issue from it.

Another novel innovation during the Trump presidency was the symbiotic relationship between the White House and *Fox News*. The White House went nearly a year without a press briefing.[44] The Departments of Defense and State also effectively ended daily briefings.[45] But Trump routinely spoke with *Fox News* hosts. He watched *Fox News* incessantly, and rage-tweeted (before he was permanently banned) about the agitprop he saw there.[46] For its part, *Fox* shows relentlessly defended virtually anything Trump did, even when the actions were deeply unpopular for their cruelty. *Fox* wasn't just friendly towards a Republican-controlled White House the way they were during the Bush Administration. They were effectively the official media outlet and propaganda arm of the federal government.

This insular information environment results in conservative outlets speaking in code, which is often full of racial dog whistles.[47] The language is something of a mix between a "twins secret language," and the "Darmok and Jalad at Tanagara" allegory language from *Star Trek: The Next Generation*. It relies on shared cultural views and experiences to express ideas and emotions in a word or two.[48] The words themselves have no meaning without them.

For example, the word "caravans" in Fox-ese means desperate criminal indigent Central Americans coming to leach jobs and resources away from "real, good" Americans. "Socialism" evokes atheism, lazy brown people, burning cities, bread lines, empty shelves, and the hated Alexandria Ocasio-Cortez. "American Carnage" means criminal Black people in cities who loot, murder, and burn everything and should be shot by police to restore law and order. Building these associations would not be possible if it were not for the repetitive language and coverage.[49] Trump uses a rhetorical shorthand to evoke images and feelings, while conveying nothing new or substantial.[50]

Conservative media figures are fine with this state of affairs. *Breitbart* Washington News Editor, Matt Boyle, observed that "journalistic integrity is dead. There is no such thing anymore. Thus, everything is about weaponization of information. We envision a day when *CNN* is no longer in business. We envision a day when *The New York Times* closes its doors."[51]

We, as a nation, are no longer able to have rational political discourse in great part due to this ecosystem. We are incapable of operating from a common set of facts, or even from facts that vaguely resemble one another. This is one reason why the guardrails of our democracy are failing, and we're experiencing a political hyper-polarization not seen since the days before the Civil War. The RAND Corporation described this phenomenon in their publication *Truth Decay*. It is characterized by an inability to agree on fact or analysis, a blurring of the line between fact and opinion, increasing influence of anecdotes over analysis, and a loss of trust in formerly respected sources of information.[52] The study concluded that truth decay is a threat to U.S. national interests. Perhaps because they were trying to be non-partisan, RAND also concluded that these effects were "mostly unintentional."

The preponderance of evidence, however, indicates otherwise. This is the culmination of nearly thirty years of deliberate destruction of established media by conservative operatives like Limbaugh, Ailes, Hannity, and Bannon. They never meant to demonstrate journalistic integrity or adhere to the truth. They always wanted a media echo chamber for their base. Their goal from the start was to dismantle faith in mainstream media and make the Republican Party look more like Limbaugh and Hannity than John McCain. They got exactly what they wanted. It wasn't an accident; it was premeditated murder of our ability to discern truth.

Pravda, Istina, and Vranyo

> *"Truth isn't truth."*
> Rudy Giuliani

> *"You think the right question will get you the truth? There is no truth."*
> Anatoly Dyatlov, *Chernobyl*

> *"The real opposition is the media. And the way to deal with them is to flood the zone with shit."*
> Steve Bannon

In Russian, there are two words for truth: *pravda* and *istina*.[53] Americans are more familiar with *pravda*, which means the surface truth, which can be both subjective and infinitely malleable. Think of Obi-Wan telling Luke Skywalker that Darth Vader killed his father: this is true from a certain point of view. *Istina*, on the other hand, is the concrete, universal, and unalterable truth—the real truth. Darth Vader is Anakin Skywalker, and he is Luke's father regardless of his name after turning to the dark side. There is also a third word in Russian, *"vranyo,"* that helps us understand where our country currently is in regard to truth and information. While *vranyo* has no literal English equivalent, the general idea is "useful bullshit."[54]

When Russia invaded the Crimean Peninsula, they used *pravda* to twist the truth and inflame anti-Ukrainian sentiment in Russia.[55] They used *vranyo* to lie and claim they didn't shoot down Malaysia Air Flight 17, and to declare that all the soldiers causing trouble in Ukraine were simply Ukrainians who happened to be ethnic Russian patriots. According to several Russian experts, most Russian civilians had come to regard *istina,* objective factual truth, as impossible to separate out from all the *pravda* and *vranyo.* The population had self-segregated into three groups: the first bought government-provided *pravda* and *vranyo* hook, line, and sinker, the second regarded *istina* as essentially unknowable and willingly went along with the status quo, and only a small remaining percentage was willing and able to distinguish *istina* from *pravda.*

The purpose of obscuring the factual truth was to paralyze the target audiences. Peter Pomeranstev, a Soviet-born British journalist, echoed Hannah Arendt and described this approach as, "nothing is true and everything is possible."[56] Gleb Pavlovsky, an oligarch, technologist, and advisor to Putin until 2011, explained the strategy as: "You can just say anything. Create realities."[57] This eerily echoes what Karl Rove, who filled a similar role for George W. Bush, told a reporter:

> "That's not the way the world really works anymore. We're an empire now, and when we act, we create our own reality. And while you're studying that reality—judiciously, as you will— we'll act again, creating other new realities, which you can study too, and that's how things will sort out. We're history's actors... and you, all of you, will be left to just study what we do."

In other words, facts and truth were *passé.* Seeing events like these, Pomeranstev concluded that "here is going to be there," meaning that he saw the west becoming more like Russia. The over-abundance of misinformation would inevitably overwhelm the audience's ability to discern the truth. Political polarization has helped feed these phenomena. During the 2016 election, Russia deliberately injected fake news into targeted social media streams that was designed to inflame existing social tensions. Indeed, their preparation of their own populace for the invasion of Ukraine was done similarly. It made matters worse that the GOP's base were the most avid consumers and disseminators of this *pravda* and *vranyo.*[58]

Russia had plenty of practice before meddling in the 2016 election. After Russian forces shot down an airliner in Ukraine in 2014, Russian media circled the wagons and began throwing speculation, misleading questions and misinformation at the public in much the same way that *Fox News* does in the U.S. The many stories explaining what happened didn't need to be consistent, they merely needed to cast doubt on what had actually occurred. Russian media claimed or suggested Ukraine itself had shot the passenger plane down, or there was proof that Russian forces were blameless. Regardless, the Russian government's official story changed constantly.[59]

Eighty-six percent of Russians ended up blaming Ukraine for shooting down Malaysia Air Flight 17, even when shown indisputable proof that Russia was responsible.[60] At the end of 2014, only eight percent of Russians believed that they bore any responsibility for events in the Ukraine, and 79 percent agreed with the statement, "the West will be unhappy no matter what Russia does, so you should not pay attention to their claims."[61] Russian propaganda even infected Trump, who in August 2016 stated, "[Putin]'s not going into Ukraine, OK, just so you understand. He's not going to go into Ukraine, alright? You can mark it down. You can put it down."[62] This, despite the fact that Russia had already gone into Ukraine in 2014.

Bálint Magyar, who studied Viktor Orbán's authoritarian efforts to influence media in Hungary, also concluded:

> "Where totalitarian regimes of the past sought to control media, today's autocracies seek to dominate it; and where a totalitarian regime sought to suppress media rights, the autocrat seeks to neutralize them. The end result is not a controlled communications sphere where reality is dictated from above, but a weak one, where nothing can be known and no reality is tangible."[63]

This is happening on a grand scale in the U.S. From Trump's first days in office, we could see efforts to make truth unknowable. The goal was always to get people to regard lies by the White House as equivalent to facts, making truth and reality seem unknowable. When Kellyanne Conway went on *MSNBC* to defend Trump's claim that his inauguration crowd was the biggest ever, despite hard facts and photographic evidence to the contrary, she replied, "I don't think you can prove those numbers one way or another. There's no way to really quantify crowds. We all know that."[64] This is an example of Masha Gessen's rule, "being right was a question of power, not evidence."[65]

Trump was using the power of his office, and the U.S. government, to try to assert control over reality itself. He was also more than willing to punish anyone who spoke truth if it differed from the reality that the White House was presenting.[66] In an autocratic state, telling the truth is always more dangerous than telling lies, even after the RBMK reactor explodes, or hundreds of thousands of people die of a preventable disease.

The majority of Americans cannot tell the difference between real and fake news, either.[67] Eighty-four percent of the population are confident they can spot fake news,[68] although, in a stunning display of the Dunning-Kruger effect, nearly all Republicans have been taught to believe that this "fake news" is coming from traditional media sources.[69] Their paranoia about gays, Mexicans, Muslims, Hillary Clinton, "socialism," and other bugaboos make them particularly susceptible to any conspiracy theory put in front of them via social media, no matter how far-fetched. The PizzaGate and QAnon conspiracy theories are prime examples.[70] The terrible danger of the Republican base believing utter falsehoods was put on display when they stormed the U.S. Capitol and killed five people in the process. They attempted to overturn an free and fair election by force based on the completely false belief that the election had somehow been stolen by nefarious Democratic forces.

The fact that an unending stream of misinformation is available to people is made worse by science fiction writer Theodore Sturgeon's observation that "90 percent of *everything* is "crap." While Sturgeon's Law is a ballpark figure, and the exact ratio of "crap" to reality on the internet is debatable, there is an inexhaustible supply of misinformation out there, and there are forces arrayed to ensure people absorb it.

Rob Pommer in 2007 jokingly proposed what became *Pommer's Law*: "A person's mind can be changed by reading information on the internet. The nature of this change will be from having no opinion to having a wrong opinion." Once this happens, it's often too late. Research shows that when people with factually incorrect political beliefs are presented with factual, incontrovertible evidence they are wrong, they will often dig in their heels and become even more strongly convinced of their false belief.[71] This phenomenon is known as the "backfire effect." Social media also introduces people to more false beliefs by showing them things similar to what they already like and agree with. This leads to the "conspiracy theory singularity" where all of the beliefs begin to merge together. Once people believe one conspiracy theory, they're likely to end up believing many others, because social media algorithms and tribal epistemology guide them to it.[72]

Former Facebook executive, Tim Kendall, testified before Congress that they designed their product to be more addictive than tobacco. "Allowing for misinformation, conspiracy theories, and fake news to flourish were like Big Tobacco's bronchodilators," he confessed. In the end, though, he was mortified by what they had done. "The social media services that I and others have built over the past 15 years have served to tear people apart with alarming speed and intensity...At the very least, we have eroded our collective understanding—at worst, I fear we are pushing ourselves to the brink of a civil war."[73] As a result, we now have a federal government that uses proxies like *Fox News* to convince their base of anything they want, as long as it coincides with the base's existing worldview. If someone already believes that brown people and immigrants are bad, it is much easier to persuade them that Guatemalan toddlers are drug mules for MS-13 and should be locked in cages.[74]

Some Americans are aware of the confusion and misinformation being disseminated but feel powerless to do anything about it.[75] Much of the population is unable to discern the truth, however, and don't care to. This is part of the cause of American political apathy. The fraction that does learn the truth and cares is unable to do anything at all, given that they have no real power in any branch of government, and their ability to affect the course the U.S. is taking is dwindling to nil.[76]

Donald Trump and the Republican Party embraced the use of disinformation as a tool crucial to their political survival.[77] It's no secret that Trump lies the way most people breathe, even about things as trivial as the weather.[78] However, he is capable of using lies tactically.[79] Trump even discussed using *vranyo* with donors, though he did not use the word. During a meeting with Canadian Prime Minister, Justin Trudeau, Trump claimed that the U.S. had a trade deficit with Canada. Trudeau was taken aback and tried to argue that Trump was mistaken. However, without the exact numbers in that instant, his response was weakened to, "I believe you're wrong." Later, Trump admitted he made up this "fact" just to put Trudeau off balance.[80]

This helps to illustrate the power of lies and why strategies relying on disinformation are so successful. The apocryphal maxim, "a lie can travel halfway around the world while the truth is still putting on its shoes," is true. A recent study found that misinformation spreads much more quickly than facts, and to an order of magnitude more people.[81] It doesn't help that once a false "fact" goes out to the public it sticks in their minds, even if it is later proven to be false.[82]

Another related strategy used by Trump, and other Republican media figures, is the "Gish Gallop."[83] This technique involves telling a steady stream of vaguely plausible lies, knowing that it takes longer to disprove the lies than it does to spew them out. It is named after Duane Gish, a creationist who used it to good (or bad) effect during debates in the 1980's. The Gish Gallop is effective for two reasons. First, you can spew lies faster than your opponent can address them in a debate. In practice, it means that Trump and the right-wing media could generate false information faster than it can be debunked, and many of these lies end up "sticking" in people's minds as facts, or potential facts. The other reason it is so effective is that if you fail to disprove every single spurious point made, it allows them to claim victory on the points that slipped by unchallenged.

84

Caitlyn Dewey, who used to debunk internet hoaxes and myths for the *Washington Post*, explained why there is almost no way to combat this tactic: "no one has the time or cognitive capacity to reason all the apparent nuances or discrepancies out." She gave up in disgust, and the column was discontinued shortly thereafter.[84] There's plenty to gain from disinformation and literally nothing to be lost. One study reported that Trump supporters finding out (and even accepting) that he lied or spread misinformation had no significant impact on their opinion of him.[85] However, these same lies, distortions, and half-truths feed their fears and grievances, create a tribal knowledge, and are an effective way to mobilize people.

The other tool used is the active suppression of factual information by reputable sources. When Facebook brought on media sources to fact check articles posted on their site, they included *The Daily Caller* as one of the fact checkers.[86] Unfortunately, the *Caller* is an ultra-right-wing site created by *Fox News* host Tucker Carlson. Inevitably, it began flagging factual information about Trump from reputable sites like *Politico* as "Fake News," adding to the confusion over what was real while simultaneously ensuring fewer people saw the real information.[87]

For its part, Facebook started, in 2015, to carefully craft its rules to make sure Trump and his campaign didn't violate them.[88] In 2020, Facebook announced that they would not do any fact checking of political ads purchased on the site for the upcoming election, continuing a policy that did massive damage to the American political system just four years prior and likely contributed to the insurrection after the election.[89] The danger becomes even clearer when you find that 45 percent of Americans get most of their news from Facebook.[90]

This is a recipe for chaos, and it is intentional. The Russians took a keen interest in seeing Trump elected in 2016 and helped it along by setting Americans against each other. They used their own media outlets like *RT* (formerly *Russia Today*) and *Sputnik*.[91] They bought ads on Facebook to promote pro-Trump, pro-Sanders and anti-Clinton messages.[92] They created over 500 fake Facebook groups, fake social media accounts, and bots to control many of them in order to spread divisive memes and stories and to manipulate voters into action, like rallies.[93] The Mueller investigation concluded that Russia's efforts were years in the making, sweeping and systemic.[94] These efforts continued even after the election. The Seth Rich murder conspiracy, promoted endlessly by Sean Hannity on *Fox News*, was revealed to have been planted and promoted by Russian intelligence.[95] As Brian Barrett in *Wired* magazine noted about the Russian disinformation attempts directed against democracies, "The point has always been to find democracy's loose seams, and pull."[96]

The RAND Corporation looked at Russian messaging and also concluded that, "We characterize the contemporary Russian model for propaganda as 'the fire hose of falsehood' because of two of its distinctive features: high numbers of channels and messages, and a shameless willingness to disseminate partial truths or outright fictions. In the words of one observer, '[N]ew Russian propaganda entertains, confuses, and overwhelms the audience.'"[97] Digging a bit deeper, RAND found four distinctive features of contemporary Russian propaganda:

1. High volume and multichannel
2. Rapid, continuous, and repetitive
3. Lacking commitment to objective reality
4. Lacking commitment to consistency

Republicans and conservative media outlets have adopted this model.[98] Rightwing media sites that peddle conspiracy theories and agitprop, like *The Daily Wire*, are shared relentlessly by bot accounts and pages on Facebook, which refuses to shut them down despite the fact that the pages violate Facebook's terms and conditions.[99] Conservative media outlets are happy to coalesce around talking points about Benghazi or Burisma, or to defend whatever Trump did. These defenses need not be based in any sort of reality, nor do they need to remain consistent.[100] They are, however, blasted *ad nauseum* from conservative outlets until the faithful are immune to fact, and much of the public is just confused.

It doesn't help that traditional and reliable news outlets still believe they are playing by the old rules. They seem reluctant to call out falsehoods and feel obligated to present "both sides" of an issue, even though they know full well that one of those sides is propaganda ungrounded in any sort of reality. *The New York Times*, in particular, has been guilty of this. Both-sideism not only makes things worse by further obscuring truth, but it widens the Overton Window a bit further each time, eventually making political positions that would have been unthinkable a few years ago part of the mainstream conversation.[101]

Traditional media's paradigm of how American democracy works did not include an administration that lied this way, which left them vulnerable. They are used to journalistic objectivity, which treats both sides with equal respect, as if each set of arguments is equally true and presented in good faith. However, this faith in journalistic objectivity is misplaced when the government weaponizes lies and misinformation against its citizens. As journalist Norman Ornstein observes, "a balanced treatment of an unbalanced phenomenon distorts reality."[102] In this situation there is only one side: the truth. Daniel Okrent, journalist and inventor of fantasy baseball, also summarized this concept in what became known as *Okrent's Law*: "The pursuit of balance can create imbalance because sometimes something is true."[103]

American media has failed at fighting this source of democratic decline because they were extremely hesitant to call the un-truths that came out of the White House, GOP, and right-wing media sources as lies. For something to be a lie there must be intent, and as the character George Costanza on the 1990's TV comedy "Seinfeld" observed, "It's not a lie if you believe it." Trump repeatedly demonstrated that he was both ignorant of facts, intellectually incurious, and existed in his own weird little universe (and it's not a happy place). Thus, media outlets felt they could not call what he said "lies" when there was the chance that he believed what he was saying, no matter how ridiculous or stupid. Given that Trump claimed wind turbines cause cancer, and that American troops captured British airports during the Revolutionary War, it is hard to underestimate the depths of his ignorance.[104]

With someone like Richard Nixon, the distinction was far clearer. He may have been many things, but stupid or ignorant were not among them. Accordingly, forty-five years ago it was far easier for the *Washington Post* or *The New York Times* to call his statements lies than it is for them to do with Trump's outlandish pronouncements. In this, we all became the Danish Prime Minister, who observed of Trump's lies and irrational outbursts: "I strongly hope that this is not meant seriously."

It is one thing to create the lies. It is another to ensure they reach the right eyes and ears, as part of the information warfare "kill chain." It has become easier to target individuals with ads and news meant to influence them in specific ways. Cambridge Analytica developed psychological profiles of about 30 million voters using Facebook data.[105] From this, targeted information meant to manipulate voters was placed via Facebook and Google ads. For example, Black Facebook users were targeted in the final days of the 2016 election with newsfeed headlines announcing, "Hillary Thinks African Americans are Super Predators," in order to suppress their vote.[106] Conservatives were shown headlines and videos meant to stoke fears of violent immigrants and racial replacement in order to boost their turnout, and articles presenting Trump as the only one who could protect them from the invasion.

Progressives and liberals watching this situation have been bewildered. The old expression, "Sunlight is the best disinfectant," doesn't seem to apply anymore. While the *Washington Post's* motto is "Democracy dies in darkness," one humorist wryly noted that "maybe it dies in broad daylight too."[107] People opposed to the Trumpist movement have come to the horrifying, dawning realization that there are few, if any, effective counters to the movement's disinformation strategies and tactics. Dr. Christopher Browning, Professor of History Emeritus at the University of North Carolina at Chapel Hill and an expert on the Holocaust and Nazi Germany, described how he felt while watching Trump rise to power. "[My] feeling is bewilderment. As a rational thinker, someone who believes in the Enlightenment project and liberal democratic norms, I assumed that the truth and basic facts were a type of sunshine. If you put enough of this light out there for the public, they would make good decisions. But now, with Trump and his enablers, systemic serial lying is rewarded."[108]

How do you fight propaganda whose sole requirement is that it needs to be plausible to a target audience already untethered from reality who is inclined to believe anything they hear that confirms their views? Mostly, you can't. As RAND put it, "Don't expect to counter the firehose of falsehood with the squirt gun of truth." You can't out-firehose them. They have more outlets, more money, a more devoted audience, and the supply of misinformation is effectively infinite. You can't shut down the propaganda outlets, whether they're *Fox News, RT,* or social media giants. You could try to get Facebook, Twitter, and other social media outlets to cut down on propaganda and micro-targeting, but these efforts appear to have failed. There is a strong demand signal for all this disinformation, because it is what Trump's base wants to hear. There's a lot of money to be made spreading it, and power in giving the customer exactly what they want, even if it is cyanide for democracy.

In the end, *istina* is absolutely no match for the *pravda* and *vranyo* that Trumpists prefer. When former Tea Party Republican Joe Walsh briefly ran for President against Trump in 2020, he pleaded with the Republican caucus in Iowa.

> "I said the party is going to be a party of old white men unless we become more inclusive. More boos. I said we shouldn't be okay with a president who lies all the time. I said we need a president who's decent, not cruel. I said, you might enjoy Trump's mean tweets, but most people don't. I said we must be better than a president who makes every day about himself. Boos. And more boos. One woman yelled that she loves the president's tweets. The crowd cheered her." [109]

Conversely, when McKay Coppins at *The Atlantic* asked a Trump supporter at a rally whether it mattered if the things Trump said were true or not, he replied, "He tells you what you want to hear. And I don't know if it's true or not—but it sounds good, so fuck it."[110]

How do you compete with that?

Five

Idiocracy

"To be a scientist is to be naive. We are so focused on our search for truth we fail to consider how few actually want us to find it."

Valery Legasov, *Chernobyl*

O ur society requires expertise. Whether it is landing a military helicopter on the pitching and heaving flight deck of a destroyer in the dead of night, performing heart surgery, designing rockets, or virtually any other profession, our civilization depends on specialization and trust. To use an example from Tom Nichols' book, *The Death of Expertise*, we don't expect that the architect, metallurgist, and beam welder building a skyscraper should be able to do each other's jobs, even though each is competent in their own field.[1] If we did make them do each other's jobs, common sense dictates that the results would be catastrophic.

Yet, somehow that common sense has been lost. The conservative base believes that anyone can do the job of some "lazy government bureaucrat," because they believe government workers are inherently untrustworthy and have easy jobs. Trumpists have been convinced that proper ideology is more important than the right experience or education. As a result, we ended up with a conservative radio host leading the United States Department of Agriculture (USDA), a religious billionaire in charge of the Department of Education, a medical doctor running housing policy… and Trump's real estate-developer son-in-law managing national the COVID-19 pandemic response.

The result is much like what would happen if the beam welder and architect switched places: many horrible and needless deaths. The true tragedy, however, is that the people who didn't trust the experts still don't trust them, even after those experts were repeatedly proven right and hundreds of thousands of people have died. Such blindness to the obvious took a long time to cultivate and was intentionally developed over a period of decades.

89

Expertise Matters

"There is a cult of ignorance in the United States, and there has always been. The strain of anti-intellectualism has been a constant thread winding its way through our political and cultural life, nurtured by the false notion that democracy means that my ignorance is just as good as your knowledge."

Isaac Asimov

The modern Republican Party has worked relentlessly for decades to discredit mainstream media and become the sole trusted source of information to their base. However, to accomplish this they also needed to destroy something else: their base's faith in science, academia, and subject matter expertise, particularly in government.

The assault on expertise within the government goes back decades. Two of Ronald Reagan's most famous quotes touch on these themes. When Reagan said, "In this present crisis, government is not the solution to our problem; government is the problem," it was echoed by the Trump Administration in its response to COVID-19. Another of Reagan's quotes was: "The nine most terrifying words in the English language are 'I'm from the government, and I'm here to help,'" which implies that any sort of government assistance or intervention only makes the situation worse. These belie a fundamental misunderstanding of how science, and expertise, are vital to a functional government that provides basic services to the public under normal circumstances, and particularly in a crisis like COVID-19.

One of the most familiar conservative misuses of science in the 20th century was the effort to confuse the public over the link between tobacco use and cancer. By 1953, it was clear to the tobacco industry that their product caused cancer.[2] Their response was to hide the evidence as well as they could. They created the Tobacco Institute to provide plausible sounding pseudo-science propaganda denying the tobacco-cancer link. The goal was to confuse people and encourage "debate" when there really wasn't any. The scientific consensus was overwhelming, yet it took 40 years for Republicans to turn on the tobacco industry.

In the 1990's, in the largest class action lawsuit in U.S. history, the courts found that the tobacco industry waged a decades-long fight against science and research while deliberately muddying the waters with their own deceptive, low quality studies.[3] Conservatives from the south were the biggest proponents of attempts to confuse the issue. Mitch McConnell was a "special friend" to the tobacco industry for decades.[4] He regurgitated tobacco industry talking points nearly word for word, including denying the connection between the product and cancer. Rush Limbaugh was an avid cigar smoker who, as late as 2015, also denied the link.[5]

He was later diagnosed with terminal stage 4 lung cancer in 2020, and died of it a year later.[6]

The Republican Party hasn't only been hostile to science related to tobacco; it is hostile to any science that threatens the cash flow of its corporate sponsors, contradicts the religious beliefs of its base, or runs counter to conservative ideologies in general. Belief in anthropogenic climate change has become a heresy to Republicans because it might hurt fossil fuel industry profits,[7] and because the base literally believes God will not let it happen.[8] Most Republican Party members believe people choose to be LGBTQ and oppose efforts to ban harmful conversion therapy, despite ample research and proof to the contrary.[9] Republicans reject any studies by economists that cast doubt on the efficacy of supply-side economics, or the thoroughly discredited belief that tax cuts pay for themselves.[10]

They reject research on abortion, and instead force doctors to lie about the procedure to their patients.[11] They have joined ranks with the anti-vaccination movement in the name of "parental control" and "religious freedom" to oppose strengthening vaccination laws, in some cases working to tear down these laws in conservative states.[12] White evangelicals were the demographic least likely to get the COVID-19 vaccine as well. The GOP categorically rejects the overwhelming evidence and research by Nobel Prize winning economists on the effects of wealth inequality.[13]

They adamantly oppose any effort to research gun violence,[14] because they know it will show that easy access to firearms is the cause of high gun homicide rates in the U.S.[15] Accepting this blindingly obvious fact would run counter to their dogma that being awash in guns somehow makes us safer.[16] Instead, their leadership blames mental illness (which also exists in countries with low gun violence),[17] video games (gamers in countries with little gun violence have played until they die of exhaustion),[18] and lack of prayer in schools.[19] The list of rejections of science in the name of ideology is nearly endless.

You get people to reject scientists, academics, and subject matter experts by making them *want* to disbelieve them. The conservative movement in the U.S. has been doing this for decades. For example, people who believe in climate change are portrayed, and then seen, as weak or womanly.[20] They paint anyone who supports abortion as evil, and then ask their base: you wouldn't listen to someone who supports murdering babies, would you?[21] Conservative leaders declare that anyone barring unfettered access to assault rifles and high-capacity magazines is a gun-grabbing closet dictator, and then ask: you wouldn't listen to some freedom-hating commie, right?[22]

These sorts of narratives are frighteningly effective. For example, only 17 percent of Republicans believe climate change is a critical issue, compared with 72 percent of Democrats (and 97 percent of experts).[23] Given that climate change represents the gravest threat to the survival of *homo sapiens* as a species, the fact that propaganda can make 83 percent of Republicans dismiss it is stunning.

This might seem simplistic, but over time the basic "us vs. them" narrative lures people into orthodoxy.[24] This sort of messaging creates an "us" that sets Republicans against the evil "them." Trump railed in one of his speeches: "Our radical Democrat opponents are driven by hatred, prejudice, and rage. They want to destroy you, and they want to destroy our country as we know it."[25] Republicans are significantly more likely to see their Democratic counterparts as lazy, immoral, and unpatriotic.[26] Disagreement is a sign of both immorality and treasonous intent.[27] This is true for Republicans more than Democrats, due to homogeneity within the GOP.[28] Data from the Varieties of Democracy (V-Dem) Project show that demonization of the opposition in the U.S. is asymmetric as well. Figure 3 (below) shows how it has shifted over time. The anti-democratic Hungarian Fidesz and Polish Law and Justice (PIS) parties' scores are provided for comparison.

Figure 4. How Often Party Leaders Demonize Opposition

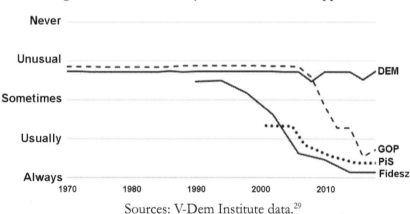

Sources: V-Dem Institute data.[29]

Rush Limbaugh called academia, government, science, and media the "four corners of deceit."[30] For decades conservative voices like his cultivated distrust in all four by using flawed logic encouraging the belief that someone's down-home common sense was intrinsically more capable of discerning truth than people who have studied these things their entire lives. Perhaps nothing better embodies this outlook than Senator James Inhofe (R-OK) bringing a snowball to the Senate floor as "proof" that climate change isn't real.[31]

Years of denigrating expertise have taken a measurable toll. Conservatives are now less likely to trust scientists than independents or liberals, regardless of whether the issue is climate change, nuclear power, genetically modified organisms, evolution, or vaccines.[32] Only a third of conservatives trust scientists on evolution and climate change, and a slim majority (56 percent) on vaccines (though this survey was taken before the COVID-19 pandemic, and the number has almost certainly fallen since). These attacks have also destroyed faith in academia and college educations. When writing about a topic, citing experts and journal articles actually dissuades conservatives, as they see appeals to authority as "sure signs of elitism."[33] In 1990, a roughly equal number of Democrats and Republicans had college degrees. Today, Democrats have become the party of the college educated.[34] Seventy-four percent of Democrats said they believe graduating from college is important to being successful, compared with only forty percent of Republicans.[35] In fact, fifty-nine percent of Republicans believe that colleges are bad for America, and that number has been growing.[36]

Religious conservative and former U.S. Senator Rick Santorum (R-PA) made it clear that his wing of the party was waging war against institutions of higher learning during a speech in 2012. "We will never have the elite smart people on our side, because they believe they should have the power to tell you what to do. So, our colleges and universities, they're not going to be on our side."[37] Conservatives are literally afraid to send their kids to college because they will presumably be exposed to "liberal" ideas like climate change. Dennis Prager, of the ironically-named "PragerU" propaganda videos on YouTube, went on *Fox News* and told people not to send their kids to college to prevent them from being infected with such nonsense.[38] "Sending your child to college is playing Russian roulette with their values," he concluded.[39]

The sad irony is that studies show colleges don't actually make kids more liberal; on the whole they come out with the same attitudes they went in with.[40] Nor are college professors disproportionately liberal; their political beliefs are roughly what you would expect of members of the public, with similar educational backgrounds.[41] However, Trump's push for a "1776 Commission," and his executive order to only teach patriotic material clearly showed conservatives aren't concerned about bias in education. Rather, they are arguing for the "proper" kind of bias.

It has already been noted that Americans generally aren't able to discern the difference between reliable and unreliable sources. Republicans in particular have been persuaded to distrust centrist media outlets, journal articles, and experts. While people who work in academia and research have been taught to evaluate a source's reliability, most Americans don't have that sort of training. Indeed, Republican-aligned forces are trying to discourage this capability. In 2012, the Republican Party of Texas wrote into its 2012 platform that they reject the teaching of "Higher Order Thinking Skills (HOTS), critical thinking skills, and similar programs..."[42]

Trump was apparently their poster child. He is an anti-intellectual who "goes with his gut," rather than relying on research or expertise, and didn't place a lot of value on education when he was in school.[43] A professor at Wharton called him, "the dumbest goddamn student I ever had."[44] Trump doesn't read,[45] his briefings consisted mostly of pictures,[46] and he has "the attention span of a gnat."[47] Yet, Trump enjoyed support from anti-intellectual pundits like Hannity and Limbaugh from day one of his campaign, much to the initial consternation of the Republican establishment.[48]

Trump has been described as a "fucking moron," "dope," "fucking idiot," "dumb as shit," and having "the understanding of a fifth or sixth grader."[49] Shockingly, every one of those quotes came from members of his own cabinet and staff, not his Democratic opponents. He was, however, exactly what the base wanted. They didn't want Republicans who sounded like Ivy-League educated lawyers, especially not after Barack and Michelle Obama (who were exactly that). They wanted someone who saw the world the way they did and sounded like the political voices they listened to the most. Which is to say, they wanted someone who resembled loud-mouthed college drop-outs like Rush Limbaugh and Sean Hannity.

Trump had made it clear from the beginning that he had no intention of trusting experts within the government. During the 2016 campaign, when asked who he was consulting with on foreign policy, he responded, "I'm speaking with myself, number one, because I have a very good brain, and I've said a lot of things."[50] At a rally in Wisconsin, he disparaged foreign policy experts within the government and made it clear they would be marginalized during his administration: "The experts are terrible... They say, 'Donald Trump needs a foreign policy adviser.' Supposing I didn't have one, would it be worse than what we're doing now?"[51]

His utter disregard and disdain for expertise extended to the presidential transition team: he didn't see the need for one. Christie had to tell him that it was legally required. Trump and his supporters believed government was easy. At one point, he told former New Jersey governor and campaign advisor Chris Christie, "Chris, you and I are so smart that we can leave the victory party two hours early and do the transition ourselves." When Trump found out that putting together the transition team had cost the campaign money, he was furious. "Fuck the law.

I don't give a fuck about the law. I want my fucking money. Shut it down," he reportedly yelled at Christie and Bannon.[52]

Regardless, eventually Trump went along with standing up a transition team led by Christie. The former governor ran the team in something resembling a professional manner, building 20 binders of guidance on how to conduct the turnover if Trump won. Three days after the election, Trump fired Christie, and his binders were thrown out. Responsibility for the transition was passed to Trump's children (Eric, Don Jr., and Ivanka) and his son-in-law Jared Kushner, none of whom had any experience in government.[53] The utterly predictable result was that the transition was a fiasco, and the administration unprepared to govern from day one.

While previous presidents, both Democratic and Republican, had worked to ensure a smooth transition of power, Trump made little to no effort. Many Federal agencies never saw landing teams. The ones that did show up were woefully underqualified, often just recent college graduates selected mainly for their ideological purity. At the Department of Energy, the Trump transition representative "didn't bring a pencil or a piece of paper. He didn't ask questions. He spent an hour... He never asked to meet with us again."[54] There was never an intention to work with these departments and institutions, only to remake or destroy them.

As senior government official Max Stier noted, "A bungled transition becomes a bungled presidency." According to *The New York Times*, so little effort had been put into the transition that White House staffers hadn't even learned to use the light switches, and ended up conducting meetings in the dark after the inauguration.[55] This particular consequence seems funny, but among the things lost during this bungling was the detailed Obama pandemic response plan, which would end up costing hundreds of thousands of American lives.[56]

When Trump talked about "draining the swamp" during the 2016 campaign, he couched it as getting rid of lobbyists, foreign and corporate influence, and term limits. Naturally he did the opposite: "draining the swamp," turned into an all-out assault on the "deep state" and the "administrative state," Trump's phrases for experts within the federal government. [57] The Trump Administration began systematically dismantling federal expertise in areas Republicans and the President didn't like, or found inconvenient.[58] At the same time, he filled government posts with former lobbyists who stood to make a profit from destroying the agencies they were put in charge of.

Civil servants made the cardinal mistake of believing that they were seen by Trump, his administration, and the Republican base as high-minded individuals working for the betterment of the country as a whole. However, as George Packer observed in *The Atlantic*, "Trump didn't want true professionals. Either you were loyal, or you were not, and draining the swamp turned out to mean getting rid of those who were not."[59] Civil servants were tools to be used to further an agenda, and if they hindered it, they would be discarded.

One of the first acts of the Trump Administration at the Department of Energy was to issue a questionnaire to all employees. It pointedly asked whether individuals had been involved in anything to do with work on anthropogenic climate change. The meaning was clear: they were going to find anyone who supported the scientific consensus on climate change, and then either sideline them or force them out. "It reminded me of McCarthyism," remarked one DOE official.[60]

From day one, Trump installed people who were hostile to the agencies they led, were former lobbyists helping their former clients get richer, or were comically unqualified.[61] Former Secretary of State Rex Tillerson, former CEO of Exxon-Mobile, was frustrated by the fact that the State Department didn't operate like a company.[62] Secretary of Energy Rick Perry reportedly didn't know what his department actually did until a month before he took the reins.[63]

The lower-level transition team members weren't any better. Former workers at the DOE described them as "a handful of young ideologues" who "mainly ran around the building insulting people." According to a former Obama administration official, "There was a mentality that everything the government does is stupid and bad, and the people in it are stupid and bad."[64] All Obama appointees were forced out immediately, most without replacement. Thus, critical roles like CFO at the Department of Energy went unfilled for months or years.

Secretary of Education Betsy DeVos, who did not have any experience in government, teaching, or school administration prior to her appointment, was nominated to head the Department of Education specifically because she wanted to tear down the public education system. Her confirmation hearing went so badly as to be a farce. She couldn't answer the most basic questions about her department, and opined that teachers need guns in the classroom to fend off grizzly bear attacks.[65]

Ben Carson is a former brain surgeon (with offensive views about a lot of things) who was inexplicably put in charge of Housing and Urban Development (HUD).[66] He believed poverty motivates people to work harder, implying that poor people are poor because they're lazy, which is why he supported cutting HUD's budget.[67] He didn't grow into the job at HUD either. During a May 2019 hearing when Representative Katie Porter (D-CA) asked Carson about REO

(Real Estate Owned) properties (a common term for foreclosures), he thought she was talking about Oreo cookies. At that point, he had been the head of HUD for over two years.[68]

ProPublica compiled an expansive list of lies told by Trump cabinet nominees Scott Pruitt, Betsy DeVos, Steven Mnuchin, Tom Price and Jeff Sessions during their confirmation hearings.[71] Many of them were ridiculous in their flimsiness: DeVos had apparently plagiarized her answers from the American Legislative Exchange Council's website. As Masha Gessen described it in her book, *Surviving Autocracy*: "They were lying to the swamp. They couldn't be bothered with the conventions of government because they found government itself contemptible."[70]

The Soviets also believed that the correct communist ideology would always result in the right solution, pouring millions of rubles into researching Lamarckian evolution.[71] Likewise, modern Republicans seem to believe that education, expertise, and experience are far less important to running a government than the correct ideology. Their solution for dealing with inconvenient ideologies, and the people who hold them within the federal civil service, is to make them go away, either by firing them, giving them a "window seat," or making their lives so miserable they simply leave.

Putting people of limited intellect, experience, ability, imagination, and education in positions of authority in government was a common tactic of past authoritarian regimes. Loyalty and the right ideology were the most prized attributes and protected leaders from being challenged by ambitious people smarter than they were. Despite the misperception that Nazi Germany functioned like a finely tuned piece of German engineering, it was in fact corrupt, inefficient, and filled with people promoted past their level of competence. Extreme competence was the exception, not the rule.[72]

Tom Nichols describes the phenomenon where Americans in particular believe that, "All things are knowable and every opinion on any subject is as good as any other."[75] This is part of what's known as the Dunning-Kruger effect: people who know the least about a subject are the most likely to believe they know a lot more than they really do. To put it simply, "The dumber you are, the more confident you are that you're not dumb." Because they radically overestimate how much they know, they are also much more likely to have strong opinions about things they know almost nothing about. For example, people who can't find Ukraine on a map were the most likely to favor U.S. military intervention there.

Because of the amount of misinformation being pumped into the GOP base by their media ecosystem, social media silos, and politicians willing to exploit their ignorance, Republicans are particularly vulnerable to the Dunning-Kruger effect. When asked if the U.S. should bomb Agrabah (the fictional kingdom in Disney's *Aladdin*), 30 percent Republicans said we should, and only 13 percent said no. This survey was taken during the 2016 election, and found that Trump voters were more than twice as likely to support the bombing campaign against a fictional nation in a children's cartoon as were Republicans who supported another candidate.[74] When asked if Arabic numerals (the number system we already use) should be taught in school, 72 percent of Republicans said no, about twice as many as Democrats. John Dick, the British pollster who administered the survey, said the results were "the saddest and funniest testament to American bigotry we've ever seen in our data."[75]

The internet jokingly reinforces this delusion of knowledge. "Rule 34 of the Internet" states that if you can think of something, you can find pornography of it on the web. A corollary to this is that no matter what opinion you have, you can find a web page that supports the idea. You can always surf Google until you find confirmation of the conclusion you want. People with social media accounts and far too much time on their hands can easily find "evidence" to support whatever they already believe and call it "research."

Combine the "90 percent of everything is crap" idea with the Dunning-Kruger effect, freely available misinformation, universal access to Google, and Pommer's law regarding how people's minds are usually changed for the worse by reading information on the internet, and you end up with a large population of people who almost universally (mistakenly) believe they are experts. Tom Nichols compared it to an entire nation of Cliff Clavins, the know-it-all mailman from the old sitcom *Cheers*.[76]

Lies that people want to believe trump factual information. When reporters asked believers in the QAnon conspiracy where their information came from, or challenged them to prove their beliefs, the responses they got were almost always some variation of "go online," or "dig deep."[77] There have always been conspiracy theories and bad information in human history, but this is the first time that every crackpot and kook can broadcast them to the world at nearly the speed of light. This completely undermines the ability of actual experts to implement coherent public policy.

Filling positions of power with people who have no experience, and making the actual experts treat their ideas as valid, takes a toll on the experts in question. You could see the light leaving the eyes of Dr. Birx as she shared the stage with Trump, pretending that his suggestion to use bleach to kill the novel corona virus inside of people wasn't a phenomenally stupid idea. This is in part the reason for the mass exodus of government experts under Trump and his incompetent, corrupt cronies and sycophants.

The Trumpist "America First" policies, combined with a series of deeply unpopular appointees,[78] led to low morale and mass resignations.[79] Sixty percent of all career ambassadors from the Department of State resigned.[80] The Department of Justice was similarly devastated. It was turned into a tool for attacking Trump's enemies and defending his crimes, while tearing down civil rights for women, people of color, and LGBTQ individuals.[81] Career litigators who could no longer bear the ethical burden of what they were being asked to do resigned in disgust. The entire Department of Justice prosecutorial team on the Roger Stone case resigned rather than drop charges under political pressure from the White House.[82] The National Labor Relations Board, under the leadership of Trump appointees, actively undermined workers' rights. Its civil work force was utterly demoralized. The Department of Education and Consumer Financial Protection Bureau, also actively destroyed from within, fared even worse.

At the same time, those left behind were given the nearly impossible task of turning Trump's venal mafioso instincts into a coherent policy. Kiron Skinner, the State Department policy director under Trump, described her assigned duties: "The President provides the hunches and instincts, and it's my job, and that of Secretary Pompeo, to turn those hunches and instincts into hypotheses." This is the basis for what has been called the "Trump Doctrine" in foreign policy, which former State Department policy director Anne-Marie Slaughter described as "the United States is a sovereign nation guided by its national interest – we'll do for you if you do for us."[83]

Scientists who deal with the realities of climate change were systematically forced out, leaving empty offices and a government incapable of performing vital services for agriculture. According to the Office of Personnel Management, the U.S. has "lost a generation of research," as over 1,600 scientists left federal service in the first two years of Trump's presidency alone.[84] Morale at the Environmental Protection Agency (EPA) was destroyed by Trump appointees rolling back decades of progress. What happened at the EPA went far beyond anything done during previous Republican administrations. "I've never seen such an orchestrated war on the environment or science," said Christine Todd Whitman, former head of the EPA under George W. Bush.[85]

The Administration's disdain for science extended into foreign policy, where it abdicated the country's role as a global leader. The U.S. withdrawal from the Paris climate agreements allowed China and the European Union to claim leadership, while giving other bad actors an excuse. Given the projected consequences of doing nothing about climate change over the next decade, this could have devastating consequences for all life on the planet.

One of Trump's final maneuvers before the 2020 election was to issue Executive Order 13957 stripping anyone in federal service in "confidential, policy-determining, policy-making, or policy-advocating positions" of their civil service protections. In practical terms, this means that doctors, scientists, economists, and lawyers who provide expert, fact-based advice could be fired at will for failing to provide the "advice" the administration wants. It also converted many politically appointed positions into permanent ones, ensuring that ideologues put in place by the Administration would remain when he left. [86]

Similarly, the Trump Administration also withdrew from the World Health Organization in a fit of pique during the COVID-19 pandemic.[87] It also withdrew from the Iran nuclear deal, not because Iran had violated it, but simply because Trump and the base didn't like it. As a result, the U.S. reputation for upholding treaties was damaged, as well as its international standing and leadership.[88]

While these transactional approaches to science, expertise, and foreign policy might be marginally acceptable for a someone running quasi-legal schemes in the New York real estate market, it was hardly a winning approach to a complicated multilateral world, where long term U.S. national security interests are critically affected by relations with our allies and adversaries. The Trump Doctrine did enormous harm to U.S. interests, and both Russia and China perceive our position in the world as critically diminished.[89]

The consequences of policies based on anti-science animus are rarely felt quickly, or while the people implementing them are still in office. It will take decades for climate change to create the "dystopian hellscape" predicted by experts on the subject.[90] If we stopped providing public education, it would take decades for the country to run out of educated workers. If the EPA stopped doing its job entirely, large numbers of people won't drop dead from hexavalent chromium poisoning next week, next month, or even next year.

However, the Trump Administration finally encountered an issue where it went up against science, and the consequences were clear almost immediately in the form of the novel coronavirus. Trump and GOP leaders didn't give a damn about the science, and tried to imagine it away to save the economy and their reelection chances. The Trump Administration's anti-science and expertise policies were compared to previous efforts by the tobacco and petroleum industries to shut down government research into their products.[91] The old and well-respected journal *Nature* concluded: "The U.S. president's actions have exacerbated the pandemic that has killed more than 200,000 people in the United States, rolled back environmental and public-health regulations, and undermined science and scientific institutions. Some of the harm could be permanent."[92]

Even exiting the White House, Trump ensured that Biden would struggle to restore expertise to government. During the final months of his presidency he purged Pentagon and Department of Defense boards and replaced their members with unqualified ideologues who were loyal to him. This included placing campaign managers Corey Lewandowski and David Bossie on the Defense Business Board, and Kellyann Conway on the Air Force Academy Board of Visitors.[93]

The other thing we learned, with the entire world watching, is that Trump's base—47 percent of the American population—simply didn't care how many people died. Hundreds of thousands of Americans needlessly succumbed to COVID-19 between March 2020 and the election on November 3rd, 2020 but this had no effect on their support of Trump.

Trump and *Fox News* Made the Pandemic Inevitable

"Every lie we tell incurs a debt to the truth. Sooner or later, that debt is paid."
Valery Legasov, *Chernobyl*

"For whatsoever a man soweth, that shall he also reap."
Galatians 6:7, *KJV*

COVID-19 brought an entirely new dimension to the conservative war on science and expertise. The failures of the Trump Administration to contain, prevent, and quarantine the spread of the novel coronavirus had the potential to be felt well before the 2020 election. Rather than taking decades for the failures to be measurable, the consequences came within months. Finally, something happened to the Trump Administration which exposed the "Fifth Risk" of "responding to long-term risks with short-term solutions."[94]

Trump was never one to listen to experts or scientists, and is nearly incapable of accepting information he doesn't want to hear.[95] Briefers were told not to present him with information that contradicted something he had said in public. COVID-19 was no different; his aides warned Health and Human Services Secretary Azar against briefing the President on the coronavirus in January, and Trump was consistently presented with only best-case scenarios.[96] Thus, when he finally was briefed, he was motivated to downplay it for several reasons.

The Trump Administration wasn't in a position to respond effectively even if they had taken it seriously, however. Trump and John Bolton had disbanded the National Security Pandemic Response Team in 2018.[97] President Obama had left behind a comprehensive pandemic response plan for the Trump White House. Like almost everything else in the bungled transition, it was lost or simply thrown away out of incompetence, disregard for expertise, or disdain of anything related to the previous administration.[98]

Trump had made the economy the focus of his pitch to be re-elected,[99] and used the stock market as a barometer of his economic policies.[100] Thus, he was reluctant to do anything about the coronavirus that might negatively affect consumer confidence, the stock market, or the economy as a whole (and thereby his re-election chances). Trump also never admits mistakes and dislikes backtracking or giving the appearance of ever having been wrong.[101] Unsurprisingly, he declared that the administration's initial responses to COVID-19 Centers for Disease Control (CDC) tests were "…all perfect like the letter was perfect. The transcription was perfect. Right? This was not as perfect as that but pretty good."[102]

He also vastly overestimated his knowledge of epidemiology in a disastrous demonstration of the Dunning-Kruger Effect. "Every one of these doctors said: 'How do you know so much about this?' Maybe I have a natural ability," he boasted during a visit to the Centers for Disease Control (CDC) in early March 2020.[103] To put this "natural ability" in perspective, he also believed that vaccines cure disease, and that the flu vaccine would prevent the spread of COVID-19.[104] He was surprised to hear that people could die of the flu, even though it killed his grandfather.[105]

Just days prior to this visit, he had replaced HHS director Azar with Mike Pence as head of the COVID-19 response team. During the press conference announcing Azar's ouster, Trump blamed the outbreak on "open borders" and immigrants. His son and surrogate Don Jr. claimed Democrats wanted to "kill millions" of Americans with their policies, a notion which Vice President Pence seconded.[106] Azar was a former executive at a pharmaceutical company and a lawyer, with no other experience in public health. As such, his qualifications to lead HHS were mediocre. But he was still more qualified than the sycophantic and religiously conservative Pence.[107] The Vice President's most prominent previous foray into public health had been during his time as governor of Indiana, when he went against the opinion of experts and banned needle exchanges. This led to the largest HIV outbreak in the history of the state.[108]

The Soviet response to the Chernobyl disaster was to force all information regarding the disaster to flow directly to Moscow bureaucrats, apparatchiks, and the Secretariat first. Similarly, the first order of business for Pence's task force was making sure all HHS and CDC information on COVID-19 went through the Vice President's office first before the public, or the world, could see it.[109] Days after replacing Azar, Trump declared that the danger had passed, and the situation was contained completely. "We closed it down; we stopped it. Otherwise — the head of CDC said last night that you would have thousands of more problems if we didn't shut it down very early. That was a very early shutdown, which is something we got right."[110]

Trump overruled experts' handling of the outbreak in several ways. He decided to quarantine passengers on a cruise ship off the coast of California, risking another mass outbreak like the *Diamond Princess* in Japan.[111] He also overruled CDC experts and decided against issuing a warning to the elderly and frail to avoid air travel, for fear that it would disrupt the economy and send a message that everything might not actually be perfect and under control.[112]

The initial U.S. response to the virus was slow, weak, and ineffective compared to other developed nations with similar outbreaks.[113] Countries hit early and hard, such as South Korea, Japan, and Italy, managed to tamp down the infection to low levels within months. This pushed a second wave farther into the future, unlike the U.S., which never really got past the first wave.[114] President Trump, by comparison, was promising to continue to hold his campaign rallies on March 7th, long after other countries had locked down. "We're going to have tremendous rallies," he told reporters at his Mar-a-Lago estate in Florida. "I'm not concerned at all."[115]

Trump and his media surrogates worked diligently to downplay any sort of concern among the base, working to silence the voices of experts at the CDC, and obscure anything that might cause worry. Rush Limbaugh declared coronavirus an "overhyped hoax" meant to derail the president's reelection chances.[116] He also promoted the conspiracy theory that Dr. Nancy Messonnier, a senior CDC official handling the COVID-19 response, was part of a plot to hurt Trump.[117] A guest on Laura Ingraham's *Fox News* show told people not to listen to the CDC about COVID-19 because it's a "highly politicized [liberal] organization."[118] White House National Economic Council Director Larry Kudlow went on *CNBC* to contradict the CDC's warnings: "We have contained this, I won't say airtight but pretty close to airtight."[119] Trump even went so far as to call in to the *Sean Hannity Show* on *Fox* and claim that people with coronavirus get better, "by, you know, sitting around and even going to work."[120] He also contradicted the CDC's mortality rate numbers and insisted there's little difference between COVID-19 and the flu.[121]

During the 2020 campaign, Trump made it clear that scientists and the experts were the enemy. During his rallies he repeatedly threatened that if he lost the election, Biden would, "listen to the scientists."[122] *Fox News* host Laura Ingraham picked up on this messaging as well during her show: "When Biden says we're going to let science drive our decisions that means unelected medical experts will dictate when kids can go to school, when we can go to church, and when we can drive or travel anywhere to see relatives or friends."[123] Trump also repeatedly claimed that the virus would simply go away when warmer weather came.[124] This unfounded hypothesis ignored Australia's mid-summer outbreak. It was also the second wave of Spanish Flu in the fall of 1918 that caused most of the fatalities in the U.S.[125] Regardless, U.S. COVID-19 cases surged throughout the summer, peaking in mid-July 2020, and again that winter.

Despite top experts at the CDC being gagged,[126] the organization had been trying to warn the public of the danger of COVID-19 since early January 2020.[127] Later, during the phase where containment might have been possible, the tests issued by CDC were failing to reliably detect COVID-19 due to contamination of the reagents. FDA policy made it difficult for other organizations from developing their own tests.[128] To make matters worse, only people who had traveled to an infected area, or had contact with a person known to be infected, were allowed to be tested.[129] This made it difficult to detect community transmission, creating a situation where there was a high degree of uncertainty over how many people were infected and artificially lowering the number of confirmed cases.[130]

This was, in part, intentional. Trump actively encouraged Pence and the CDC to keep the numbers low.[131] The CDC obliged and stopped tracking how many people were being tested. Thus, CDC reported cases lagged behind European Union and Johns Hopkins University estimates. At the same time, Trump hinted that he wanted even less testing because that would lower the number of confirmed cases. "Every time you test, you find a case, and it gets reported in the news: We found more cases. If instead of 50 [million], we did 25, we'd have half the number of cases," he complained during an interview with Chris Wallace on *Fox News*.[132]

Defying Trump in late February of 2020, the CDC warned that the spread of coronavirus in the U.S. "appears inevitable,"[133] and that hospitals "may be overwhelmed."[134] Despite White House claims that there was no danger, numerous epidemiologists agreed that the high transmission rate of coronavirus and the lack of any immunity meant that anywhere between 40 to 70 percent of the world's population could become infected if steps were not taken to keep it in check.[135] Dr. James Lawler, a professor at the University of Nebraska Medical

Center, briefed the American Hospital Association to be prepared for 96 million infected and 480,000 dead based on his calculations.[136] Behind closed doors, scientists within the government secretly fumed over the damage Trump's misinformation was doing to public health.[137] Later, the Trump White House installed the equivalent of *zampolits* (Soviet political officers) at the CDC to keep an eye on director Robert Redfield, and ensure that what came out of the CDC conformed with expected political messaging.[138]

Tests remained in short supply for months, and first responders were woefully unprepared in terms of both equipment and training.[139] Lack of communication, federal guidance and coordination meant that many of them had no idea they were dealing with suspected cases of the virus.[140] At the same time, the U.S. was uniquely vulnerable among the developed world nations to an epidemic due to lack of insurance, high individual health care costs, no federal sick leave laws for workers, and people being told, "Come in to work or you're fired."[141] The U.S. also ranked 32nd out of 40 Organization for Economic Co-operation and Development (OECD) countries in hospital beds per 1,000 people to begin with.

On March 3, 2020, Jennifer Wright, author of *Get Well Soon: History's Worst Plagues and the Heroes Who Fought Them*, identified four ways governments fail at dealing with epidemics: deny the disease is a problem, suppress scientific information, blame minorities, and claim those who fall ill are doing so because they are sinners. She noted the U.S. had "achieved" the first three immediately.[142] Other experts offered similar warnings. Only days before the U.S. shut down in March 2020, Dr. Joshua Sharfstein, Vice Dean at Johns Hopkins Bloomberg School of Public Health and author of *The Public Health Crisis Survival Guide*, offered prescient guidance as well. When he reviewed the history of such crises, he found, "One of the huge lessons is: don't politicize the communications. You really need credible communicators who people believe."[143]

The Trump Administration did the opposite. They elevated misinformation, politicized it on *Fox News* such that most of the GOP base was unwilling to accept truth. Experts like Dr. Fauci were demonized and sidelined because his message didn't match the party line. Trump and *Fox News* touted miracle cures that were pure quackery, like hydroxychloroquine. The White House later put cardiologist Scott Atlas, who advocated for letting everyone get the devastating disease to build "herd immunity," in charge of the response instead of actual experts.[144] As such, it came as little surprise to those paying attention that by election day 2020, about 235,000 Americans were dead of the disease. The toll would continue to rise to eventually surpass the worst case numbers described by Dr. Lawler.

Trump and *Fox* were preaching to a credulous audience. Research from 2015 showed that Christian nationalist ideologies (i.e., the Trump base) are correlated with anti-vaccine beliefs.[145] Ultimately, Trump was successful in spreading the messages he wanted. Unfortunately, those messages were both wrong and dangerous. A study by researchers at Cornell University, which examined 38 million English language social media posts, concluded that, "The President of the United States was likely the largest driver of the COVID-19 misinformation 'infodemic.'"[146] This observation of Trump's disastrous influence on the American digital information ecosystem was confirmed when, after Trump was banned by Twitter, misinformation about the 2020 election plunged by 73 percent.[147]

Polling data by the Public Religion Research Institute (PRRI) showed that President Trump was the only source of information a majority (58 percent) of *Fox News* Republicans believed provided accurate information and advice about the coronavirus pandemic. No *Fox News* Republicans surveyed (out of hundreds sampled) reported a lot of trust in Joe Biden to provide accurate information or advice. Only 30 percent of *Fox* News Republicans agreed that Trump and people in his administration contracted the coronavirus because they behaved irresponsibly, compared with 69 percent of all Americans.[148]

Thus, despite Trump's inept leadership and chaotic messaging, he succeeded in his goal: discrediting the CDC and convincing the Trumpist base that everything was just hunky-dory.[149] Pew Research found that 94 percent of people who relied on Trump for information on COVID-19 thought his messaging on the outbreak had been completely or mostly right. Similarly, those who got their information from *Fox News* or talk radio thought the same.[150] According to a Reuters/Ipsos poll from March 2020, only 20 percent of Republicans saw coronavirus as an imminent threat to the U.S. Less than half were washing their hands more, and only 3 percent changing their travel plans. In every case, Democrats were significantly more likely to take the threat seriously.[151]

On election day 2020, 93 percent the 376 counties with the highest COVID-19 rates per capita went for Trump.[152] Other studies returned similar numbers: Republicans were much less likely to socially and physically distance themselves during the pandemic, and were thus much more likely to contract COVID-19. They also found that those who watched *Fox News* were more likely to contract the deadly disease.[153] After decades of undermining and demonizing academics, scientists, and subject matter experts, conservatives and *Fox News* had successfully managed to convince the vast majority of their political base to ignore the people trying to save them from a pandemic highly lethal to people over the age of 60.[154]

The median age of a *Fox News* viewer is 68.[155]

The Worst Danger of a Post-Truth World

"But it was all right, everything was all right, the struggle was finished. He had won the victory over himself. He loved Big Brother."

George Orwell, *1984*

While Valery Legasov observed that the debt to truth must eventually be paid, the Trump Administration came very close to paying none whatsoever in the 2020 election. Despite the carnage of 2020, despite the truths emerging before the election, the Republican base looked up, and still loved Big Brother. On January 1st, 2020 Trump's aggregate net approval rating per FiveThirtyEight was at -11.5. Heading into the election, it had improved to -9.5 points. Despite roughly 235,000 Americans needlessly dying before the election, he had become more popular.

Estimates by epidemiologists in April 2020 showing that an effective and timely response could have reduced the death toll by 90 percent had no effect on Trump's approval ratings.[156] Conservative media simply pushed the narrative that the number of deaths reported by the CDC was greatly inflated. The base believed it and moved on, secure in their knowledge that it was an overblown hoax, especially after Trump re-tweeted a post in support of COVID-19 conspiracy theories.[157] Later, once the deaths started to mount, they moved the goalposts: despite the virus being on track to kill more Americans than World War II in one-fourth the time, 57 percent of Republicans saw the losses as "acceptable."[158]

It didn't matter that as the summer of 2020 wore on, it increasingly came to light that Trump's mishandling of the crisis lined the pockets of the rich and those seeking to curry favor.[159] Nor that early in the crisis the White House nixed plans by the United States Postal Service to send five high-quality masks to every household in the U.S.[160] Or that Trump handed over the COVID-19 industrial response to his completely unqualified son-in-law Jared Kushner, who botched the entire effort and produced nothing more than 3,500 "spoiled and unusable" kits at a cost of 52 million dollars.[161] Nor that Kushner's solution to people in blue states with COVID-19 was "that's their problem."[162]

Bob Woodward of the *Washington Post* later released an audio recording of Trump saying on March 19th, 2020, "I wanted to always play it [COVID-19] down. I still like playing it down because I don't want to create a panic," (presumably in the financial markets which he was counting on to get him re-elected). Trump also admitted on tape to knowing that the virus was deadly, and far, far worse than "just the flu," as he had repeatedly dismissed it. "You just breathe the air, and that's how it's passed. It's also more deadly than even your strenuous flus... This is deadly stuff."[163]

These revelations had no effect on his supporters. This was in part because their preferred media sources hardly spoke of it.[164] The day the news of Woodward's recordings broke, *One America News* never directly mentioned it, and Lou Dobbs at *Fox* declared Trump had a "great day" for being nominated for a Nobel Prize. Other Trump-aligned talking heads on *Fox* explained it away as meaningless, because the American people knew that they were being lied to from the start.[165] This was uttered apparently without any awareness of what Hannah Arendt had to say on the subject: namely that devoted fascists admire the cleverness of leaders who lie effectively.

Multiple sources also confirmed that Trump had called troops who died in the service of their country "suckers" and "losers."[166] It had zero effect on his ratings, as his base refused to believe the "fake news." *Fox* went so far as to bash the reports, even after their own reporters confirmed them.[167] They dismissed them as a symptom of "Trump Derangement Syndrome," which assumes all critics of the president harbor an irrational hatred of him (rather than a rational one borne out of watching hundreds of thousands of people die needlessly).[168]

Thus, literally nothing can dissuade Trump's base from full-throated support of him. Not screaming children in cages. Not the lies that led to the carnage that Bob Woodward recorded. Not his disdain for American troops. Not his observation that COVID-19 might be a good thing because he wouldn't have to shake hands with so many "disgusting" people at rallies.[169] Not even hundreds of thousands of Americans dying due to his lies, incompetence, and desire to put the stock market and re-election first. Given the age demographics of those who died, a great deal of them were his own supporters. The fact that all of this barely moved the needle is astounding. These suggest the cult of personality and degree of hyper-polarization involved.

Even though Trump lost the election, it was by less than a total of 43,000 votes in a handful of swing states. Biden's margin in 2020 was only about two points better than Clinton's in 2016. Republicans almost held the Senate in an election cycle that didn't favor them, and made unexpected gains in the House, as well as in state legislatures. All in all, it was not a repudiation of Trumpism. Like the protagonist in Orwell's seminal novel, no matter what Trump did to his base they still loved him. GOP and white evangelical turnout during the 2020 election was record setting. Historian Timothy Snyder called this phenomenon sadopopulism in his book *The Road to Unfreedom*. He describes sadopopulism as a political movement wherein an oligarchy makes great promises to its base but ends up hurting them deliberately so that the base will look to the leader more to stop the pain.[170]

Other researchers found that Republicans were likely to believe the basics of QAnon, even if they had never heard of QAnon itself. Almost half of Trump voters believe that Democrats run a secret child sex-trafficking cabal, and that Trump was trying to dismantle it, regardless of whether or not they had ever heard of QAnon.[171] This suggests that Trump supporters are already primed to believe absurdities whenever they are applied in a way that paints Democrats as evil beyond description. Which then begs the most uncomfortable question of all: if Trump's supporters (i.e. the vast majority of Republicans) were willing to enthusiastically support him when he callously allowed the deaths of hundreds of thousands of his followers and American troops, how would they have reacted if it were their mutual enemies being imprisoned or killed? And what if the base generally believes the people targeted are pedophiles and child murderers?

The evidence we have on hand suggests that they would have either fallen in line in support of it or deny it was happening, just as they have with everything else he has done, no matter how awful. The danger is closer, more profound, and more real than most people choose to believe, because doing so requires us to look into a Nietzschean abyss within ourselves as self-identified Americans. As Voltaire observed, **"Those who can make you believe absurdities can make you commit atrocities."**

Trump may be gone from the White House, but every other thing that made him possible remains, and this creates an incredibly dangerous environment in the long run.

Six

Christian Nationalism

"I reject your reality and substitute my own!"
Adam Savage

White evangelicals have their own set of tribal epistemologies, which do not necessarily conform with reality as the rest of us know it. Consider David Barton, the evangelical "scholar" with no formal background as a historian. In 2012 he wrote a book titled *The Jefferson Lies: Exposing the Myths You've Always Believed about Thomas Jefferson.* He argued that Jefferson was really a conservative and opposed the separation of church and state. The book was so riddled with errors that the publisher retracted it, and it was voted the "least credible history book ever" by readers of the *History News Network.*[1] (Lest you think this was liberal bias, the book that came in second was *A People's History of the United States,* and the scholars who initially debunked Barton's book came from the Grove City College of Pennsylvania, a conservative Christian institution.)

The lack of factual evidence didn't matter to evangelicals, however; the book made *The New York Times* bestseller list. Leading conservatives like Newt Gingrich and Mike Huckabee lined up to endorse it. The lesson from this is that evangelicals are a demographic eager to reject objective reality and substitute their own. This is a major reason why they believed that Trump was the best person to be president of a nuclear armed superpower.

No demographic has been a stronger supporter of Trump and Trumpism than white evangelicals. Based on a 2018 survey, broadly speaking, Republicans fall into three "tribes": moderates, traditional conservatives, and devoted conservatives.[2] Moderates tend to be your chamber-of-commerce-style Republicans, who don't actively hate or fear minorities, but take a more libertarian approach to policy. When it comes to others, their attitude is, "Can't we all just get along?," although they are uninterested in doing the things needed to lift up traditionally marginalized people.

The religious right falls across "traditional conservatives" and "devoted conservatives," being strongly motivated by both "freedom of religion" (making America a Christian nation) and xenophobia toward immigrants and Muslims. The primary difference between these two groups is that "traditional conservatives" are more motivated by conservative Christian beliefs, while "devoted conservatives" (though generally conservative and Christian) are more motivated by xenophobia. By this taxonomy, roughly 63 percent of conservatives are what would be considered part of the Christian right.

Figure 5. A Taxonomy of Voter Types

Progressive Activists	Traditional Liberals	Passive Liberals	Politically Disengaged	Moderates	Traditional Conservatives	Devoted Conservatives
younger	older	unhappy	young	engaged	religious	white
highly engaged	retired	insecure	low income	civic-minded	middle class	retired
secular	open to compromise	distrustful	distrustful	middle-of-the-road	patriotic	highly engaged
cosmopolitan	rational	disillusioned	detached	pessimistic	moralistic	uncompromising
angry	cautious		patriotic	Protestant		patriotic
			conspiratorial			
			26%		19%	
8%	11%	15%		15%		6%

Wings	Exhausted Majority	Wings

SOURCE: D. A. Yudkin,
Hidden Tribes: A Study of America's Polarized Landscape.[3]

Some people in the field, such as Daniel Yudkin (above), Andrew Whitehead, and Samuel Perry in *Taking America Back for God* try to separate Christian Nationalism from white supremacy and racism. However, data analysis by Robert P. Jones demonstrates a tight correlation between white supremacy and Christian nationalism that cuts both ways. Using surveys that measure racist attitudes and beliefs among religious groups in the U.S., he found prevalent racist attitudes among most white Christians, particularly among evangelicals. Jones found that racist attitudes were strongly predictive of whites identifying as Christian,[4] and that evangelicals with the most racist attitudes were four times more likely to be weekly church goers.[5]

The religious right has a long history of courting overt racists. Paul Weyrich observed that Klansman David Duke, who ran for governor of Louisiana in 1990, raised important issues "of fundamental fairness and colorblindness in race relations, welfare, and destruction of families, and unchecked crime."[6] Tony Perkins, current president of the highly influential Family Research Council, paid

Duke $82,500 for his mailing list when he ran for office in Louisiana in 1996, and has spoken at the white nationalist Council of Conservative Citizens.[7] Sarah Posner, in her book *Unholy: Why White Evangelicals Worship at the Altar of Donald Trump*, describes over the course of several chapters the myriad ways that white nationalism, and white evangelicals as a political entity, are inextricably entwined. Her observation is backed up by the data in this chapter: white evangelicals hold generally hostile views towards the same groups that white nationalists do.

Polling data by the Pew Research Center backs up the accuracy of the observation. About 60 percent of Republicans would be considered part of the Christian right. When looking at all Republicans, including those who lean Republican, only 44 percent support same-sex marriage as opposed to 88 percent of Democrats. Remove the Republican leaners and only 37 percent of core Republicans support it. This serves as a reasonable proxy for conservative religious beliefs, and demonstrates that no matter how you slice the data, the GOP is dominated by people with conservative (or intolerant) religious beliefs, not just of LGBTQ people, but also of immigrants, Muslims, Blacks, and other minorities.[8] According to Pew, 25.4 percent of the U.S. identifies as evangelical Protestant (of all races), and 20.4 percent identify as Catholic.[9] About 16 percent of the U.S. self-reports as white evangelicals, according to another survey.[10]

Within the Christian right, white evangelicals are the dominant group. Conservative Catholics exert a very strong influence on politics, but they are a small minority within a divided Church where most members actually support same-sex marriage, oppose the religious right to refuse service to LGBTQ people, support access to birth control, and support other issues where the laity is at odds with the clergy. Mormons are another religiously conservative group, but constitute only 2 percent of the population, and really only hold significant political power in two states, Utah and Idaho, where they are overrepresented in the majority party in government, which is, of course, the GOP.

There is a toxic confluence of whiteness and Christianity, where 64 percent of white Catholics and 57 percent of white mainline protestants also voted for Trump in 2016.[11] Conversely, only 26 percent of whites with no religious affiliation, and 24 percent of non-whites, voted for Trump. This difference between non-religious whites and non-whites isn't statistically significant.[12] Thus, while white evangelicals weren't the only white Christian group that supported Trump, they are the largest group within the GOP that also happened to be the most staunchly pro-Trump. Ryan Burge of the Eastern Illinois University used General Social Survey data to look at the religious evolution of Republicans. He has similarly found that white evangelicals are a plurality of the party, with (presumably) conservative Catholics being the second largest group within the party. You can also see that since 1988 the GOP has been the party of white evangelicals, and to a lesser extent, highly conservative Catholics.

Figure 6. Religious Composition of the Republican Party Over Time

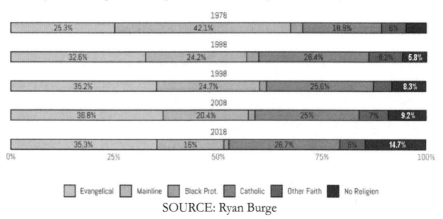

SOURCE: Ryan Burge

These figures show why Republicans are now beholden to evangelicals and their beliefs. In elections where every vote matters, it isn't enough to carry evangelical voters; if you are a Republican you must energize them. George W. Bush beat McCain when unknown surrogates used racial animus against the Senator from Arizona in South Carolina in 2000, floating rumors that his adopted daughter from Bangladesh was actually his secret love child.[13]

When McCain ran in 2008 against Barack Obama, evangelical support was lukewarm at best.[14] During the 2012 presidential election, Obama should theoretically have been beatable, with his low approval numbers, the country digging out of a recession, and a Tea Party fueled by racism leading a frenzied pushback against him.[15] But Republicans lost, in great part due to the tepid support from evangelicals for the Mormon ex-governor of Massachusetts Mitt Romney, whom they suspected of being a fake Christian and a closet liberal.[16] The lessons to the GOP couldn't be clearer: If you want to win presidential elections, you must put someone out there who stirs up the evangelical base. The Public Religion Research Institute (PRRI) found that in 2004 white evangelicals were 23 percent of the population and 23 percent of voters. By 2018, they had shrunk to 16 percent of the population but grown to 26 percent of voters.[17] Given this, you wouldn't think that Trump, a thrice-married, philandering, serial liar who cheats his contractors would attract much evangelical support, but he did so by deliberately courting them with his campaign rhetoric, and during a meeting with over a thousand conservative Christian leaders.[18]

He told them exactly what they wanted to hear: that conservative Christians like themselves were being persecuted, and that they didn't really have religious freedom. He promised them an administration that would grant them broad latitude to discriminate and bring religion into government, schools, and the workplace. His campaign singled out Muslims and immigrants as a danger to the U.S., and resorted repeatedly to racial dog whistles like "American carnage" referring to crime in cities (presumably caused by Blacks and Latinos).[19]

He promised to strike down the Johnson Amendment, which prevented churches from making unlimited political contributions and supporting specific candidates without losing their tax-exempt status.[20] He promised to put conservative Supreme Court justices on the bench who would interpret religious freedom as broadly and as favorably as possible to them. These same justices would also presumably strike down *Roe v. Wade* (right to abortion) and *Obergefell v. Hodges* (same sex marriage). In addition, he catered to their racist and xenophobic biases by repeatedly singling out immigrants and Muslims as a threat. After two days of meetings, evangelical leaders were ready to crown him as their King Cyrus (a non-believer who, according to the Bible, nevertheless freed a population of Babylonian Jews[21]). When confronted with Trump's many indiscretions, the white evangelical response has often been, "Yes, we know he's going to hell. But we don't care because he's furthering the cause of God."

In a 2011 poll, 60 percent of white evangelicals surveyed said that a public official who "commits an immoral act in their personal life" cannot still "behave ethically and fulfill their duties in their public and professional life." By 2016 that number had dropped to 20 percent in response to Trump.[22] This embraced the Gingrich-ian belief that Christians are in a war for power over America, democracy be damned. In the end, 81 percent of white evangelicals voted for Trump in 2016.[23] They remained his strongest supporters.[24] You cannot separate the beliefs of the base of the Republican Party from those of white evangelicals; the Venn Diagram is effectively a circle.

Perhaps the most stunning statistic comes from what white evangelicals believed about Trump. One of the primary tenets of evangelical Christianity is that only Christians can go to heaven. Yet, of southern white evangelicals, only 38 percent believe that Trump is a Christian. Despite this belief that Trump is a non-believer, 84 percent of southern white evangelicals still voted for him.[25] Many don't believe he's a good person, or that he shares their beliefs; he was simply hurting the people that they wanted him to hurt.[26]

As a result, the GOP positions on law and policy are essentially in lockstep with the beliefs of white evangelicals, conservative Catholics, and Christian nationalists in general. Because of the makeup of the Supreme Court, this is likely to be true for decades to come; and the results will be disastrous. Evangelical beliefs are opposed to the majority on every major touchstone social issue in America today: race, police violence, immigration, LGBTQ rights, women's rights, health care (both reproductive and non-reproductive), voting rights, and wealth inequality. White evangelicals also have strong beliefs about things that normally have nothing to do with religion, including gun control and the environment. In every single case, evangelicals take positions that go against virtually all the data, expertise, and research we have. Their policy goals aren't just unpopular, but also detached from reality. In the process of trying to make America into a Christian nation, they are adopting positions that are dividing the county, destroying our environment, tearing down civil rights, and subverting our democratic institutions at an exponentially increasing rate.

It's cute when Adam Savage said, "I reject your reality and substitute my own," on Mythbusters. It's not so cute when the people dictating environmental policy decide that climate change isn't real, and we need to burn more coal.

They are why we can't have nice things now—or potentially ever.

The White Evangelical Mindset

First and foremost, the evangelical backlash is driven by fear. Fear of changing racial demographics, fear of a loss of political and social power, fear of "Islamic Terrorism," fear of growing acceptance of social values that are contrary to their beliefs, and fear of the decline of white Christian evangelicals as a demographic. While many of the beliefs of white evangelicals are not rooted in reality, their instinctive understanding that the American landscape is changing is correct.

The U.S. Census Bureau estimates that regardless of how we set immigration policy, whites in the United States will be a minority by 2044 (i.e., the U.S. will become a majority-minority nation). [27] The percentage of Republicans who identify as white evangelical has slowly started to slip, and not because they are defecting to the Democratic Party; instead, the number of unaffiliated, churchless "nones" in the party is growing. About two-thirds of Americans support same-sex marriage, while white evangelicals are the group least likely to support it. [28] At the same time, evangelical populations are aging without replacement. According to 2016 data, 26 percent of Americans over the age of 65 identify as white evangelicals. For 18-29-year-olds, the number is 8 percent. [29]

Some of these evangelical fears, however, are completely irrational—they are fueled by right-wing news outlets stoking the fires of paranoia. Perhaps the best example of this is their out-of-proportion fear of "Islamic Terrorism," which they rated as their number one issue according to a 2016 survey. (No other group had it rated anywhere close to the top).[30] They're also afraid that the government will ban their Bibles, force their churches to perform gay weddings, punish people for saying "Merry Christmas," and that the changing American landscape will make their religion illegal.[31]

In addition to fear, White evangelicals are also motivated by a powerful sense of nostalgia.[32] According to John Fea, author of *Believe Me: The Evangelical Road to Donald Trump*, this is related to their belief that America was better when it was less racially diverse and when there was a single-dominant culture in the South, where prayer and Bible reading were mandatory in schools, gender roles were clearly defined, men were in charge, and LGBTQ people stayed in the closet for fear of discrimination and moral opprobrium.[33] Donald Trump's slogan "Make America Great Again" tapped into this yearning for a past that was worse for most of America except them.

Fea also cites a need for power as a dominant characteristic of white evangelicals.[34] With their cultural influence waning, and their deep fear of where America is going, they have dropped any pretense of being a movement based primarily on morality (except perhaps where LGBTQ people are concerned, and even now they advise their members to couch their objections in secular terms) and have embraced their intrinsically authoritarian instincts.[35] Researchers have noted a consistent link between authoritarian beliefs and voting Republican since the 1964 Presidential Election.[36]

Another peculiar trait of white evangelicals, according to Dr. Robert P. Jones, is what he calls "the white Christian shuffle." They can admit the horrific racism of slavery, admit that Jim Crow was evil, and that the church had some role in them. But they believe that because they have apologized, they are now absolved and are thus blind to racism and its effects today.[37] They ascribe different outcomes for Black people to intrinsic flaws in their character or culture, rather than acknowledge any institutional or cultural barriers remaining in the U.S. This creates an inability to see any but the most blatant expressions of racism.[38] In those cases, white Christians ascribe racism to isolated incidents or individuals, and do not see them as a part of a larger problem.[39]

In the 1950's, scholars introduced the concept of authoritarianism to describe "ideological receptivity" to "ethnocentric, antidemocratic, proto-fascistic messages in societies that emphasized threatening circumstances and nationalist propaganda."[40] Later, it was boiled down to three essential traits: "(1) submission to 'strong' or charismatic leaders, (2) aggression against deviants and 'weak' scapegoats, and (3) the holding of traditional, conventional views about politics and morality."[41]

Authoritarian beliefs are often triggered by fear.[42] This explains why white evangelicals have supported harsh measures to address largely imaginary problems like immigrants destroying America, or transgender people in bathrooms. Numerous studies have found that Trump voters demonstrated significantly more authoritarian values than the general public.[43] However, despite holding traditional views about morality in general, authoritarian voters are much more likely to support politicians who lie, which helps explain the unwavering support of evangelicals for Trump despite his non-stop series of well-documented falsehoods.[44.]

Another feature common to Trump voters is Social Dominance Orientation (SDO). This is a personality trait that is highly predictive of political views. People exhibiting SDO desire to maintain or expand the existing social hierarchy and prevent "out groups" (people not like them) from narrowing the gap.[45] The SDO trait is associated with a lack of empathy, a belief in social Darwinism, opposition to actions which encourage equality, racism, and an authoritarian outlook.[46] This SDO worldview is also more commonly found in men than women.[47] When you consider that white evangelicals represent conservative whites in the south who believe they need to make the U.S. a Christian nation again, it is not difficult to see how the SDO trait folds into their world view.

Outgroup prejudice, which is related to Social Dominance Orientation, is bias or antipathy against otherwise marginalized groups. Polling data shows that white evangelicals hold the most strongly negative views of atheists, immigrants, LGBTQ people, Blacks, and Muslims of any demographic.[48] Authoritarianism and SDO are also both strongly correlated with a belief in rigid gender roles.[49] This makes sense, when you consider that one of the guiding principles of evangelicals, and conservative Christianity in general, is that men are leaders and women's proper role is to support them and make babies.[50]

Other studies have shown that they are also more likely to act on prejudices than other groups. One study of American Christians and atheists found that Christians consistently favored other Christians and discriminated against non-Christians in economic cooperation games. Conversely, the same study found that atheists didn't favor other atheists or discriminate against Christians.[51] Another showed that Trump supporters value ethnic antagonism over democratic norms. Researchers found that the strongest predictor of anti-democratic values (e.g., the government shouldn't ensure freedom of the press or prevent politically motivated violence) is a person's hostility towards ethnic, religious and racial minorities. In other words, Trump supporters' values appear highly correlated with a willingness to destroy democracy in order to maintain a white ethno-state.[52]

There are other demographic characteristics which set white evangelicals apart. They tend to be older and live in more rural environments where their population is becoming more homogeneous as their children leave the area and the church itself.[53] As a result, they have less contact with people unlike themselves, an isolation that tends to feed and intensify authoritarian beliefs, xenophobia, and SDO traits.[54]

Economic angst has often been cited as a factor in Trump support among "blue collar" Republicans. However, the data does not back this up. Some studies show that his supporters are about as well off as the average American, while[55] others show that, on average, they are significantly better off.[56]

What Sets Evangelicals Apart from Other Americans

We have explored many of the traits that are highly correlated with white evangelicals: authoritarianism, social dominance orientation, fear, nostalgia, belief in traditional gender roles, geography, and a lack of exposure to different kinds of people. However, these traits translate into some very specific beliefs and behaviors that differentiate evangelicals from the rest of the American public. When you look at evangelical beliefs, and how out of step they are with the rest of the U.S., keep in mind that this is the group setting domestic policy and federal/state law. They are the group bringing impact litigation to the Supreme Court of the United States (SCOTUS), which will happily sign off on it now that there is a 6-3 conservative supermajority. In the long run, this will only serve to heighten tensions between evangelicals and the rest of the U.S. population.

Evangelicals are first and foremost Biblical literalists, who believe that the King James Version (KJV) of the Bible is the literal word of God. This makes them fairly unique; other major denominations, including Catholics, generally do not consider the Bible to be the actual word of God.[57] Indeed, the 24 percent of Americans who believe the Bible is "the actual word of God, and is to be taken literally, word for word," is almost identical (within the margin of error) to the 25.4 percent of American adults who identify as evangelical.[58] This belief in Biblical literalism is the lowest percentage seen since Gallup polling first started asking this question in 1976, and makes evangelicals even more of an outlier as time goes by.[59] This literal, fundamentalist stance has wide-ranging effects on evangelicals' views of other Americans. For instance, 57 percent of white evangelicals say it is *very* important to be a Christian to be a "true American."[60] Just 29 percent of Catholics, 27 percent of white mainline Protestants, and 9 percent of the religiously unaffiliated agree with this statement. It becomes even more harsh when one considers the fact that the unaffiliated (or "nones") are now the largest religious demographic inside the U.S.[61]

The white evangelical belief in Trump was unwavering and greater than any other religious group by a wide margin. They are the only religious demographic where only a minority (47 percent) believe that Trump has damaged the dignity of the office of President. One-quarter of all white evangelicals say there is literally nothing Trump could do that would affect their support of him, the highest among any group surveyed.[62]

An interesting correlation is that evangelical denominations are typically among the least educated religious groups in the United States. Educational attainment is negatively correlated with support for Trump (i.e., less educated people are far more likely to support Trump).[63] Research shows that religious fundamentalists are also much more likely to believe the sorts of fake news and conspiracy theories that got the base out during the 2016 election and permeated the environment in the period.[64]

Evangelicals were also isolated in their support of his agenda and the direction he was taking the country.[65] Sixty-one percent of white evangelical protestants thought the country was on the right track, whereas only 37 percent of white mainline Protestants and 39 percent of Catholics agreed with this statement. Among all Americans, the number was even lower at 35 percent.

Another key difference related to racism and xenophobia is the white evangelical attitude towards changing demographics in the United States. White evangelicals are the only religious group where a majority (52 percent) believe that becoming a majority non-white country is a bad thing. Only 39 percent of white mainline Protestants, 32 percent of Catholics, and 23 percent of the religiously unaffiliated agree.[66] This statistic touches on a lot of other major divisive issues, from race relations to immigration to wealth inequality (discussed further in this chapter). It isn't religious scripture or doctrine shaping evangelicals' ideas on race; rather it is their whiteness. Black and Hispanic evangelicals are far less conservative than white evangelicals.[67]

White evangelicals are the only group where a majority (60 percent) believes that churches are doing a good job responding to issues of sexual harassment and assault. Only 42 percent of white mainline Protestants and white Catholics hold this view. Hispanic Catholics (who have been hit hardest by the shuffling of pedophile priests between dioceses) take an even dimmer view, with only 29 percent approving of the Church's handling of the issue. As for the religiously unaffiliated, only 17 percent believe churches are doing a good job handling these. At the same time, while there have been well-documented cases of systemic sexual abuse and cover-ups within evangelical churches, white evangelicals are the least likely to be aware of them.[68]

Attitudinally, white evangelicals are very different from the rest of the United States. Their outlier beliefs also translate into being an outlier on law and policy like no other group.

Positions on Specific Issues

As described in the section above, white evangelicals are very different from the rest of the United States in their views. The GOP, the Trump Administration, and white evangelicals are almost entirely in lockstep on policy. The same cannot be said for any other religious group, who go against at least some of the GOP's policies. (For instance, the Vatican and U.S. Catholics aren't supportive of U.S. immigration, asylum, and refugee policies under the Trump Administration.)

White evangelicals, however, are supportive across the board. When it comes to the "hot button" issues in American politics, white evangelicals have pushed the GOP further and further to the right.

Race Relations

"Whites, it must frankly be said, are not putting in a similar mass effort to reeducate themselves out of their racial ignorance. It is an aspect of their sense of superiority that the white people of America believe they have so little to learn."

Martin Luther King, Jr.

When discussing the history of racism, several facts are inescapable. The first is that white evangelicals were more-or-less running the American South during slavery and Jim Crow and fought desperately to preserve both. The second is that the modern Republican Party is the party of the white southern evangelicals and, by association, the American South (which is solidly Republican, with their strongest supporters being white evangelicals). Given everything we know about white evangelicals described so far in this book, one would have to assume that they magically became totally unbiased, and that some other group picked up the racism ball and ran with it, to come to the conclusion that white evangelicals and the party they control are not fundamentally responsible for the dismal state of race relations today.

Occam's razor, and the empirical evidence available, both strongly suggest that the people who were the worst racists and the most dead set against civil rights 55 years ago have similar demographics today. The data supports this conclusion. White evangelicals hold beliefs about race that are wildly out of step with the rest of the nation. They are the least likely, by a wide margin, to believe that racism against black people actually happens. While 57 percent of Americans believe there is "a lot" of discrimination against black people, only 36 percent of white evangelicals believe this.[69] Conversely, an astounding 57 percent of white evangelicals believe there is "a lot" of discrimination against Christians in the U.S.[70] Two-thirds of white evangelicals believe that discrimination against whites is as big a problem as discrimination against black people.[71]

It takes a particular level of detachment from reality to conclude that you, as the dominant group within the dominant party that controls most of the U.S. government, are more put-upon than the people you enslaved who have very little financial clout or representation in government and are still the victims of iron-clad factually-documented, endemic institutional racism.

White evangelicals are more or less blind to overt racism. While 54 percent of the public believe President Trump's decisions and behavior have encouraged white supremacists, only 26 percent of white evangelicals do. This is by far the lowest of any group, including white Catholics and white mainline Protestants.[72] A Quinnipiac University poll put the number of white evangelicals who believe Trump is racist even lower, at 21 percent.[73] If they could not see it in Trump, who has a long history of documented and recorded race-baiting, it is no wonder they can't see it in themselves. Fifty-three percent of white evangelicals believe that black people could earn as much as whites if "they just tried harder," which is simply a euphemism for calling black people lazy.[74] Seventy-two percent of white evangelicals believe that killings of unarmed black people are "isolated incidents." Fifty-seven percent of white evangelicals believe that the criminal justice system treats whites, blacks and minorities equally,[75] despite a mountain of empirical, peer-reviewed evidence that says exactly the opposite.[76] Black Americans see it much differently. Eighty-one percent of Blacks believe that such shootings are not isolated incidents, but rather part of a pattern of police hostility and indifference to black lives.[77]

It was noted earlier that white evangelicals have a social dominance orientation, which leads to hostility towards efforts to make society more equal. This applies to race issues as well, where 63 percent of white evangelicals (higher than that of any other religious group) believe that enough has been done already to compensate Blacks for slavery, Jim Crow, and the racial inequities of the past.[78]

Efforts by Blacks to speak out peacefully against the system are met with absolute apoplexy by white evangelicals and the religious right. When African American athletes knelt during the national anthem, 90 percent of Republicans believed they should have been legally compelled to stand.[79] Conversely, 85 percent of white evangelicals see Confederate monuments and flags as more a symbol of Southern pride than of racism. Only about 20 percent of Black Protestants agree.[80]

One of the worst side-effects of white evangelical influence is that Republicans, usually have no fear of challenges from the left in general elections due to gerrymandering. They do fear challenges from the right and are thus susceptible to "ethnic outbidding." This is the phenomenon where "political leaders competing for support from an ethnically homogeneous group (in this case, the majority-white, majority-Christian GOP) have really strong incentives to demonize outgroups to gain political support. Once that process has started, this rhetoric increases the hostility, and each candidate may try to one-up the others to compete for a bloc of voters who hate or fear that outgroup."[81] This would explain why Republican dog-whistles are growing stronger.

Guns

> *"The problem is not the absence of laws. It's an absence of morality. It's really the result of a decades-long march through the institutions of America, driving religion and God from the public square."*
>
> Tony Perkins

The United States suffers from gun-related violence and mass shootings at a rate higher than anywhere else in the developed world, and higher than most developing countries. Gun laws are lax compared to almost everywhere else in the world, and the number of guns per capita is twice as high as the next nearest country.[82] Support for additional gun control after numerous mass shootings during the Trump Administration was as high as it has ever been, particularly since most of the mass shootings have been carried out using assault rifles with high-capacity magazines.[83]

White evangelicals, however, are the group most opposed to any sort of gun control. After the mass shooting in Odessa, Texas in 2019, Senator Ted Cruz objected to new gun control laws, calling self-defense a "God given" right that rules out any sort of new gun control.[84] National Rifle Association President Wayne La Pierre echoed these sentiments, and Jerry Falwell, Jr. went a step further by urging students at his Liberty University to get concealed-carry permits after the San Bernardino mass shooting in 2015.[85]

White evangelicals are the demographic most likely to own guns, in part, because of these attitudes. Some believe that owning a gun isn't just a God-given right, but a Biblical commandment.[86] Forty-four percent of white evangelicals own a firearm, compared with 30 percent of the overall population in a 2019 study by Pew Research. Evangelicals are most likely to be satisfied with current gun control laws (44 percent, compared to 30 percent nationally). They are also the least likely to favor new gun control measures.[87]

Some studies have pointed out that a wide majority of white evangelicals support broader background checks.[88] However, their support is lower than any other group examined, and evangelicals on the whole don't support background checks for person-to-person sales, mental illness diagnoses preventing gun purchases, or "red-flag" laws.[89] Indeed, this same study found that Mormons and white evangelicals were the only groups where a majority of respondents believed that it should be easier to get a concealed carry permit. One study found that a belief in supernatural evil is bound up in policy attitudes that protect or expand gun rights, which points shows the connection between white evangelical Biblical literalist beliefs and gun ownership.[90]

Evangelicals and Mormons are also the only two groups where a majority oppose a ban on assault weapons. This sets them apart from even the rest of the Republican Party in which 55 percent of members favor an assault weapon ban.[91] Evangelicals and Mormons are also the least likely to support a ban on high-capacity magazines.[92] Even a plurality of rural adults supports an assault weapons ban, although there is a high degree of overlap between evangelical and rural voters.[93]

The evangelical belief about what causes mass shootings is very different from the rest of the public. Most subject-matter experts agree, based on facts and analysis of mass-shooting data, that the widespread availability of assault rifles and high-capacity magazines are the most significant cause of deadly mass shootings. More centrist Republicans blame mass shootings on video games or mental illness (both of which exist in other countries that don't have mass shootings).[94] White evangelical leaders, on the other hand, blame it on secularism. Family Research Council President Tony Perkins claims that the teaching of evolution in schools causes mass shootings.[95] Texas Lieutenant Governor Dan Patrick blames gun violence on the fact that Texas no longer has state sponsored mandatory prayer in school.[96]

The NRA, weakened as it is by scandals and investigations, remains a powerful lobby. However, they have to represent a sizable portion of the GOP's constituency in order to dictate policy effectively, while simultaneously thwarting the overwhelming will of the majority. The data clearly shows that the NRA constituency draws more heavily from white evangelicals than any other group.[97]

LGBTQ Issues

"Stonewall, many people may not be aware of, was a move of New York of homosex-uals that were pushing back for special rights."

Tony Perkins

White evangelicals are consistently one of the most hostile groups toward LGBTQ people. While Jehovah's Witnesses tend to be even less accepting of LGBTQ people than evangelicals and Mormons, they are a small group, and their religious beliefs prohibit them from participating in the political process, including voting, because Jesus refused to hold office according to their inter-pretation of the Bible.[98] Mormon views on LGBTQ people track fairly closely in polling with white evangelicals; but again, Mormons are a small group, and their political clout is primarily in the Republican strongholds of Utah, Idaho and Wyoming. Indeed, the Utah legislature passed a law banning job discrimination against LGBTQ people (with significant religious carve-outs).

Such laws in southern states, where white evangelicals dominate the political landscape, are unimaginable. Only 36 percent of white evangelicals believe gay people should be accepted, compared to 70 percent of Catholics and 54 per-cent of Christians. They are also, conversely, much more likely to believe that homosexuality should be "discouraged." This translates to discrimination, moral opprobrium, and making homosexual relationships illegal again by overturning *Lawrence v. Texas.*[99] Sodomy laws remain on the books in 12 states, most of which are southern (i.e., where slave holding was legal), plus the two states with the larg-est per capita Mormon population, Utah and Idaho.[100] White evangelical support for legal same sex marriage is significantly lower than every group but Mormons and Jehovah's Witnesses, at 34 percent. Compare this percentage to Catholics, of whom 66 percent support same-sex marriage despite their religion's doctrinal opposition.[101] Indeed, for all the conservative talk of how hostile Muslims are to LGBTQ people, significantly more American Muslims believe homosexuality should be accepted (45 percent) and support same sex marriage (51 percent) than white evangelicals.

Support for a law that would protect LGBTQ people from discrimination in the same ways that the Civil Rights Act of 1964 protects other groups of people is lowest among white evangelicals (54 percent), and far below that of Mormons (70 percent).[102] The sampling in this polling may skew high, since it did not ask about religious carve-outs in the legislation. Conversely, white evangelicals are the group that most wants to enshrine a religious right to discriminate, and the only one where a majority supports it.[103] Republicans are significantly more likely to re-gard same-sex marriage as an important issue than Democrats or Independents.[104]

The dramatic shift in public attitudes towards LGBTQ people over the past 20 years has exacerbated the white evangelical persecution complex. When asked in a PRRI study which groups "face a lot of discrimination," white evangelicals were by far the least likely to mention LGBTQ people (which is ironic, given that white evangelicals are the group most desirous of the right to discriminate against them in this same study). Only 43 percent of white evangelicals believe LGBTQ people face a lot of discrimination. Conversely, white evangelicals were the group most likely to believe Christians face "a lot" of discrimination at 57 percent. Evangelicals were the only religious group to believe that LGBTQ people face less discrimination than Christians, despite evidence to the contrary.[105] The study found the same pattern elsewhere; white evangelicals felt more put upon than other historically disadvantaged groups such as immigrants, Blacks, and Muslims.

When the Supreme Court ruled in 2020 that LGBTQ people have protections under "sex discrimination" laws, it reinforced religious conservatives' perceived need to replace Ruth Bader Ginsburg at any cost, even if it tore the country asunder. However, as the largest bloc within the Republican Party and one that cares more about LGBTQ issues than any group but LGBTQ people, white evangelical influence on the GOP is why no federal law will protect LGBTQ people from discrimination for the foreseeable future, unless the filibuster is abolished. It is worth noting that the filibuster also played a critical role in preserving white supremacy in the south.[106]

Climate Change

> *"A consensus of peer reviewed literature has nothing to do with truth."*
>
> Trump's National Security Council on climate change

Anthropogenic (human-caused) climate change is likely to be the most dangerous long-term threat to not only our national security, but to the world and to mankind as a whole.[107] Climate change causes crop failure and refugee migration, which in turn leads to political instability.[108] Because of it, humans are responsible for the sixth great extinction event in Earth's 4.5 billion-year history, and our survival as a species is in doubt.[109] What is *not* in doubt by actual experts is that humans are the driving force behind climate change. There is no remaining meaningful debate within the mainstream scientific community as to whether the planet is warming, and whether humans are responsible.[110]

However, white evangelicals are the group least likely to believe in climate change. A Pew Research study found that only 28 percent of white evangelicals believe in anthropogenic climate change, compared with 50 percent of all U.S. adults. Thirty-three percent of white evangelicals believe the earth is warming but that humans aren't responsible, while the plurality (37 percent) don't believe the earth is warming at all. No other group comes close to this level of scientific rejection; 41 percent of main-line Protestants and 45 percent of white Catholics believe in anthropogenic climate change; still lower than anywhere else in the developed world, but significantly better than white evangelicals in the U.S.[111] White evangelicals are also the only religious group where less than half believe that climate change is a crisis or a major problem. Almost twice as many that believe it is not a problem at all as believe that it is a crisis. Fifty-seven percent are "unconcerned" about climate change, and 30 percent say they are not concerned at all, more than any other group surveyed.[112]

They are also the religious group least likely to be scientifically literate, or even to believe what scientists have to say. Fewer than 1-in-5 (17 percent) of white evangelical Protestants say they pay a lot of attention to news reports about developments in science, compared to at least one-quarter of all other major religious groups. Forty-nine percent of white evangelicals say scientists treat religion and religious people with disrespect. These numbers are almost identical to the percentage of Tea Party members (51 percent) who answered similarly. White evangelicals are the group most likely (52 percent) to say that science conflicts with their religious beliefs.[113] Which helps explain why white evangelicals are much more likely to attribute the severity of recent natural disasters to the biblical "end times" (77 percent) than to climate change (49 percent). The majority believe that if there is anything going wrong with the environment, it should be up to industry and "the market" to address the issue.

There are many reasons why it is more or less the official position of evangelical churches that humanity cannot adversely affect the global environment, that CO_2 does not cause climate change, that renewable energy sources are not viable, and that we should continue to burn fossil fuels at an ever-increasing rate while opposing any government effort to fight climate change.[114] Chapter seven discusses how oligarchs and corporations have deliberately co-opted evangelicals to support their positions.

The statistics above show they distrust science and scientists (as described in the last chapter), and oppose government doing anything on general principle. They literally believe that government action to stop climate change goes against God and the Bible, on the grounds that it would hurt poor people. Which is ironic, given that they have pushed policies that hurt poor people of color for decades. There are other psychological factors at play, as well. White evangelical culture is deeply patriarchal and strict about enforcing gender roles. Being environmentally conscious is seen as weak, unmanly, and effeminate.[115] This leads to bizarre virtue signaling behaviors to show how much white southern evangelicals despise people who believe in climate change like "rolling coal," wherein trucks are modified to dump additional diesel fuel into the engines of their trucks causing them to spew forth a dark black cloud of partially burned hydrocarbons. Like voting for Trump, it is essentially a "**** you and your liberal tears" to people they see as elitist, politically correct, ungodly, and effeminate.

White evangelical leadership encourages these views. Evangelical megachurch pastor Robert Jeffress has been one of Trump's closest, most loyal, and powerful allies since early in the 2016 campaign.[116] Jeffress praised Trump in a *Fox News* interview for skipping a U.N. summit on climate change. Instead, Trump opted to give a speech on "religious freedom," bemoaning how Christians are so horribly oppressed. "It is a remarkable thing that this president would skip a U.N. climate change summit **on an imaginary problem** (emphasis added) to address the very real problem of global persecution of believers. Think about it. What president in history would have the guts to do what President Trump is doing? And it's this kind of leadership that is absolutely infuriating the president's enemies, but it's also energizing his base, especially his religious base of voters."[117]

Not 24 hours later, Jeffress addressed Greta Thunberg's U.N. speech by denying science, claiming that God wants us to exploit the planet, and expressing the religious belief that God would never let humanity cause ecological devastation. "God said he created the environment to serve us, not for us to serve the environment. This Greta Thunberg, the 16 year old, she was warning today about the mass extinction of humanity. Somebody needs to read poor Greta Genesis Chapter 9, and tell her the next time she worries about global warming, just look at a rainbow; that's God's promise that the polar ice caps aren't going to melt and flood the world again."[118]

The result of all of this is that a group of people who are scientifically illiterate, don't believe science or scientists, believe that climate policy should be left to corporations, believe that God will step in to save humanity from itself, and reject all the key tenets of climate change research, are able to block most legislation meant to address the issue. Which is to say: The U.S. will do nothing, so long as white evangelicals are calling the shots. Which they will be for the foreseeable future after rigging the game and preserving the filibuster.

While the title of this chapter is "White Evangelicals Are Why We Can't have Nice Things," in reality, white evangelicals are why 90 percent of life on earth is probably doomed to extinction in the relatively near future. If there was any chance of staving off or mitigating devastating levels of climate change, white evangelicals are ensuring that we miss the opportunity.

Immigration

"Why are we having all these people from shithole countries come here?"

Donald J. Trump

The Trump Administration enacted some of the most draconian immigration policies in U.S. history. From the travel ban on Muslim countries, to forcibly separating (sometimes permanently) parents and children crossing the border seeking asylum, to putting asylum seekers in overcrowded camps and prisons, to cutting the refugee cap to the lowest it has been since the program was instituted in 1980, the Trump Administration's policies have been remarkable in their cruelty. However, the administration would not be doing these things if it did not have the absolute support of its base, which is white evangelicals.

As has been described above, white evangelicals believe more than any other group that immigration and increasing racial diversity is bad for America. They are also more hostile to immigrants than any other group by a wide margin, with 53 percent describing immigrants as a "threat to American values."[119] They are the religious group most likely to support the Trump family separation policy.[120] Sixty-eight percent believe the U.S. has no moral obligation to take in refugees, far higher than any other group, but perfectly in line with Republican policy positions.[121] They are the group most likely to support building the expensive and ineffective wall (65 percent), and the group least likely to support letting adults who were brought to the U.S. as children become citizens.[122] Seventy-five percent of white evangelicals described "the federal crackdown on undocumented immigrants" as a positive action, compared to just 46 percent of Americans overall.[123] (Presumably, this includes support for the unsanitary camps and asylum courts where three year olds are forced to represent themselves in front of a judge.)[124]

White evangelical church-goers almost never hear about immigration from the pulpit.[125] The attitudes seen above are based on the intrinsically xenophobic and racist attitudes of white evangelicals, whose biases and fears of an immigrant "invasion" are stoked by Republicans and conservative media outlets like *Fox News, One American News Network, Breitbart, Daily Caller* and others.[126] The constant stream of misinformation leads to uniquely white evangelical beliefs, including "immigrants hurt the economy"—demonstrably false—and that immigrants are responsible for more crimes than other groups, which is equally false and easy to debunk if one does minimal research.[127]

President Trump was directly tapping into these fears during the 2016 election when he said of Mexican immigrants, "They're bringing drugs. They're bringing crime. They're rapists."[128] Thanks to Trump, immigration issues are far more important to white evangelicals than other groups, because it directly stimulates their biases and fears. It was successful enough that President Trump again used anti-immigrant agitprop to try to get the base to turn out for the 2018 election.[129] Trump's highly unpopular efforts to overturn the Deferred Action for Child Arrivals (DACA) executive order and throw hundreds of thousands of Dreamers out of the country were also an appeal to white evangelical elements of his base.

Muslims

"There's a sickness. They're sick people. There's a sickness going on. There's a group of people that is very sick."

Donald J. Trump on Muslims

White evangelicals place more importance on "religious freedom" issues than any other group. Polling around the 2016 Election showed that white evangelicals were 3.5 times more likely than the general population to say religious freedom was the most important issue to them.[130] The Trump Administration made "religious freedom" a top priority at the State Department, and the Department of Health and Human Services, forming commissions to punish infringements on "religious liberty," and treating religious freedom as the most important (and perhaps only) human right.[131]

In practice, these beliefs in religious freedom only apply to white evangelicals who want to be free to discriminate against anyone they don't like. Freedom from religiously-based discrimination doesn't extend to Catholics and Jews who want to adopt children via government-funded evangelical agencies.[132] And it most certainly doesn't apply to Muslims, according to most white evangelicals.

Evangelicals, by a wide margin, hold the most negative views of Muslims of any religious group in America.[133] Seventy-two percent of white evangelicals believe there is an inherent conflict between Islam and democracy. (Their concern for democracy is ironic, considering that they are supporting voter suppression and gerrymandering throughout much of the U.S., which is explored further in Chapter 8). Sixty-three percent of evangelicals believe that Islam encourages violence more than other religions, and two-thirds believe that Muslims are not a part of mainstream society. Almost 4-in-10 believe that "half or more U.S. Muslims are anti-American."[134] A 2015 PRRI survey found that 73 percent of white evangelicals believe that "Islam is incompatible with American values and way of life," far more than any other group surveyed.[135] When President Trump accused two Muslim congresswomen of being anti-American and told them to "go back" to the countries they came from, he was tapping directly into these sentiments, and taking advantage of the general ignorance of his audience; Representative Rashida Tlaib (D-MI) was born in Detroit in 1976.[136]

White evangelicals were by far the most supportive group of the ban on travel by people from predominantly Muslim countries. Three-quarters of white evangelicals supported a ban, as opposed to only 38 percent of the general population.[137] If religious discrimination is defined as adverse government action towards people based on their religious beliefs, the Muslim travel ban certainly qualifies.

However, white evangelicals are generally only concerned about "religious freedom" when it affects them. Most white evangelicals generally think of religious freedom as, "Can I refuse service to LGBTQ people?" Thus, when white evangelicals are asked if Christian business owners should have a religious right to refuse to serve LGBTQ people, 60 percent say "yes." But when asked if Muslim business owners should have that same right to refuse service, only 46 percent of white evangelicals answered in the affirmative.[138]

White evangelicals also believe they face more discrimination than Muslims.[139] This is part of their wider persecution complex, where they believe that somehow the people who control the majority of U.S. government and an entire political party are the most put-upon people in the nation. Some would chalk it up to a singular lack of ability to see irony, but more realistically this is part of their drive to "Make America Great Again" by permanently making their brand of Christianity the dominant socio-political force.

Islamophobia by white evangelicals doesn't just interfere with our ability to function as an increasingly pluralistic society, it also affects our foreign relations and national security posture. For instance, white evangelical eschatology (study of the end time or the apocalypse) was a motivating factor behind the unpopular (except with white evangelicals and the Netanyahu government) decision to move the U.S. Embassy in Israel from Tel Aviv to Jerusalem. To many, this symbolized the end of any hope for a two-state solution.[140]

Women's Health

"If it's a legitimate rape, the female body has ways to try to shut that whole thing down. But let's assume that maybe that didn't work or something. I think there should be some punishment, but the punishment ought to be on the rapist and not attacking the child."

Republican Senate Candidate Todd Akin

As noted in Chapter 2, white evangelicals were essentially ambivalent towards reproductive rights and women's health in the 1960's and 1970's. It is easy to for-

131

get that the 1963 case that took down prohibitions on birth control was *Griswold v. Connecticut*, a northern state. Before *Roe v. Wade*, Deep South states were more likely to allow abortion under some circumstances than were mid-western and northern states. This can be seen in Figure 6. Paul Weyrich found that overturning *Roe v. Wade* wasn't of particular interest to white southern evangelical leaders, but that retaining federal dollars for segregated schools was.

Figure 7. Abortion Laws Prior to *Roe v. Wade*

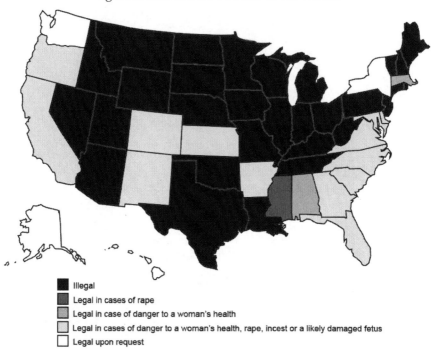

■ Illegal
▨ Legal in cases of rape
▦ Legal in case of danger to a woman's health
▢ Legal in cases of danger to a woman's health, rape, incest or a likely damaged fetus
□ Legal upon request

The Southern Baptist Convention passed a resolution in support of abortion rights in 1976. Abortion was seen primarily as a Catholic issue at the time.[141] It wasn't until 1978 and 1979 that Weyrich and a few evangelical leaders were able to galvanize white evangelicals around the issue, once the fight to keep federal money in segregated schools was effectively lost (and a losing issue in the court of public opinion). Since then, white evangelicals have been the driving force behind the push to rescind access to reproductive health care. While ultra-conservative white Catholics have played a significant role, their numbers are much smaller as a total of the pro-life movement, and their power is more diluted, as they are more concentrated in traditionally blue states where they have little political influence. Of the 10 states with the largest per-capita Catholic populations, nine are solidly blue and one (New Hampshire) is purple. Southern states have the smallest Catholic populations per capita, typically less than 10 percent of the total adult population.[142]

Conversely, evangelical protestants dominate the south. The states with the least religious diversity are Mississippi, Alabama, Arkansas, South Carolina, and North Carolina. The politically and socially dominant strain of religion in each of these states is white evangelical Protestantism. It is also no coincidence that these states are the ones passing the most draconian laws challenging *Roe v. Wade*.

In 2019 and 2020, conservatives saw an opportunity after Brett Kavanaugh replaced Anthony Kennedy on the Supreme Court and passed a slew of anti-abortion bills. Alabama passed a complete ban, with no exceptions for rape or incest. Mississippi, Georgia, Kentucky, Louisiana, and the newly red Ohio banned it after 6 weeks without exceptions for rape or incest. Missouri did the same at 8 weeks. All of them allow exceptions for life of the woman.[143] However, there has been a push to remove those exceptions as well.[144]

Bans such as these are immensely unpopular with the American public. A Gallup poll found that 77 percent of Americans think that there should be exceptions for rape or incest.[145] Conversely, 77 percent of white evangelical protestants believe that abortion should be illegal in most or all circumstances. Only 42 percent of Catholics, and 38 percent of the public overall, believe the same.[146] According to Pew 70 percent of the American public do not want *Roe v. Wade* overturned, 56 percent of white evangelicals do, according to PRRI.[147]

While leading conservative publications push against life of the woman exceptions, only 9 percent of the American public supports abortion laws that do not include any exceptions.[148] Unsurprisingly, the exception is white evangelicals. They are almost three times more likely (25 percent) to support "no exceptions" laws than the general public.[149] When the question is phrased as "Abortion should never be permitted," they express an even higher support for a ban without exceptions. Polling data using this wording again shows white evangelicals hold the most extreme position on abortion, with 53 percent believing that it should never be permitted, not even to save the life of the woman. The same survey only found this to be true for 27 percent of Catholics.[150]

Additionally, white evangelicals on the whole oppose access to birth control. This is ironic, given the wealth of data showing that access to birth control is the most effective way to bring down demand for the abortions that evangelicals so hate.[151] Only 22 percent of white evangelicals support government health plans covering contraceptives, compared with 64 percent of Republicans over all, and 78 percent of independents.[152] They are more than twice as likely than mainline protestants (38 percent to 18 percent) to say pharmacists should not have to fill prescriptions for birth control.[153] Catholics are also far less staunch than evangelicals in their opposition to access to birth control, as only 21 percent believe pharmacists should have the right to refuse to fill these prescriptions.

Utah provides an interesting case study on how white evangelicals are dragging the Republican Party far to the right on abortion and access to birth control. Utah has a religious diversity score somewhere between Tennessee and North Carolina, and the Mormon church more or less dominates the social and political landscape in the same way that white evangelical denominations dominate the South. The state's attitudes towards abortion look very similar to the Deep South; only 41 percent of people in both Mississippi and Utah believe abortion should be legal in most or all cases.[154] However, when Utah challenged *Roe v. Wade* with a law in 2019, it set the cutoff date at 18 weeks, and included exceptions for rape, incest, and life of the woman.[155] This seems to show that white evangelicals track well to the right of even the Mormon Church on abortion…a rather high bar.

#MeToo and Sexual Abuse

"I moved on her like a bitch… I just start kissing them. It's like a magnet. Just kiss. I don't even wait. And when you're a star, they let you do it. You can do anything… Grab 'em by the pussy. You can do anything."

Donald J. Trump

As mentioned above, white evangelicals are the group least likely to believe their church has a problem with sexual abuse, and have the strongest confidence that, if it happened, it would be handled appropriately. This belief is completely out of step with women who credibly accuse the powerful men the religious right depends on (e.g., Donald Trump and Brett Kavanaugh) of sexual misconduct.

While approximately 80 percent of white evangelicals supported Trump and the job he was doing, they were perfectly willing to overlook his "grab 'em by the pussy" comments unearthed during the 2016 campaign, which is more or less an admission of sexual assault. Nor have they turned on him despite allegations he had sex with a 13 year old at one of Jeffrey Epstein's parties in 1994.[156] (In 2019, Epstein killed himself in prison after being convicted of repeatedly having sex with underage girls.) Only 40 percent of white evangelicals believe Trump had sex with pornography star Stormy Daniels, despite the evidence, including receipts for hush money payments.[157] The short version is that they don't believe the women, or simply don't care even when the President admits guilt in an audio recording.

Similarly, white evangelicals overwhelmingly supported Roy Moore, who also had a long history of trolling for teenage girls as a thirty-something district attorney.[158] His pederasty was such common knowledge that he was reportedly banned from the local mall. Regardless, 80 percent of white evangelicals in Alabama voted for Moore, while seventy-six percent of everyone else in the state voted against him.[159] It was almost enough to elect Moore anyway, who lost by only 1.5 points. He was popular, despite his well-known sexual exploitation of minors, because he was unabashedly running on a "God, guns, and gays" campaign that appealed to the grievances and fears of white evangelicals.

Evangelicals were also the driving force behind Brett Kavanaugh's appointment to the Supreme Court, despite multiple credible accusations of sexual misconduct against him.[160] They were the demographic least likely to believe his accusers. Worse, 48 percent said they would support him even if the allegations were true.[161] In the end, 64 percent of white evangelicals supported his confirmation, while only 40 percent of the American public did.[162]

The response to the #MeToo movement by the GOP and white evangelicals is to declare that the movement has gone too far and that it's unfair to men.[163] In the aftermath of the Kavanaugh hearings, Republicans were more likely to say that the #MeToo movement leads to unfair treatment of men than they were to say it helps address sexual harassment.[164] You can see this coming out in the form of policies from the Department of Education that make it harder for schools to investigate sexual assault, and providing far more protections for students accused of rape than for the students actually assaulted.[165] Given that very few, if any, sexual assault cases are actually adjudicated, this hurt people who already have an uphill battle.

The takeaway from all of these examples and polling data is that white evangelicals desire power more than any other concern, including even the minimal levels of acceptable morality. They are inherently hostile to women who accuse men of sexual assault, and inherently receptive to the excuses of (white) men who claim it didn't happen, or excuse their sexual assaults as just "boys being boys." Evangelicals believe that rapists shouldn't be punished, because it would ruin their lives. Betsy DeVos' proudest achievement as Secretary of Education was making it easier to get away with rape on college campuses in order to protect men accused of it.[166]

White evangelical culture is highly patriarchal and fosters a belief that if a woman is raped, it is her fault for leading the man on.[167] When it comes to the #MeToo movement, white evangelicals are the reason it has made little practical headway. As of this writing, the Violence Against Women Act (which provided funding and law to prosecute individuals who commit violent crimes against women) has expired, and there is no sign that Republicans in the Senate have any intention of ever giving it another hearing. Nor is it likely to pass, without abolishing the filibuster. Which is to say, the VAWA is effectively dead, permanently because of white evangelicals and the GOP.

Wealthiness Is Next to Godliness

"It's alright to tell a man to lift himself by his own bootstraps, but it is a cruel jest to say to a bootless man that he ought to lift himself by his own bootstraps."

Martin Luther King, Jr.

During Ronald Reagan's 1976 primary run for president he gave a speech which is credited with popularizing the term "welfare queen." He cited a single instance of a woman who scammed the U.S. welfare system by using 80 aliases and at least four fake dead husbands.[168] Based on this anecdote, Reagan promised to fix the welfare system by deterring people from using it. The term "welfare queen" became a 1980's racial dog whistle to evoke images of the lazy, indigent Black person, who scammed the system and had no right to government assistance.

Reagan also used latent racism to undermine support for government assistance with his references to "some strapping young buck" during message testing to southerners.[169] He evoked the image of an able-bodied black man using food stamps to buy steak while everyone else worked to afford hamburger. These racist messages directed at white southerners were appallingly, if predictably, effective. Even Bill Clinton, as a centrist Democrat, used this false stereotype of overly-generous welfare benefits to cut welfare in the bipartisan Welfare Reform Acts of Personal Responsibility and Work Opportunity Reconciliation Act of 1996.

Racial stereotyping played to the Republican base, both to its religious right members and the more secular hard-right that coalesced around racial grievances. The religious right also has a distinctly racist streak: it is primarily built around white evangelicals (who are concentrated in the U.S. South). As described in Chapter 1, The Southern Baptist Convention, the largest protestant denomination in the U.S., was founded on providing biblical justification for slavery during pre-Civil War debates on the issue. During the Civil Rights Movement, they again were responsible for providing the biblical justification for segregation and using religion as a way to opt out of civil rights laws. Today, white evangelicals still hold the most regressive opinions on race of any religious group in the U.S.

Over time, the evangelical right has come to believe, more than any other religious group, that people are poor because they are lazy or sinful.[170] Indeed, white evangelicals are more than twice as likely as non-Christians to believe people are poor because they are lazy. Conversely, white evangelicals believe that wealth is a sign of divine favor for leading a good life. Forty percent of white evangelicals (again, more than any other group surveyed) believe in the "prosperity gospel," which teaches that people who give money to churches will be rewarded by God with more wealth.[171] President Trump kept huckster proponents of the prosperity gospel like Paula White close to his administration.[172]

Influential evangelicals, such as "historian" and Christian nationalist David Barton, preached on the biblical nature of Reaganomics. According to Barton, the Bible "takes a very clear position" against the capital gains tax, the estate tax, the progressive income tax, and the minimum wage. "All of these are economic issues that we should be able to shape citizens thinking on because of what the Bible says."[173] Jerry Falwell once wrote that, "The free enterprise system is clearly outlined in the book of Proverbs." Thus, historically the religious right leadership has generally treated free market economics as being on a par with social issues in the "war for the soul of America," as arch-conservative Pat Buchanan called it at the 1992 Republican Convention. [174]

Finally, the "I've got mine" attitude underlying support for reverse Robin Hood policies is also associated with the base of the Republican Party. Nate Silver of FiveThirtyEight.com found, counter intuitively, that Trump's supporters were wealthier than the average American. This makes sense; they are older, whiter, and less likely to be queer than the general population, all factors likely to make individuals more financially secure.[175]

This adds up to a worldview in which God supports all the policies that make wealth inequality worse. Poor people shouldn't get assistance because they are lazy and sinful. In turn, this feeds the racist paradigm that minorities are poor because they are lazy, stupid, or sinful. At the same time, there is a belief that slashing benefits encourages hard work, even though the economic data shows that people are working more hours at more jobs just to survive. They believe that rich people worked hard for their money, and God is rewarding them for their efforts. Thus, any sort of taxes on the rich are an attempt to undo the will of God and punishing "hard work."

Corporations and oligarchs have encouraged these beliefs from their end as well. Their efforts are explored in the next chapter on the corrosive effects of wealth inequality on democracy and living conditions in the U.S.

The White Evangelical Persecution Complex

All of these beliefs illustrate how differently white evangelicals see the country, and the world, from the rest of Americans. While many pundits try to pin the blame for polarization on progressives, black people, the LGBTQ community, or the Democratic Party, the data most strongly suggests that the white evangelicals who control the Republican Party are the outlier that has pulled away from the rest of society.

White evangelicals understand their beliefs are outside the mainstream, but they reject the mainstream as either "elites," or as godless people. This growing distance between their beliefs and the rest of society's, coupled with long-held grudges dating back to the Civil War, has resulted in a deep-seated persecution complex. White evangelicals effectively believe they are right, and everyone else is wrong. Under previous administrations, they lost the battle over civil rights for Black people, and society moved on without them. They lost the public opinion war against the first Black American president; Obama remained the most admired man in America three years after he left office.[176] They feel they've lost the war of public opinion on separation of church and state, LGBTQ issues, climate change, keeping *Roe v. Wade* intact, prayer in schools, assault rifles, high capacity magazines, believing women who are assaulted, and virtually every other position they hold as a group. This leads to all the polling showing that evangelicals see themselves as more discriminated against than Muslims, immigrants, Jews, black, lesbians and gays, or any other group, with the exception of transgender people (they're a statistical tie).[177]

Ironically, while they have been losing cultural battles for hearts and minds, they are winning the war for power. They controlled the Senate, the Presidency, the Courts, two-thirds of state legislatures, and over half the Governorships. They have gerrymandered themselves near perpetual control of most state legislatures, and non-proportional representation makes it nearly impossible for Democrats to build a filibuster proof majority in the Senate. Chapter 8 takes an in-depth look into how Republicans, and by extension white evangelicals, have deliberately subverted the system and decimated democratic processes.

This only describes how they have reacted politically to their conviction that they are being persecuted. Emotionally, white evangelicals want revenge against the people they believe took "their" country away from them. The groups of people white evangelicals want to take revenge upon also tend to be core Democratic constituencies: people of color, Muslims, urbanites, LGBTQ people, immigrants, atheists, feminists (read: uppity women), economic progressives, and people who believe in separation of church and state. This explains the mindset of a Florida Trump supporter, whose home was destroyed by a hurricane and was bewildered by the inadequate government support for her disabled family. She remarked, "I voted for him, and he's the one who's doing this. I thought he was going to do good things. *He's not hurting the people he needs to be hurting.*"[178]

Evangelical culture and theology are unyielding, exclusive, and discourage empathy. If someone gets sick, they must have displeased God. If they're LGBTQ, they're making a choice to go to hell. Anyone who got handed the wrong religion at birth is going there, too. Even minor infractions of the law, God's or man's, deserves the harshest penalties, and they believe that everyone besides themselves (and maybe a few really conservative Catholics) deserve no quarter for having picked the wrong side in the battle between heaven and hell. Adam Serwer explored the results of such angry, intolerant, beliefs in his seminal article, "The Cruelty is the Point."[179]

Part of the white evangelical persecution complex stems from the fact that they believe the media is biased against them.[180] This leads to increased consumption of favorable, but far less reliable news sources such as *Fox News* and talk radio, which then feeds their fears and further stokes their beliefs that they are persecuted and that the rest of the media is biased against them.[181] It did not help that President Trump also fed these fears with his attacks on the media, and by decrying any negative coverage of himself as "fake news," thus amplifying the echo chamber they are already in.[182]

After what they feel to be decades of persecution for being white and Christian, they now held almost all the power at the state and federal level. Their goal is to re-imagine America as a Christian nation, and their plan is actually available publicly as part of Project Blitz. This document wraps their desire for revenge, anger, authoritarianism, Social Dominance Orientation, nostalgia, and religion into one legislative agenda meant very deliberately to shatter the barriers between church and state, and ensure that it is their kind of churches directing the state in perpetuity.

Project Blitz: The White Evangelical Plan for America

"We're on a mission from God."
Elwood Blues

The long-term goals of white evangelicals go far beyond simply re-shaping the federal judiciary and federal policy on "religious freedom." This isn't just about carving out vast religious exemptions to civil rights laws, destroying the so-

139

cial safety net, ending abortion, trying to hold back the "browning" of America with draconian immigration policies, and throwing dreamers out of the country. These are merely their immediate goals. Their true ambition is to Make America Great Again by restoring the country to its Christian roots at a fundamental level, by destroying the separation of church and state, and putting their brand of theology front and center in all facets of life. They want a country where their brand of religion is effectively the state religion.

This was a common view within the Trump Administration. Neither Secretary of State Mike Pompeo nor Attorney General William Barr believed that separation of church and state is in the constitution; they saw the First Amendment as only barring government interference in religion, and not vice versa. The Trump-appointed head of the Federal Election Commission, James Trainor, III, didn't believe in it either. He called the 2020 election a "spiritual war."[183] Barr went even a step further, believing a lack of religion in governance is a threat to democracy, and that religion (presumably his conservative brand) must be central to governance in the U.S.[184] Thus, to Barr and other Christian nationalists, tactics such as "voter suppression, gerrymandering, and the use of the Supreme Court to hand electoral victories to the Republicans are no longer dirty tricks. They are patriotic imperatives. They are not last resorts but first principles."[185] And Project Blitz was their playbook on how to accomplish this.

After the Republican success in winning at the state and local levels in 2010, and using that success to gerrymander their way to permanent majorities in most state-level legislative bodies in the U.S., the religious right recognized an opportunity to begin tearing down the walls separating church and state at the local level. After Trump's election, and his three nominations to the Supreme Court (all of whom are very friendly to freedom of religion claims), they have run towards this goal full tilt. Project Blitz acts as the mechanism to introduce legislation that erodes this separation over time.

The Congressional Prayer Caucus Foundation (CPCF) was founded by former Congressman Randy Forbes in 2005 to "protect religious freedom, preserve America's Judeo-Christian heritage, and promote prayer."[186] Another organization linked to CPCF is WallBuilders, LLC, which is run by Christian-nationalist and revisionist historian David Barton, who believes America should be a Christian nation and rejects separation of church and state.[187] The National Legal Foundation is an organization which also advocates ending the separation of church and state via the courts in order to gain "a broad acceptance of explicitly Biblical arguments in legal and policy debates."[188] In 2015 ,the CPCF, along with WallBuilders and the National Legal Foundation, created Project Blitz, along with a number of other state-level, mainly white, conservative evangelical groups.[189]

The idea behind Project Blitz was to do for religion what the American Legislative Exchange Council (ALEC) did for big business.[190] The basic premise is to create a robust network of religiously conservative legislators who oppose separation of church and state (and want to make America Christian again), produce sample draft legislation that can be passed in multiple states at once, and share tips and strategies. This is why the first order of business of Project Blitz in 2015 was to begin forming state level "Prayer Caucuses" modeled on the CPCF. To date, there are Project Blitz affiliated prayer caucuses across 29 states, claiming over 600 members.[191] Iowa alone has 65 members in their prayer caucus, including the governor and lieutenant governor. At the federal level, about 100 senators and representatives belong to the CPCF.[192]

In late 2016, they introduced their first "playbook," somewhat innocuously titled *Report and Analysis on Religious Freedom Measures Impacting Prayer and Faith in America (2017 Version)*.[193] The basic plan starting in 2016 was to work in three phases. The first goal was to pass (seemingly) innocuous legislation like bills requiring "In God We Trust" to be posted in schools, office buildings, and on license plates. Others included teaching kids about Federalism and limited government, teaching the history of Christianity and Christianity in America, teaching the role of religion in shaping U.S. law since 1620, and requiring schools to offer elective "Bible Literacy" classes for credits.

The second phase (or category) was titled "Resolutions and Proclamations Recognizing the Importance of Religious History and Freedom." It went a step further by trying to use the power of government to officially "focus more on our country's Judeo-Christian heritage," and worked towards making Christianity the *de facto* state religion. Both the 2017 and 2019 playbooks called for proclamations or resolutions recognizing "Religious Freedom Day, Recognizing Christian Heritage Week, Recognizing the Importance of the Bible in History, Recognizing the Year of the Bible, and Christmas Day."

Phase three is where they enter Republic of Gilead territory.[194] This is where they planned to use their brand of Christianity as a legislative weapon to attack groups that white evangelicals really don't like in the name of religious freedom, particularly LGBTQ people. The 2019 version of the playbook expanded phase three based on the success they were having accomplishing phases one and two, and the phase three goals described below are drawn directly from the most recent 2019 version.[195] The playbook called for resolutions establishing public policy favoring sexual relations only between heterosexual people, forbidding gender marker changes on government IDs and documents, and favoring adoption by married heterosexual couples.

The document also provided model bills for creating a "Marriage Tolerance Act," which in reality is a law that enshrines a right to discriminate against lesbians and gays. It calls for a "Preserving Religious Freedom Act," which would grant special rights to Christians who want to discriminate not just against LGBTQ people, but literally anyone, including people of other faiths. The mis-named "Child Protection Act" would create a situation in which adoption agencies which refuse to serve people based on their religious beliefs would be granted preferential treatment (i.e., more and better government contracts and money). It also provides a model for a "Clergy Protection Act" and a "Licensed Professionals Civil Rights Act" model bill that would allow anyone with a state license to refuse service to anyone based on their religious beliefs. It provides no exceptions for things like race or religion: It is a blanket "get out of jail free" card for discrimination and effectively neuters the Civil Rights Act of 1964.

The "Student Prayer Certification Act" model bill is meant as a direct challenge to the Supreme Court's 1962 decision in *Engel v. Vitale*, which ruled against school mandated prayers. The "Teacher Protection Act" would shield teachers, schools, and districts that discriminate based on religious beliefs from lawsuits. The "Preserving Religious Freedom in Schools Act" prohibits any sort of action against students or teachers for expressing their religious beliefs. This sounds innocuous, until you realize that this makes it impossible to stop students and teachers from wearing "God Hates Fags" buttons to school, or verbally abusing students who are LGBTQ or non-Christian. The playbook also includes a section on what sorts of bills to fight against, including bills that protect LGBTQ people from discrimination, bans on conversion therapy, and bills that counter the power of state-level Religious Freedom Restoration Acts.

This should sound bad to anyone who isn't a big fan of discrimination against everyone else in the name of God, and forcing people to listen to your theology in school. When you drill down into the details of the document, though, it becomes even more apparent how radical and frightening their plans really are. It portrays lesbians and gays as disease-ridden and unhealthy in order to claim compelling governmental interest in discouraging homosexuality. It also claims that being transgender is simultaneously unhealthy and contagious, and that governments have a compelling interest in preventing the "spread." With Amy Coney-Barrett creating a 6-3 conservative super-majority on the Supreme Court, such odious laws are likely to stand up in court.

While Project Blitz is not explicit in the governmental powers they intend to use, literally everything is on the table. Banning transition-related health services for transgender people, putting LGBTQ people on the sex offender watch list, enforcing sodomy laws (which still exist in 12 states) with the intention of over-turning *Lawrence v. Texas*, quarantining transgender children from schools, deem-ing LGBTQ Centers a threat to public health and minors, mandating conversion therapy for LGBTQ people: these are all logical, legal steps under the guidance of Project Blitz and similar laws passed in Russia. They do not care that this runs counter to all the reputable scientific evidence about LGBTQ people. Their goal is not good policy, it is policy based on their particular interpretation of Christi-anity and the Bible, and they openly admit that this is their desired goal.

The worst part is that they are succeeding. The number of model bills they are passing is increasing at an exponential rate. In 2016, they passed 4 model bills. In 2017, they proposed 200 bills and passed 31 in 17 states. In 2018, they proposed 300 and passed another 33 in 16 states. Almost all of these had to do with schools and education. In 2019, they proposed 14 bills in 11 states mandating teaching of "Biblical Literacy" classes in schools. All but two of them were proposed in former Confederate states (i.e., by white evangelical dominated legislatures), and one of the others in Mike Pence's home state of Indiana. The sole non-Southern state, North Dakota, voted the bill down 5-42.[196]

The sponsors of these mandatory Bible lessons all use language similar to that of Project Blitz and its beliefs about eliminating the separation between church and state. Senator Dennis Kruse of Indiana said, "[W]e need more Christianity and religion in our society, in our state." In North Dakota, Rep. Aaron McWilliams re-marked, "[W]e are Christian, and you know a lot of the founding principles of the country are based on Christian principles and philosophies." In Florida, Rep. Kim Daniels attributed opposition to her Bible bill as "anti-Christ spirits."

What the reader should take away from this is that CPCF and Project Blitz are powerful forces within the Republican Party for white evangelicals. CPCF has over 100 members in Congress which included Vice President Mike Pence when he was a Representative from Indiana. They have shown us their plan and success in implementing it. We know what their end goal for America looks like, and that they have the governmental clout to make getting there not just a non-trivial possibility, but a more than reasonable fear. Even worse, they now have a court system that is potentially willing to uphold what they pass.

Some might scoff at the idea that white evangelicals would push this far. But, to reiterate Masha Gessen: "Believe the autocrats. They mean what they say. Whenever you find yourself thinking, or hear others claiming, that he is exaggerating, that is our innate tendency to reach for a rationalization."[197] As radical and unthinkable as Project Blitz sounds, you must always bear in mind that this demographic supported two great sins of our nation: slavery and Jim Crow. Project Blitz lays out their desired goals in no uncertain terms, and they have rigged the game in their favor.

Conclusion

Pew Research made an interesting finding in 2019: people who know a lot about other faiths besides their own tend to have the warmest feelings towards other faiths, with one faith being a key exception. More knowledgeable people had significantly more negative feelings towards evangelical protestants than towards atheists, Jews, Catholics, and Muslims.[198] It should not be hard to see why.

White evangelicals, the politically dominant strain of Christianity in America, have views that are not only out of touch with everyone else in America, but are actively hostile to large swathes of Americans. They are the most negatively predisposed group in America towards Blacks, immigrants, Latinos, LGBTQ people, women, members of progressive religious traditions, feminists, and Muslims. Their views on issues like guns, abortion, and climate change are far to the right. People who (rightly) see climate change as an existential threat to their progeny perceive white evangelicals' views as a threat to humanity and future generations. This dynamic is unlikely to change, as the data shows that young white evangelicals are not, in fact, getting more moderate over time.[199]

Researching the evangelical mindset in more depth uncovers an ugly pastiche of anger, authoritarianism, a desire to keep others in their place, and to hurt groups who have made social progress. Those who dig deeper find plans to remake America into something dark and theocratic, where everyone but white evangelicals are at best second-class citizens. At worst, they plan to drive swathes of the population out of public life using the full force of the government to do so.

The white evangelical lust for unfettered power has broken the American democratic system of government and generated a ruling party that is authoritarian in nature, unconcerned with the consent of the governed, and is steered by a fundamentalist religious minority whose values differ radically from the rest of the population. When they discovered that there was no hope to achieve their goals through democratic processes, they decided to break democracy.

Sadly, the religious right is destroying liberal Christianity, too. They are "poisoning" the brand name with their hard-right out-of-touch political stances, their hypocrisy in supporting Trump, and their assertion that they are the only real Christians. The Democratic Party has reluctantly had to admit that due to the growth of the religiously unaffiliated, the "nones" are now by far the largest religious component of the Democratic Party.[200]

This sets the stage for a scenario where a small ethnic and religious fundamentalist minority reigns undemocratically over people who do not share their religion, culture, nor ethnicity, while oppressing and disenfranchising the majority. It is no coincidence that during the attempted coup in 2021 the insurrectionists bore flags proclaiming "Jesus Saves," "Make America Godly Again," and bearing other Christian iconography.[201] Unsurprisingly, the government they have made has most of the classic hallmarks of modern single-party authoritarian regimes, complete with the characteristics of a fascist movement. All the while their values are drifting farther and farther from the mainstream. In short, the tension between white evangelicals and the rest of the country is building, and white evangelicals are only making it worse with their desperate attempts to hang on to power through gerrymandering, voter suppression, court packing, police brutality, and militias.

Something's going to give way eventually. And it's likely to be even uglier than the insurrection on January 6th, 2021, when it does.

Seven

The Runaway Train to Oligarchyville

"Let me tell you about the very rich. They are different from you and me."

F. Scott Fitzgerald

During the 2016 Democratic primaries, Bernie Sanders (I-VT) called out economic inequality and student loan debt forgiveness as major issues. His target audience was primarily Millennials, and it resonated well. A primary that was supposed to be a cake-walk for Hillary Clinton turned into an uncomfortably tight race. The Russians also capitalized on this sudden (and unexpected) opportunity by churning out pro-Sanders propaganda, and stoking the narrative that Clinton had "cheated" in the primary.

The fact that Sanders did far better than expected speaks to his message more than the messenger. In 2016, he was 75 years old. He is a Jewish atheist and an avowed socialist who ran for Senator as an Independent rather than as a Democrat (though he caucused with them). His appearance and demeanor are similar to Doc Brown in *Back to The Future*, that manic uncle who explains animatedly to the entire family over Thanksgiving dinner how time travel is possible with a flux capacitor. And, like Doc Brown, Sanders was right.

Sanders' message resonated with younger people because he was the only candidate who correctly identified one of the fundamental problems facing not just younger people, but the country as a whole: wealth inequality. The reason why it worked best with Millennials was because they are disproportionately affected by it. They are the first American generation to have less than a 50-50 chance of being financially better off than their parents, and the odds are likely to be even worse for Generation Z (people born after 1995 or so).[1]

Before exploring this in depth, the term wealth inequality deserves definition beyond simply "the rich get richer and the poor get poorer." It is a measure of not only the difference in how much people make every year, but in how much they have accumulated. There are many ways to measure inequality.[2] One commonly used statistical measure of economic inequality is the Gini coefficient. It is a continuous scale that goes from 0 if everyone had the same accumulated wealth or income, to 1 if one person had all the wealth or income in a nation. Income distribution and household consumption costs are other common metrics.

All of these measures indicate that wealth and income inequality in the United States have been increasing for decades. The Gini coefficient is rising steadily, as is the wealthiest 10 percent's share of pre-tax income. Consumption rates agree. There is a general consensus among economists that we have entered a second gilded age, with income inequality at a level not seen since the late 1920's, just before the Great Depression. Even conservative economic think tanks, like the American Enterprise Institute, have noted the trend in their studies.[3] By 2018, after the Trump tax cuts kicked in, the top 400 wealthiest individuals in the U.S. paid taxes at a lower rate (23 percent) than the bottom 50 percent of wage earners, who pay 24.2 percent of their income.[4]

Figure 8. Top 10 Percent Pre-Tax Income Share in the U.S.

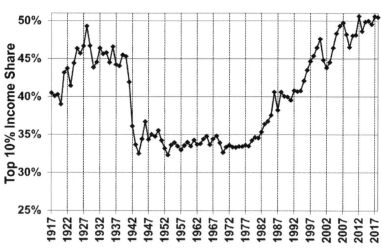

Source: Piketty and Saez[5]

It is also important to understand the difference between income inequality and wealth inequality. The former measures how much people make in a year compared to others, and the latter measures how much they (and their forebears) have accumulated. In the U.S., as bad as income inequality is, wealth inequality is worse, and there is a strong racial component to it.[6] The differences between white and Black net household worth are stark reminders of this, and it has only accelerated since the Great Recession of 2008.[7]

Wealth inequality exists everywhere, of course. Some people will always have more money than others, and conversely no society will ever exist where a single person has all the money in the country. There is a great deal of space in between these two extremes, though, and the Gini coefficient provides a continuous, quantitative measure with which to compare countries against each other, as well as states within the U.S.

Generally speaking, progressive, wealthy, democratic, socialist countries have the lowest wealth inequality as measured by the Gini coefficient. Among wealthy nations, Nordic countries such as Sweden, Finland, Norway, and Iceland have the lowest levels of economic inequality. Japan, and progressive western nations such as Belgium, Austria, and Denmark also have relatively low levels of wealth inequality. Conversely, places with high levels of inequality tend to be places that few people would want to immigrate to. High crime, rampant corruption, low life expectancy, poor civil rights records, teeming slums, and shanty towns are typical of the countries with very high Gini coefficients. Among nations with large populations, Mexico, Brazil, and the United States have some of the highest levels of wealth inequality. Indeed, wealth inequality in the U.S. has risen to a level higher than that of Russia and China, both of which are known for their bloated, corrupt oligarchies.[8]

Conservatives tend to argue that wealth inequality is only natural, and that the benefits (some cheap goods and services and the way in which it incentivizes hard work) outweigh the negatives. However, a review of the relevant literature clearly shows the opposite. Wealth inequality is a leading cause of a wide array of damaging social ills and prevents people from getting ahead simply through hard work.[9] Indeed, the availability of cheap goods and services in a deeply unequal society means only that those who have wealth can enjoy luxuries like pointless consumer items.

In *The Spirit Level*, British epidemiologists Richard Wilkinson and Kate Pickett looked at the overall societal effects of inequality across a number of wide-ranging factors, among them life expectancy, incarceration rates, drug use, homicide rates, and educational performance. First, they compared countries and U.S. states using per capita income. Then, they repeated their data analysis using measures of inequality. Using data collected by the United Nations, they measured wealth inequality in countries by comparing the ratio of income between the top 20 percent and bottom 20 percent of the population. They made similar comparisons between U.S. states using Gini coefficients collected by the U.S. Census Bureau.[10]

Their findings were startling. When comparing developed countries, total societal wealth (Gross Domestic Product per capita) had little to no influence on the results. For example, there was not a significant correlation between life expectancy and average income in developed nations. However, there is a significant correlation between life expectancy and wealth equality. This pattern held true throughout the analysis: Wealth inequality, not income per capita, was more predictive of a host of social ills. Societal problems associated with higher wealth inequality included lower life expectancy, higher incarceration rates, a lower percentage of people who say others can be trusted, higher infant mortality rates, lower scores on standardized tests, more drug use, and higher murder rates.

You could dismiss these findings by noting that these countries are very different culturally, legally, politically, and economically. However, when the same analyses are performed on a state-by-state basis within the U.S., we see the same results. States with higher levels of wealth inequality have worse outcomes across many of the same metrics (life expectancy, incarceration rates, educational attainment, etc…). Thus, it isn't the culture, or the location, or the political structure that are primarily responsible. It seems to be the highly unequal distribution of wealth.

Another data point damaging to the conservative talking point that wealth inequality increases incentives to work harder is the evidence that wealth inequality decreases social mobility. In other words, the more unequal the wealth and income distribution of a country is, the more difficult it is to change your station in life. Thus, the opposite of the conservative narrative is true: wealth inequality disincentivizes hard work because in more unequal countries, it is harder to get ahead, and there is less connection between how hard you work and how much you make.

The trend in the U.S. is the same. As wealth inequality has risen since World War II, social mobility has declined precipitously. Today, people born after 1985 (Millennials) have less than a 50 percent chance of earning more than their parents. This has colloquially come to be known as "The Great Gatsby Curve," seen below in Figure 9.

The lack of social mobility isn't because of social Darwinistic self-sorting, where the rich have risen to the top because of their supposedly superior genetics and intelligence. When scientists studied some of the genes predicting academic success and compared them with income, they found that there was no link between the two. In other words, the "good" genes were spread evenly across all income levels. Instead, academic attainment was primarily determined by the income of a child's father.[13]

Wealth and poverty in the U.S. are self-perpetuating. Poor children are far less likely to go to college. Even poor kids who do well academically in high school are less likely to graduate from college than the children of the wealthy who were poor students. Even after they graduate from college, children of the poor are worse off economically than low achieving children of the rich. At elite universities, 74

Figure 9. Global Social Mobility vs. Wealth Inequality

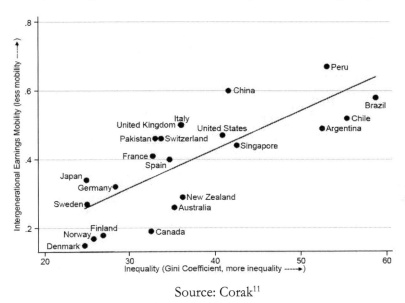

Source: Corak[11]

Figure 10. Percentage of Children Earning More than their Parents by Birth Year

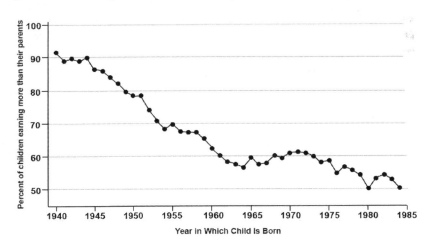

Source: Chetty, Grusky, et al.[12]

percent of students come from families in the top quarter of the population economically. Only 9 percent come from the bottom half.[14]

It's not a matter of "lazy Millennials" either. Data from 2015 showed U.S. Millennials work an average of 45 hours per week. This is higher than most of western Europe, as well as Australia and Canada. By comparison, Japanese Millennials work 46 hours per week on average. Other than Japan, countries where Millennials work as many, or more hours than the U.S. tended to be nations with horrific poverty, terrible human rights records, high crime, and either weak or despotic governments (China, Mexico, India, Brazil).[15] Indeed, there appears to be a correlation between wealth inequality and number of hours spent working in awful conditions.

The butcher's bill for the continual, rapid rise of wealth inequality in the United States is starting to come due. In 2017, the U.S. set records for alcohol, drug, and suicide deaths per capita. According to the Centers for Disease Control and two public health non-profits, the national rate for deaths from these causes rose from 43.9 to 46.6 deaths per 100,000 people. This was a 6 percent increase, according to the Trust for America's Health and the Well Being Trust. The 4 percent increase in suicides in 2017 was double the average rate in the past decade.[16]

Data shows that jobs that pay a living wage are becoming scarcer. Forty-four percent of American workers are in low paying jobs.[17] Forty percent make less than the minimum wage as it stood in 1968 (adjusted for inflation), and that number is growing as wages stagnate and the cost of living increases.[18] Wealth inequality has soared as a result. Members of the *Forbes* 400 list are worth more than every Black family in the U.S., and more than the bottom two-thirds of households in the U.S. combined.[19] The three richest Americans are worth more than the bottom 50 percent.[20] During the COVID-19 pandemic, the worth of billionaires soared, while working class families (disproportionately minorities) suffered.[21]

Millennials are forced to work far more hours just to survive than Gen Xers or Boomers, while making relatively less.[22] They are keenly aware of this issue, which is likely why Bernie Sanders' message resonated so strongly with them; he was the only major candidate directly addressing the problem. They instinctively know that Republican *laissez faire* capitalism, and economic favoritism of the rich and corporations, is the cause of wealth inequality. Clinton failed to take the issue head on for fear of sounding too extreme or being branded a socialist. This may be part of why it has been so maddeningly difficult for Democrats to get younger voters to the polls.

It is worth noting that most of this occurred in a supposedly "booming" economy with low unemployment. Thus, work truly does not make you free. Quite the opposite; wealth inequality is a huge part of the problem. The truth is that economic inequality destroys opportunity, while forcing people to work harder for less. At the same time, democracy has been collapsing. This all runs counter to the conservative narrative that economic freedom results in more freedom and democracy for everyone. *Arbeit macht frei* (work sets you free), the slogan appearing above the entrance to the Auschwitz concentration camp, was a cruel lie 80 years ago, and it remains so today.

Wealth Inequality is the Death of Democracy

"I'm not a big believer in democracy. I always say that democracy can be two wolves and a sheep deciding what's for dinner."

Stephen Moore, The Heritage Foundation

Runaway wealth inequality is not only socially destructive, it is also corrosive to the democratic processes that spawned it in the first place. It is incompatible with democratic governance where the will of the people is executed by their elected representatives. It results in national leadership that may or may not be competent, but which definitely ensures that economic and political systems favor the rich, disfavor everyone else, and create a government unresponsive to the actual desires of the vast majority of the population.

Thomas Piketty estimates that 60 percent of U.S. wealth (or more if you count "gifts" to offspring) is inherited. This is up from 50 percent in the 1970's and 1980's.[23] Perhaps no better case study of how the inheritance of great wealth can easily overcome gross ignorance, incompetence, and a singularly unpleasant personality can be found than Donald J. Trump.

Case Study: Donald Trump

"On some great and glorious day the plain folks of the land will reach their heart's desire at last, and the White House will be adorned by a downright moron."

H. L. Mencken

The rich really are very different from you and I, but perhaps not in the way F. Scott Fitzgerald meant. The Trump presidency was a stark and disturbing illustration of what underlies those differences, and of the overwhelming power of wealth in the United States.

Trump is not a smart man. He's not intellectually curious. He has read almost nothing and cannot even manage to work his way through bullet-pointed intelligence briefings. He is, by all accounts, unteachable about anything. His personality isn't suited for leadership or success either. He is ill-tempered, mercurial, petty, vindictive, and garrulous. Nor is he eloquent, stringing buzzwords and dog-whistles together into a stream of consciousness that only those in tune with his brand of politics can follow or understand. He's not particularly strategic or deep in his thinking. He is impervious to information that does not already fit his worldview. He pits subordinates against each other in a belief that "survival of the fittest" makes things work, as though his cabinet was an episode of *The Apprentice*. He belittles them, mocks them, and turns on them in an instant. Nor does he listen to them. And when they do speak their minds, he fires them.

He assumes that because he's rich, he must also be smart, but he's not particularly hard working. He rarely started his official duties before 10 a.m., and frequently not until 11. He spent 60 percent of his time in the White House in unstructured "executive time."[24] His frequent golf junkets to Mar-a-Lago cost more in one year than all 8 years of travel in the Obama Administration.[25]

He delights in fawning praise, like the roundtable love-fests staged by his cabinet. The evangelical right fed this by praying over him and claiming he was sent by God, and, in turn, he granted them their fondest wishes. The same is true with *Fox News*; they flattered him, and he tweeted exactly as on their shows. Thus, his vanity, pride, and ignorance make him easy to manipulate. His primary "gift" is sharing pettiness, vindictiveness, and cruelty with people who are similarly ignorant, petty, vindictive, and racist. He has a talent for appealing to the lowest common denominator at the right times in ways that they understand.

"Trump the Successful Billionaire" is a fiction; a mirage created by TV and his showmanship. His hotels are chintzy money-pits. His casinos are bankrupt, their empty husks scheduled for demolition. He has declared bankruptcy at least six times and is in debt up to his eyeballs. His shadowy creditors may plausibly be the kind that ensure people "accidentally" fall out of windows if they don't repay their debts. Even his inaugural cake was a knock-off of Obama's. Unlike the 44th President's cake, Trump's cake was mostly made out of Styrofoam and frosting.

Trump is not a great businessman or deal-maker; he would be far better off financially today if he had done absolutely nothing after his father gave him his money, and just dumped his inherited wealth into an indexed stock fund in the 1970's. He paid $130,000 for two minutes of sex with porn star Stormy Daniels. His Twitter feed was ample evidence of his loose affiliation with the truth and poor impulse control.

For all his bombast, Trump is a failure. If he hadn't inherited his father's fortune, or had to answer to a board, he would have been fired long ago. He'd be that loud-mouthed uncle who sells time-shares in Boca Raton and unfortunately shows up to Thanksgiving dinner, boasting, brazenly lying, spouting racism, groping your wife, and making creepy innuendos about your daughter. He's sound and fury, signifying nothing.

Trump is not a good human being. Willful ignorance, mocking the disabled, preying on women, lying, cheating on his spouses, cruelty, bullying people, and inciting violence are all examples of his personal failings. His chief of staff, General John Kelly, reportedly called him "the most flawed person I have ever met in my life."[26]

In almost any alternate universe where he didn't inherit hundreds of millions of dollars, Trump would be a spectacularly unsuccessful person. To quote Tom Nichols, "Bad teachers over time tend to get bad evaluations, lousy lawyers will lose clients, and untalented athletes will fail to make the cut."[27] However, bad millionaires and bad billionaires will remain millionaires and billionaires, even if they are spectacularly bad at not just business, but life in general.

But, because Trump was born rich, people have had to put up with these failings his entire life. They have had to genuflect to him because of his wealth. They make excuses for him, cater to him and allow him to get away with anything. He never had to learn or grow or consider how or why he has failed. He has never had to ponder how he could be better. He never needed to improve himself or consider the moral implications or consequences of anything he does. He is the perfect example of how a life utterly devoid of introspection and replete with narcissism is possible because he was born with a silver spoon in his mouth. He also illustrates how meritocracy fails in a system where there are no checks and balances on the ultra-rich; they exist above the law and outside the Peter Principle.[28]

The rich do not play by the same rules as the rest of America, and they know it.

Wealth Inequality and Democracy

> *"You work three jobs?... Uniquely American, isn't it? I mean, that is fantastic that you're doing that."*

George W. Bush to a divorced mother of three in Omaha, Nebraska

Political scientists Jacob Hacker and Paul Pierson identified three types of threats that extreme inequality poses to democracy. The first is greatly unequal power within society, where a few rich people have far more power than the rest of society combined. The second is diverging interests: as the rich grow increasingly wealthy, and the poor grow poorer, what the rich want becomes more unaligned with what the majority of the population wants. Finally, there is elite fear. When the rich worry that a democratic government may harm their interests, they "become more willing to contemplate and support political alternatives to democracy."[29]

In the U.S., the unequal power has become increasingly evident. In 2014. Benjamin Page of Northwestern University and Martin Gilens at Princeton University shocked the world by publishing a paper which seemed to show quantitatively that the United States was no longer functionally a democracy. They reached this conclusion by comparing the clout of rich Americans (top 10 percent) vs. the middle 85 percent on 1779 policy issues between 1980 and 2002. They found that the middle class' views on policy had no statistical impact on it being adopted. However, the opinions of the wealthiest 10 percent had a dramatic impact on whether a policy was passed.[30]

It's not hard to think of cases where the American public feels very strongly about an issue, but money and interests override the popular will. This includes even the simplest forms of gun control (88 percent of the population supported enhanced background checks after the Sandy Hook massacre), protections for LGBTQ people (~70 percent support), and the Trump Tax Cut (which passed with only 29 percent of popular support in December 2017).[31] Without a doubt, it is the rich who are driving U.S. tax policy. A 2011 poll of rich Americans making more than $14 million per year found that only 17 percent said they would support raising taxes to reduce inequality.[32]

Nor do the wealthy support policies that are in the best interests of the public if it means less money for them. Seventy-eight percent of Americans believe that the government should make it affordable for people to go to college, but only 28 percent of the wealthy agreed. In this same survey, sixty-one percent of Americans support national health insurance of some sort, but only 32 percent of the wealthy do. It's difficult to find a reason why a society shouldn't aim for a healthier, more educated, and less indebted society, but we have ended up with a system that caters to the people who want the exact opposite.

Another danger is what Nobel Prize winning economist Joseph Stiglitz describes as "regulatory capture," which hastens the process of government working against the interests of the public. When government entities meant to regulate businesses turn to protecting them instead, it's the public that suffers, whether it's financial institutions like the Securities and Exchange Commission, environmental ones, or agencies that supposedly protect workers. When corporations control these institutions, it creates a hazard to the public.[33] For instance, during the COVID-19 pandemic, Tyson Foods successfully pressured the government into letting it keep plants open. As a result, workers were among those who were most affected by the disease in many midwestern states.[34] Managers at Tyson allegedly had betting pools on how many workers would get sick.[35] They were secure in the knowledge that the Supreme Court had already ruled that workers would struggle to collectively sue them, or the company, as a group after the Supreme Court decision in *Epic Systems v. Lewis.*[36]

Finally, the fears of the wealthy fuel decline in their belief in a democratic system. This is where it gets dangerous, and there's ample quantitative evidence to support this relationship. If you look at Gini Coefficient vs. the Democracy Index scores of Organization for Economic Co-operation and Development (OECD) nations, there is a statistically significant ($p = .022$) relationship between how unequal wealth within a country is, and how democratic its government is. The democracy index ranges from zero (perfectly totalitarian state) to a perfectly democratic one at 10 (Norway has the top score at 9.87).

Figure 11. OECD Gini Coefficient vs. Democracy Index

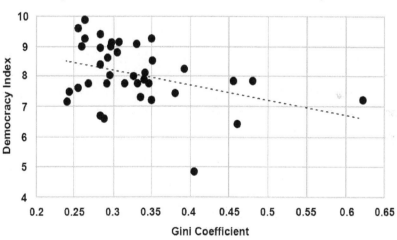

Data Sources: Economist Intelligence Unit (Democracy Index), OECD (Gini coefficient)

Other studies have shown that high levels of wealth inequality reduce support for democracy.[37] This fits the pattern we see in the U.S. and elsewhere around Europe, where wealth inequality has increased and support for democracy has decreased. We also see the lowest level of support for democracy amongst younger people, who are the hardest hit by the issue of unequal wealth distribution.[38] Analyst Paul Howe looked at this same data set and concluded, "Disregard for democratic norms is part of a larger social transformation that has seen rising disengagement and alienation, particularly among younger generations and lower socioeconomic classes."[39]

The view that massive disparities in wealth endanger democracy is held by many subject matter experts, and the data presented here seems to support this hypothesis. The mechanism for this effect is not hard to understand. When oligarchs or plutocrats pursue aims that are actively harmful to most of the population but have far more influence than the people being harmed, they diminish democracy and society. It also reduces democratic participation when these oligarchs and plutocrats have so thoroughly captured the system that meaningful change via the ballot box appears impossible. The plutocrats and oligarchs, for their part, are motivated to subvert democracy. If their ideas and goals are so unpopular that they cannot be passed through a free and fair democratic process, then they will likely seek to achieve those aims by other means.

"It's very dangerous," said Ngaire Woods, Dean of the Blavatnik School of Government at the University of Oxford. "If people can't aspire to succeed within the system, they will aspire... outside the system, in ways that break the system."[40] These experts point out that by 2030, the top 1 percent of the U.S. population will earn 37-40 percent of the income. The bottom 50 percent will earn 6 percent. Nick Hanauer, a former venture capitalist and now head of Civic Ventures, summed up what this sort of disparity represents. "That's not a capitalist market economy anymore. That's a feudalist system. And it scares me."

When comparing GDP per capita to the Gini coefficient, the U.S. is an outlier with a higher-than-average GDP per capita and higher Gini coefficient. However, economic growth for the middle class and poor has stalled out or reversed, and the fact that the U.S. is becoming less democratic may be a phenomenon known as reverting to the mean. In other words, while the U.S. is democratic for a nation with such high wealth inequality now, it is becoming more like undemocratic countries that also have high wealth and income inequality. In this case, the U.S. may be becoming more like Russia, China, and Brazil politically because in some ways it resembles them economically.

If a capitalist system with a healthy middle class and strong consumer spending as an economic driver is the intended goal of U.S. economic policy, wealth inequality works against it. When the International Monetary Fund (IMF) studied the issue, they found that high levels of wealth inequality create significant economic drag. Extremely low levels of wealth inequality reduce economic growth to a lesser extent, but the U.S. is far above the .27 Gini coefficient threshold where there appears to be a "Goldilocks zone" for inequality.[41]

As wealth inequality grows, GDP growth slows. This makes sense intuitively. If the only people able to afford niceties are a very select few, and everyone else is barely capable of making ends meet, this is a disaster for retailers. We can see this effect with Millennials and their spending habits. While Millennials have been accused of "killing" numerous businesses and industries, it's not their fault. The Federal Reserve studied this and concluded the reason Millennials aren't buying things is simply because they do not have the disposable income that Gen X and the Boomers did, which is attributable to rising wealth inequality.[42]

Republicans (Mostly) Created This Issue

"Since 1920, the vast increase in welfare beneficiaries and the extension of the franchise to women—two constituencies that are notoriously tough for libertarians—have rendered the notion of 'capitalist democracy' into an oxymoron...I no longer believe that freedom and democracy are compatible."

Peter Thiel, billionaire and Trump Supporter

Who is to blame for the rise of economic inequality and all the ills that come with it? While Democrats can take some of the blame for failing to emphasize policies that reduce wealth inequality (neo-liberalism), the Republican Party and its base (corporations and religious conservatives) are the ones actually demanding policies that exacerbate the problem.

Since Reagan, it has been conservative dogma that the best thing for the economy and the country is to slash taxes and social services. All welfare programs, in their view, should be the province of churches and charitable organizations. As previously discussed, the religious right leadership rallied behind Reaganomics. These policies intentionally did enormous damage to minorities. They also hurt democracy and our society in the long run by widening wealth and racial inequalities.

The basis for Reaganomics was the Laffer Curve, which postulates that maximum tax revenue is generated at some point between 0 and 100 percent. Arthur Laffer believed that the optimum tax rate was far lower than other, more mainstream economists believed. He argued that U.S. tax rates were far above the theoretical optimum point and claimed that if the U.S. reduced tax rates, it would spur so much economic growth that the amount of taxes collected would, counter-intuitively, go up in the long run. Laffer sold this theory to Dick Cheney and Donald Rumsfeld on the back of a napkin in 1974, and unfortunately it caught on. When it was finally implemented under President Reagan, U.S. tax receipts fell

159

far behind the rest of the Organization for Economic Co-operation and Development and the deficit skyrocketed.

So, what to do about these deficits? The GOP, predictably, settled on the Lee Atwater-approved messaging of slashing benefits for the poor. An anonymous Reagan staffer reportedly called it "starving the beast." This economic philosophy "used tax cuts to discipline government spending,"[43] believing that if revenues were unilaterally reduced, the reduction would lead to a higher budget deficit, which would force legislators to enact spending cuts.

The theory that tax cuts will enforce fiscal discipline has permeated the GOP, and been adopted by lobbyists like Grover Norquist, and the George W. Bush administration. It also worked about as well as buying pants that are too small in the hopes that this will motivate weight loss. Budget deficits ballooned under Reagan under successive Republican administrations. Thus, to no serious economist's surprise, theory and reality differed. Since the Reagan Administration, deficits under tax-cutting Republican presidents have generally increased at a higher rate than under Democratic presidents. Post-World War II, top marginal tax rates in America varied between 94 percent and 70 percent. When Reagan entered office, they were at 70 percent, where they had been since the mid-1960's. In 1980, both debt as a ratio of GDP and wealth inequality were at near historic lows.

Then came Reagan's sweeping tax cuts for the wealthy, dropping top marginal rates to as low as 28 percent by 1987. The result was an exploding deficit and ballooning wealth inequality. For people of color, the growth in wealth inequality since Reagan's time has been even more pronounced.[44]

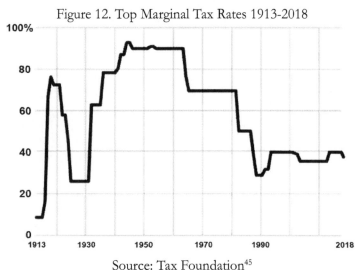

Figure 12. Top Marginal Tax Rates 1913-2018

Source: Tax Foundation[45]

160

The Republican assault on unions was part of the problem, and it accelerated under Reagan. Countries with healthy unions have less wealth inequality. When Reagan broke the air traffic controllers' strike of 1981, it further weakened that institution and paved the way for growth in wealth and income inequality.[46]

While never immensely popular, Reaganomics has been the dominant economic theory in the U.S. for four decades now. What the rich want, the rich get. And they want policies that allow them to become richer, regardless of whether they benefit society. To get such policies, they go to the Republican Party. Of the 100 wealthiest Americans on the *Forbes* 100 list, two-thirds give exclusively or mainly to Republicans or conservative causes. Overall, individuals on this list gave three times as much money to conservative causes as liberal or progressive ones.[47] This same study found that of these 100 individuals, none were seeking to lower taxes. Even progressive billionaires like George Soros and Bill Gates aren't pushing for "socialism," despite the fears of the conservative base. Executives in the relatively socially liberal tech sector are more conservative than average Republican voters on issues like government regulation of corporations and labor unions.[48]

After 40 years, The Laffer Curve and the economic theories surrounding it have been extensively field tested and disproven. A 2020 study of 18 OECD nations over 50 years found that tax cuts for the wealthy do not boost the economy, nor do they "trickle down." It also concluded that raising taxes on the wealthy had little or no impact on the economy. This effectively debunks both conservative talking points that low taxes on the rich help the economy, and that increasing tax rates on them would harm it.[49] (But more on that later.)

As noted previously, unequal societies have great difficulty balancing protections between the 1 percent and everyone else. As a result, most conservative parties face the following conundrum: how do they represent the interests of businesses and the rich, while appealing to enough voters to get elected, even if their economic policies are deeply unpopular? Simple: they find divisive social issues based on race, sex, xenophobia, religion, and other areas where they will have long-term opportunities to exploit fears and hatreds that induce their supporters to ignore the damage their economic policies cause. This right-wing, populist, 1-percenter-friendly, us vs. them politics is the basis of *fascism*.

The list of policies that contribute to worsening economic disparities reads like a Republican letter to Santa: low top marginal tax rates, low taxes on corporations, slashing the social safety net (Medicare, social security, Medicaid, Affordable Care Act, the Special Supplemental Nutrition Program for Women, Infants and Children (WIC), etc.), opposition to unions, weakened labor laws, opposition to raising the minimum wage (or having a minimum wage at all), the Bankruptcy Reform Bill of 2005, and acceptance of medical bankruptcy. These are all GOP positions that are generally unpopular, but core tenets of their party platform nonetheless. The base has been conditioned to see this as simply the price of "freedom." You know, the freedom to work two jobs until you die on your greeter's chair at Wal-Mart at the age of 72.

Each Republican wish is effectively the government acting as a reverse Robin Hood, taking from the poor and giving to the rich and corporations. Any one of these individually isn't enough to create the runaway wealth inequality that we see now. Together, however, they are sufficient to create the free fall we are observing across society. Conversely, fixing one of these problems (say, the top marginal tax rate) is not enough to overcome the effects of all the others.[50] Conservatives use this to effectively argue, "Whelp, that won't fix everything, so let's not do it." We are effectively on a path to social, governmental, and economic oblivion (unless you really want to live in a third-world theocratic oligarchy where elections are incapable of changing anything).

Thus, halting the runaway train to Oligarchyville will take an "all of the above" strategy. All of the things necessary to prevent going to "The Bad Place" are vehemently opposed by the GOP, while generally favored by the majority of the public. Eighty-two percent of the public wants to raise the federal minimum wage, and 55 percent want to more than double it to $15 per hour.[51] Fifty-nine percent of registered voters support raising the top marginal rate on people earning more than $10 million per year to 70 percent, while only 12 percent of Americans want to see cuts to Medicare and Social Security.[52] The Affordable Care Act is significantly more popular than the Trump Tax cuts for the wealthy.[53] Support for labor unions is at a 15-year high, and has been rising since 2008.[54] Indeed, modern analysis suggests that tax revenue is maximized when the top marginal rate is set to about 70 percent, even accounting for economic growth.

Instead, we're going in the opposite direction under Republican rule. The 2001 Bush tax cuts gave 40 percent of the benefits to the top 1 percent.[56] The 2017 Trump tax cut, by comparison, gave 80 percent to the top percentile.[57] At the end of World War II, the effective tax rate on the richest 400 families in America was over 70 percent. By 2018, it had fallen to 23.[58] Despite virtually every Republican economic policy being wildly unpopular with the general public and contributing to worsening social and economic conditions for most Americans, they still pursue these goals. Why? Because corporations, Republican politicians, and Christian nationalist community leaders have convinced some of their religiously conservative base that these policies are what God wants.

Others simply don't care about economic policy, as long as the government is hurting people that want to see hurt.

Figure 13. Theoretical Tax Revenue vs. Tax Rate

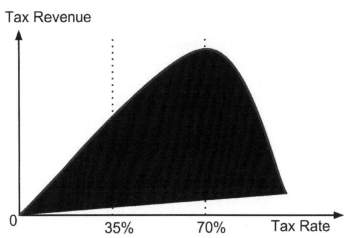

Source: Mathias Trabandt and Harald Uhlig (2011).

"The Laffer Curve Revisited"[55]

Joseph Stiglitz has looked at solutions to wealth and income inequality in detail and proposed solutions to the wealth and income gaps in America: laws preventing monopolistic competition, higher tax rates on the wealthy, affirmative action in education, removing incentives for "too big to fail" risk taking, ending corporate welfare, estate taxes, collective workers' rights, and health care for all.[59] Every one of these solutions is anathema to Republicans. Indeed, Attorney General William Barr sued Yale University to force them to accept *fewer* minority students, while simultaneously supporting lawsuits to end the Affordable Care Act.[60] This is why Stiglitz concludes, "Inequality is the result of political forces as much as of economic ones."[61]

However, rather than responding to the conservative dilemma by moderating its economic policies to attract more voters, the GOP relied on cultural divisions to stoke hatred and fear of others to pull people to the polls for them, regardless of their economic policies.

Plutocracy vs. Populism

> *"The aristocracy, in a desperate last struggle, tried to ally itself with the conservative forces of the churches—the Catholic Church in Austria and France, the Protestant Church in Germany—under the pretext of fighting liberalism with the weapons of Christianity. The mob was only a means to strengthen their position, to give their voices a greater resonance. Obviously they neither could, nor wanted, to organize the mob, and would dismiss it once their aim was achieved. But they discovered that antisemitic slogans were highly effective in mobilizing large strata of the population."*

> Hannah Arendt

While evangelical attitudes towards wealth have already been discussed in Chapter 6, it is worth noting this has been something of a two-way street. Corporations and the wealthy have worked hard to encourage the "pull yourself up by the bootstraps" narrative that anyone can get rich if they simply work hard enough, which bolsters the white evangelical religious belief that morality in the form of work ethic determines personal economic success. It also dovetails with the observation that demographic groups associated with Republicans are far more likely to believe that poverty is caused by personal faults rather than circumstances, along with the converse. Rakeen Mabud, the director of the Roosevelt Institute's 21st Century Economy and Race and Gender programs, puts the lie to this narrative:

> Conservative lawmakers have long been selling the misleading notion that Americans can change their destinies simply by working themselves to the bone, distracting from the structural forces that make economic upward mobility extremely difficult. But the truth is that in America today, hard work can get most people only so far. In fact, those who are working hardest have fallen behind the fastest. These days, working as a home health aide, a restaurant worker, or in any minimum-wage job is not a gateway to the middle class. According to some reports, a quarter of all individuals living in poverty are working or seeking work, and in many states, people working full time at minimum wage still live below the poverty line.[62]

At the same time, Republicans always knew this was something of a shotgun wedding. The average Republican voter is far more socially than economically conservative: there is significant overlap between Republican and Democratic voters on some economic issues.[63] This renders Republican voters more receptive to populist messages than might be expected. Even Lee Atwater (of the infamous n-word observations) remarked on white southern economic values: "The South is not conservative. If one label had to be ascribed to the whole South, that label should be 'populist'. Populists are not *laissez-faire* free-marketers."[64] This is part of why Trump's trade protectionist policies were so popular with the base.

However, any hope that Republicans might take the steps necessary to turn things around for Millennials and Gen Z is entirely misplaced. Leading conservative religious figures like Franklin Graham denounce any attempt to raise tax rates, empower unions, or raise minimum wage laws as "godless" and "evil" socialism.[65] FiveThirtyEight's analysis observed that the U.S. is probably too religious to institute the progressive economic policies necessary to turn the tide.[66] Given the Republican stranglehold on the U.S. Senate due to non-proportional representation, the odds of getting enough votes to raise tax rates, close corporate loopholes, protect unions, guarantee health care, and bolster the social safety net are just about zero. Even then, the 6-3 conservative Supreme Court is likely to strike some of these down, even if they are passed.

Jacob Hacker and Paul Pierson described this phenomenon of "reactionary economic priorities and right-wing cultural and racial appeals" as "plutocratic populism."[67] As noted in Chapter 5, this is related to Timothy Snyder's concept of "sadopopulism," where a plutocratic government works against the interests of its own base, thereby ramping up their feelings of grievance. Hacker and Pierson postulate that what keeps the populist base aligned with plutocrats is the exploitation of "resentment, racialization, and rigging." Resentment and racialization prey upon their fear that they are losing their place in society, and that Blacks and others who are "less American" are receiving benefits that exceed their value to society (e.g., welfare queens). This, and what Hannah Arendt described, fit with how billionaires such as the Kochs and their allies in the media used their fortunes and assets to help bootstrap the Tea Party as a movement.

Similarly, political scientists William Howell and Terry Moe write that "populists don't just feed on socioeconomic discontent. They feed on ineffective government—and their great appeal is that they claim to replace it with a government that *is* effective through their own autocratic power."[68] After decades of Republicans trying to make government less effective and do fewer things, and Democrats more or less going along with it, people no longer believe government can provide essential goods and services to the public. Worse, because of non-proportional representation, there are few avenues to restore this lost functionality, and thereby disempower these populists.

Ultimately, the relationship between Christian nationalists and the oligarchs is mostly one sided: other than the oligarchs spending money to elect socially conservative politicians, most Christian nationalists do not benefit economically from the relationship. Quite the opposite. The oligarchs profit greatly from control of the U.S. political system handed to them by white Christian nationalist voters, but not vice-versa. This was always the weak link: Christian nationalists always got less from businesses than businesses got from Christian nationalists.

Part of our collective blindness to inequality comes from the late 19th century economic philosophy of "marginal productivity theory," which posited that those with the highest incomes earned this because they contributed the most to society.[69] In reality, however, productivity has soared while wages have stagnated for all but the super-wealthy. They often engage in non-productive activities (rent seeking[70]) that pull money from society and redistributes it to the wealthy, such as the work Mitt Romney did as a corporate raider at Bain Capital.[71] As Romney's gaffe showed, Republican oligarchs and social conservatives divide the world into "makers" and "takers," while believing that the poor "have only themselves to blame."[72]

Franklin D. Roosevelt's New Deal and Lyndon B. Johnson's Great Society are examples of governmental action to reduce inequality. Obama had two terms in office, as did Clinton. During both their administrations, wealth inequality continued to worsen, because the GOP was able to block any attempts at fixes, while Democrats were reluctant to anger the donor class. Thus, any efforts by Democrats to turn the tide were half measures at best. However, history teaches us that reversing runaway wealth inequality is somewhere between extremely difficult and impossible without catastrophic black swan events.

A historical example of how to raise the value of labor, and overall standard of living, is to kill a large percentage of your workforce. The lowest level of wealth inequality in the U.S. in modern history came not during the New Deal, but starting in the early 1940's when we went to war, lost 407,000 men, and another 671,000 came back wounded. This trend held true for virtually every country that fought major battles in WWII.

Other historians credit the black plague (aka The Black Death), which killed a third of the people in Europe and hit Italy the hardest, with reducing inequality more than any other event in Western history. Indeed, historian Dr. Walter Scheidel makes the argument that violence and catastrophes (like the plague) are the most effective ways to reduce inequality, and that the Renaissance was only possible because of the preceding pandemic.[73] Thus, he looks at the situation in the U.S. with regards to inequality, and finds it irreversible without violence and catastrophe sufficient to nearly collapse society.

Another element that makes recovery from runaway wealth inequality nigh impossible is that religious conservatives and oligarchs have something in common: they both realize that time and demographics are not on the side of the wealthy and religious conservatives. The goals and beliefs of the religious right are less and less popular. Weyrich, who died in 2008 at the age of 66, knew by 2005 that the culture war was lost. The rest of the Christian right caught up by 2015 with the ruling in *Obergefell.* So did the Heritage Foundation, which realized by 2018 that, "fiscal issues are a complete wasteland… and the donors know it." Wall Street backers of Heritage and the GOP urged a pivot to social issues to get out the base.[74] The elections of 2018 pivoted to focusing on immigrants and dark commercials associating them with violence and crime.

Similarly, the Millennials and Gen Z have had enough of *laissez-faire* capitalism: the word "socialism" had lost much of its stigma with them. Tax cuts for the wealthy and the use of the Laffer Curve weren't fooling them with promises that a rising tide lifts all boats. Hucksters like Grover Norquist (who headed the anti-tax group Americans for Tax Reforms and forced Republicans to sign a pledge to never raise taxes) have ensured the GOP will never moderate their economic policies.

Both evangelicals and the wealthy recognized that in order to get what they wanted, they would have to win back the White House once more, and then ensure that no more meaningful elections ever took place. They had made a Faustian bargain with each other to break American democracy once and for all based on their fears: one of losing a fraction of their money, and the other of losing their place in society. The unholy spawn of that union was Donald Trump and the modern GOP. As Pierson and Hacker described it:

> "The result is an especially volatile mix—a party coalition that is capable of changing policies and institutions, but fearful it will not long control them; a party coalition that is able to achieve its priorities, but only by disregarding majorities, dividing and lying to citizens, and distorting democracy."

By the end of 2020 it was clear that most of the GOP wasn't just distorting democracy, it was intent on destroying it.

Eight

Permanent Single Party Rule

"Tell me why you kept kicking him? You had already won."

"Knocking him down won the first fight. I wanted to win all the next ones, too."

Ender's Game

When former Republican Speaker of the House Newt Gingrich first called politics a "war for power," he was spelling out the philosophy of the future of his party.[1] They don't see politics as a game where "you win some, you lose some," but rather as a life-or-death struggle for permanent dominance. The problem with this is that when one side stops playing the "Democracy game" and ends up permanently on top, the system breaks down and is no longer a democracy.[2] What emerges may be totalitarian, fascist, authoritarian, plutocratic, oligarchic, or some other form of dystopia.

After the 2008 presidential election, conventional wisdom in the GOP was adapt or die. Some Republicans and pundits believed that they needed to change their message, become more inclusive and less reliant on white voters, and generally adapt to America's shifting demographics and attitudes on social issues.[3] Instead, GOP operatives built a plan called the REDMAP Project, designed to ensure Republicans could win forever with their (shrinking) base at the state and federal level via gerrymandering, court packing, voter suppression, and other anti-democratic methods.[4] When Republicans swept state legislatures in 2010 and conducted reapportionment, they gerrymandered Democrats out of existence across much of the U.S.[5] In effect, they created single-party states impervious to the popular vote across much of the country.

Creeping permanent minoritarian rule is insidious. The fall from democracy in modern times is usually a slow and deliberate process of tearing down defenses and rigging the game one rule at a time. It's not loud and explosive. There aren't tanks rolling in the streets, nor is there secret police spying on everyone. There aren't gulags and death camps. Instead, it's a legalistic death by a thousand cuts.

169

Formal and informal constraints on the autocrat and the ruling party fall by the wayside one at a time, over a period of years, until finally the Republic dies not with a bang, but a whimper.

When the interests of people on top of the societal pyramid become increasingly minoritarian, they feel threatened and outnumbered. This creates a powerful incentive for democratic backsliding. Democracy becomes part of the threat, something that needs to be destroyed every bit as much as the things they were afraid of in the first place, whether it was immigrants, gays, or higher marginal tax rates. The American system of government was never intended to protect a tyranny of the minority. Rather, the goal of the Constitution was to "make it difficult to for majorities to rule without broad agreement."[6] In the U.S. today there is broad agreement on a great many issues, but a minority prevents action on any of them.

In this, the Constitution has failed. A functional democracy requires at least two competing parties committed to playing the democratic game, as well as competitive elections that represent the majority vote. Instead, in states that were taken over by Republicans using the strategies of REDMAP, politicians pick their voters rather than voters picking their politicians. The Supreme Court looked at this sort of partisan gerrymandering and decided that it was outside their jurisdiction to address, thereby enshrining illiberal democracy and sham elections as constitutional.[7] They have done the same with voting rights, as Republicans have rolled back the ability of democratic constituencies to vote. The result is an America that may no longer meet the definition of a democracy, or even a republic.

Republican suppression of democracy takes two general forms: gerrymandering and voter suppression. Another anti-democratic force in the U.S. is the system itself, which emphasizes non-proportional representation that tends to heavily favor the GOP.

Gerrymandering

> *"Most Americans conceptualize a hypothetical end of American democracy in apocalyptic terms. But actually, you usually learn that you are no longer living in a democracy not because The Government Is Taking Away Your Rights, or passing laws that you oppose, or because there is a coup or a quisling. You know that you are no longer living in a democracy because the elections in which you are participating no longer can yield political change."*
>
> Thomas Pepinsky

Efforts to suppress voters have exploded since the Supreme Court struck down key portions of the Voting Rights Act (VRA) in *Shelby County v. Holder* in 2013, in which southern states argued that they weren't really racist anymore and could be trusted not to suppress the votes of minorities (which they did the minute the enforcement provisions of the VRA were struck down).[8] What is left of the VRA appears unlikely to survive Trump's 6-3 conservative Supreme Court. The Roberts Court was inclined to either overturn the Voting Rights Act or interpret standing in such a way as to make it unenforceable, even when there were clear cases of racial gerrymandering (which remains illegal, for now).[9]

The results of elections influenced by gerrymandering and voter suppression resemble those where ballot boxes have been stuffed or voting machines have been hacked. In states like Wisconsin and North Carolina, where Republicans have gerrymandered the political boundaries using optimizing computer algorithms, there is no plausible path for Democrats to win control of the state legislatures even when they win the popular vote by wide margins.[10] The only reason Virginia flipped in 2019, despite Democrats winning by nearly 9 points, was realignment of a district that the courts found to be racially gerrymandered.[11]

North Carolina is perhaps the best case-study in gerrymandering, given that the behind-the-scenes election rigging efforts of the Republican Party eventually became a matter of public record. In 2010, the Republican Party of North Carolina enlisted the help of Thomas Hofeller, who specialized in creating heavily gerrymandered districts. He liked to describe his work as "the only legalized form of vote stealing left in the United States."[12] He also described redistricting as "like an election in reverse… Usually voters get to pick the politicians. In redistricting, politicians get to pick [their] voters."[13]

Obama had won North Carolina in 2008, but after the 2010 redistricting the state's legislature and congressional delegation became unassailably red. Despite winning only 50.3 percent of the vote in the 2018 election, Republicans carried 10 out of the 13 seats for the U.S. House. North Carolina Republican representative David Lewis had endorsed this gerrymander when it was put forward, noting: "I propose that we draw the maps to give a partisan advantage to 10 Republicans and three Democrats, because I do not believe it's possible to draw a map with 11 Republicans and two Democrats."[14]

Literally, the day after the Supreme Court struck down the enforcement provisions of the Voting Rights Act in 2013, North Carolina Republicans requested voter data by race to help craft a sweeping elections bill. This bill eliminated a week of early voting and out-of-precinct voting, and required voters to show specific types of photo ID, all of which were intended to prevent as many Blacks as possible from voting. In 2017, a federal court found that the laws "target African-Americans with almost surgical precision."[15]

Proving that North Carolinian Republicans intended to target people by race rather than "improving election security" proved maddeningly difficult. It might not have been possible except for an unlikely chain of events. The data analysis for the 2013 law had been run by Hofeller. After his death in 2018, his estranged daughter, a Democrat, stumbled across his hard drives and turned them over to Common Cause, a voting rights advocacy group. They, in turn, used them to support claims in court that the 2013 laws intentionally targeted voters by race.[16] This undeniable evidence was finally enough to swing the courts, which ruled: "The Court finds that in many election environments, it is the carefully crafted maps, and not the will of the voters, that dictate the election outcomes in a significant number of legislative districts and, ultimately, the majority control of the General Assembly."[17]

This happy ending is likely a one-off, however. It's unlikely that a smoking gun like Hofeller's drives will be found in other gerrymandered states like Michigan, Wisconsin, Florida, and Pennsylvania. However, given how coordinated the REDMAP Project was, and how similar the gerrymandering is across states with Republican controlled legislatures, there is little doubt that the only thing different about North Carolina is that the perpetrators got caught.

Worse, the Supreme Court decided in 2018's *Gill v. Whitford* that no political gerrymander is so outrageous or oppressive that the courts should be involved. Chief Justice Roberts wrote in his decision: "Excessive partisanship in districting leads to results that seem reasonably unjust. But the fact that gerrymandering is 'incompatible with democratic principles' does not mean that the solution lies with the federal judiciary." Thus, the Roberts court, like the court that gave us Jim Crow, is dedicated to freedom and democracy in the abstract only. Like Chief Justice Taney and *Dred Scott*, this court would easily make decisions ending the United States as both a democracy and a union.

Voter Suppression

"If conservatives become convinced that they cannot win democratically, they will not abandon conservatism. They will reject democracy."

David Frum, former speechwriter for President George W. Bush

Extreme polarization also reduces states' ability to move one way or another or to flip voters.[18] Some election theorists, notably Rachel Bitecofer, have arrived at the conclusion that swing voters are becoming a smaller portion of the electorate, and therefore less important to winning elections than mobilizing the base of a party. Thus, competitive elections are primarily determined by existing population ratios and "Get Out The Vote" efforts.[19] Because younger, more liberal voters are more likely to have jobs and children, it is more difficult for them to vote than seniors, who tend to be more conservative and have more time on their hands to vote. Republicans have steadfastly resisted efforts to make it easier for younger people to vote, making it much more difficult for Democrats to follow Bitecofer's proposed path to electoral success.[20]

This does not bode well for Democrats. The highly effective Republican strategies to suppress turnout now include deliberate and sustained disinformation campaigns.[21] Paul Weyrich described this strategy decades ago: "I don't want everybody to vote. Elections are not won by a majority of people. They never have been from the beginning of our country, and they are not now. As a matter of fact, our leverage in the elections quite candidly goes up as the voting populace goes down."[22]

Gerrymandering works wonderfully in rigging legislatures, but there are still offices that are won by popular vote. This is where suppression comes in. Functionally, this means making it as hard as possible for people who tend to be Democrats to vote. This includes voter ID laws requiring forms of ID that Black people are least likely to have,[23] voter-roll purges that mostly affect Black Americans,[24] and limiting the number of polling places in areas where Black voters are concentrated.[25] Since 2013, 17 million Americans have been purged from voting rolls, disproportionately affecting areas with a history of discrimination.[26]

These efforts are supported by the GOP base, often for reasons that are likely rooted in racism. One post-election poll in 2020 found that 46 percent of Republicans believe that "some people are not smart enough to vote" (27 percent among Democrats). Forty-three percent of Republicans (compared with 15 percent of Democrats) say that people should have to pass some sort of test before they can vote.[27] This clearly signals a desire among the base to bring back the sorts of literacy tests that the Voting Rights Act (VRA) banned, and could return if the Supreme Court finishes it off.

Quantitative research backs up the supposition of a desire by Republicans to disenfranchise blacks being the real reason behind laws seeking to restrict voter access. Erin O'Brien, a political scientist at the University of Massachusetts, conducted a study using over 600 examples of restrictive voter access bills introduced between 2006 and 2011. She used regression to test both the explanations used by both conservatives and liberals for why these bills were introduced. None of the right-wing claims held up, but she found that minority turnout in the previous election, increase in minority turnout between the previous two elections, increase in low-income turnout between the previous two elections, African-American population, and non-citizen population were the significant predictors of the legislation being introduced. Only two were predictive of passage: percentage of Republicans in the state legislature, and having a Republican governor.[28]

On the flip side of the coin, GOP efforts to maximize turnout of their base have been wildly successful. By playing on the fears and grievances of white Christian nationalists about abortion, immigrants, Muslims, and transgender people, they have consistently boosted turnout of their core demographic.[29] In 2004, white evangelicals were 23 percent of the population and 23 percent of the vote. In 2018, they were 15 percent of the population and 26 percent of voters.[30] However, white evangelical voters cannot push their relative turn out much higher than it already is (they're already among the most likely to vote), which incentivizes the GOP to rig the elections via voter suppression.

We may have entered a death spiral of electing politicians who select judges who let the politicians pick their voters in order to keep them in power, which allows them to pick more judges and so on. How Republicans and Democrats respond to losing statewide elections is telling. When Democrats won control of the governors' offices in the heavily gerrymandered states of North Carolina, Michigan, and Wisconsin, Republican legislatures with super-majorities passed bills stripping those governors of their powers during the lame duck session.[31] However, when faced with the same situation, Democratic legislatures in Maryland, Massachusetts, Vermont, and New Jersey did not retaliate with similar laws.[33]

Republicans are also uninterested in following through with voter-initiated ballot initiatives. When 65 percent of Florida voters approved allowing ex-felons to vote, Republicans put a poll tax on ex-felons to ensure that none of them could do so without potentially facing new felony charges.[53] When Utah's voters passed a ballot initiative to expand Medicaid, Republican legislators made the expansion so narrow that almost no one qualified.[34] Arizona Republicans have waged a two-decade-long battle to take away the ability for citizens to put initiatives on the ballot, because the unwashed masses had the temerity to mandate independent districting commissions to prevent gerrymandering.[35] Michigan Republicans succeeded in making ballot initiatives nearly impossible after a Democrat gained control of the governor's office in 2018.[36]

The ultimate goal is to ensure that the will of the people is irrelevant, and that only the will of the GOP and its base matters in a functionally minoritarian, single-party state.

Non-Proportional Representation

"The rule of a minority, as a permanent arrangement, is wholly inadmissible; so that, rejecting the majority principle, anarchy or despotism in some form is all that is left."

Abraham Lincoln

The deck is stacked against Democrats in federal elections as well, making reclaiming the White House or the Senate difficult even when the public votes for Democrats by a wide margin. The Senate, as defined in the Constitution, is mandated non-proportional representation—a concession to slave states at the time. Low-population states are much more likely to be Republican-leaning. As a result, Republican senators will usually hold the majority, despite representing significantly less than half the population.[37] Wyoming's voters have sixty-seven times more voting power and representation per person in the Senate than Californians. This ratio is unheard of in other democratic countries, even those with upper and lower house legislatures.[38] Nor did the framers of the Constitution envision this, as the largest disparity in 1787 was only 6:1.[39]

Because of non-proportional representation, Republicans have a nearly insurmountable 20-seat advantage going into elections in the Senate.[40] Elliot Morris, a statistician and election wonk for *The Economist*, estimated that in order for Democrats to claim a veto-proof super-majority in the Senate, they would need to win the national vote by about 19 points. This has never happened in the modern era. Conversely, Republicans only need to win the national vote by two points to achieve a similar super-majority, which happened in the 2014 off-year elections.

Election forecaster and statistician Nate Silver described the near impossibility of this situation for Democrats in the Senate in an interview:

> "We talked before about what a landslide it was when Obama won in 2008. He won by 7 points. The GOP has about a 6- to 7-point inherent advantage in the Senate, meaning that the median state is around 6 points more Republican in the country as a whole. So Democrats can win, but only if they win in a landslide."[41]

He concluded that Republicans do not need to govern for the median voter. They will govern for people far more conservative than most Americans.

Mitch McConnell launched over 500 filibusters during his tenure as Senate Minority Leader under Obama. Some of these were on legislation supported by nearly 90 percent of Americans.[42] Over-representation of rural, white, evangelical voters in the Senate, plus hyper-polarization, makes it nearly impossible for Democrats to put justices on the federal bench. This results in a non-representative federal judiciary as well.[43] Senators representing as little as 11 percent of the population can sustain a filibuster. Or, put another way, you can get 41 votes in the Senate with just the states that Trump won in 2016 by 20 points or more.[44] This disparity in representation and lack of action on popular legislation caused Morris to observe that, "Republics are supposed to have indirect representation for voters—and under no reasonable national parameterization can you call what the Senate is doing today 'representation.'"

Given the increasing polarization of Americans, state-level voter suppression, and the growing concentration of Democrats in deep blue urban areas, there is no viable path for Democrats to create a filibuster-proof Senate in the foreseeable future.[45] This concentration of Democrats in deep blue areas is increasing,[46] as people with college educations,[47] who increasingly favor Democrats,[48] are more likely to end up in blue urban or suburban areas.[49]

The path to the White House is inherently biased towards Republicans as well, primarily due to the Electoral College.[50] Because of this demographic clustering, we see a gerrymander-like effect: Democrats are concentrated into a small number of states where they win handily, such as New York and California, while the Electoral College votes of the closest states with lots of Electoral College delegates (Michigan, Pennsylvania, Wisconsin, Florida, Arizona, North Carolina, and Ohio) tilt Republican based on tipping-point analysis and how they vote in comparison with the national average. It doesn't help that in smaller, low population states (which tend to be red) individual votes are worth more than in larger population states.[51] Urban shift and wastage of Democratic votes[52] are a major factor in why the inevitably shifting demographics of the U.S. may not be enough to save Democrats in presidential elections in the long run.[53] We are in a race between demographics and authoritarianism, and the latter seems to be winning. The bias in the Electoral College is likely to be between 4 and 5 points in 2024, meaning that Republicans are likely to again retake the executive branch despite winning the popular vote only once since 1988.

Why We Should Be Afraid

"Democracy isn't the objective; liberty, peace, and prosperity are. We want the human condition to flourish. Rank democracy can thwart that."

Senator Mike Lee (R-UT)

This descent into permanent single-party rule is by definition the end of democracy. It is far worse when you consider what the two groups supporting the

GOP, namely oligarchs and white Evangelicals, want. No group is a bigger outlier in its views on every major issue in American politics than white Evangelicals. Whether it is guns, LGBTQ rights, race relations, climate change, immigration, Muslims, abortion, or wealth inequality, white evangelicals stand out as the most conservative group and far to the right of the American public as a whole.[54]

The other group that the GOP represents, oligarchs and plutocrats, want to get richer, even at the expense of everyone else. Paying McDonald's workers $15 dollars per hour would raise the cost of a Big Mac by 17 cents.[55] A nation of a few rich people in gated communities, and everyone else living as wretched wage-slaves in service to them, is an outcome they are more than fine with. (It's also the premise of the prescient dystopian novels *Parable of the Sower* and *Parable of the Talents* by Octavia Butler.)

The motivations of Trump supporters bode ill for both democracy and most Americans who disagree with them. A study found that Trump supporters tend to be motivated by authoritarianism, social dominance orientation, prejudice, and lack of contact with people different from themselves.[56] Other more recent studies have found that racism and fear were more significant motivators of Trump voters than economics.[57]

The GOP base is driving the entire system further to the right regardless of what the majority of Americans want. Primaries are the only elections that matter to most Republican legislators, and this encourages Republican politicians to adopt even more extreme positions to cater to their base. Those who won't go along with the extreme positions of the base are generally replaced by people who will.[58] As a result, the Republican party has shifted dramatically to the right over the past 30 years.[59] Since the game is rigged for the GOP, most of the rest of us are just along for the ride. Only 10 percent of House seats and 15 percent of Senate races are competitive.[60]

These factors combine to create a highly unstable situation. Imagine a population of severely economically depressed young people who widely despise a minoritarian government that cannot be voted out of office.[61] State governments will have to make hard decisions as well if the GOP has its way. For instance, what would California do if the federal government attempts to begin mass deportations of the 200,000 Dreamers living in the state?

In *Ender's Game,* the protagonist Andrew "Ender" Wiggin is a tactical and strategic genius who wins an interstellar war for humanity. The recurring theme of the book is that when you fight a war, you must destroy your enemy so thoroughly that they will never be capable of opposing you again. This analogy describes the modern Republican approach to politics: They have Democrats beaten down, and they are systematically ensuring that they will never get up again, even if it destroys the nation. Even if Biden is President, he has little power to move anything through Congress, without using the reconciliation process and his executive orders are likely to be challenged in the courts left behind by Trump.

So, in the final analysis, are we doomed to decades of eroding civil rights, rising wealth inequality, inertia on climate change, civil unrest, and racial and religious minoritarian rule in an illiberal democracy?

Given how the GOP has abandoned any pretense of representing anyone but their base, stacked the courts, and ensured they control most state legislatures in perpetuity, the Magic 8-Ball says: "All Signs Say Yes."

Nine

Is Trumpism Fascism?

"Nothing perhaps illustrates the general disintegration of political life better than this vague, pervasive hatred of everybody and everything, without a focus for its passionate attention, with nobody to make responsible for the state of affairs—neither the government nor the bourgeoisie nor an outside power. It consequently turned in all directions, haphazardly and unpredictably, incapable of assuming an air of healthy indifference toward anything under the sun."

Hannah Arendt

In the aftermath of the first Senate impeachment trial, Trump had lost what few previous constraints he had. Whatever Senator Susan Collins (R-ME) might have hoped, there was no contrition in the man.[1] Indeed, he was unbound. He instinctively realized that the guardrails of democracy were down.

The Senate would not exercise oversight over him or his administration, nor hold anyone within his administration accountable. He would not be convicted of any crimes, and the second impeachment trial after the insurrection demonstrated he was correct. He could pardon anyone he wanted to.[2] He used the Department of Justice to investigate those who had crossed him, or threatened his political power.[3] He interfered with the parts of judiciary he did not put in place himself, and actively asked why he couldn't eliminate the parts of the judicial branch that defied him.[4] He gave his cronies the ability to replace anyone in federal service who was insufficiently loyal or had the wrong ideology.[5] Trump used the immunities of his office to retaliate against witnesses and stonewall any Congressional oversight of his administration.[6] It has been noted more than once that recent events in the U.S. drove it even deeper into "Banana Republic" territory.[7] As early as 2019, Trump had a committee looking at how he could run for a third term despite the Twenty-Second Amendment and bragged in his speeches that he would win a fourth term in 2028.[8]

Among those watching closely, there was an emerging consensus that if the U.S. was not already under authoritarian rule, four more years of Trump would

179

move it across that line.[9] Under Trump, we moved toward a type of competitive authoritarianism that emerged at the end of the Cold War and has grown like a malignant tumor since.[10] These types of regimes are known by different names. Putin describes it as "managed democracy."[11] In Hungary, Viktor Orbán has referred to the government he and the Fidesz Party created as "illiberal democracy."[12] Regardless, they represent the same phenomenon.

These regimes don't fit the 20th century paradigm of silly-looking dictators and military juntas in gaudy uniforms. They don't take power by rolling tanks on the capitol; rather, they maintain a veneer of democracy and normalcy through elections that don't actually change anything, and a marginalized free press that is effectively screaming into the void due to the deluge of misinformation put forward by the government and its proxies.[13] This is the difference between autocracy and totalitarianism: Nazi Germany looked very different from autocratic illiberal democracies like Hungary, Poland, and Turkey, but that difference doesn't mean that the movements driving them don't share most, if not all, of the characteristics of fascism.

Authoritarian regimes are almost always corrupt, nepotistic, and rife with cronyism that enrich the autocrat, his family, and sycophants who latched onto the system.[14] However, not all autocracies are fascist. Many don't have an overarching ideology beyond greed and power. The current Thai monarch, Maha Vajiralongkorn, is one example of an authoritarian ruler who is light on unifying ideology.[15] Which brings us to the question few want to ask and fewer to answer: Is the Trumpist movement fascist?

The word "fascist" conjures images of goose-stepping soldiers, book burnings, gray and black uniforms, ridiculous mustaches, over-the-top architecture, military conquest, and death camps. However, scholars who study fascism do not see these as its defining characteristics. Germany was fascist long before it built Auschwitz or invaded Poland. Instead, what defines fascist movements are their outlooks on gender, history, religion, human rights, roles of government, egalitarianism, and a host of other factors that describe a society.

Unfortunately, the concept of "American Exceptionalism" prevents most Americans from seeing the danger, much less the possibility, that the U.S. could turn down a dark path. Sanford Levinson described the unerring belief that the Constitution is the perfect and eternal blueprint for politics as "the American civil religion."[16] Some conservative religions and religious figures, including Mormonism, take this further and believe that the U.S. Constitution is divinely inspired.[17] In The Road to Unfreedom, Timothy Snyder calls the American belief that the free market and democracy will always lead to freedom and happiness a form of the "politics of inevitability."[18] Sinclair Lewis explored this blindness in 1935 in his dystopian novel, *It Can't Happen Here*. This sort of myopia about democratic decline and fascism isn't unique to America; European states like Hungary and Poland thought they had learned their lessons from World War II, yet failed to recognize authoritarianism taking root again because it looked somewhat different this time. The flaw in American thinking has been in the belief that our institutions are stronger than the autocratic impulses of demagogues and their parties.

For the most part, we have been wrong. The Constitution was not designed to simultaneously deal with a demagogue president, a party supporting his autocratic efforts, and a judiciary suddenly flooded with loyalist appointees willing to grant the aspiring autocrat the power he desires. It could handle one failure (Nixon), nearly buckled and gave way with two, and stands no chance against all three of the above happening simultaneously.

People reach for rationalizations to feel better. Since there aren't death camps and swastikas, it's not really fascism, right? They believe America is intrinsically good, or favored by God, and thus could never happen here. The belief that the U.S. is somehow different and better than other countries made us deaf, dumb, and blind to the emerging reality of how our democracy is being subverted, and to the nature of the entities causing such damage to the world's oldest republic.

All politics are local, and fascism looks like the country from whence it came.[19] Prominent scholars on fascism and American history have argued that the post-Reconstruction south was the first fascist state.[20] Hitler looked to the Jim Crow south for ideas on how to marginalize and oppress hated minorities. Father Coughlin was a fascist and functioned much like Limbaugh or Hannity. Sinclair Lewis predicted in the 1930's that American fascism would have a particularly white evangelical bent and *laissez faire* capitalist flavor. Scholar Robert Paxton agreed with Lewis that religion would shape the American expression of fascist ideas.[21]

Thus, when fascism re-emerged in America, it would likely look like the Jim Crow south, carry a cross, and wrap itself in the flag.

What Defines Fascism?

Scholars have looked at what defines fascist movements for decades. This book approaches this question by reviewing what scholars and texts on the subject see as the characteristics of fascism.[22] This lit review included works by Hannah Arendt, Umberto Eco, Jason Stanley, Laurence Britt, Emilio Gentile, Roger Griffin, and Robert Paxton. The following are an amalgam of the traits identified most commonly by these sources.

1. Misogyny and sexual anxiety

Fascist movements have highly traditional views of sex and gender.[23] They believe women are there for "*kinder, küche, kirche*" (children, kitchen, and church). Though they may exalt the feminine in the abstract, they consider it generally inferior in practice. Men are the protectors and providers; this division is the natural order of things. It uses fears that women will be raped by "bad people" (Blacks, Jews, transgender people, etc.) to appeal to the masculine code of protecting women. It hates homosexuality and gender theory because it threatens that "natural" order.[24]

In modern Russia, Putin has offered masculinity as an argument against democracy.[25] His bear-wrestling, shirtless horseback riding, helmetless hockey-playing persona is a quintessentially Russian ideal of masculinity, and every bit a fabrication. Conversely, Trump's faux wise-guy billionaire act is a uniquely American expression of manliness. It's also seen in how the GOP campaigns: manly men can run the country better than "mom-jeans" Obama[26] or a supposedly purse-carrying Biden.[27] As a result, polling before the 2020 election showed a record setting 43-point gap between men and women in their support for Trump.[28]

In the U.S., Steve Bannon, former editor of *Breitbart* and Chief Strategist for Trump, published articles alleging that there should be fewer women in science and technology fields, and that women would be better off without dishwashers and birth control (i.e., they should be staying home, doing chores, and incubating babies). Glenn T. Stanton of the highly influential evangelical Christian think-tank Focus on the Family,[29] has echoed traditional views of sex and gender while blaming homosexuals for declining marriage and birth rates.[30] Ralph Drollinger, the influential leader of the Bible study group for Trump cabinet members, held similar views on women and LGBTQ people.[31]

Other research finds that people with traditional "masculine honor beliefs" overwhelmingly supported Trump.[32] Data suggests that sexual anxiety is much more common in regions that supported Trump as well.[33] One of the defining characteristics of the conservative cultural wars has been the manufactured fear of transgender people in bathrooms, or of them mutilating children, in an appeal to "real" Christian men to protect women and girls.[34] Underlying it all is deep seated misogyny and sexual anxiety surrounding gender roles. Fascist movements use these as a wedge to build up the belief that they need a single, hyper-masculine father-like figure to lead the nation.

2. Contempt for the poor, the weak, and human rights in general

One of the hallmarks of fascism is contempt for anyone who is not part of the in-group considered *übermensch*. The poor, homeless, disabled, mentally ill, and people of "inferior" races are seen as a valueless drain on the resources of society.[35] It is notable that the Nazis first claimed they wanted to help the homeless, but this took a dark turn quickly.[36] They also took the Malthusian view that letting the poor starve was natural, proper and in the best interests of a healthy society.[37] Hannah Arendt described the Nazi approach to unemployment as, "[they] will not be satisfied to assert, in the face of contrary facts, that unemployment does not exist; it will abolish unemployment benefits as part of its propaganda." As Laurence Britt also observed, "The poor formed an underclass, viewed with suspicion or outright contempt. Under some regimes, being poor was considered akin to a vice." Jason Stanley's analysis in *How Fascism Works* concurred: "…one 'earns' one's freedom by accruing wealth in struggle. Those who do not "earn" their freedoms do not deserve them."[38]

Trump's base sees many of these groups in a similar light. Poverty, especially among racial minorities, is seen as a sign of laziness, sin, lack of intelligence, or personal failing.[39] The evangelical prosperity gospel also teaches that sickness is a sign of God's disfavor. During the 2016 Election, Trump mocked a reporter for his physical disabilities while his jeering audience laughed.[40] Unlike any other modern country, the U.S. does not regard health care as a human right. The GOP base is adamantly opposed to any effort to establish it as such, and opposition is getting stronger.[41] The Trump Administration also supported the lawsuits to nullify the Affordable Care Act, which would strip millions of their access to health care during the COVID-19 pandemic.[42]

Columbia University has tracked many of the ways the Trump Administration has attacked human rights. It worked to implement deep cuts to social services for the poor and elderly.[43] They also scouted locations to establish federal camps to relocate homeless people to.[44] Trump urged more involuntary psychiatric commitments and withdrew the U.S. from the U.N. Human Rights Council.[45] Secretary of State Pompeo's council on "unalienable rights" was stacked with Christian religious conservatives, and their mandate was to return a determination that only religious freedom is an "inalienable right." All other rights defined since the end of World War II were merely "ad hoc," including the right to food.[46]

The Administration was also preparing to deport thousands of Dreamers if it had gotten a second term, despite it being likely that many would die as a result..[47] The child separation policy for asylum seekers and immigrants was a deliberate attempt to deter immigrants,[48] using brutal policies that resulted in permanent separations, lost and stolen children, and a spike in deaths of children in custody.[49] Despite these naked desires to harm the poor, the elderly, the sick, and the disabled, Trump's approval among Republicans hovered around 90 percent, which again supports Adam Serwer's observation that "the cruelty is the point."[50]

3. Belief in a better mythic past followed by a descent into depravity

Another hallmark of fascism is the belief in a past (that usually didn't exist) where everything was better. This past was ruined by some sinister evil force that made everything bad for all the good, real, salt-of-the-earth citizens of the country. This mythical setting usually involves a population that was homogeneous and undiluted by people (Jews, Blacks, Queers, Muslims, immigrants, or whatever scapegoat is needed) and liberal values (feminism, high top marginal tax rates, atheism, tolerance in general). Then, decadent cosmopolitan cities wrecked everything and cast their national culture into depravity. Fascism uses this narrative to urge people to reclaim that non-existent time by imposing a traditionalist moral code as law and oppressing groups of people blamed for the fall into depravity.

Nazi Germany calling itself the "Third Reich" was clearly a call back to times they considered better. Trump's "Make America Great Again" 2016 campaign slogan was undoubtedly an appeal to this narrative—a nostalgia for the 1940s and 1950s—and a dog whistle to his base.[51] It hearkened back to a time before *Brown vs. Board of Education*, the civil rights movement, the Civil Rights Act, and the Voting Rights Act. It was a time when everyone was socially compelled to go to church, government-compelled prayer was mandatory, and almost everyone's religion was Christianity. Non-Christians generally kept it to themselves and went to church anyway.[52]

It was also a time before *Griswold v. Connecticut*, *Roe v. Wade*, feminism, and the ERA. Before *Lawrence v. Texas* and *Obergefell v. Hodges*, when queers had the good sense to stay in the closet if they knew what was good for them.[53] A time when segregation and redlining made sure whites didn't have to actually co-exist with people of color.[54] This mythic past was also supposedly far safer and free of crime, with the unspoken reason being that this was because there were fewer immigrants, and Blacks knew their place.

In short, this mythic past was worse for everyone except white southern Christians. Which brings us to a related phenomenon:

4. Anti-egalitarian and xenophobic fear of changes in the social ordering

Umberto Eco noted that, "The first appeal of a fascist or prematurely fascist movement is an appeal against the intruders. Thus, Ur-Fascism is racist by definition." Fascism feeds into xenophobic fears, stokes them, and moves people to actions that would otherwise be unthinkable. One of the easiest fears to stoke is that of being replaced or displaced as a member of the highest caste in society. Being "Aryan," "Brahmin," etc. made you special and put you at the top of the social order.

Similarly, being white and evangelical put you at the top of the social order in the 1950's, and a fascist ideology would exploit that fall. As President Lyndon Johnson described the phenomenon: "If you can convince the lowest white man he's better than the best colored man, he won't notice you're picking his pocket. Hell, give him somebody to look down on, and he'll empty his pockets for you."[55] It's little wonder that Jim Crow laws served as the template for German anti-Semitic laws of the 1930's[56], or that racist views and anti-immigrant beliefs were one of the strongest predictors of support for Trump.[57]

Trump's base is deeply fearful of losing their privileged status, as was described in great detail in Robert P. Jones' book, *The End of White Christian America*.[58] Other studies have shown that fear of demographic change was one of the most significant factors motivating people to vote for Trump,[59] and that a social dominance orientation was associated with voting for him.[60]

The push to make "religious freedom" the most important, singular, universal human right above all others is an attempt to undercut laws that would level the social playing field for LGBTQ people, women, and religions other than some form of conservative Christianity. They attempted to use the same arguments with race in the past.[61] It is also why civil rights legislation of any sort cannot seem to move through the Republican-controlled Senate, including renewing the Violence Against Women Act or the Voting Rights Act.[62]

Trump and his media proxies fed these fears. Trump's speeches painted lurid tales of immigrants raping and gruesomely murdering (mostly white) Americans.[63] His proxies in the media, such as *Fox News* host Tucker Carlson, repeated these stories, while more explicitly feeding racist fears of replacement by brown people: Democrats "want to replace you, the American voters, with newly amnestied citizens and an ever-increasing number of chain migrants."[64] American politics is littered with anti-immigrant sentiment, from the "Yellow Peril" and Chinese Exclusion Act of the 19th century, to the mass deportation of hundreds of thousands of Mexican-Americans in the

1930's. However, rarely has a party in the U.S. made xenophobia so central to it's political identity as today.

5. Religion and government intertwined

Emilio Gentile wrote extensively about "political religion" and its role in fascism in Italy.[65] He observed of political religion in a fascist system that, "The essential characteristic distinguishing 'political religion' from 'civil religion' is the extremist and exclusive nature of its historical mission…"

In Germany, the Nazis unsuccessfully tried to co-opt Protestant religions and had a contentious (at best) relationship with the Catholic Church. While some Protestant churches in Germany embraced the hybrid Nazi theology, it was far from universal. In modern times, however, authoritarians like Russia's Vladimir Putin, Polish President Anderzej Duda, Turkey's President Recep Erdogan and Hungary's Prime Minister Viktor Orbán have made religious identity one of their primary talking points. In each country, religion has come to take a more and more central role in public and social policy.

In the U.S., white evangelical Protestantism was more than happy to become one of the most influential aspects of the Trump Administration and the GOP. They saw themselves as the only ones capable of "Making America Great Again" via a religious renewal.[66] Their religion rejected cosmopolitan beliefs and was aligned with the GOP efforts to create single-party rule. They frequently accepted violence against abortion clinics and providers, as well as against migrants and asylum-seekers, as scripturally justified.[67] Later, they were likely one of the driving forces behind the violence at the U.S. Capitol.

At the same time, "Lost Cause Theology" has been described since the 1960's as a revivalist movement aiming "to restore a golden age believed to have existed in the society's past." This connects with the public religion of the Republican Party, with its yearning for a mythic past that draws upon the distinctly fascist yet uniquely American mythos and cultural narrative described above.[68] Trump, for his part, reveled in being treated like some sort of God-king. Christian nationalists scorned any religion that dared disagree with the Trump Administration, casting a wary eye at Catholic and Papal disagreement with the Administration's treatment of immigrants, but were willing to coexist with them based on shared animus for abortion and LGBTQ people.[69] It is also the belief of many of their leaders that liberal churches "deserve to die."[70]

Compulsory religious participation (in their particular brand of religion) is one of their greatest goals. Project Blitz has developed a complete legislative strategy to tear down the wall between the separation of (their) church and state.[71] Drollinger openly called for Trump to create a "benevolent" dictator-ship guided by Christian laws.[72] Trump, in turn, effectively blocked the IRS from enforcing the Johnson Amendment, which forbids all charities, including churches, from endorsing candidates or giving them money. He packed the court with judges who took a more Scalian view of using religion to create law, and allowed them to ignore federal civil rights laws (while taking federal money) at the expense of LGBTQ people, Jews and Catholics.[73]

Lawrence Britt noted of Nazi Germany that, "The fact that the ruling elite's behavior was incompatible with the precepts of the religion was generally swept under the rug." This holds true for the relationship between white evangeli-cals and Trump as well.[74] It contributed to a public perception of hypocrisy, though.[75] Others noted this fascist relationship between religion and govern-ment and attributed it to sadism in Trump's evangelical supporters.[76]

At this point, white Christian nationalism is essentially synonymous with being a Trump-supporting conservative to the point where it is driving other brands of Protestantism out of business.[77] White evangelical Protestantism, and a particular strain of *opus dei* Catholicism, has become the *de facto* state religion in a one-party authoritarian state, and it is difficult to tell where white Christian nationalist beliefs stopped and where Trumpian views begin.

6. Rejection of expertise and anti-intellectualism

Fascist movements tend to promote and tolerate open hostility to higher ed-ucation. Any politically unacceptable ideas that come from universities are met with extreme hostility. Studies centered on the arts and humanities are seen as useless, or actively harmful. For example, one of the first acts of the Nazis when they took power was to storm and burn Magnus Hirschfeld's *Institut für Sexualwis-senschaft* (Institute for Sex Science).[78] Hungary's Viktor Orbán has also led a cru-sade against liberal higher education, particularly women's and gender studies.[79]

The right-wing attack on science, academia and expertise is described in detail in Chapter 5. It is worth reiterating that thirty years ago, people with college de-grees were roughly evenly split between the Republicans and Democrats.[80] Today, a wide majority of Americans with college degrees are democratic leaning vot-ers. During the 2016 primaries, Trump was the overwhelming favorite of people without college degrees. He was effectively the candidate for the least educated people in the least educated party.[81]

This appeal was deliberate. Both Trump and his supporters showed a broad-ly anti-intellectual streak.[82] He exclaimed, "I love the poorly educated," at a ral-ly.[83] He also cited himself as his top foreign policy advisor: "I have a good brain."[84] The language used in Trump's speeches was very simple, clocking in at a third or fourth grade level of comprehension.[85] This, too, is troubling, given that Umberto Eco saw "newspeak" and "impoverished vocabulary" as a sign of fascist movements as well.[86]

This broad anti-intellectualism also translates into a Republican disdain for universities. Fifty-nine percent of Republicans see universities as having a negative overall effect on the U.S.[87] In this same polling sample, Democrats considered the biggest problem with higher education to be high costs. The majority of Republicans believe that professors indoctrinate students with liberal ideas, and that students are not getting the skills they need to succeed in the workplace. They consider these issues, and their belief that students are being protected from (presumably conservative) views, as the biggest problems with higher education. When these Republican respondents bemoan the lack of work skills being taught, in reality they are espousing a belief that the arts, humanities, and philosophy-based critical thinking have no value.

In response to their perception that universities are attacking their values, these conservatives have launched efforts to discredit institutions of higher learning. They have manufactured repeated, baseless accusations that colleges are suppressing free speech.[88] Turning Point USA, an ultra-conservative and antagonistic group for college students, compiled a "Professor Watchlist" to call out liberal professors who cross them.[89] President Trump even issued an executive order to address this non-existent crisis while conservative outlets pushed him to go even further.[90]

One of the more perverse ideas propagated by anti-democratic movements world-wide is that they are saving freedom of speech and expression by fighting "political correctness" or "censorship." They invariably use these excuses to attack minority groups, whom they accuse of enforcing a tyranny of the minority. Viktor Orbán has used this successfully to suppress the media and academia throughout Hungary.[91]

This anti-intellectualism leads to a distrust of science and expertise that has been growing for decades.[92] Republicans reject any research that contradicts their views on the environment, guns, LGBTQ people or economics. Indeed, Republicans who accept anthropogenic climate change and the need to take action to slow it are treated as heretics and are not re-elected.[93] They have stifled or shut down many government researchers and policy makers, particularly those working on environmental or public health issues.[94]

Perhaps the most damaging part of this attack on higher education and intellectualism is its effect on the critical reasoning capacity of the population.

Umberto Eco noted that "Fascism devalues intellectual discourse and critical reasoning as barriers to action, as well as out of fear that such analysis will expose the contradictions embodied in a syncretistic faith." One of the primary purposes of a higher education is the development of critical thinking, which is the first line of defense against propaganda and conspiracy theories.[95] Which brings us to the next aspect of fascism...

7. Powerful and continuing expressions of nationalism

One of the frequently cited factors in fascism is overt nationalism. Laurence Britt noted that "catchy slogans, pride in the military, and demands for unity were common themes in expressing this nationalism. It was usually coupled with a suspicion of things foreign that often bordered on xenophobia." This xenophobia encompasses not only foreign people, but foreign cultures, and even people deemed to not be "real" citizens.

Trump openly embraces his identification as a nationalist. "You know what I am? I'm a nationalist, O.K.? I'm a nationalist. Nationalist! Use that word! Use that word!" he declared at one of his rallies.[96] "Make America Great Again," was Trump's campaign slogan from beginning to end in 2016, and immensely popular. His self-described foreign policy philosophy was "America First."[97] His 2020 campaign slogan initially was "Keep America Great," implying that he and his movement had made America great again.

Trump engaged in grandiose displays of patriotism such as hugging flags,[98] military hardware in parades,[99] and million-dollar fireworks displays excessive even by American standards.[100] His 2016 campaign speeches frequently included the phrase, "One people, under one God, saluting one flag."[101] This is an eerie echo of an earlier German slogan which even more closely resembles the one used by Trump: "*Ein Reich. Ein Volk. Ein Gott.*" (One nation. One people. One God.), which was a slogan used in Germany prior to 1933. It then became "*Ein Volk, Ein Reich. Ein Führer!*" which roughly translates as "One people. One Nation. One Leader!" and was effectively the national motto of Germany between 1935 and 1945.[102]

There is a great deal of cultural xenophobia as well. Trump ridiculed the idea of a Korean film (*Parasite*) winning the 2020 Academy Award for Best Picture, with the clear implication to his audience that American movies are always superior.[103] He called African and Caribbean nations "shit-hole countries."[104] The Administration put a ban on visas from several African nations because they claimed they would never "go back to their huts" if they were allowed in the U.S., according to Trump.[105] He also opined that anyone who refuses to participate in their nationalistic displays should just "go back" to wherever they came from.[106]

The movement behind Trump was similarly nationalistic. Republican representatives and senators led chants of "U-S-A! U-S-A!" during the State of the Union addresses.[107] Trump supporters such as Ben Shapiro expounded at great length on how Western (white) culture was superior to all others because "we're Christian monotheists implementing Greek philosophy" (which he regards as the pinnacle of reason).[108] The editor of the influential and religiously conservative magazine *First Things* embraced nationalism and laid out in an interview how nationalism will be the force that saves America.[109]

The Trump Administration's *1776 Report*, written by Federalist Society members rather than historians, concluded that racism was a necessary evil, everyone did it, and that the biggest threat to America was people who still think racism was, or is, a problem. The solution was, of course, patriotic education teaching kids that the U.S. is the best country ever at everything and shouldn't be criticized for slavery or racism, and that anyone who did so was an enemy of the people.[110]

Americans were already one of the most nationalistic people in the world before Trump was elected, and Republicans are more than twice as likely as the general population to believe the U.S. stands above all other nations.[111] This pride, and belief that the U.S. is the best at everything is tragically misplaced.[112] The U.S. ranks at or near the bottom of OECD countries in terms of poverty, wealth inequality, social mobility, obesity, health care costs, life expectancy, child mortality, maternal mortality, literacy, education costs, domestic violence, murder, gender inequality, green energy, infrastructure investment, and voter participation.[113] American nationalism prevents us from even seeing that we have problems, much less permitting us to look to other countries to see how they have addressed these issues successfully.

8. Corporate power and the wealthy are protected

Laurence Britt observed that in fascist movements, "…The ability of large corporations to operate in relative freedom was not compromised… Members of the economic elite were often pampered by the political elite to ensure a continued mutuality of interests, especially in the repression of 'have-not' citizens."

The Darwinistic and Malthusian inclinations of fascism, that the strong should triumph over the weak, lead fascists to take a somewhat *laissez-faire* approach to capitalism, taxes, and regulation of the economy. Thus, while some of these movements have had "workers" or "socialist" in their names, their economic libertarianism meant that in practice their economies were not socialist.[114] Indeed, both Italy and Germany privatized a number of state industries.[115] Many companies that prospered in Germany, such as BASF, Bayer, Daimler-Benz, Volkswagen, and Junkers, still exist today despite their roles in atrocities, war crimes and the Holocaust. The rule for corporations was essentially "do not cross *der Führer*, go along with things, and you will be fine."

In modern times, the Trump Administration promised economic expansion through extensive deregulation, privatization, and tax cuts.[116] Deregulation included dismantling a host of government oversight functions including environmental, financial, monopolistic, and billing laws.[117] As a result of tax cuts, corporate tax revenue has plummeted, along with penalties for violating regulations.[118] Because of generous tax loopholes and low corporate tax rates, 91 of the *Fortune* 500 companies paid no taxes, or even paid a negative rate, in 2019. The money corporations saved under Trump did not "trickle down" to workers or create new jobs; rather it was primarily used by corporations to inflate their stock values via buy-backs.[119] After the Trump tax cuts, the overall tax rate on the richest 400 households in 2018 was lower than what the poorest half of Americans paid.[120] The U.S. has become one of the first modern countries to have a functionally regressive tax system.[121]

But woe betide the corporate owner who crossed Trump! Jeff Bezos owns Amazon and the *Washington Post*, which has published articles critical of the Trump Administration. Amazon reportedly lost a $10 billion dollar government contract for cloud computing services because of the latter, and Amazon attempted to depose the President in its bid protest.[122] This allegation is based on statements made by former Defense Secretary James Mattis, who wrote in his memoir that Trump instructed him to "screw Amazon" out of the contract.[123] Similarly, the Trump Department of Justice launched an investigation into auto makers who reached an agreement with the State of California on vehicle emissions that the Administration opposed.[124]

A related question to how corporate power is protected is: "How are corporations allowed to treat their workers?" under the regime. This brings us to the next characteristic of fascism:

9. Suppression of labor

According to Laurence Britt, "Since organized labor was seen as the one power center that could challenge the political hegemony of the ruling elite and its corporate allies, it was inevitably crushed or made powerless." One of Hitler's first acts was to crush trade unions in May of 1933, and Mussolini effectively banned them in 1925.

The Trump Administration was nothing short of disastrous for unions and workers' rights. While unions have been in decline since the late 1950's, the Trump Administration attempted to actively destroy their ability to represent their workers. Newly installed Associate Justice Neil Gorsuch helped deliver a devastating decision in 2018 that undermined unions of government workers, effectively making the U.S. a "right to work" country.[125] Trump issued executive orders that rolled back the rights of federal workers, and engaged in union "busting," including a plan to effectively eliminate unions within the Department of Defense.[126] Shortly before the 2020 election, he issued an executive order allowing any unionized federal employee who is in a policy making position to be fired at will by political appointees. It also allows the unionized federal employees in these positions to be replaced with political appointees.[127]

On a wider scale, the Trump National Labor Relations Board (NLRB) delivered policies and case law that undercut the rights of workers, including letting employers force arbitration, undermine collective bargaining, and forbid workers from discussing workplace issues while in the workplace.[128] The administration also made it more difficult (if not impossible) to successfully sue corporations for violating wage laws.[129] The Trump Administration sided with employers at the Supreme Court in *Lamps Plus, Inc. v. Varela*, and as a result class action lawsuits by employees are now nearly impossible.[130]

The Department of Justice successfully argued at the Supreme Court in *Our Lady of Guadalupe School v. Morrissey-Berru* that anyone who works for a religious organization can be exempted from most labor and civil rights laws under the ministerial exception.[131] Millions will be affected by this case: one in six hospitals in the U.S. are Catholic,[132] and most private schools are religiously affiliated.[133] Religious freedom claims that degrade worker rights are likely to continue succeeding in courts Trump and McConnell have stacked with justices who see it as the chief constitutional right above all others. The decline of workers' rights is highly correlated with the decline of the middle class, stagnant wages, and growing wealth inequality, which cause a whole host of issues in and of themselves.[134] Unions act as a guardrail against high income inequality. Harvard political scientist Dr. Archon Fung found that no OECD country had both high wealth inequality and high labor union participation rates.[135]

Given the state of the federal judiciary after four years of Trump and McConnell, the rulings of those courts, and the difficulty in raising taxes on corporations and the wealthy, American workers will be getting poorer, more abused, more desperate, and more angry in the foreseeable future.

10. Anti-urbanism and agrarianism: who the "real" people are

One element that sets other kinds of authoritarianism apart from fascism is whether the base of support is drawn from urban or rural areas. Anti-urbanism also tends to separate communist or socialistic populism from more fascist populism. For example, the junta propping up the Thai monarchy of Maha Va-jiralongkorn, and the monarchy itself, draw most of their support from urban areas, but aren't particularly socialist.[136] Both the pro-and anti-monarchy factions practice populist economics to woo rural areas.[137] Similarly, the Bolshevik revolution made appeals to both rural farmers and urban factory workers: the hammer and sickle were meant to represent unity between the peasantry and industrial workers.[138]

What sets fascism apart is the "us vs. them" dynamic pitting traditionalist, conservative, monocultural, rural populations against the more cosmopolitan urban "elites." Fascist leaders and movements hold up rural people as the true keepers of national virtues, while cities are dens of decadence that degraded the character of the country. In *Mein Kampf*, Hitler idealized the village he grew up in and despised Vienna. "I hated the mixture of races displayed in the capital. I hated the motley collection of Czechs, Poles, Hungarians, Ruthenians, Serbs, Croats, and above all... Jews." Cities, to his mind, were the source of corruption.

Trump's base is rural, and he made his disgust with cities that harbor immigrants well known.[139] He called Brussels a "hellhole" because it had Muslim immigrants.[140] He called Chicago "embarrassing to our nation," because they weren't anti-immigrant enough.[141] Trump described Los Angeles and San Francisco as "disgusting," due to homelessness, and seemed obsessed with people defecating in the streets.[142] He saw homelessness as part of the same progressive moral rot that promises safety to immigrants. Trump also played on racist stereotypes of cities with large Black and Latino populations as incredibly violent and dangerous. He baselessly claimed the murder rate in Baltimore was "significantly higher than El Salvador, Honduras, and Guatemala," and egged the audience on for more examples of dangerous, decadent, "blue" cities.[143] He seemed to believe that Black people in cities all live in "war zones."[144] During his inaugural State of the Union Address he declared, "This American carnage stops right here and right now."[145]

This anti-urbanism streak also fits right into the populist rhetoric Trump employed. So does the fascist narrative of a better, mythical past and the belief that a fall into decadence was caused by immigrants, brown people, secularists, queers, and anything else that came from cities. Trump's vision of what life in American cities is like was a caricature of reality. It is what someone living in a white, rural area would imagine if they never lived in a city. They are certain that things went from bad to worse (they didn't),[146] and that this was the fault of Democrats, immigrants, and people of color.[147] They also believed that LGBTQ people are a product of the morals of tolerant cosmopolitan cities: It's what conservatives really mean anytime they reference "San Francisco values."[148]

The anti-urbanism streak of the Trump base also fits right into the xenophobic populism Trump employed and exploited.[149] Trumpists see Republicans and rural (white) people as the "good" and "real" Americans.[150] Even some Democrats fell into this trap of revering rural populations of the "heartland" as somehow more American than their urban counterparts.[151] Trump, for his part, used this as a key part of his messaging in the 2020 campaign.[152] How this dichotomy is weaponized by fascist populists brings us to the next characteristic:

11. Selective populism headed by a single man from which all political power flows

In fascist movements, there is a single leader who claims to be a uniter of the country. He is the interpreter of the will of the people, and the undisputed head of the party and regime from which all direction and authority flows. This leader claims to be the only one who can do this. He is a populist, but his message is for people who believe themselves to be the true and rightful population of the country. Umberto Eco called this selective populism and described the leader's relationship with the public: "Since no large quantity of human beings can have a common will, the Leader pretends to be their interpreter."[153] Anyone who rejects the leader's interpretation is accused of no longer representing the will of the people.

Trump repeatedly claimed he would "unify the country" throughout his campaign and Presidency.[154] He also claimed that the country was more unified than ever due to his leadership.[155] He repeatedly made statements announcing himself a savior of the nation: "I will give you everything. I will give you what you've been looking for 50 years... I'm the only one."[156] His message of unification and leadership was only for his base, however. They believed themselves to be the only "real" Americans. In their world, immigrants, non-Christians, non-whites, and people living in big cities and blue states weren't "real." After visiting the Daytona 500 NASCAR race, Charlie Kirk of Turning Point USA proclaimed Trump had "historic levels of support with real Americans."[157]

Cas Mudde of the University of Pennsylvania describes fascist populism as the antithesis of uniters because they split society into two, "homogeneous and antagonistic groups: the pure people on the one end and the corrupt elite on the other."[158] During the 2016 campaign, Trump set himself up as the man fighting Republican "elites" to take back the party for "Real Americans." Populism is thin on actual policy, however, so it tends to fall back on either socialism or nationalism for ideological underpinnings. There is a sense that even if they are outvoted, they have the votes of all the "good" people, which (in their minds) justifies anti-democratic actions such as the disenfranchisement of their political adversaries.

Trump claimed he spoke for this "silent majority" of Americans, and was doing and saying what they really want.[160] In reality, he derived support from oligarchs and the aggrieved Christian nationalist minority that held themselves on a pedestal as the only "good people."[161] "Populists only lose if 'the silent majority'—shorthand for 'the real people'—has not had a chance to speak, or worse, has been prevented from expressing itself," says Jan-Werner Müller, a professor at Princeton University and the author of *What Is Populism?*[161] All of this seems to align Trumpism with Eco's concept of selective populism.

Trump also established himself as the single source of political power and direction for the party that controls most state and federal government. Republicans used to be for free trade, states' rights, and separation of powers.[162] Trump wasn't and as a result the GOP embraced all of his positions.[163] If you wanted to stay in politics as a Republican, you had to stay in Trump's good graces. This was put on display several times for the media, where the cabinet went through ritualistic praise of Trump, or prayed to God giving thanks for sending him to the nation as its leader.[164]

In the end, nothing summed up how Trump had become the Republican Party more than the Republican National Committee party platform of 2020.[165] It was only one page long and boiled down to: "We're good with everything Trump is doing, and our vision for the future is whatever President Trump thinks it should be at the moment." It thus seems apropos that Hannah Arendt observed in *The Origins of Totalitarianism* that, "The chief qualification of a mass leader has become unending infallibility: he can never admit an error."

Never was this more on display than in the aftermath of the election where instead of booking a press conference at the Four Seasons Hotel in Philadelphia, Trump's legal team accidentally booked it at the Four Seasons Total Landscaping Company, right between an adult novelty shop and a crematorium. Rather than admitting error, they gamely went out and held it in a parking lot just off of I-95. As of this writing, the Trump team still has not admitted they made a mistake.

12. Enemies are both weak and strong, creating a sense of victimhood and power

Umberto Eco noted of fascist movements that, "The followers must feel humiliated by the ostentatious wealth and force of their enemies... Jews are rich and help each other through a secret web of mutual assistance. However, the followers must be convinced that they can overwhelm the enemies. Thus, by a continuous shifting of rhetorical focus, the enemies are at the same time too strong and too weak." Jason Stanley also noted the related phenomenon of a sense of victimhood amongst people in a fascist movement.

These two ideas are closely related. The base within a fascist movement must be both powerful enough to control a party, and even a government. At the same time, a common trait of this base is a belief that their enemies are so powerful that they have victimized the rightful "real" and "good" citizens of the country. They see these enemies as disgusting enough that society is better off without them, and weak enough to be stopped.

In pre-war Italy and Germany, people were told that Jews were incredibly rich, powerful, and had Illuminati-like networks. Germans, in particular, believed that they were victimized because of Jews. Most notable was the "stab-in-the-back" conspiracy theory that Jews and Communists had cost Germany The Great War and were the reason Germany was subjected to the humiliations and economic devastation brought by the Treaty of Versailles.[166] Yet, at the same time, Jews were also portrayed as weak, wretched sub-human creatures who could easily be defeated by the big, strong, moral Aryan people of Germany... if real Germans just stood up to them. Thus, Arendt noted that anti-Semitism peaked "when Jews had similarly lost their public functions and their influence and were left with nothing but their wealth."

In the United States today there is a similar overwhelming sense of victimhood shared by white evangelicals. They see themselves as the primary victims of discrimination by employers insisting that they use a transgender person's preferred pronouns,[167] by being legally required to serve gay customers,[168] and by not being allowed to force people to pray in schools. County clerks are victimized by being forced to do their jobs and marry gay people.[169] These are essentially the same grievances they suffered in 1970: They feel discriminated against because they're no longer allowed to discriminate against those they feel they are superior to. The list of actual grievances isn't that long or convincing, and don't exactly count as crimes against humanity. But they feel humiliated by this shift in the social order. Their power and superiority are dwindling as society becomes more equal. They find LGBTQ people repulsive and weak at an individual level,[170] but ascribe to them vast political power and a sweeping conspiracy-theory-driven agenda.[171]

Much like previous fascist movements, white evangelicals and Trump's base fail to grasp the irony of a constitutionally-protected religious class, one which is the dominant force within the dominant party at both the state and federal level, feeling powerless and victimized. Nor do many remember that while they call protections for LGBTQ people "special rights," Andrew Johnson likewise called civil rights for Blacks "discrimination against the white race" when he vetoed the Civil Rights Act of 1866.

White Christian nationalists experience a similar dynamic when it comes to immigrants. The idea of white people becoming a minority fills them with dread and makes them more receptive to right-wing policies.[172] Of all demographic groups, they are the most hostile to immigrants due to their fear of a change in their respective social statuses. They embrace false stereotypes about immigrants being lazy, illiterate, violent, criminal, rapists, disease carriers, and a burden on society.[173] They believe immigrants to be individually weak and detestable, yet simultaneously powerful enough take over and destroy America.

Trump himself voiced these beliefs, and they were warmly received. He rarely missed an opportunity to cast himself as a victim, even when it was entirely inappropriate. His unhinged rant in front of the national Boy Scout Jamboree was cringe-worthy, and filled with hints of how he felt things weren't fair to him.[174] He used his "unfair treatment" to justify a third term in office, or more, regardless of the Constitution.[175] While this might seem irrational to the majority of the public, it resonated with his base. Trump was more than happy to encourage these irrational fears and sense of victimhood, while promoting the belief that people who are at the bottom of the heap socially, politically, legally, and economically are the real bullies.[176] So, too, were the media outlets that had become *de facto* organs of the state. Which brings us to the next characteristic of fascism:

13. Conspiracy theories and propaganda create an unreality that feeds into fears and scapegoating

Hannah Arendt saw propaganda as a crucial component of the rise of fascism in Germany. She noted, "Only the mob and the elite can be attracted by the momentum of totalitarianism itself; the masses have to be won by propaganda." To her observation, Jason Stanley adds: "Fascist politics exchange reality for the pronouncements of a single individual, or perhaps a political party." Umberto Eco identified a related phenomenon: namely that fascism is obsessed with plots and conspiracy theories. "The followers must feel besieged. The easiest way to solve the plot is the appeal to xenophobia."

Perhaps the most famous conspiracy theory of the 20th century was the *Protocols of the Elders of Zion*, a fabricated document purporting to prove that a rich cabal of Jews was killing babies, drinking their blood, and planning to take over the world. It has not gone unnoticed that the fundamental beliefs of QAnon were strikingly similar.[177] Regardless, fascist leaders are more than happy to embrace these sorts of beliefs to further their own ends. The Trump base and conservative media exist in a symbiotic relationship feeding one another. There is no shortage of conspiracy theories that have taken root with the base, many of which have been discussed in previous chapters: PizzaGate, QAnon, birtherism, the Seth Rich murder, the "deep state," etc. While conspiracy theories are not unique to the right wing, they flourish unfettered there.[178]

Trump himself is obsessed with conspiracies theories about internal opposition and "the deep state." He launched extensive investigations to root out those in government who might be disloyal to him and to purge them from the system.[179] He was reportedly obsessed with the idea that there was a conspiracy within the federal government (the deep state) to thwart him or remove him from office.[180] He put his top trade advisor Peter Navarro in charge of hunting down a former administration official who criticized him anonymously.[181]

Even as the Trump Administration came to a close, it embraced the belief that there had been massive election fraud, which rigged the election in favor of Joe Biden. His base proved very likely to believe this, even as conservative media repeated the Trump campaign's innuendos and allegations. Eighty-six percent of Trump voters believe that Biden "did not legitimately win the election," and another 73 percent say that we'll "never know the real outcome of this election." Almost 9 out of 10 Trump voters believed that "illegal immigrants voted fraudulently in 2016 and tried again in 2020."[182] Over time, these have melded into one giant conspiracy theory.[183] People that believe one half-baked idea tend to believe most, if not all, of them.[184] In a previous age, these ideas would have been too fringe to make it into mainstream political discourse. Today, they're literally dogma to Trump's base and members of the Administration.

Trump was one of the first people to accuse President Obama of being born in Kenya, and *Fox News* promoted this conspiracy relentlessly.[185] Sean Hannity, who is exceptionally close to the president, was the chief advocate of the theory that Seth Rich was assassinated by Hilary Clinton. He pushed this conspiracy almost every night for weeks.[186] QAnon supporters were a staple at Trump rallies, and the theory eventually crept into mainstream Republican politics.[187]

Senator Tom Cotton (R-AR) has aggressively pushed his belief that the novel coronavirus is an escaped bio-weapon, calling his position "common sense."[188] *Fox News* has been happy to repeatedly give a platform to individuals pushing anti-Semitic conspiracy theories about George Soros.[189]

Right-wing media outlets contribute significantly to this ungrounding from reality. They present information in ways that encourages entirely false beliefs about what is real and true. Individuals who watch *Fox* know less about current events than people who watch nothing at all.[190] The purpose of *Fox News*, *Newsmax* and *One America News* was to create an alternate reality in which the President could do no wrong, and *Fox* was by far the most popular source of information on impeachment for Republicans.[191] It selectively edited impeachment coverage, and showed live-video without audio,[192] except for pro-Trump *Fox* hosts who provided their own narration.[193] As a result, *Fox News* viewers came away with impressions of the impeachment that were completely false.[194] One survey showed that only 40 percent of Republicans believed that Trump asked Ukrainian President Zelensky to investigate Joe Biden[195], despite the fact that Trump literally asked for this exact thing in the pseudo-transcript released by the White House.[196] Making matters worse was Trump's own lack of "truthiness." The *Washington Post* cataloged over 20,000 or misleading claims in his first three years in office, and the rate increased through 2020.[197] Despite this obvious evidence, *Fox News* hosts insisted that the President has never lied and then tried to shape reality to conform to those lies.[198]

Breaking this cycle is nigh impossible. People can wrap themselves inside insular information ecosystems like the one provided by *Fox* and *OAN* and become unreachable by mainstream factual media. A study commissioned by the *Columbia Journalism Review* found that consumers of "legacy media" (like the *New York Times*) were exposed to a wide variety of stories and opinions. Conservatives, however, existed in their own "insular sphere"[199] where there is intense social pressure to ignore "Fake News" that provides contrary information.[200] By labeling journalists as "enemies of the people," they imply that anyone who believes them is guilty of un-American thoughts as well.[201]

What Fascism Looks Like in Practice

These thirteen aspects of fascism are the most prevalent across experts' analyses. Some of the less agreed-upon characteristics, however, are also worth mentioning. Some authors, including Umberto Eco, noted that fascism is always at war with something internal or external, and thus thrashing about from self-inflicted crisis to self-inflicted crisis. As Eco described it, "Life is permanent warfare" in fascist ideology. These fascist nation-states then engage in knee-jerk action for the sake of action. As cynical as it may sound, the U.S. has had a "war on something-or-other" since the Lyndon Johnson administration. While people bemoan what isn't normal under the Trump Administration, this Administration's manufactured crises, poorly thought-out policy, and over-reaction isn't unique. It has been par for the course since the Gulf of Tonkin. Trump merely turned it up to 11.

Tim Snyder observes that this perpetual state of warfare is related to what he terms the politics of eternity, which "places the nation at the center of a cyclical story of victimhood. Time is no longer a line into the future, but a circle that endlessly returns to the same threats from the past… Eternity politicians spread the conviction that government cannot aid society as a whole but can only guard against threats."[202]

This description of a state that provides little to its citizens other than a parade of threats which the leader alone can save them from captures many elements of the Trumpist Republican Party today. The GOP dogma dictates that government can't, and shouldn't, provide anything besides national defense and law and order. The Republican base is still making "Islamic terrorism" a top priority 20 years after 9/11, despite evidence that white nationalist terrorism is a much greater threat.[203] Indeed, Trump's sales pitch to the LGBTQ community wasn't that he would protect their rights, rather that he would instead protect them from Muslims.[204] It's these same xenophobic fears that Trump and the GOP tried to use to rally the base before the 2018 election, spreading fears of an "army" of immigrants coming to invade America, commit crimes, steal jobs, and sell drugs.[205] As Tim Snyder notes of Putin and his modern-day form of fascism, "If citizens can be kept uncertain by the regular manufacture of crisis, their emotions can be managed and directed."[206]

Violence and the use of police to stifle opposition are also mentioned in some of the literature on fascism. However, this is also a characteristic of authoritarianism in general. It should be noted, though, that police in the U.S. are becoming increasingly less accountable to the public, and the courts that Trump and Senator McConnell have filled are hastening this process towards fully militarized police forces that are completely unaccountable under the law.[207] Police actively worked with armed, pro-Trump militias during his tenure. These militias increasingly filled the same role as the Nazi Party's paramilitary supporters, known as the *Sturmabteilung*, or "Brown Shirts."[208] This dovetails with the "Law and Order" message some researchers also saw as a common trait of fascism.

Some authors have cited supremacy of the military and conquest as a characteristic of fascism. This was only cited by some, and it doesn't fit well with what we have seen in the U.S. While the Trump Administration put a priority on military spending, it was fundamentally uninterested in expanding U.S. territory through conquest (though they did inquire about buying Greenland).[209] Several experts on fascism mentioned elections that don't matter, or a single party state. These are more rightly categorized as characteristics of authoritarianism, which may or may not be fascist (although U.S. elections are, in fact, getting less democratic).[210]

Another commonality of fascist movements is hatred of socialism and communism.[211] This permeates some of the other fascist traits. The fascist opposition to labor movements and protection of corporate interests (and the wealthy) put them at odds with both groups. The Malthusian views of fascist movements are hostile to the underlying communist philosophy of "to each according to his needs," as well. Thus, based on their values and beliefs, fascists are the natural enemies of people who believe in taking care of the weakest and poorest members of society. Fascist movements exploit fear, and part of their appeal is to a middle class that is afraid that socialism and communism will take from them and give to the poor, whom they see as unworthy. In the U.S., we can see this expressed in Trumpism as they label everything they dislike as socialist or communist, even when the person or thing they oppose isn't either.[212] Paranoia over socialism and communism was used effectively as a scare tactic in Florida in the 2020 election.[213]

Still, the question remains: Are we a fascist country? The answer isn't simple.

Is Trumpism fascist? Based on this analysis, the Trumpist movement has almost all the characteristics described by scholars as hallmarks of some form of fascism, and now includes an attempted violent overthrow of the American government.

Is the Republican party fascist? Difficult to say, given that some "just followed orders" out of fear of Trump and his base, while some were true believers. Like Arendt's elites, even those who don't believe the propaganda, certainly profited from it politically and financially. If Ted Cruz or Mike Pence were President, they would likely leverage the same fears, biases and divisions to their own advantage and move forward with many of the same policies, albeit more quietly and with less tweeting.

Is Trump a fascist? He probably wouldn't call himself one, and it's unlikely he's read enough books to effectively evaluate himself.[214] However, his instincts for how to get elected and stay in power permanently absolutely fit the description of a selectively populist leader ruling over a movement that has fascist motivations and beliefs, and who actively encourages and leverages those beliefs for his own benefit. He certainly helped incite the conditions that led to a violent coup attempt on the Capitol, which was part March on Rome, part Beer Hall Putsch, but distinctly American in its flavor. However, he undoubtedly emerged at the forefront of a fascist movement and encouraged its beliefs and violent tendencies, even if he didn't create it.

Are we a fascist country? Not yet, but we are moving in that direction. Judicial and legal guardrails slowed things down temporarily, but with Associate Justice Amy Coney Barrett and a 6-3 conservative court, that's unlikely to be the case going forward. A Biden administration will work against a descent into fascist autocracy, but there's little he can do to reverse the tide, with an evenly divided Senate and without the courts. When another right-wing populist like Trump comes to power, any constraints on a right-wing authoritarian regime will eventually give way as the courts become rubber stamps, civil servants who were insufficiently loyal to the autocrat leave or are forced out, and people get used to the new normal.

None of this means we're going to end up looking like Nazi Germany though. There has only ever been one Nazi Germany, and it was the product of a specific time, place, and individual. Trump isn't Hitler. Only Hitler could be Hitler. Just because the movement we are seeing is fascist doesn't mean we'll end up with the specific horrors of Germany any more than it means we're doomed to fight a land war in Russia in the winter. Those are not essential characteristics of fascism; rather, they are historical outcomes of one particular fascist movement, leader, and country in a specific time. This is not a new perspective: scholars on the subject of fascism have known for decades that it is not limited to Germany and Italy in a particular time period. Theodor Adorno, a German Jewish philosopher who escaped the country in 1933, recognized fascism as something that emerges from within democratic societies naturally under the right conditions. He was warning us in the 1950's and 1960's that it could grow within any democracy, and that understanding the causes of fascism required a multidisciplinary approach (which was the point of this book).[215]

It does, however, mean that we are in growing danger of "very bad things." What might these be? Let's assume that the GOP base only gets what they are asking for currently.

Even with Trump ousted, the conservative Supreme Court will cause incredible harm. It means rolling back civil rights we take for granted and giving corporations powers we haven't seen since the infamous case of *Lochner v. New York*.[216] They will likely grant religious employers and institutions a broad right to ignore civil rights and labor laws, while forcing the federal government to provide such discriminatory institutions with taxpayer dollars.[218] Indeed, the Trump Administration argued that Christian organizations receiving federal funding have a constitutionally guaranteed right to refuse to serve Jews.[218] Federal courts are also more likely to sign off on further GOP attempts to use gerrymandering and voter suppression to ensure they remain in power.

Beyond just the courts, future Republican administrations will take many more actions deeply unpopular with the American public but supported by their base. Social safety net programs like Medicare, Medicaid, and Social Security will be cut in order to provide additional tax cuts, thereby worsening the corrosive effects of wealth inequality.[219] The forecast gets even worse when you consider the economic circumstances that will surround all of this. Wealth inequality and all the social ills that come with it are going to continue to worsen.[220] The U.S. was well past due for another recession before COVID-19 hit.[221] The U.S. is already at record low tax rates, deficits are above $2 trillion per year, and lending rates are near zero, meaning that we have few of the usual tools to deal with a recession.

Members of Gen Z and Millennials have been hit the hardest. They have no savings, no wealth compared to previous generations, and may not even have health insurance.[222] At the same time, Senate Majority Leader Mitch McConnell (R-KY) refused to hold a vote for further economic assistance before the election, and suddenly rediscovered "fiscal restraint" when Biden won the election.[223]

The fascistic hatred of immigrants will lead to drastic policies under the next GOP administration, which will likely have to leverage the Trumpist base to win. Land mining the border with Mexico was reportedly on the table for a second Trump term.[224] The head of ICE under Trump indicated he planned to deport hundreds of thousands of Dreamers if DACA was overturned.[225] Trump Senior Adviser Stephen Miller planned to try to overturn birthright citizenship via an executive order during a second Trump term, despite it being in the Constitution. This might seem impossible, but don't forget that it's constitutional if the 6-3 conservative Supreme Court says it is.

Over the first four years of a Biden Administration, the Supreme Court will sign off on whatever the Alliance Defending Freedom plans for LGBTQ people. It means an end to bans on conversion therapy, and it likely means federal money being poured into religious organizations claiming they can cure LGBTQ people. If Project Blitz succeeds in legally treating transgender people as a communicable public health hazard, it opens up a Pandora's Box of bad things that governments can do to any minority group under the guise of "promoting the health and social welfare" of the public.[226]

Birth control will follow a similar fate as *Roe v. Wade*, as the religious right goes after *Griswold v. Connecticut*.[227] *Obergefell, Windsor, Lawrence v. Texas* and *Romer v. Evans* are likely on the chopping block as well due to the court undermining the implied right to privacy, opening the door to criminalizing LGBTQ people and allowing government sanctioned discrimination against them under the guise of "community morals." Social services will be slashed.[228] Christian religious beliefs will be granted a get-out-of-jail-free card for discrimination, mooting much of the Civil Rights Act of 1964 and other civil rights laws. The religious right has every intention of challenging *Engel v. Vitale*, which forbade government led prayer in schools, and conservative justices have telegraphed their intentions on it.[229] Associate Justices Alito, Thomas, and Kavanaugh appear ready to overturn it.

Republican election rigging through gerrymandering, voter suppression, and foreign interference will become exponentially worse as the Voting Rights Act is cast down, and other laws protecting voting rights are found unconstitutional, to the point of making elections a moot point.[230] After the 2020 elections, Republican legislatures in swing states are already proposing legislation to make voting far more difficult, and the Supreme Court will sign off on it.

It means militarized police forces that are even more effectively immune from everything. It also means that nationalist paramilitary groups, working with or unhindered by the police, will become even more brazen and dangerous in their support of a future fascist administration. This likely leads to increasing civil unrest, as oppressed people of color push back against a police force that can murder them with impunity.

Corporations will be able to abuse employees in ways we haven't seen since the days of the company store, usury, and *Lochner v. New York*. The next GOP administration will resume flooding government with loyalists and ideologues, remove anyone they see as potentially disloyal or ideologically impure,[231] and replace them with people willing to lie to Congress and the public.[232] The guardrails would essentially disintegrate after another four years of Republican misrule, and the next GOP autocrat's ability to exploit the office and target his enemies would no longer have any functional opposition.

The U.S. is going down a path that guarantees nothing will be done to mitigate climate change, and another GOP administration ensures this continues. Nepotism and corruption in government is likely to run amok in the next GOP administration just as it did under Trump, as all the gatekeepers against these have been captured. It also means a system so corrupted that anyone associated with the administration is virtually immune from prosecution, investigation, subpoena or indictment. Government will increasingly become nothing more than an arm of the administration and the oligarchs serving to enrich and protect them, while punishing their enemies, including people who live in blue states.

The scariest part, though? These are the best-case scenarios for what happens if the Trumpist wing of the GOP re-takes the White House and the GOP controls the Senate. Many of these outcomes are already "baked in" by courts that Trump and McConnell built. It has also been demonstrated by Trump and the 2020 election that the next GOP nominee must tap into the Trump base's desires in order to win the nomination.

Umberto Eco observed that, "For Ur-Fascism there is no struggle for life but, rather, life is lived for struggle… Since enemies have to be defeated, there must be a final battle, after which the movement will have control of the world. But such a "final solution" implies a further era of peace, a Golden Age, which contradicts the principle of permanent war." Thus, Fascist movements need an enemy. They need conflict.

Eco's observations on fascism suggest that it is highly likely that once the Trumpist movement achieves the goals they state now, they will find new and even more extreme ones. From 1933-1939, the German goal was "just" to marginalize the Jewish population and chase it out of the country. When they had taken this about as far as it could go, they then decided to liquidate the population. Thus, once the guardrails are completely down, as they almost certainly will be during the next autocratic attempt, the future goes completely grimdark.[233] We will almost certainly lose the power to prevent the fascist movement from going even further than they've indicated they will today. The scholars who have studied fascism suggest that they almost certainly will keep taking it to the next step, and the next one, and so on, until they are overthrown, or the nation disintegrates.

So, if "going further" means heretofore unthinkable things, there's nothing we can do to stop them after a certain point. That point of no return, where we lose any collective power to stop horrors we swore would never happen again, are inevitable if we elect another person devoted to giving the fascist movement what it wants: too many of the protections against future potential atrocities have already been permanently degraded.

For those of us who are not part of the "in-group," it means that we live hoping that whatever groups we belong to never fall afoul of the Trumpist movement. It means praying that this reality-challenged movement, founded on xenophobia, sexual insecurity, misogyny, power, purity, fear, paranoia, religious extremism, and victimhood, exhibits (heretofore) unseen restraint and decides to go no further once it has achieved its currently stated goals.

This was, and is, what's at stake. This is the future we are trying to prevent given the ascendant fascist movement currently controlling the GOP.

Ten

Death of Democracies

"Mass propaganda discovered that its audience was ready at all times to believe the worst, no matter how absurd, and did not particularly object to being deceived because it held every statement to be a lie anyhow. [...] instead of deserting the leaders who had lied to them, they would protest that they had known all along the statement was a lie and would admire the leaders for their superior tactical cleverness."

Hannah Arendt

One of the most constant refrains we heard in the age of Trump was, "this is not normal." Almost every day, something new tore down norms that had existed for decades, if not hundreds of years. It happened so often that we grew numb to it, and greater and greater outrages were required to provoke any sort of immune response. When the Mueller report revealed Trump's connections with Russia, it spawned an impeachment. The Senate refused to provide anything more than a *pro forma* hearing. Later, the Senate Intelligence Committee report was released, and it contained numerous new revelations of how deep the corruption went. It was a tacit acknowledgment that the Senate would not provide any checks on the executive branch.[1] The framers of the Constitution had hoped that Congress would put the good of the country ahead of party and prevent demagogues, autocrats, and criminals from controlling executive branch; instead, the legislative branch was enabling a man who was all three.

This has people who study how modern democracies fall into autocracy and fascism extremely worried. The Trump Administration closely hewed to the model of other failed democracies in the post-Soviet era. Indeed, there are some who believe that the likes of Vladimir Putin and Viktor Orbán of Hungary were actively coaching the Trump Administration and the religious right on how to re-make America in the image of their autocratic, Christian, ethno-nationalist states.[2]

This chapter examines the characteristics of how post-Cold War governments have been de-democratized from the inside, using Russia, Hungary, Turkey and Poland as examples, and points to similarities occurring in the United States under Trump.

Warnings of Authoritarian Behavior

Harvard professors Steven Levitsky and Daniel Ziblatt provided one of the most eye-opening analyses of how modern countries fail in their book, *How Democracies Die*. They outlined four key indicators of authoritarian behavior. The Trump Administration failed, or nearly failed, all of these tests. This is more startling given that when Levitsky and Ziblatt wrote their book in 2018, they judged that Trump only ran afoul of 7 of the 15 indicators listed above. After two additional years in power, it was 15 out of 15 when he left office.

Rejection (or Weak Commitment to) Democratic Rules of the Game

"A society becomes totalitarian when its structure becomes flagrantly artificial: that is, when its ruling class has lost its function but succeeds in clinging to power by force or fraud."

George Orwell

"I have to see. No, I'm not going to just say 'yes.' I'm not going to say 'no.' And I didn't last time, either,"

Donald Trump,
when asked in July 2020 if he would accept election results

Trump continually expressed a desire to violate the Constitution. He suggested delaying the 2020 elections in violation of the Constitution's dictates that Congress sets the election date.[4] He repeatedly stated that he should be allowed to seek a third term in office, in violation of the 22nd Amendment that limits presidents to two terms in office.[5] Indeed, he went so far as to say he should be allowed to seek a fourth, fifth, or sixth term, which (at his age) was expressing a naked desire to become president for life.[6] Trump implied validity of the use of violence to overthrow normal democratic processes and the government. During the 2016 election, he hinted that if Clinton won, the only way to "fix" the courts would be to assassinate federal judges. "If she gets to pick her judges, nothing you can do folks… Although the Second Amendment people—maybe there is."[7]

Trump encouraged protests against state governments that took measures to contain COVID-19, with tweets such as, "LIBERATE MICHIGAN!"[8] His encouragement was clearly aimed at the most dangerous parts of his base, and as a result, protesters carrying assault rifles swarmed capitols in displays that were

Table 2. Key Indicators of Authoritarian Behavior

Rejection (or weak commitment to) democratic rules of the game
1. Do they reject the Constitution or express a willingness to violate it?
2. Do they suggest a need for antidemocratic measures, such as cancelling elections, violating or suspending the Constitution, banning certain organizations, or restricting basic civil or political rights?
3. Do they seek to use (or endorse the use of) extraconstitutional means to change the government, such as military coups, violent insurrections, or mass protests aimed at forcing a change in the government?
4. Do they attempt to undermine the legitimacy of elections, for example, by refusing to accept credible electoral results?
Denial of the legitimacy of political opponents
1. Do they describe their rivals as subversive, or opposed to the existing constitutional order?
2. Do they claim their rivals constitute an existential threat, either to national security or to the prevailing way of life?
3. Do they baselessly describe their partisan rivals as criminals, whose supposed violation of the law (or potential to do so) disqualifies them from full participation in the political arena?
4. Do they baselessly suggest that their rivals are foreign agents, in that they are secretly working in alliance with (or the employ of) a foreign government, usually an enemy one?
Toleration or encouragement of violence
1. Do they have any ties to armed gangs, paramilitary forces, militias, guerillas, or other organizations that engage in illicit violence?
2. Have they or their partisan allies sponsored or encouraged mob attacks on opponents?
3. Have they tacitly endorsed violence by their supporters by refusing to unambiguously condemn and punish it?
4. Have they praised (or refused to condemn) other significant acts of political violence either in the past or elsewhere in the world?

Readiness to curtail the civil liberties of opponents, including media
1. Have they supported laws or policies that restrict civil liberties, such as expanded libel or defamation laws, or laws restricting protest, criticism of the government, or certain types of political organizations?
2. Have they threatened to take legal or other punitive action against critics in rival parties, civil society, or the media?
3. Have they praised repressive measures taken by other governments, either in the past or elsewhere in the world?

Source: Levitsky and Ziblatt[3]

clearly meant to intimidate elected officials with threats of violence or insurrection.[9] Governors who defied Trump were inundated with credible death threats.[10] Later, the FBI foiled a plot by a militia group to kidnap, try, and extrajudicially execute Michigan Governor Gretchen Whitmer.[11] The members of the plot had been part of the groups openly carrying in the Michigan state house.[12] This presaged the assault on the U.S. Capitol only a few months later, when some of the same people from the state protests stormed it.

Trump worked tirelessly to undermine the legitimacy of U.S. elections. He called the 2016 elections fraudulent based on the demonstrably false conspiracy theory that millions of undocumented immigrants were not only allowed to vote, but all voted for Hillary Clinton.[13] He repeatedly refused to commit to accepting the results of the 2020 election.[14] Trump also claimed that the only way he could lose the 2020 election was if it was rigged.[15]

At the same time, Trump and sycophant Postmaster General DeJoy were tearing down the capabilities of the Postal Service in order to prevent Democratic votes from being counted during the pandemic.[16] Trump promoted the conspiracy theory that absentee and mail in ballots were subject to fraud.[17] Thus, he first made sure that as few Republicans as possible were encouraged to submit their votes by mail, and then he attempted to destroy the voting mechanism which Democratic voters were more likely to use to cast their ballots.

Denial of the Legitimacy of Political Opponents

"I have been in two elections. I won them both and the second one I won much bigger than the first, okay?...We will not be intimidated into accepting the hoaxes and the lies that we've been forced to believe. Over the past several weeks, we've amassed overwhelming evidence about a fake election."

Donald Trump to his supporters, minutes before
they stormed the capitol and attempted a coup

Donald Trump made bizarre, outlandish claims about Joe Biden and Kamala Harris a staple of his campaign and stump speeches. He described his opponents in apocalyptic terms as dangerous radicals who would destroy the First and Second Amendments of the Constitution. In Trump's world, Biden and Harris were an existential threat to the Constitution and the prevailing way of life. He claimed Democrats would eliminate all police forces, buying ads that showed elderly people calling the police during home invasions only to find that they had been disbanded by Biden.[18] Guns would be confiscated.[19] Suburbs destroyed by hordes of poor, brown, and presumably criminally violent people moving in.[20] He claimed Biden would ban religion, the Bible, "hurt God," and "wipe away every trace of religion from national life."[21] Trump even made the bizarre claim that if Biden were elected, he would cancel Christmas, which speaks to the mindset of the audience that believes these sorts of claims.[22]

Trump also relentlessly pushed the narrative that his political rivals, namely Clinton, Obama and Biden, were all criminals who should be prosecuted and imprisoned. He spent years leading chants of "lock her up," and pushing the Department of Justice to reopen investigations into Clinton. Trump repeatedly accused former President Obama of "treason," alleging that he had spied upon the 2016 Trump campaign using the FBI.[23] He and his Senate enablers pushed the easily falsifiable narrative that Biden and his son were foreign agents of the Ukraine and should likewise be prosecuted.[24] It was enough for Trump loyalists in the Senate to hold hearings to try to smear Biden.[25]

A corollary to this is Masha Gessen's observation that "autocratic power requires the degradation of moral authority–not by the capture of the moral high ground."[26] Republicans made no attempt to seize the moral high ground during Trump's presidency or the 2020 election. Their justifications were either that the 2016 election validated their actions, or to attack the morality of Biden based on his stance on abortion. The GOP never claimed to be the good guys, only that nothing could be worse than people who support executing newborn babies.[27] By this risible standard, anything done by Republicans short of gas chambers and crematoriums is morally defensible.

Toleration or Encouragement of Violence

> *"Power and violence are opposites; where the one rules absolutely, the other is absent. Violence appears where power is in jeopardy, but left to its own course it ends in power's disappearance."*

Hannah Arendt

Trump has consistently embraced anti-democratic violence against those who oppose him. At a 2015 campaign rally, he suggested that a Black Lives Matter protester should have been "roughed up" by the crowd and security.[28] Before the 2016 Iowa caucus, he told his fans, "…Knock the crap out of them. I'll pay the legal fees."[29] At other rallies where they hauled out protesters, he declared, "Try not to hurt him. If you do, I'll defend you in court." He also defended the "old days" where protesters were "carried out on a stretcher."

During the protests against police violence in the summer of 2020, Trump was more than happy to escalate the use of violence against protesters. A source within the White House said that he enjoyed watching police and National Guard troops clear out Lafayette Square across the street from the White House with tear gas, stun grenades, rubber bullets, and truncheons. He followed it up by posing with a Bible in front of Saint John's Episcopal church in a photo-op clearly designed to appeal to his white evangelical base.[30] Later, Trump deployed unmarked police forces to Portland and other cities. Simultaneously, he threatened to use the National Guard in states that displeased him in order to suppress protests.[31]

Violent Christian nationalist militia groups such as the Proud Boys, the Three Percenters, and Patriot Prayer militia groups all have ideologies that are misogynistic, Islamophobic, transphobic, and anti-immigration.[32] They are strongly supportive of Trump, whose views, methods, and goals align closely with theirs.[33] They recognize him as one of their own. During the first Presidential debate of 2020, Trump told the Proud Boys militia group to, "Stand back and stand by." This was widely seen as a call for political violence if things didn't go the President's way during the election.[34] When Kyle Rittenhouse shot three Black Lives Matter (BLM) protesters in Wisconsin, killing two, he was with the "Kenosha Guard" militia group.[35] His social media posts were littered with support for Trump and "Blue Lives Matter" posts. Only minutes before the shooting, police were recorded handing him and other members of the militia water and thanking them for turning out.[36] After the shootings, Trump refused to denounce Rittenhouse's actions, while right-wing media hailed him as a hero.[37] Ultra-conservative pundit and former *Fox News* regular Ann Coulter tweeted, "I want him as my president."[38] Trump defended Rittenhouse during one of his press briefings.[39]

Later, supporters of Rittenhouse crowd-sourced over $2 million dollars to pay his bail.[40]

Trump embraced a both-sideism when it comes to violent extremists who support him. After the 2017 violence in Charlotte between white supremacists and counter-protesters that resulted in the vehicular homicide death of Heather Heyer (who opposed racism), Trump called them "very fine people, on both sides," when addressing the violence.[41] Worse, Trump had a long history of admiring how dictators handle protesters. In 1989, after the Tiananmen Square massacre, he praised the military response: "When the students poured into Tiananmen Square, the Chinese government almost blew it."[42] Three decades later in 2019, he reportedly gave Chinese President Xi Jinping approval to continue building concentration camps for the Muslim Uighur ethnic minority in northwest China.[43]

Let that sink in for a moment: Trump seems to believe that genocide is an acceptable response to political dissent, and to maintain "law and order," if the people being liquidated are labeled terrorists. His public actions all supported the observation that he wanted violence and encouraged it against political adversaries and protesters with a wink and a nod.

Despite all of this, people still seemed shocked that Trump got up in front of an angry mob on January 6th, 2021 and told them to march on the capitol. After every ounce of conservative media and the Trump campaign had been telling his base for months that they needed to fight for him, that they were being robbed of their country, and that it would be the end of America if Biden controlled the White House, it still came as a surprise to some when Trump's devoted base stormed the capitol. They had every intention of taking the Vice President hostage, and potentially killing him, along with Democratic legislators like Nancy Pelosi, Alexandria Ocasio-Cortez, and James Clyburn.[44] They nearly succeeded, but for the quick thinking and bravery of Capitol Police officer Eugene Goodman.

Trump initially watched the assault on TV with glee, feeling happy that "his" people were standing up for him and he might prevail in remaining president.[45] When he was forced to denounce the violence, it was half-hearted, flat, and sounded like a POW reading from a script. Hours later, almost two-thirds of Republicans in the House tried to give the insurrectionists what they wanted and voted to overturn a free and fair election. Some admitted they were afraid to vote to affirm it.[46] However, when given a chance to repudiate violence, and the President who encouraged it, the vast majority of Republican legislators chose instead to reward it.

Readiness to Curtail the Civil Liberties of Opponents, including Media

> *"What makes it possible for a totalitarian or any other dictatorship to rule is that people are not informed; how can you have an opinion if you are not informed? If everybody always lies to you, the consequence is not that you believe the lies, but rather that nobody believes anything any longer. This is because lies, by their very nature, have to be changed, and a lying government has constantly to rewrite its own history. On the receiving end you get not only one lie—a lie which you could go on for the rest of your days—but you get a great number of lies, depending on how the political wind blows. And a people that no longer can believe anything cannot make up its mind. It is deprived not only of its capacity to act but also of its capacity to think and to judge. And with such a people you can then do what you please."*

> Hannah Arendt

Trump repeatedly called for expansion of libel and slander laws against media outlets, while at the same time calling them the "enemy of the people," a phrase with distinctly Nazi and Stalinist histories.[47] While he wanted to broaden libel laws so he could sue news outlets, he was thwarted by the legal system.[48] This didn't stop him from suing *CNN*, *The New York Times*, and the *Washington Post* for libel in a wave of expensive nuisance litigation, hoping that something would stick in the courts he was filling with loyalists.[49]

Trump heavily favored news sources that spoke glowingly of him and his actions, while attempting to punish those who didn't.[50] In 2019, 92 percent of Trump's interviews were on *Fox News*. The White House went nearly a year without holding a formal press conference.[51] When they did, the Trump White House forced the press corps to let in reporters from hyper-conservative, conspiratorial networks like *One America News* during the COVID-19 pandemic to press briefings, even when it wasn't their turn to have a spot.[52] They even issued White House passes to conspiracy blogs like *The Gateway Pundit*, at the expense of actual news outlets.[53] At the same time, the White House attempted to revoke the press credentials of *CNN* reporter Jim Acosta for asking difficult questions during pressers.[54]

When Trump did hold press conferences, there was a distinctly Russian autocratic flavor to them. Vladimir Putin hosts one press conference a year in which he lies, throws out trivial factoids, dodges questions, calls on favorite reporters to throw him softballs, and insults the ones who don't. He treats them the way an indulgent uncle might react to badly behaved, petulant children.[55] Trump's approach to press conferences was broadly similar, as is the point of the exercise; both men are demonstrating who is in charge, not conveying actual information.

At the same time, Trump and the conservative media monoculture worked diligently to demonize protesters, often using misleading information and sources, including video footage of riots that didn't even happen in the U.S.[55] He repeatedly endorsed heavy-handed methods to suppress not only protesters, but political opponents, too. Governors in red states passed slews of laws designed to make it easier to punish peaceful protesters with long, harsh sentences, at the same time making it far easier to get away with murdering them.[57]

Tearing Down the Guardrails

"It's one thing to win a fair game. It is quite another to be able to write the rules of the game—and to write them in ways that enhance one's prospects of winning. And it's even worse if you can choose your own referees…Economists refer to this as regulatory capture."

Joseph Stiglitz

It is not simply enough for a would-be authoritarian to have these leanings. There are concrete actions they must generally take to tear down the guardrails that would otherwise prevent them from seizing the power and authority they need to implement their vision. Their goal: permanent, single party rule under a single, unitary executive branch beholden to no one and nothing, which in turn rules by fiat. These guardrails can be laws or norms. Attorney General Bill Barr had long been a proponent of this idea that presidents can rule by executive order under Article II of the Constitution.[58] Trump, for his part, quickly endorsed the idea that, "I have an Article II, where I have the right to do whatever I want as president."[59] This illustrates how constitutional means can even be used to ensure democracy can quickly fall under the determined onslaught of an authoritarian party in power.

Hard Guardrails

Hard guardrails are the written, legal norms of a democratic society. These usually start with a constitution and are reinforced by the legal system. Many actions of would-be authoritarians are theoretically proscribed by both. Despite the name, these guardrails are incredibly fragile. The 20th and 21st centuries are rife with examples of how theoretically stable democracies, with constitutional and legal systems designed to withstand any foreseeable challenge, fall quickly into despotism. For example, the constitution of the Weimar Republic had been designed by Germany's finest legal minds. There was a longstanding cultural and political tradition of *Rechtsstaat* (rule of law) that many believed would be sufficient to prevent abuse of power. However, the Weimar Republic survived only 51 days after Hitler was sworn into office on January 30, 1933. The passage of the Enabling Act of 1933 granted Hitler unitary power, thereby ending the Republic.

A more modern (and perhaps germane) example is the Philippines. The Philippine constitution was drafted in 1935 and was almost a word-for-word translation of the U.S. Constitution. Its legal system was based on U.S. law as well. However, when President Ferdinand Marcos didn't want to step down after his second term in 1972, he simply declared martial law and assumed autocratic power.

Just because a law exists does not mean that it will be enforced. The Hatch Act supposedly prevents the use of public spaces for political activities. However, because of the blind loyalty of William Barr at the Department of Justice, the law was not enforced during the Trump Administration (at least against Republicans). Trump took the unprecedented step of using the White House to deliver his Republican National Convention acceptance speech from the Oval Office, while the First Lady delivered hers from the Rose Garden. Later, he held campaign rallies on the South Lawn.[60] Internally, Trump's aides scoffed at the law and took pride in violating it publicly. This demonstrates how a law is useless, if the system has been so subverted that the bodies responsible for enforcing it no longer do so, in order to support the party in power.[61]

Additionally, anything is constitutional in the U.S. if the Supreme Court says it is. If Donald Trump decreed that all Muslims were to be rounded up and put in camps as a national security threat, and the Supreme Court said "yes, the President can do this," then it's absolutely constitutional and legal. If an American autocrat personally picked most of the justices on the court based on their loyalty to him, you can see how this quickly goes from a thought exercise to terrifying possibility.

Nothing in the Constitution defines how many justices there should be on the Supreme Court either, which makes it theoretically easy to expand the Court. This is one of the greatest weaknesses in the Constitution. For instance, Republicans in the Senate could vote to end the filibuster and then vote to expand the Supreme Court. A would-be authoritarian could fill those seats with blind loyalists to rubber stamp any decision he makes. At that point, he could rule by fiat with executive orders, with the courts repeatedly confirming his broadened Presidential authority. This is an example of how "hard guardrails" like the Constitution can come down quickly, even in the United States.

Soft Guardrails

Levitsky and Ziblatt identify *mutual toleration* and *institutional forbearance* as the norms most fundamental and critical to a functioning democracy. These "soft guardrails," wherein people of both parties agree to not exploit legal and constitutional loopholes to subvert the democracy and eliminate opposition, are the only thing remaining to prevent a calamity if the "hard guardrails" go down.

Mutual tolerance is "the idea that as long as our rival plays by the same constitutional rules, we accept that we have an equal right to exist, compete for power, and govern."[62] The belief that political opponents are not enemies is a fragile and remarkable concept. It's also one that is effectively dead in America.

As late as 2008, mutual toleration was still something observed within the Republican Party. While on the campaign trail in October 2008, Republican presidential nominee John McCain was confronted by an angry voter who said she couldn't trust (then) Senator Barack Obama. "I can't trust Obama. I have read about him, and he's not, um, he's an Arab," a woman said to McCain at a town hall meeting in Lakeville, Minnesota in October 2008.[63] McCain seized the microphone and cut her off. "No, ma'am. He's a decent family man and citizen that I just happen to have disagreements with on fundamental issues, and that's what the campaign's all about." Just before McCain died in 2019, he left instructions that former Presidents George W. Bush and Barack Obama should deliver eulogies. He also let it be known that President Trump was absolutely not invited.[64]

Today, it's impossible to imagine Donald Trump doing the same for Biden if a Trump voter had said similarly false things about his opponent, especially given how thoroughly Trump demonized them. It's also impossible to imagine other Republican leaders like Senator Josh Hawley, Senator Cotton, Sean Hannity, Tucker Carlson, Matthew Gaetz, or Senate Majority Leader McConnell leaping to Biden's defense. Indeed, doing so would probably be political suicide, earning them the label of RINO (Republican in Name Only) or "squish."

After the 2016 Election, outgoing President Obama issued a statement from the White House stating, "We go forward with a presumption of good faith in our fellow citizens. That presumption of good faith is essential to a vibrant and functioning democracy." However, this hope was entirely misplaced in Trump, the Republican Party, and its base.[65] Trump set himself apart as the first American president dedicated to ending democracy and becoming an autocrat. His base enthusiastically supported the attempt, and the GOP let it happen with their implicit approval.

Institutional forbearance is loosely defined as "avoiding actions that, while respecting the letter of the law, obviously violate the spirit." Here again, Republicans have deliberately fallen off the wagon. In their quest for raw, unfettered political and cultural power, Republicans have deliberately subverted the system in a myriad of ways that diminish the system as a functioning democracy.

Previous chapters have discussed how gerrymandering has become a Supreme Court-sanctioned tool to ensure that state legislatures remain in Republican hands in perpetuity, regardless of how the people as a whole vote. The same is true of voter ID laws, voter roll purges, and other attempts to prevent democratic constituencies from voting. Similarly, Republican legislators in gerrymandered states have deliberately subverted voter ballot initiatives to expand voting rights or end gerrymandering.

The presidential power to pardon or commute sentences is also a powerful tool, and one that the founding fathers recognized as so "broken" that Alexander Hamilton wrote in Federalist 74 that it would "naturally inspire scrupulousness and caution." Hamilton never dreamed that Americans would elect, and Congress would tolerate, a president so venal and corrupt that he would use pardons as a carrot to persuade people to commit crimes for him and then refuse to testify, as Trump did for Roger Stone. Hamilton never imagined it would be used to protect loyalist politicians who committed gross violations of civil rights and defy the U.S. court system[66], or people who commit war crimes against civilians.[67] There was the assumption that Congress would punish a President who was so nakedly partisan and corrupt.

Pardons were meant to be a way for presidents to be a check on judicial abuses or injustices. Trump instead used them as leverage or favors to his loyalists. Overall, Trump offered very few pardons compared to most modern presidents, and most of them went to co-conspirators or right-wing politicians who had fallen afoul of the law.[68] Before he left office, Trump had pardoned or commuted the sentences of Steve Bannon, Roger Stone, Paul Manafort, Duncan Hunter, George Papadopoulos, Michael Flynn, and dozens of others.[69]

In other words, while pardons are constitutional, the way they were used by the Trump Administration undermined democracy. It subverted the independence and power of the judiciary, while shielding the Administration and its cronies from any judicial or legal checks. With the Senate held by Republicans and a two-thirds majority required for conviction during impeachment, it also meant that there were no legislative checks on the executive branch either. Which, in effect, meant no checks at all.

Another prime example of institutional forbearance destroyed by the Trump Administration was nepotism. There's nothing that says you cannot put your completely unqualified (and generally incompetent) son-in-law in charge of the Middle East Peace process and the nation's pandemic response team at the White House, but here we are.[70] There's nothing that says you can't send your completely unqualified daughter to diplomatic events rather than professionals from the State Department, but again, here we are.[72] The reason this hasn't happened before is not because it is illegal, but because everyone assumed no president would be so openly corrupt, or that the Senate would not let such acts stand.

Nor did the founders contemplate a president who would deliberately destroy or subvert government agencies. They might have packed them with party loyalists or relatives in days past, but outright destruction was new. Trump intentionally exploited a loophole in the rules to install his unqualified ideologues as "acting" secretaries of various agencies, thereby bypassing Senate approval.[72] The Senate never confirmed a new secretary of the Department of Homeland Security after Kirstjen Nielsen left on April 19, 2019, because the White House never nominated one. Nor did they anticipate a President installing unqualified ideologues like Ben "Oreos?" Carson, Betsy "Grizzly Bear Attacks" DeVos, or Rick "What does my agency do?" Perry in charge of essential government functions like the country's nuclear weapons stockpile.

Worse, there are people who stand to make a substantial profit from undermining the missions of their own agencies. Before being the head of the Environmental Protection Agency and tearing down laws and policies protecting the environment, Andrew Wheeler was a lobbyist for the coal industry.[73] Between Wheeler, and his predecessor Scott Pruitt, inspections of industrial sites were cut in half, and monetary penalties against offenders dropped by 94 percent. Wheeler also increased allowances for mercury and methane emissions and attempted to strip California of its ability to regulate vehicle emissions.[74] Postmaster General Louis DeJoy, who made a series of catastrophic decisions to undermine his organization, has financial holdings in companies that would make significant amounts of money if the Postal Service was destroyed and its parts sold off.[75]

There used to be a functional Office of Government Ethics (OGE), but it was one of the first organizations Trump destroyed. Walter Shaub, who left the OGE in despair in 2017, summarized why and how the Trump Administration has obliterated norms for ethical governance by abandoning institutional forbearance. According to Shaub, the White House's attitude was:

> "We're going to do the bare minimum of what is legal, and we're going to do things that are questionable, as long as there is an argument that, maybe, it's legal, is completely at odds with the way the program has been run for forty years, because we've all understood that there is a practice and a body of things that you do to make these bare-bones rules work."[76]

The most damaging of all these violations of norms, however, was Mitch McConnell's drive to prevent President Obama from filling the late Antonin Scalia's seat on the Supreme Court with Merrick Garland. There is nothing in the Constitution that says you have to vote on a nominee, or when. McConnell made up a "Calvinball" rule that you can't fill a Supreme Court seat in an election year.[77] Four years later, in 2020, he openly admitted this was a lie when he promised to fill Associate Justice Ruth Bader Ginsburg's seat if she died prior to the election. Or, even if Biden won, he would fill it during the period between the election and the inauguration.[78] He did exactly this by ramming through Amy Coney Barrett's nomination in record time, one week before the 2020 election.

Prior to the fiasco with Merrick Garland, the Senate had long accepted the President's traditional authority to appoint Supreme Court justices, even when they disagreed with them ideologically, so long as they were fully qualified. For example, Antonin Scalia was approved in 1986 by a vote of 98-0. However, McConnell's reversal of his own rule signaled how far Republicans were willing to go to begin the shift to autocracy and single party rule by "capturing the referees" as Levitsy and Ziblatt describe.

Stepping into Competitive Authoritarianism

"We're not above the rules. We're not above the law. That's the essence of our democracy."

Barack Obama, on being an elected official

The goal of modern authoritarian governments is to win an election, and then use this power of government to tilt the playing field such that the opposition has no meaningful chance of ever winning again. Or, to paraphrase *Ender's Game*: "We won the first election. We want to win all the next ones, too."

In 2010, Steven Levitsky and Lucan A. Way described the emergence of a new kind of government in their book, *Competitive Authoritarianism: Hybrid Regimes After the Cold War.*[79] What they observed was neither democratic nor fully authoritarian (or totalitarian), but somewhere in the middle. They named this new phenomenon *competitive authoritarianism*. These types of governments are known by many names—managed democracy, electoral authoritarianism, illiberal democracy, hybrid regimes—but they all describe the same phenomena.

In competitive authoritarianism there are still elections, but the playing field is so heavily tilted that the opposition has almost no chance of winning. There's still a legal system, but court rulings almost invariably favor the ruling party. There is still law, but it is applied unequally to the ruling party and the opposition. There are still protests, but they yield no real political change or results, other than occasional beatings by police and paramilitary groups aligned with the ruling party.

Historian Christopher Browning observed how modern competitive authoritarianism employs economy of effort in doing the absolute minimum to stay in permanent power. He calls it "illiberal democracy," but it is essentially the same thing.

> "Democracy [in the U.S.] is beleaguered. But it is in the form of a new kind of authoritarianism, what I call "illiberal democracy," where the whole system does not need to be changed entirely. You don't need a vast army of secret police. You don't need concentration camps. You don't need to lock up all your opponents. Now, in America or other liberal democracies, if an enemy of democracy or a would-be authoritarian manages to tweak the electoral system, infiltrate and stock the judiciary, control information and pollute the public discourse against truth—using language such as "fake news"—people basically lose faith. The fig leaf of democratic appearance is preserved. Elections are held but the opponents have no chance of winning." [80]

"Free" media still exists under competitive authoritarianism, but it either self-censors to avoid angering the regime or is available only to liberal elites. The rest of the media, available to the masses and the most widely seen, are all effectively controlled by the ruling party.

In the end, it creates a system where the opposition party can run whatever candidates they wish, hold rallies, collect donations, and function almost normally. They can even win seats in the legislative branch, but never enough to actually make anything happen. Alternately, the legislative branch can be so weakened, and the executive branch become so strong, that it hardly matters who wins control of the legislature. Because the ruling party has deliberately weaponized the functions of government against the opposition, opponents will almost certainly never regain sufficient power through elections to effectively oppose or challenge the ruling party.

Nor are these states totalitarian; the average person can criticize the government (if not too loudly). There isn't 24/7 surveillance for thought crimes. There are no gulags for political enemies, though a few top leaders might be imprisoned. The government isn't going to waste effort on the rank-and-file members of the opposition, because they have made protesters powerless to effect change. For most people, living under competitive authoritarianism is boring and stable.[81] This sums up the difference between modern authoritarianism and totalitarianism of the past: There is a certain efficiency to forgoing secret police and gulags when you can just as easily stay in power without them.

Stability has, surprisingly, turned out to be a hallmark of such regimes. Social scientists up until the mid-2000s believed that governments that were neither democratic nor authoritarian (or totalitarian) were weak, and likely to collapse. This may have been true of developing nations during the Cold War but has not been true since. There are now about twenty competitive autocracies that have endured for more than 15 years. Most of these governments are right-wing, religiously conservative, xenophobic, and populist: they tend to frame everything as us vs. them. Immigrants and LGBTQ people, as well as religious, racial and ethnic minorities, tend to be scapegoated for the nation's ills. The government promises to return to a mythic past when these sorts of people, and tolerance of them, were far scarcer. Part of the us vs. them philosophy is a seething hatred of cosmopolitan values. The ideology of many competitive authoritarian states is essentially fascist. Current examples of competitive authoritarian governments include Russia, Turkey, Poland, and Hungary. Brazil and India are well on their way. And so is the United States, even with Trump out of office (more on this later).

According to Levitsky and Ziblatt, the three strategies by which authoritarians seek to take power are: "capturing the referees, sidelining the key players, and re-writing the rules to tilt the playing field against opponents." All three were well underway prior to the 2020 election. They are also likely to continue going forward, as the GOP has worked actively to do many of these things for decades.

Capturing the Referees

> *"My goal is to do everything we can for as long as we can to transform the federal judiciary, because everything else we do is transitory."*

Senator Mitch McConnell

Rarely in recent history are there moments like the "Reichstag Fire," in which politicians use a singular event to rapidly seize absolute power. Rather, modern autocrats tend to tear down the guardrails slowly. Their actions tend to go unnoticed by most. Sometimes the public is willing to accept excuses by the soon-to-be autocrats as to why the changes are necessary (e.g., restricting access to voting is necessary to prevent fraud). Most of the time, the autocratic party has introduced so much *pravda* and *vranyo* that the public has no idea what is real, or what truth is anymore. By the time the guardrails give way entirely, people are numb to the autocrat's violation of norms, hardly anyone notices, and it's too late to stop what's coming.

"Capturing the referees" means subverting systems, individuals, or institutions that would hinder the autocratic attempt. Courts, police, law enforcement agencies, and legislatures can all serve as checks on autocratic power and are thus frequent targets for capture. However, once subverted, either through coercion or packing, these institutions can become a weapon as well. One of Viktor Orbán's first actions upon reclaiming power in 2010 was to pack various legal and oversight offices in the Hungarian government with loyalists and cronies. He also expanded the Constitutional Court from eight to fifteen. Vladimir Putin has forced out any judges on the Russian Constitutional Court who have displeased him or spoken out about the lack of judicial independence. In Poland, when the Law and Justice Party came to power in 2015, they immediately manipulated the system to place five loyalist judges on the fifteen-member Constitutional Tribunal, and imposed a rule that all decisions must have a two-thirds majority to take effect, thereby granting the party veto power over all court decisions.

Similarly, Trump placed the loyal William Barr at the head of the Department of Justice, a man who believed that all power should rest with the executive branch. Barr attracted Trump's attention in June 2018 when he wrote an unsolicited memo to the Department of Justice with the subject line "Mueller's Obstruction Theory." In it, Barr basically argued that the president can do whatever he wants without repercussion.[82] Barr was essentially making the legal case for the concept of *rex non potest peccare* (literally "the king can do no wrong"), which is the basis for crown or sovereign immunity. Thus, he was exactly what Trump was looking for after Jeff Sessions failed to prevent the Mueller investigation—an attorney general who would treat Trump like a God-King and usher in autocratic power.

McConnell did his part, too. He prevented the Merrick Garland appointment and later placed a hard-right loyalist (who was credibly accused by multiple women of being a drunken rapist) on the court.[83] Trump has placed a historic number of judges on the federal bench in his first term, and Mitch McConnell always made it his top priority.[84] They dispensed with the normal American Bar Association process, resulting in a record number of unqualified people being placed on the bench. The goal was an ideologically loyal and pure judiciary, not a competent one.[85]

The Office of Government Ethics was gutted, as were insufficiently loyal attorney general and inspector general offices.[86] The Senate confirmed its blind loyalty during the perfunctory 2019 impeachment trial. Trump used his power to pardon or commute sentences as a carrot to induce witnesses to refuse to testify. The Trump Administration made it clear: crimes committed in the name of the President will not be prosecuted, and if they somehow are, they will be pardoned so long as the President is protected.

In turn, these legal and administrative bodies captured by autocratic attempt can then be used to launch investigations of political enemies, such as the Senate hearings into Hunter Biden at the behest of Trump and Republicans like Senator Lindsey Graham (R-SC) who were trying to curry his favor.[87] The police can turn a blind eye to thugs and paramilitary forces who brutalize or murder protesters. Opposition leaders can be charged on the flimsiest of evidence. Conversely, members of the ruling party are free to flout the law, such as openly violating the Hatch Act without fear of being held to account.

Sidelining Key Players

"If we nominate Trump, we will get destroyed… and we will deserve it"

Lindsey Graham, 2016

Key players that may need to be sidelined include the independent media, opposition political figures, and even figures within one's own party who might offer up resistance. Capturing the referees often makes this easier. Sometimes this sidelining can be through simple bribery, as was used with the porn star Stormy Daniels, whom Trump had sex with. Coercion (support me or I'll support your opponent in the primary) is another technique, as is simple favoritism.

One of the most crucial players in any modern political system is the media. Some autocrats, like Putin and Orbán, responded by using the powers of the state to take over major independent sources of news. Putin did so as early as 2001 and 2002, wresting the influential *ORT*, *NTV* and *TV-6* stations away from oligarchs and into the hands of state-owned companies. He has also used the power of government to revoke licenses of stations that displeased him. Russia is now one of the world's most dangerous places for journalists, who seem to routinely have "accidental" falls out of windows. Russian independent media has been systematically dismantled as a result.[88] Putin has also used libel suits to bankrupt journalists and entire media outlets.[89]

Speech in Russia has been significantly curtailed as well. Libel is now a criminal offense. So is offending anyone's religious sensibilities, making the police an enforcer for the Russian Orthodox Church. As Tim Snyder points out, you can go to jail for a stick figure cartoon of Jesus or playing Pokemon Go in a church.[90] Russia's "no promo homo" laws make any sort of discussion of LGBTQ issues a potentially criminal activity, thus stifling a group who might otherwise dissent. Similar laws remain on the books in the U.S., though they are rarely enforced, but that could change in the future.[91] Hungary's Orbán has similarly absorbed, nationalized, shut down, or constrained independent media into oblivion. Supporters of Orbán have taken control of most Hungarian media outlets.[92] Between the state and supportive oligarchs, 80 percent of Hungary's media outlets have fallen under his control.[93] Additionally, he has weaponized friendly tabloids to smear his political opponents with scandals, both real and imaginary.[94]

As discussed in previous chapters, Trump captured or sidelined the largest media outlets in the U.S. through a variety of means. He controlled *Fox News* by granting them special access to his White House and by threatening to take that access away and give it to rival network *OAN* whenever *Fox* displeased him. Trump-aligned Sinclair media broadcasting, like Orbán's supporters in Hungary, has been buying up local TV stations and filling them with "must run" propaganda pieces.[95] The Trump-appointed head of the Federal Communications Commission changed the rules to allow Sinclair to control more than one station in a given market to facilitate this. At the same time, far-right media content dominates social media, particularly Facebook.[96] The Republican base has also been conditioned to never believe more reliable news sources, dampening whatever effects they might have.

Perhaps the worst example of Trump's love of dictators and hatred of journalists is the murder of Jamal Khashoggi. Khashoggi was a Saudi Arabian resident of the U.S. who wrote for the *Washington Post*. In 2018, he was lured to the Saudi Consulate in Istanbul, where he was immediately killed and dismembered by a team of Saudi agents. According to multiple reports, Saudi Crown Prince Mohammed bin Salman personally ordered the killing. Two years later, Trump bragged to journalist Bob Woodward that he protected Mohammed bin Salman from any sort of repercussions from the incident.[98]

While Trump has threatened to expand libel laws and has filed numerous frivolous lawsuits against media outlets like the *New York Times* and the *Washington Post*, he doesn't need to because his base only believes the media outlets he endorses. At the same time, major media outlets have tried to treat the actions of the Trump Administration as quasi-normal, while shying away from accurate characterization of his words and deeds as "lies," "fascistic," or "autocratic." This has lulled the middle into a false sense of normalcy, while ignoring a GOP and its base that is becoming increasingly radicalized and anti-democratic. When not enough people trust the media, or are so confused as to be unable to know what is true and what is not, the autocrat doesn't actually need to have control of everything. He just needs enough control to paralyze the opposition prior to the autocratic breakthrough.

The other key piece that Trump sidelined was opposition within the Republican Party. It's easy to forget, but when Trump ran in 2015 and 2016, he set off antibodies within the Republican party, some of whose members recognized him for what he was. Lindsey Graham tweeted that the GOP deserved to be destroyed if they nominated Trump and called him a "kook,," "idiot," and "jackass."[99] Marco Rubio called Trump a "con artist" and "an embarrassment." John McCain refused to attend the Republican Convention in 2016 and withdrew his support for Trump before the general election.[100] Ted Cruz remarked, "We're liable to wake up one morning, and Donald, if he were president, would have nuked Denmark."[101]

Trump, for his part, attacked Republican contenders for the nomination in ways that were shocking by American political standards. He accused Ted Cruz's father of conspiring to kill President Kennedy in 1963 and called Cruz's wife "a dog."[102] He said of John McCain, "I prefer people that weren't captured."[103] He referred constantly and insultingly to "Little Marco" Rubio while on the campaign trail.[104] All but McCain would eventually become enthusiastic supporters of Trump regardless of what he did, or the outrages coming out of the White House. They ceased to be a check on any of his impulses. Indeed, if Trump did wake up one morning and "nuke Denmark," it seems likely these Senators would be lining up for interviews on *Fox* to explain why this action was both justified and proportional.

In the end, it didn't matter. Once Trump was president, Republicans either fell in line or left elected office. Senators Jeff Flake (R-AZ) and Bob Corker (R-TN) retired and McCain passed away. Representative Justin Amash (R-MI) left the party and retired. Republican establishment figures put in place to check Trump's worst impulses, like former RNC Chair Reince Priebus as the Chief of Staff, were swept away by loyalists who would simply let Trump be Trump. Tea Partiers like Mark Meadows would go on to encourage some of his worst impulses.[105]

The authors of the Constitution had expected members of the president's party to put country first, and they did so for most of U.S. history. It was arch-conservative Senator Barry Goldwater (R-AZ) who delivered the news to Nixon that there were "ten at most, maybe less" votes to acquit him if Watergate went to trial in the impeachment. In 2020, on the other hand, there were 52 votes to acquit, despite overwhelming evidence of crimes far worse than Nixon's. Trump had co-opted the most crucial players in the game: Republican senators who could vote to convict him of high crimes and misdemeanors.

Nor were Republicans willing to resist Trump's usurpation of Congressional powers. Congress is charged with the powers of the purse by the Constitution. When Richard Nixon tried to "impound" funds allocated to Congress, he was denounced by his party, which voted unanimously to block the action. However, when Trump bypassed Congress by reapportioning Department of Defense money to fund his border wall, only 12 Republicans voted to block him—a mere symbolic action, and far too few to override a veto.[106]

Not that it was a particularly difficult task for Trump to capture Republican Senators. Decades of politics without compromise, labeling Democrats the enemy, conservative media radicalizing the GOP base and spinning them into a state of unreality, made it far too easy. In the end, whether or not they were true believers in Trump, Republican Senators correctly concluded that the white evangelical base was no longer concerned with democracy and entirely concerned with power.

Trump had hand-picked over a quarter of the federal judiciary and a third of the Supreme Court by the 2020 Election. Most government watchdogs such as inspector generals and attorney generals had been similarly corrupted. Government agencies had become instruments of the campaign who twisted reality to reflect whatever the President said, enrich oligarchs, and advance the goals of the religious right over the interests of the rest of the public. Thus, with most of the regulatory bodies captured or destroyed, a Trump re-election in the 2020 election would have been catastrophic. Instead, it left behind a tilted judiciary and a federal government riddled with loyalists.

Re-writing the Rules

"The only permanent rule of Calvinball is that you can't play it the same way twice."

Calvin, of *Calvin and Hobbes*

The basic strategy of competitive authoritarianism is to win once, and then change the rules to ensure you keep winning while keeping up the pretense of democracy. If the opposition looks like it has found a strategy that might threaten their power, competitive authoritarian governments use the power of government to simply change the rules again to reclaim the advantage. Often, these changes are framed as being for the public good.

Viktor Orbán's government in Hungary is one of the best examples of this. In 2010, they legitimately won the election. However, by 2012, internal support for Orbán's Fidesz party fell below 20 percent during an election year, threatening the continuation of their rule. Thus, Fidesz set about to alter the game. They aggressively changed rules for how seats in the legislature were allocated via hyper-partisan gerrymandering. Campaign ads were only allowed to run on public channels, which were run by loyalists. Orbán also had legislation passed that allowed ethnic Hungarians living abroad, who were not actually citizens of Hungary, to vote in the election as well. These ballots were not carefully monitored, and a staggering 95 percent of these sketchy votes went for Orbán.[108] In combination, these actions allowed Fidesz to retain a 66 percent supermajority of seats in the legislature, while winning 44 percent of the vote, much of which came from "near abroad" ballots of dubious authenticity. Observers called the election, "Free, but not fair."[108]

Levitsky and Way set three criteria for elections being unfair:

1. State institutions are widely abused for partisan ends.

2. Incumbents systematically favored at the expense of opposition

3. The opposition's ability to organize and compete in elections is seriously handicapped.

We see all of these in the autocratic attempts in the U.S. today. Chapter 8 on permanent single-party rule by the GOP covers many of the strategies being used by the Republican party to tilt the playing field in their favor. Like Hungary, gerrymandering in states like Wisconsin and North Carolina results in legislatures that look nothing like who the people voted for. In turn, these legislatures enact agendas that are at odds with the wishes of the public.

At the same time, rather than expanding the voter base as Orbán did, Trump and the GOP worked to ensure that as few Democrats as possible could vote. They went so far as to put a Trump loyalist in charge of the Postal Service with the intent of destroying it, because Democrats were about three times as likely as Republicans to vote by mail or absentee ballot in a year marred by the COVID-19 pandemic. Polling places in precincts where Black people vote were dramatically cut, as were the number of hours given to voting.[108] Millions of voters were purged from the rolls, deliberately and disproportionately affecting minorities and poor people.[110] Many of those purges were done so wrongfully: in Georgia alone it is estimated that 200,000 eligible voters were removed.[111] Voter ID laws targeted Blacks and young people, both of which are core Democratic constituencies.[112] At the same time, Senate Majority Leader Mitch McConnell refused to bring the Voting Rights Act up for renewal.[113] While these are somewhat more subtle than the Jim Crow laws that disenfranchised black people, the intent is the same: prevent people that white evangelicals and the GOP dislike from voting to the maximum extent practical.

In recent years, spending on U.S. elections has grown dramatically and tilted sharply against Democrats. The 1976 Supreme Court decision in *Buckley v. Valeo* permitted corporate spending as freedom of speech in elections, and the 2010 decision in *Citizens United* opened the floodgate. Spending on Republican candidates by PACs and Super-PACs doubled between 2010 and 2012.[114] At the same time, the influence of labor unions decreased, as did their spending power in campaigns. The influence of the wealthy increased as well: as few as 25 individuals provide half of all super-PAC money.[115] Scholars who looked at *Citizens United's* effect on American elections concluded it has a significant effect of driving Democrats out of elections and putting more Republicans in office.[116]

One of the lesser known effects of *Citizens United* is that corporations can effectively force employees to use their work hours to support political candidates or causes, such as phone banking. Workers who refuse can be punished. Sixteen percent of workers claim to have seen such retaliation, and nearly half of all managers admit to mobilizing workers on behalf of corporations. Thirty to forty percent of workers report being pressured by their companies to vote a certain way. One study concluded that corporations have become "political machines" who use their workers as a "mercenary grassroots army."[117]

Perhaps nothing exemplified Republican Calvinball more than the replacement of Justice Ruth Bader Ginsburg with hard-line religious conservative Amy Coney Barrett. In 2016, Senate Majority Leader Mitch McConnell had refused to bring Judge Merrick Garland's Supreme Court nomination up for a vote, saying that because it was an election year, voters should decide. At the time Republican senators like Lindsey Graham all lined up and agreed that this was a real rule, and that they would absolutely uphold it if something similar happened in 2020. When it did happen, they quickly reneged, finding various implausible excuses for why this time was different.[118] Which sums up how a broken, captured, system works: "rules and laws for thee, but not for me."

Republicans had been in a war for power for 30 years, and they were preparing to win it once and for all in the 2020 Election. They had captured most of the referees, sidelined anyone that could stop them, and re-written the rules to suit them. All that was left was the autocratic breakthrough.

Little Hope of Meaningful Recovery

> *"Do not go gentle into that good night. Rage, rage against the dying of the light."*
>
> Dylan Thomas

It is one thing to note how the United States appears to be following the template for a slide into autocracy. It is another to quantify it. This has been done by the Varieties of Democracy (V-Dem) Project at the University of Gothenburg in Sweden. This project has 50 social scientists, working with over 3,000 country level subject matter experts to curate and analyze a data set of 470 variables, 82 indices, and five high level indices. These high-level indices are meant to measure the principles of democracy (electoral, liberal, participatory, deliberative, and egalitarian) within a given country.[119]

Their findings are chilling. Democracy is in retreat around the world. For the first time since the project started in 2001, there are more autocracies than democracies in the world. Fifty-four percent of the world's population lives in autocracies. Hungary has become the European Union's first. NATO now has two (Turkey and Hungary). And nowhere else in the world has democracy been falling harder or faster than the United States. Anna Lührmann, the deputy director of the V-Dem Project, called the Republican-led descent into autocracy "certainly the most dramatic shift in an established democracy."[120] Figure 14 shows how far and fast the U.S. has fallen. It adds to the body of evidence that Republicans have drifted toward authoritarianism, while their economic policies were always far to the right. Note that the data only goes up to 2018, and does not represent the events of 2020 in the U.S.

Figure 14. V-Dem Project Data Shows Lack of GOP Commitment to Democracy

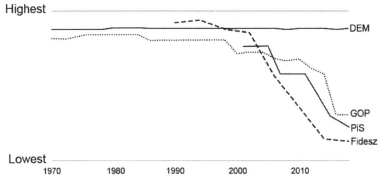

Sources: V-Dem Institute data.[121]

For all the Republican fear mongering that Democrats are radical socialists or communists, the V-Dem data finds the opposite. In its report on democracy in 2020, V-Dem concluded, "Most Democrats also fall to the right of the median party in democracies in this millennium in terms of the role of religion in politics, immigration, and support of state measures to enhance the equal participation of women in the labor market."[122] In other words, the Democratic Party in the U.S. is significantly more conservative than most "liberal" or "center-left" parties in other democratic countries.

Lührmann's analysis of the V-Dem dataset showed the same phenomena observed by Levitsky and Way: when democracies have fallen since the Cold War, it hasn't been because of a violent takeover; rather, "contemporary democracies tend to erode gradually and under legal disguise."[123] Erosion of democratic norms using legal mechanisms means "multi-party regimes slowly become less meaningful in practice making it increasingly difficult to pinpoint the end of democracy."[125] However, it is possible to ascertain in retrospect. One political scientist, when asked if there is a litmus test for democracy, replied, "Yes: the power of elections to remove incumbents. If that's gone, it's not a democracy. It's just not."[125]

Another tantalizing piece of data that points to the U.S. departure from being a democratic republic is its response to COVID-19. *The Economist* compared deaths per capita during epidemics between 1960 and 2020, and compensated for GDP per capita. It found that non-democracies fared significantly more poorly than democracies.[126] During the COVID-19 pandemic, the U.S. response was catastrophically poor and resulted in one of the highest deaths per capita rates in the world, despite its immense overall wealth.

Nancy Bermeo of Oxford University describes three modern ways of ending democracy: promissory coups, executive aggrandizement, and manipulating elections strategically. Promissory coups are where an autocrat seizes power and promises to hold elections "real soon." This isn't particularly applicable to the U.S., other than the use of promises of future elections serving as a socio-political anesthetic.

Executive aggrandizement is the vast expansion of powers for an autocrat using legal means and aided by the courts he put in place to do just this. Bermeo describes executive aggrandizement as:

> "When elected executives weaken checks on executive power one by one, undertaking a series of institutional changes that hamper the power of opposition forces to challenge executive preferences. The disassembling of institutions that might challenge the executive is done through legal channels... Existing courts or legislatures may also be used, in cases where supporters of the executive gain majority control of such bodies. Indeed, the defining feature of executive aggrandizement is that institutional change is either put to some sort of vote or legally decreed by a freely elected official—meaning that the change can be framed as having resulted from a democratic mandate."

Republicans often claim that elections, even ones that are gerrymandered or non-representational of the populace (Senate) give them a legitimate right to take the anti-democratic actions they do. There is little functional difference between the philosophies of "might makes right," "because we can," and "elections have consequences (even if the results are due to gerrymandering and nonproportional representation)." At the same time, we saw the Trump Administration work relentlessly to consolidate power within the executive branch by filling the courts, legislatures, and government agencies with loyalists. Which brings up Bermeo's second modern method of destroying democracy, which sounds suspiciously like both Levitsky and Way's competitive autocracy, and what we saw happening during the 2020 Election. She describes "strategically manipulating elections," as:

> "... a range of actions aimed at tilting the electoral playing field in favor of incumbents. These include hampering media access, using government funds for incumbent campaigns, keeping opposition candidates off the ballot, hampering voter registration, packing electoral commissions, changing electoral rules to favor incumbents, and harassing opponents—but all done in such a way that the elections themselves do not appear fraudulent."[127]

One of the defining characteristics of competitive autocracy is its stability. It is rare for states to come back from autocracy or the brink thereof: V-Dem estimates that only one-in-five democracies as far along the path as the U.S. remain democracies.[128] The other 80 percent fall into autocracy, and there's little hope of recovering via means short of violent revolution, which rarely succeed against a militarized police force willing to kill its way out of the situation.

Concerted public outcry has little effect on these regimes: for example, protesters in Belarus opposed the government after a tainted election for months to little avail. Neither does voting. One of the few cases of people voting their way out of the situation appeared to be Indonesia. The people voted the anti-democratic ruling party and parliament out of office in 2018, but the autocratic government was promptly re-installed by the courts and the monarch in 2020.[129] Similarly, Viktor Orbán's Fidesz party was voted out of office in 2002, only to take power back in 2010, re-write all the rules, and take permanent minority-rule control by the 2012 and 2014 elections.

Figure 15 illustrates the dynamic between Republicans, the religious right, the Supreme Court, and the wealthy. This diagram may be U.S. focused, but the template works just as well when applied to Hungary, Poland, Russia, Turkey, Brazil, and any of the other competitive autocracies with fascist underpinnings. The ruling party, religious conservatives, oligarchs, and the courts establish a self-reinforcing power feedback loop that only grows stronger over time. In other words, as time goes by it becomes harder to sever any one of the links. It also illustrates the dynamic that Tim Snyder's concept of sadopopulism described, wherein religious conservatives get very little back from the oligarchs.

Figure 15. American Competitive Autocracy Feedback Loop

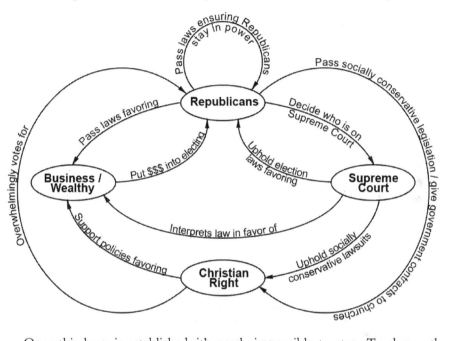

Once this loop is established, it's nearly impossible to stop. To change the court, you have to win elections. But to win elections, you need to first remove Republicans and the courts. To reduce the influence of the ultra-rich in politics, you must affect the other three. The result is a four-way "chicken-or-egg" conundrum that no one has solved to date without a violent revolution like the one seen in Ukraine in 2014.

Peaceful change from within, like Gorbachev's *glasnost* and *perestroika*, is highly improbable for the foreseeable future. Any Republican who looks like a "squish" won't make it through the primary elections. The base itself is self-selecting as well, while Republican politicians are laser focused on targeting their message to the shrinking base that decides their fate. This creates a cycle of Republicans trying to squeeze electoral wins out of a smaller and smaller group of people, resulting in more blatant and autocratic means of winning highly tilted elections.

Republicans have become increasingly reliant on extremely high levels of white evangelical turnout to be competitive in elections. According to a *Washing-*

ton Post exit poll, 28 percent of voters in 2020 identified as white evangelical.[130] This was an increase from 26 percent in 2016, despite the percentage of white evangelicals in the general population continuing to decline. They are nearing a point where it is mathematically impossible to squeeze any more votes out of this core demographic.[131]

Once a party in power loses confidence in its ability to win fair and open contestation and starts down the path of rule-breaking via democratic backsliding, it can be hard to turn back, and the quantitative evidence by V-Dem supports this observation.[132] Unless privileged classes in society "can muster enough votes to stay in the game, they are likely to desert the electoral process in favor of antidemocratic conspiracy and destabilization."[133] In the United States they have clearly done so, with the Republican Party as the vehicle for their ambitions.

Social science tells us exactly how inflammable this mixture is. The Fragile States Index shows the U.S. becoming one of the most fractured and least cohesive developed nations in the world. It is splintered along ethnic, class, racial, and religious lines, as well as escalating in brinkmanship and gridlock between ruling elites. It is also highly fractionalized "between different groups in society—particularly divisions based on social or political characteristics—and their role in access to services or resources and inclusion in the political process."[134]

Peter Turchin of the University of Connecticut has developed mathematical models and indices to reflect internal stressors within countries that could lead to revolution or civil war. The Political Stress Indicator (PSI) takes many factors into consideration, including wage stagnation, national debt, competition between elites, distrust in government, urbanization, and the age structure of the population. They believe the PSI captures how inequality escalates into instability.[135] When they applied this to the U.S. in 2010, they saw that the country was in for a turbulent decade.[136] When they revisited it in 2020, they found that the PSI for the U.S. was higher than it had been in 1860, right before the Civil War started. Decades ago, the Center for Army Analysis (CAA) described the potential for instability and violent conflict in terms of an "oily rag" analogy in their theory for how these events go from a single incident to national implosion:

> "... factors may serve as "oily rags" for a potentially combustible situation. The oilier the rags, the more likely a single spark (i.e., riot, natural disaster, or assassination) could produce an explosive situation. Conversely, the better performing a country is with respect to these factors, the less oily those rags, the more likely it can marshal the will and capacity to withstand a series of sparks or shocks to the system imploding under the weight of the event(s)."[137]

The CAA never expected their theories on failed states, revolution, and civil war to apply here. Yet, heading into the 2020 election, the U.S. had gasoline-soaked rags everywhere. Racism. COVID-19. LGBTQ rights. Women's rights. Police violence. Worsening wealth inequality. Anti-democratic disenfranchisement of minorities who fought for decades against just that. A highly unpopular autocrat elected by a minority of voters, urging his armed followers into the streets. A mis-handled pandemic that had killed hundreds of thousands of people and left even more unemployed. It turned out however that the flash point came not from the left, but from the radicalized, reality deficient members of the autocrat's cult of personality who believed the lies and propaganda. They read between the lines, and attempted to deliver the country to their leader in a coup.

These weren't so much oily rags as they were a warehouse full of sticks of old, sweaty dynamite left precariously on tall shelves in an earthquake zone. The January 6th insurrection showed how close we were to an uncontrolled, high order detonation. Many of these factors are not only still there, but will almost certainly get worse over time. Racism, violence by unaccountable police forces, voter suppression, income inequality, erosion of civil rights, non-democratic representation of the public all remain huge issues that are mostly growing worse. At the same time, the right wing will continue to radicalize under the influence of right-wing media, conspiracy theories, and GOP politicians stoking their fears and egging them on. The courts will keep adding explosives, even after Trump is out of office. Worse, the U.S. system of government makes it nearly impossible to implement solutions to any of these lingering problems.

Eleven

The (Nearly) Inevitable Plunge

"A republic, if you can keep it."
Benjamin Franklin, when asked what sort of government we have

When Joseph Biden won the 2020 presidential election, people celebrated in the streets, not just in the U.S., but all over the world. Fireworks went off in the United Kingdom and church bells rang in France.[1] The widespread celebration assumed that the U.S. was turning away from authoritarianism and returning to democracy and normalcy. However, analysis of the 2020 Election and the conditions that led to the Trump administration reveal that none of the risk factors have gone away. Indeed, most of them will only get worse over the next four years.

There is every reason to believe that the 2020 election only represents a temporary reprieve from competitive autocracy and capitulation to a fascist movement. It's like the pilot of a stricken aircraft who instinctively pulls the nose of the aircraft level, before ultimately losing the fight with physics, whereupon the aircraft stalls and plummets to the earth.

The 2020 Election

"Your bravery and quick thinking have turned a potential Chernobyl into a mere Three-Mile Island. Bravo!"

C. Montgomery Burns

By any standard measure the 2020 Trump campaign was a debacle. It blew through a billion dollars and ran out of money to advertise in key states down the stretch.[2] Campaign manager Brad Parscale got demoted and was then arrested for domestic violence.[3] The arrest was caught on tape: a crying, shirtless, and suicidal Parscale, armed and inebriated, was tackled and stuffed into the back of a police cruiser. He was suspected of skimming heavily from the campaign to fund his purchases of multi-million-dollar homes, boats, and sports cars.[4]

Thus, it was no wonder that campaign messaging was a shambolic mess. Trump described Biden in ridiculously apocalyptic terms usually reserved for describing the actions of newly installed communist dictators. According to Trump, Biden would abolish the suburbs, guns, religion, the police, ICE, cash bail, and even Christmas.[5] This fear-mongering about the suburbs was a tactical recognition that more highly educated and diverse suburbs had swung against Republicans during the 2018 mid-term elections, and Biden appeared to hold a lead in them again.[6] The GOP never had a platform outside of "do whatever Trump wants," and Trump never articulated any sort of plan for a second term other than "keep doing what we're doing."[7] Trump refused to agree to honor the results of the election.[8] He also repeatedly claimed (without justification) that the 2020 election would be riddled with fraud by undocumented immigrants and mail-in ballots.[9] Nor would he commit to a smooth transition of power.[10]

COVID-19 loomed over the election as one of the most important issues for Democrats and Independents, and the Trump White House continued to make a dog's dinner of the situation.[11] While states were trying to make it easier for people to vote absentee or by mail during the pandemic, the Post Master Louis DeJoy was working to destroy the organization he was responsible for in order to help the President's election odds. Hundreds of mail sorting machines were scrapped right before the election.[12] During the election, the USPS lost track of hundreds of thousands of ballots.[13] When a federal court ordered a sweep of locations for the missing ballots, DeJoy's lawyers refused to comply.[14]

Throughout the summer, the White House continued to downplay COVID-19. This came back to bite them. The Rose Garden ceremony honoring Supreme Court nominee Amy Coney Barrett turned into a super-spreader event at which most of the guests did not wear masks or attempt to socially distance.[15] The President, first lady, former New Jersey Governor Chris Christie, former top Trump aide Kellyanne Conway, Republican Senators Thom Tillis of North Carolina and Mike Lee of Utah, University of Notre Dame President John Jenkins, and two White House journalists (among others) became infected with the virus. Afterward, the White House refused to contact trace those in attendance.[16]

Trump did exactly as he promised to do in the aftermath of the election. He filed lawsuits, claimed election fraud, and had his conservative media mouthpieces call for state legislatures to overturn the election and send Trump-supporting slates of electors. Republican legislatures in the key swing states of Michigan, Wisconsin, and Pennsylvania did their part by refusing to allow mail-in and absentee ballots to be counted before the day of the election, resulting in a drawn-out counting process that produced a "red mirage" and a "blue shift."[17] In-person votes on the day of the election leaned towards Trump, but Biden slowly caught up as blue leaning absentee votes were counted in the days that followed. Trump and his election team had wanted this in the first place; they seized upon it to claim fraud by Democrats.[18]

Legally, their claims were laughable: Judges consistently threw out their claims or remained highly dubious given the utter lack of evidence.[19] However, the chaos was entirely expected and intentional: Even before the election, both Democrats and Republicans believed the election was likely to be rigged.[20] This tactic served as a "doomsday device," designed to de-legitimize Biden's administration from the start should he win, and allowing Republicans like Mitch McConnell to obstruct the new administration.

The primary focus of GOP attempts to throw ballots out was directed at areas with large numbers of Black people, such as Detroit, Philadelphia, and Atlanta. The success of the GOP hinged on the centuries-old playbook of disenfranchising Blacks, just as the Democrats did in the South in the 1870's.[21] As time went by and the lawsuits failed, Trump shifted focus to cajoling Republicans in gerrymandered swing states to either elect a different slate of electors, or to fail to certify the election in order to throw the decision to the U.S. House of Representatives, where Trump would presumably win based on the arcane voting rules there.[22]

Still, as the weeks went by after the election and no evidence of fraud emerged, the campaign refused to concede.[23] Trump kept furiously tweeting about how he would win, and remain President. However, as Latin American authoritarianism expert Federico Finchelstein noted, when a leader refuses to leave office, it's still a soft coup. Even if it was a stupid and clumsy attempt, this was still an attempt to tear down the democratic process.[24] Most of the GOP center tacitly accepted the soft coup attempt with its messaging of "count every legal vote," implying that there was fraud, and many of the ballots cast for Biden were cast illegally.[25] Others, such as Florida Governor Ron DeSantis, went even further, supporting Trump's efforts to get legislators to overturn the election.[26] Lindsey Graham pressured Georgia Secretary of State Brad Raffensperger (a fellow Republican) to throw out all the ballots in counties where there was a higher than average mismatch rate. When Raffensperger refused, he and his wife were inundated with death threats.[27]

The Republican National Committee wholeheartedly embraced the baseless Trump narrative of fraud, tweeting "we will not be intimidated... we are going to clean this mess up now. President Trump won by a landslide. We are going to prove it. And we are going to reclaim the United States of America for the people who vote for freedom."[28] Only "squish" Senators like Mitt Romney, Lisa Murkowski and Susan Collins accepted the results and congratulated Biden.[29] They did so long after most world leaders had already done the same, including America's closest allies in NATO.[30] The only world leaders who pointedly refused to congratulate Biden after the election were dictators and autocrats such as Vladimir Putin, Kim Jong Un, Jair Bolsonaro (Brazil), and far-right Prime Minister Janez Jansa (Slovenia).[31]

This illustrated that even if the coup was laughably bad, much of the GOP would let it happen if it benefited them. When the coup attempt turned violent, and nearly succeeded in decapitating the legislative branch of the government, Republicans still accepted no responsibility. Mere hours after insurrectionists, acting on Trump's order to march on the U.S. Capitol, almost succeeded in kidnapping and killing the Vice President and members of Congress, nearly two-thirds of House Republicans voted to overturn the election on the basis of nothing other than a naked desire for power.[32]

A smaller number would resist a full turn towards autocracy. The rest, like Ron DeSantis, would pursue it aggressively. Republican legislators in four key swing states rebuffed these attempts at a "harder" coup.[33] Perhaps they realized that it was going to be a tough sell in the courts.[34] Or, just as likely, they realized a naked attempt to steal the election would touch off violence after an otherwise (until January 6th) peaceful and obviously fraud free election.

The 2020 election showed that the GOP was more than willing to tacitly endorse lies and conspiracy theories to appease Trump and their base.[35] When 18 states and 126 Republican members of the House sued to overturn the election results in Michigan, Georgia, Wisconsin, and Pennsylvania, it showed that GOP leadership in most red states, and 64% of GOP representatives, would happily disenfranchise most of the country for their own benefit, and install an autocracy made possible by judges they had picked.[36]

Regardless, this exposed the GOP's opportunistic approach to authoritarianism: they aren't willing to force the issue, but they're willing to help it along when the opportunity arises. This is not unlike the relationship between the conservative but traditional German National People's Party (DNVP) and the Nazis (NSDAP) in the Weimar Republic; the DNVP wasn't willing to seize power itself, but it intentionally paved the way for NSDAP and the autocracy it was clearly bringing.

Yet, despite the blundering, the 235,000 COVID-19 deaths by election day 2020, the lying, and the lack of vision other than continuing to give over half the country the middle finger, Trump's campaign nearly won.[37] If not for extremely narrow margins in Wisconsin, Arizona, and Georgia, he would have had a second term. He remained extremely popular with the base, resulting in turnout not seen in a century. Republicans emerged with almost all the other big prizes. The GOP made big gains in the House, and Republicans almost retained a Senate majority, hanging on to seats that appeared to be lost in Maine and North Carolina. They gained in state legislatures, ensuring that the 2021 redistricting will overwhelmingly favor Republicans, resulting in another decade of single party rule (regardless of who people vote for) in 40% of U.S. states.[38] Republicans won almost every election where redistricting was at stake.[39] It's also highly likely that the GOP will re-take the House and Senate in 2022.[40]

Republicans have almost everything they need to complete their next autocratic attempt. At the end of the 2020 Election, all of the factors that led to the Trump Presidency were still in place: a deadlocked Senate unwilling to thwart corruption and autocratic attempts, a conspiracy-obsessed base that relies on white evangelicals, weakened democratic guardrails, destroyed institutional norms, rightwing media feeding misinformation to a credulous audience, and a court now tilted sharply to the right after the confirmation of Associate Justice Amy Coney Barrett. Even as a few key Republican leaders abandoned Trump to his electoral defeat, they had emerged from his Presidency with a blueprint for success. Next time, they would be far more likely to succeed, with even less effort. The GOP has the ideology, road map, and infrastructure they need to finish an authoritarian attempt. The 2020 Election was a narrow rejection of Trump, but not Trumpism. The conclusion was clear; in order to win permanent control of the U.S., they won't need to change anything.

The GOP Can't (and Won't) Change

"If we are to have another contest in the near future of our national existence, I predict that the dividing line will not be Mason and Dixon's but between patriotism and intelligence on the one side, and superstition, ambition and ignorance on the other."

Ulysses S. Grant.

After the 2020 Election the nation was in terrible shape. Institutions had been degraded, COVID cases were soaring, unemployment was high, and the U.S. Capitol was filled with 26,000 National Guard troops after a failed coup attempt by Trump loyalists.[41] Most of the time, when a party loses a presidential election, it causes them to reflect and potentially change course in order to alter the outcome of the next election. A normal party's leadership would take the loss in 2020 and, coupled with four years of Trump-induced chaos, engage in self-examination with resolve to change. Realistically, however, Republicans will only double down on the strategies and rhetoric of the Trump era, along with no apologetics for what happened.

For Republicans, the answer is to change nothing. Despite Trump's incompetence, odious personality, intellectual shortcomings, lack of impulse control, and general unsuitability for the job, he nearly won. He outperformed the polls, as did Congressional Republicans. The election results showed many voters picking Republicans in House and Senate races, while voting against Trump.[42] Given the popularity of most of Trump's positions with Republicans, this was a vindication of Trumpism.[43]

Trump ran campaigns in both 2016 and 2020 that were never meant to make the Republican tent bigger.[44] His acts as President were never intended to widen the base. Instead, they were, as Lindsey Graham said, meant to win with old angry white guys. In order to make GOP power durable with this strategy, anti-democratic actions became a standing requirement. Irish writer Fintan O'Toole observed from across the Atlantic, "The Electoral College, the massive imbalance in representation in the Senate, the ability to gerrymander congressional districts, voter suppression, and the politicization of the Supreme Court—these methods for imposing on the majority the will of the minority have always been available. Trump transformed them from tactical tools to permanent, strategic necessities."[45]

It is likely that if not for the COVID pandemic, Trump would have easily cruised to a victory. Back in February, before the impact of the pandemic sank in, betting markets believed the President was well on his way to a second term in an election they believed would look much like 2016.[46] In other words, if not for a *virus ex machina*, Trump would probably have cruised to an additional four, or more, years in office.[47]

Because of regional polarization, the Electoral College, and "wasted votes," the Presidential election ended up looking a lot closer than it really was.[48] In 1988, Bush won the election by 7.8 points and received 426 Electoral College votes. In 1996, incumbent President Bill Clinton won the national vote by 8.5 points and received 379 Electoral College votes. In 2008, Senator Barack Obama won by 8.5 points and received 365 Electoral College votes. Biden won the national vote by almost 4.5 percent but received only 306.

In 2020 the Electoral College conferred a 3.5 percentage-point advantage to Republicans. This meant that the tipping point state in the election (Wisconsin) was 3.5 points more Republican than the national vote. This was a historic level of bias towards the GOP, unseen since Truman defeated Dewey in 1948. There every indication is that it will continue to grow in 2024 as northern states with large white populations tilt further right, with the tipping point state potentially being as much as 4.5 percent to 5% further to the right than the nation as a whole.[49]

GOP strategists believe that few, if any, changes are needed for a GOP candidate with the same basic views and messages as Trump to win the next time around.[50] Simply flip a couple of swing states that aren't in the middle of a pandemic, and they're back in the White House. This isn't to say Trump is their guy next time around, but that his bellicose brand of anti-immigrant nationalism, mixed with a steady stream of Orwellian lies, is effective in getting out the votes they need to win. Given how Republican Senate candidates outperformed Trump in 2020, the implication is clear: even if they don't replace Trump on the ticket, they're still likely to win.[51]

Even if that analysis of voter sentiment was incorrect, GOP hardliners and party leaders couldn't change if they wanted to. Donald Trump is like Frankenstein's Monster: The Republican party created it by cultivating a base that is utterly divorced from reality, and eventually, it broke free and ran amok.[52] The Republican National Convention had no way of steering their base or reining it in. Outlets like *Fox News, OAN, Newsmax,* and *Breitbart* have a business model of outrage-driven agitprop designed to continually stir up fear, outrage, and distrust of establishment Republicans.[53] Any Republican perceived as betraying Trump was likely to be ridden out on a rail, which helped explain why the wide majority of Republicans in the House went along with the farcical claim that fraud determined the outcome of the 2020 Presidential election.[54]

Worse, candidates who embraced the QAnon conspiracy theory earned their first two seats in Congress.[55] Republican leadership was slowly learning that tolerating these theories was good for their bottom line. QAnon and other conspiracy theories give believers a sense of purpose and are a powerful draw to the polls. At the same time, any Republican politician who spoke out against the nonsense was likely to lose in the primaries.[56] Even though QAnon appeared to be imploding after the election, there was every reason to believe that the GOP faithful would simply move on to another conspiracy theory that was just as crazy, dangerous, and anti-democratic.

Moderate Republicans are abandoning the party. Gallup polling found that the GOP is hemorrhaging people who identify as Republican, increasing to a historically high gap of 11 points.[57] What is left are the true believers who support Trump, and everything he stands for, no matter what. Ultimately, these are the people who will decide the direction of the party. This base is overwhelmingly rural, white, and evangelical (or hardline Catholic), and becoming more so. They categorically reject that racism is a real problem. They don't want a pluralistic society. They want to draw a hard line on undocumented immigrants brought to the U.S. as children. They're hold-outs who still want a win in the culture war over same-sex weddings and "Happy Holidays" greetings. They are terrified of an America that looks less like them and furious at the people they blame for it. Right-wing media and the GOP will continue to exploit these fears, grievances, and sense of victimization.

Conversely, if you try to map out a way to make the GOP more moderate by taking it back to what it was only 10 - 20 years ago, it rapidly becomes apparent that there is no plausible path. It doesn't matter if the RNC wants to make the party bigger; the current base will continue to vote for people who absolutely do not. Former RNC Chairs Michael Steele and Reince Priebus both realized this after they tried to make the tent bigger, and were exiled to the political equivalent of Siberia for their transgression.[58] George W. Bush ran as the conservative alternative to McCain in 2000, and now he and his entire family are considered much too liberal.[59]

The 2020 Republican Party platform was identical to the ultra-conservative 2016 platform, complete with constitutional amendments banning gay marriage, criminalizing abortion and supporting "conversion therapy" for LGBTQ youth.[60] There is no coming groundswell of moderates to take the party back; Trump's support was consistently in the high 80's and low 90's with self-identified Republicans.[61] The 2024 nominee will almost assuredly reflect the desires of the Trumpist base.

There's no serious discussion that the GOP might embrace moderate governors like Larry Hogan (R-MD) or Charlie Baker (R-MA) to represent the party in 2024. The most often mentioned names for 2024 are Mike Pence, Ted Cruz, Ambassador Nikki Haley, Senator Josh Hawley (R-MO) and Senator Tom Cotton.[62] Haley, while sometimes pragmatic, has been a staunch defender of Trump and called him "truthful." Cotton and Hawley, however, represent a smarter, more disciplined extension of Trump's brand of politics, described as "Trumpism without Trump."[63]

Another name that has been bandied about is Tucker Carlson, arguably the most popular Trumpism cheerleader at *Fox News*. He disliked Trump's lack of discipline but loved the race baiting and culture warrior policies of the Administration.[64] Steve Schmidt, one of the founding members of the Lincoln Project for anti-Trump Republicans, specifically called out why Carlson should be considered the leader. "Look, we have almost 48 percent of this country that's voted for a statist, authoritarian movement with fascistic markers that's hostile to American democracy, to the rule of law—that venerates an individual, that's a cult of personality. I think that Tucker Carlson is the frontrunner for the Republican nomination in 2024."[65]

Hawley, Cotton and Carlson all are what the Republican base wants: white evangelical culture warriors who use racial dog whistles and grievances to exploit "us vs. them" right-wing populism while promoting further degradation of democratic norms. Let us not forget, Sen. Cotton penned a *New York Times* op-ed urging Trump to declare martial law during the Black Lives Matter protests of 2020.[66] Cotton's vision for America nearly came true under Trump when the president considered invoking the Insurrection Act.[67] We saw Federal agents in military camouflage roaming the streets of America, scooping up protesters into unmarked vehicles without charge or due process, and beating up unresisting protesters.[68] Hawley, in particular, supported the Trumpists who stormed the Capitol with the intent of decapitating (perhaps literally) the U.S. government.[69]

Despite this, Hawley, Cotton and Carlson are all likely to be the future of the GOP. They will be following the same path towards democratic decline, but with more capable, competent, and terrifying leadership at the focal point of the next autocratic attempt. The only reason the courts didn't save Trump was because his case was so bad. There was no evidence of systemic fraud. If the election had been closer, we might not have been so lucky. This is why it might appear that institutions saved us. But that is only true in the short run; after the next four years, in the long run, they may prove to be our doom.

Betrayed by Our Institutions

"The Mice once called a meeting to decide on a plan to free themselves of their enemy, the Cat. At least they wished to find some way of knowing when she was coming, so they might have time to run away. Indeed, something had to be done, for they lived in such constant fear of her claws that they hardly dared stir from their dens by night or day.

Many plans were discussed, but none of them was thought good enough. At last a very young Mouse got up and said:

"I have a plan that seems very simple, but I know it will be successful. All we have to do is to hang a bell about the Cat's neck. When we hear the bell ringing, we will know immediately that our enemy is coming."

All the Mice were much surprised that they had not thought of such a plan before.

245

But in the midst of the rejoicing over their good fortune, an old Mouse arose and said:

"I will say that the plan of the young Mouse is very good. But let me ask one question: Who will bell the Cat?"

Moral: It is one thing to say that something should be done, but quite a different matter to do it."

Aesop's Fables for Children

Much like the mice in this ancient fable who knew that they needed to have warning when the cat was around, plenty of academics, scholars, and even a few politicians have identified the structural problems underlying the causes of democratic decline in the U.S. Rather than a feline murder machine, the problems here have to do with racism, undemocratic processes, predetermined election results, single party control at the state and federal levels, stacked courts, wealth inequality, a right-wing media monoculture ungrounded in reality, and a fundamentalist political base with a fascist belief system.

Like the mice, the same scholars identifying the problems have come up with several potential solutions, none of which is remotely feasible. In most cases, the root causes of the problems are intentional features, not unintentional bugs. Rather than assess the plethora of proposed solutions based on effectiveness, it is more useful to ask a series of questions to rule out whether or not potential solutions could actually happen. If a law, executive order, or constitutional amendment addressing one of the issues is submitted, one should ask:

1. Does Republican leadership support the solution?

2. If not, do Democrats control the trifecta of the House, Senate, and Presidency?

3. If you do have all three, will you have to overcome a filibuster for laws to pass?

4. Does it require a super-majority of state legislatures to support it?

5. Will the 6-3 Supreme court overturn it?

Figure 16. Why Proposed Solutions Fail

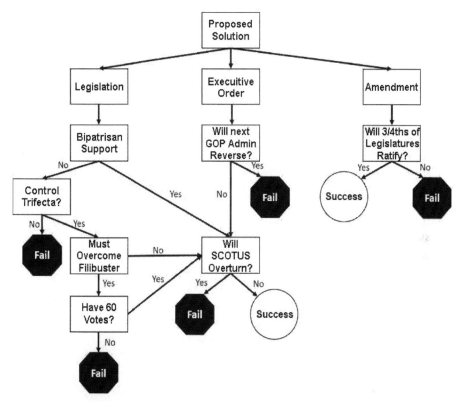

For the necessary changes to happen, potential solutions must run a harrowing gauntlet. Figure 15 (above/below) illustrates the near impossible path any proposed solutions would have to follow. This process is baked into the Constitution, and making necessary change possible requires altering the system itself. Republicans will never agree to this, given how heavily the system is stacked in their favor. From their perspective, why change the rules when they're doing so well?

Republicans, who control two-thirds of state legislatures and the Senate, will never do anything to reduce their own power in legislative bodies. This imbalance in state legislatures rules out any solutions that require constitutional amendments. The GOP will never do anything to reduce wealth inequality by slowing the flow of money to corporations and the wealthy. They will never make laws or policies that make voting easier; instead, their own self-interest dictates that, as demographic shifts make it harder and harder for them to win the popular vote, they must limit votes and gerrymander districts to guarantee a permanent Republican majority in order to succeed.

Thus, constitutional amendments are not realistic. Nor is federal legislation that cuts into the power of the GOP, cultural conservatives, or the wealthy. They are all non-starters as long as Democrats do not control the trifecta of House, Senate, and Executive Branch. Making this even more unlikely is that controlling the trifecta is becoming harder and harder for Democrats. Not because their ideas are unpopular, but because of non-proportional representation. As described elsewhere, the Senate is disproportionate at a level unseen in any other democratic society. After successive D+2.5, D+8, and D+4.5 elections, Democrats held the same number of seats as Republicans in 2021, while representing 20 million more people.

Even the Presidency is becoming increasingly out of reach to Democrats due to the Electoral College, despite Democrats winning the popular vote in seven out of the last eight election cycles. The tipping point state in the 2020 Presidential election was five points more rightward leaning than the national average, higher than any time in U.S. history. Redistricting in 2021 means that it will likely be closer to 6 or 7 points in 2024.[70] Thus, the Electoral College map is growing increasingly stacked against Democrats, even as demographics move away from the GOP.

If Democrats do beat the odds and control the trifecta, as they did at the start of the Biden Administration, they're unlikely to overcome the filibuster. Achieving a filibuster-proof majority for Democrats would require winning nationally by 15 or more points several cycles in a row. Perversely, Democrats like Biden and Sanders have been unwilling to commit to ending the filibuster, which might even be wise; given how stacked the electoral map is against Democrats, they are going to be the minority party in the Senate most of the time, despite their candidates receiving far more votes.

The wealthy and corporations will almost always act in their own self-interest, as well. They will always push for lower taxes on themselves. They will always push for laws that hold down wages and take power away from workers. They are more than happy to promote the narrative that wealth is a sign of virtuousness, and that raising taxes means stealing from the worthy. Electing Republicans and conservative judges is good for their bottom line.

The Christian Right has made the Republican party their home. They believe that electing Republicans is part of a religious holy war against the forces of darkness: feminists, Black Lives Matter, immigrants, LGBTQ people, Planned Parenthood, "cultural Marxists," etc. In order to achieve their goals, they have to vote Republican in large numbers. They would never support any sort of action that diminishes the value of their vote. They have made a host of things "religious," from guns to the top marginal tax rate. They occupy the top tier of American social strata and will never endanger it.

Executive orders suffer numerous deficiencies as a remedy. First, they can only change policy, not law. Nor can they overrule the courts, move federal dollars around in significant amounts, or contradict the law. They are temporary remedies scoped by the boundaries of Presidential power and vulnerable to the next administration's whims. They can also be overturned by the courts. As such, they lack the power to address the over-arching problems causing democratic decline.

Which brings us to the courts. The six conservatives on the Supreme Court were put there specifically by Republicans to favor businesses, uphold laws and policies that tilt elections in favor of Republicans, ban abortion, gut civil rights laws, create a "religious right to discriminate," and uphold government handouts to churches. Assuming for one moment that a conservative Supreme Court will help with the problems facing this country (wealth inequality, influence of money on politics, diminished civil rights for everyone but the Christian Right, and rigged elections, etc.) is simply foolish. These Justices were recommended by the Federalist Society specifically because they already knew how each of these justices would vote on these issues *a priori*. It's like betting against a pair of heavily weighted dice.

As witnessed in the case of *Fulton v. City of Philadelphia,* the Supreme Court seemed content to take the U.S. backwards 70 years to separate but equal, where it wasn't really discrimination to refuse service to LGBTQ people if some other business was available. It's much like saying that Woolworth's lunch counter doesn't really harm black people by refusing to serve them if there's somewhere else in the city that will sell them food. Again, to Adam Serwer's point: We are heading back to the 1890's, with justice in—and only in—the abstract.

Nor can Democrats alter the composition of the court without controlling the White House and the Senate. The only solution to make the court less anti-democratic is to expand it, and that can only happen if Democrats have the resolve to do so, which appears extremely unlikely. Nor will the courts become more democratic over time. Given that the Senate is in near-permanent Republican control, very few Democratic judicial nominees will ever make it through, even when the President is a Democrat. When a Republican is president there will almost always be a torrent of ideologues flowing into the courts, who will only make American democratic decline worse.

The solutions offered to counter the slide into competitive authoritarianism fall into four broad categories: changes to congressional procedures, making elections more democratic, reducing economic inequality, and taking money out of politics

Each of these has reasons why they will never likely happen, would have minimal effect, or potentially make things even worse by accelerating the slide into autocratic oblivion. Senate Republicans have no intention of making rules less friendly to themselves. The GOP will never support renewing the Voting Rights Act or the For the People Act to expand voting rights, limit partisan gerrymandering, strengthen ethics rules, and limit the influence of private donor money in politics. Republicans at the state level hold most state legislatures and would never vote to make Senate representation more proportional. They will never support enfranchising Puerto Rico or Washington, D.C. as states. They will never support raising taxes on the wealthy or eliminating corporate loopholes. They will never support efforts to limit carbon emissions or fight climate change. They will never support legislation guaranteeing rights for women or LGBTQ people.

The result of these is a one-way ratchet for American democracy. The system is now built such that we are much more likely to become less democratic over time, not more so. Sometimes the anti-democratic movement can slow down or stop, such as under a Biden Administration. Democrats will pull back in the direction of democracy, but the system will not move in that direction without destroying the mechanisms (i.e. constitutional governance) themselves. Conversely, when pulled in the opposite direction towards autocracy, the system moves with little resistance.

The question is, what can be done to avoid the end of American democracy? The good news is that are a few things we can do to avoid the worst cases here. The bad news is that this path is so narrow that the odds of pulling it off are almost nil.

Figure 17. One-Way Ratchet

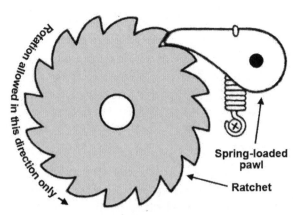

What Can Be Done

"I've been screaming, 'We need to become a big-tent party!' for some time. But I think they misunderstood me and thought I meant 'carnival tent.' Something that used to be called the Grand Old Party now stands for 'Grandpa's on Peyote.'"

Denver Riggleman, former Republican State Representative in Virginia

The American system of politics and government may be stacked towards democratic decline, and there's likely very little about it we can do directly. However, the Biden Administration has two primary tools in its limited arsenal to dissuade future autocratic attempts: passing laws that strengthen democracy, and prosecuting members of the Trump Administration for crimes while in office.

The Biden Administration, and control of the Senate on Vice-President Kamala Harris tiebreaker vote, provide an opportunity for Democrats to move legislation to the floor. Some of the legislation passed by the House during the 116th Congress would take key steps toward preserving democracy and de-radicalizing the Republican Party.

The For the People Act (HR 1) would expand voter registration and voting access, limit removing voters from voter rolls, and provide for states to establish independent, nonpartisan redistricting commissions, among other provisions supporting improved election security.[71] The John Lewis Voting Rights Advancement Act (HR 4) restores the provisions of the original Voting Rights Act of 1965, and helps ensure future conservative courts will not strike it down (as John Roberts' court did to the original VRA).[72] The Protecting Our Democracy Act (HR 8363) is aimed at preventing some of the abuses of the Trump Administration from happening again by limiting pardons, defining emoluments, preventing the President from directing funds by fiat, protecting the independence of government watchdogs, and strengthening other fundamental guardrails against kleptocracy, corruption, and autocracy.[73] The Election Security Act of 2019 (H.R. 2660) would provide additional funds and legal support for ensuring that elections are not tampered with, either by foreign or domestic agencies.[74]

These bills, taken together, would address some of the worst aspects of democratic decline in the U.S., particularly gerrymandering and voter suppression aimed at minorities. They would force Republicans to move toward the center in order to win elections, rather than catering to a base that demands theocratic autocracy. Republicans would be in a better position to ignore people that had grown too radicalized and delusional to allow for competent governance. These bills could be at least a partial solution to nearly everything described in this book.

And, as General Yeager once said to me, "if a frog had wings, he wouldn't bump his butt when he hopped."

Unless Senator Chuck Schumer (D-NY) pulls off some parliamentary magic and ties these bills to budgetary measures (allowing them to pass with a simple majority through reconciliation), they're going to require a filibuster-proof majority. Alternately, the Senate will have to strike down the filibuster, which is highly unlikely. Conservative Senators like Joe Manchin (D-WV), Krysten Sinema (D-AZ), and Jon Tester (D-MT) has already indicated they won't support ending it.[75]

Alternately, Democrats could try to rally support from ten Republicans on these bills. That seems highly unlikely to happen, given that these bills would strip the GOP of most of the institutional advantages allowing them to win elections with a shrinking minority of the population. Thus, any Biden Administration efforts to fix the worst problems facing American Democracy appear doomed to failure. The structural bias of the Senate ensures that Democratic senators will never be able to muster the necessary 60 votes to address gerrymandering and voter suppression, and in those few instances where they have a small majority, they are afraid to do the things necessary to prevent further, inevitable democratic decline.

This leaves aggressive legal action as the only credible deterrent to further attempts at insurrection and autocracy. Prosecution of Trump, his family, and assorted cronies would be a credible deterrent to further autocratic attempts, given how much Trump seems to fear it. Late Friday night on June 19, 2020, Trump and Attorney General William Barr signaled that this was their worst-case scenario by attempting to sack the man responsible for investigating Trump, his family and the Trump Organization.[76] First, Barr announced that Manhattan U.S. Attorney Geoffrey Berman had resigned. Then, Berman announced he wasn't resigning, and that only the President could fire him.[77] Trump declared that he wasn't involved, leaving Barr holding the bag.[78] While former Bush speechwriter David Frum wryly noted that this display of incompetence was "like the Saturday Night Massacre, only nobody checked whether the intended murder weapons were in fact loaded," the intent was far more worrying.[79]

Fortunately, Trump and Barr's hand-picked (read: loyal and inexperienced) replacement would not be confirmed by the Senate.[80] This particular guardrail of democracy held, if just barely. If Berman was in a red state, his replacement would likely have been confirmed by the Senate due to the arcane "blue slip" tradition, which is not an actual law.[81]

The message was clear, however: The Trump Administration was absolutely terrified of being prosecuted after leaving office, to the point of attempting to commit a second Saturday Night Massacre. Between the Mueller Report, the impeachment, and evading the release of tax returns (which turned out to be pretty dodgy anyway when released by *The New York Times*), there is ample evidence to suggest criminal activity has taken place.[82] Eight Trump associates have already been found guilty of crimes, and 29 foreign entities indicted as a result of the Mueller investigation.[83] Former Trump White House National Security Advisor John Bolton's book claims that Trump also solicited help from China in his 2020 re-election campaign.[84]

The question remains whether we should prioritize pursuing criminal investigations. Such a priority might seem hypocritical at first glance; it does not seem to fit with Biden's calls for national unity. Chants of, "Lock her up," about Hillary Clinton were a staple at Trump rallies, and he has been obsessed with having her prosecuted.[85] These calls were widely derided by both the left, and moderate Republicans, as disturbing.[86] Prosecuting and jailing previous administrations, and political opponents, is the sort of thing one expects of autocratic regimes and corrupt developing-world governments.

Given Trump's habit of projecting his own insecurities onto others, however, it provides further evidence that prosecution after leaving office is his greatest fear.[87] Additionally, the analogy between Clinton and Nixon falls apart quickly. Clinton was investigated thoroughly twice by the FBI, which declined to press charges.[88] The White House pushed hard to have her investigated again, but a 2018 internal review by the Department of Justice found that any irregularities in the investigation were insufficient to reopen the case.[89] Trump, however, has continued to call for prosecution of Clinton and pushed Barr to indict President Obama and Vice President Biden, too.[90] This attempted abuse of Presidential power was nothing new to the Trump Administration; indeed, the impeachment revolved around attempting to leverage a manufactured foreign investigation into Biden for political advantage in the 2020 election.

What is forgotten, because it happened before many Americans today were born, is that presiding administrations have prosecuted members of the previous administration for attempting to destroy democratic norms. Prosecution is also the correct response to autocratic attempts and coups. The Obama Administration was remarkably corruption-free by modern standards.[91] The Nixon Administration, however, was corrupt, and is a far more apt analogy. It is easy to forget that 69 government officials were charged as part of Watergate and 48 were convicted. It is also worth noting that Nixon's Attorney General Richard Kleindienst and former Attorney General John Mitchell both did time in jail for their roles in Watergate.

While Gerald Ford pardoned Nixon in the name of "healing," it was a deeply unpopular move, and Ford lost the 1976 Election to Jimmy Carter in great part due to this decision. Indeed, Carter ran on the tag line, "I will never lie to you," along with the promise of a transparent, ethical administration.[92] America wanted previous administrations to be held accountable, because they instinctively realized that unaccountable, imperial presidencies breed corruption that is inherently corrosive to the Republic. The situation for American democracy today is far more dire than it was under Nixon. In 1974, the guardrails of democracy held firm. Senate Republicans were going to vote to convict Nixon, and it was Barry Goldwater, along with Republicans John Rhodes and Hugh Scott, who delivered the news.[93]

In 2020, the guardrails of democracy were almost completely down. Trump has repeatedly done far worse than Nixon's "third rate burglary" by soliciting aid from foreign powers, including adversaries like Russia and reportedly China, as well as Ukraine. He also incited an insurrection that nearly overthrew the government. His Administration has repeatedly attempted to obstruct justice by pushing law enforcement agencies to drop investigations of his people, attempting to replace the people responsible for such investigations with cronies, and pushing the legal concept of a unitary executive branch that is immune from oversight or investigation, even by Congress.[94] Yet, Senate Republicans have made it clear they will never hold a Republican administration accountable regardless of the crime or evidence.

This doesn't even begin to cover the appearances of corruption and conflicts of interest. The Saudi Arabian government rented huge blocks of the Trump Hotel in Washington, D.C. in what appears to be an attempt to curry favor with the Administration.[95] Ivanka Trump was granted numerous trademarks in China, just days before Trump reversed U.S. sanctions on the Chinese telecom comny ZTE.[96] The Administration has also put a staggering number of lobbyists in the federal government, many of whom are now in positions to grant favors to industries and companies for which they recently lobbied.[97] One public citizen's group has documented more than 3,400 conflicts of interest.[98] The appearances of rampant, uninvestigated corruption have led observers to question whether the Constitution can handle an Administration so dedicated to tearing down the systems meant to prevent it.[99] Short answer: no.

Which is why, if evidence warrants it, thorough criminal investigations of the Trump Administration are necessary to the survival of the U.S. as a democracy in 2021 and beyond. For democratic governments to function, they require legitimacy and the trust of the public. The Trump Administration has eroded that trust, and the George Floyd protests were a symptom of the lack of trust that the government will actually move against entrenched conservative interests, such as the police, no matter how egregious their actions are. The same applies to both attempts to convict Trump during impeachment. The appearance of unfettered corruption, conflicts of interest, and complete immunity from legal consequences degrade the institutions necessary to a functioning society.

The Trump Administration and Republican Party have systematically torn down checks and balances. At the same time, they are immunizing themselves from prosecution by packing the judicial system and attempting to create a unitary executive branch via rulings by these courts. Democratic norms in the Senate have fallen completely under the leadership of Mitch McConnell. Other norms and guardrails are following, and when they do it is nearly impossible to restore them. If the Trump Administration is let off the hook it essentially guarantees that future administrations will feel free to further break the system leading to accelerated democratic decline and corruption.

Ensuring that administrations are not exempt from the rule of law, including the president, should not be a partisan issue. When you leave the door open to kleptocracy and the autocratic impulses of a supremely powerful executive branch, we can end up with a Hugo Chavez instead of a Vladimir Putin or Viktor Orbán. However, in the United States, we are far more prone to right-wing authoritarianism than left-wing overreach, as studies have shown that cultural conservatives are much more likely to hold autocratic beliefs here.[100]

Historically, there is grave danger in letting off people who attempt a coup off too easily. The failure of the Union to hold Confederates accountable for the Civil War and slavery led directly to the failure of Reconstruction, Jim Crow, and mass lynching. When Hitler's Beer Hall Putcsh failed in 1923, he spent his 9 months in prison writing *Mein Kampf*, and developing a plan to take Germany through political means. Conversely, the Nuremberg Trials and Denazification are hailed as some of the reasons why modern Germany has become one of the west's staunchest opponents of right-wing populism and a defender of democracy in general.[101]

Thus, the danger of Trump winning re-election, or someone worse than him, is real. The primary reason why Trump's Administration was not been more effective at destroying all checks and balances was the sheer incompetence of the administration itself.[102] The next authoritarian-leaning administration will do so far more quickly and effectively. That is, as long as they're certain that there isn't an 8' x 8' room waiting for them if they get caught, where they'll have to fight other former Trump officials for the bottom bunk.

Other countries watching the United States can clearly see what's happening. If Trump's Administration escapes scrutiny, and it becomes apparent that the Biden Administration is just the eye of the hurricane before another corrupt regime takes over again, who will want to work with us? The U.S. has already lost the trust of the world. Without taking criminal investigative measures to ensure this doesn't happen again, it will be even more difficult to begin winning it back.[103] Thus, the success of Biden's foreign policy attempts to repair U.S. standing in the world will be contingent on rooting out and prosecuting the illegal acts of the previous administration.

Letting members of the Trump Administration who have committed real crimes walk will not heal the country. The U.S. let the Confederacy walk and is still paying for it. Investigations should not be done out of animus, but to ensure that the law is applied equally and fairly. The U.S. cannot allow control of the executive branch to become an infinite pile of "get out of jail free" cards. If Biden does not use the legal system as it was intended, the U.S. will be right back at this moment in a few years. A Democratic administration has a duty to the Republic to take the measures necessary to avoid this.

What Comes Next

> *"This is the most important thing to understand about the postmortem Republican Party. The logic is not that a permanently minority party may move toward authoritarianism but that it must."*
>
> Fintan O'Toole

With Biden winning the presidency, and only 50 seats in the Senate, there are a number of "most-likely" projections on what the first term of the Biden Administration will look like, along with where the GOP, media, and courts will go as well.

Biden Administration

The Biden Administration will likely look like a repeat of Obama's second term: gridlock, with a Senate dedicated to preventing movement of any agenda or legislation, no matter how popular it is with the public. This is especially true if Democrats lose control of either the House or the Senate in 2022. As a result, Biden will attempt to run the country via executive order, as both Trump and Obama did, but for different reasons.[104] Republicans will take many of these executive orders to court, and it's likely they will shoot some of them down. Additionally, Mitch McConnell will stonewall almost all of Biden's judicial nominees throughout his term, in the hopes of continuing to fill the court with the backlog in 2025 under a new Republican administration. On the way out, Trump stacked long-term Pentagon and DOD positions[105] with completely unqualified but loyal appointees who made it a point to "start too many national security fires for Biden to put out" such that the new administration would be flailing from day one.[106]

At the same time, Trump's accusations of a fraudulent election have become part of the GOP tribal epistemology, much the way birtherism did during Obama's presidency.[107] Polling data shows that Trump, the GOP, and conservative media very effectively killed off Republican voters' faith in the democratic process in 2020.[108] The result is another president who is seen as illegitimate by the Republican base, which GOP leaders will use as justification to oppose any and all actions by the Biden Administration, regardless of their merits or popularity with the public as a whole.

The pandemic will subside by late 2021 as vaccines become widely available, and Biden will get some credit. However, the suffering will be immense. Biden said in remarks after the inauguration that he expected the death toll to rise above 500,000 Americans before this is over. Without control of the White House, Republicans will suddenly rediscover fiscal restraint, and try to prevent the sorts of stimulus bills necessary to keep Americans afloat through another long, awful, lethal year.

Biden's inability to move legislation due to conservative Democratic qualms about ending the filibuster, and the history of the President's party losing midterms, means Democrats are likely to lose the House and Senate in 2022, thereby ending any Biden legislative agenda. There's a belief that Biden, who will be 81 in 2024, will not run for a second term. Vice President Kamala Harris will be the presumptive Democratic nominee. This isn't necessarily a good thing: She polled worse versus both Trump and Pence than Biden did during the 2020 election cycle.[109] Republicans will be going all out to stop her: By 2028 the President (whoever they are) will have likely replaced Justices Breyer and Thomas, and perhaps one more.

Trump

"That was some weird shit"

George W. Bush, on Trump's Inauguration address

Predicting exactly what the notoriously erratic Trump will do, and what will happen to him, is difficult. Assuming he does not end up in prison quickly, or abscond to a country without an extradition treaty, Trump will be Trump. He's going to look to continue doing rallies and appearing on conservative media to spread conspiracy theories and pound away on the notion that the 2020 election was rigged or stolen.

His financial future looks grim. The COVID-19 pandemic has caused deep economic pain throughout his real estate empire, which is centered on the hospitality industry.[110] Simultaneously, creditors appear to be preparing to call in the hundreds of millions of dollars in debt Trump owes them. Trump has about a billion dollars in debt.[111] Deutsche Bank wants to cut ties with him and may try to collect on the $340 million USD Trump owes them. If he's unable or unwilling to pay, they will attempt to seize his assets.[112] There's also multiple reports that charges are waiting for him in the Southern District of New York, and in the State of New York, the moment he leaves office.[113]

There has been talk, including by Trump himself, that he may try to create a new network called Trump TV.[114] This seems unlikely to succeed. Trump's history of business failures revolving around selling a mediocre product at a high mark-up because his name is on it dates back decades, from Trump Airlines to Trump University. Second, the market for reality-challenged ultra-right-wing networks is already filled by bargain-bin *Fox News* knock-offs such as *OAN* and *Newsmax*.

Given how many bridges Trump has burned, and that behind the scenes Republicans and members of the media recognize how unhinged he is, Trump might follow a trajectory similar to Sarah Palin: an embarrassing flame-out that most establishment figures would like to forget the existence of as quickly as possible.[115] However, that seems unlikely. The cult-like support for him from the white evangelical GOP base means that he is more likely to remain relevant and have the potential to veto any new direction from the party. The exceptionally high turn out by both Democrats and Republicans in the 2020 Election didn't just indicate how disliked Trump was by the left, but also how effective he was at getting out the GOP base.

He has indicated he is interested in running again in 2024.[116] It would prove to be hugely disruptive for the Republican Party, even if it tries to move on from him.[117] As long as Trump is expressing interest in running again, it freezes the Republican field.[118] He would be the presumptive favorite in the primaries, and Republicans would be unlikely to run against him.[119] The Trump family intends to exert influence over the Republican Party for years to come, and many "Trumpy" politicians, such as Senators Tom Cotton and Josh Hawley, will likely wait to see what he does before deciding whether or not to run in 2024 themselves. Regardless, the GOP looks to remain the party of Trump for the foreseeable future, until he is no longer capable of calling the shots.

Regardless, it seems unlikely he will go quietly into the sunset. He craves the attention, and his sense of showmanship means he will continue to steer the public spotlight onto himself in whatever ways he can. All the polling data shows that the vast majority of Republican voters want Trump to remain the head of the Party, and the face of their movement.

Trumpism

"You know, the very powerful and the very stupid have one thing in common: they don't alter their views to fit the facts; they alter the facts to fit their views."

Doctor Who

While Trump may be out of office, Trumpism will remain. It was a dominant part of the American political scene, as was the Tea Party before Trump ran for President, and will likely only grow stronger over time. Trumpism is the purest distillation of the id of the GOP base that is still fighting the Civil War, not to mention *Roe v. Wade* and *Obergefell*.

Trump's defeat left behind an enthusiastic, reality-challenged base that believed the election had been stolen. Their values, rooted in racism and Christian nationalism, are unlikely to ever change. This is especially true in an environment where there is a smorgasbord of media and social network options built specifically to cater to their fears, hunches, and penchant for buying into conspiracies hook, line, and sinker. For instance, almost seven in ten white evangelicals believed that the Capitol insurrection was actually a false flag operation by BLM and Antifa to frame Trump supporters. Seventy percent also believe that BLM is a greater threat to the U.S. than the coup that nearly succeeded.[120]

The fascist aspects of it will remain as well. The polarization between rural and urban continues to grow, feeding the narrative of "us vs. them."[121] They still pine for a single leader. The shift of minority men towards Trump was a frightening display of how effective he was at leveraging gender norms and sexual anxiety.[122] He also used claims that Biden was a "socialist" or "communist sympathizer" to score cheap points with immigrants whose countries of origin had despotic left-wing populist leaders.[123]

Regardless of what happens to Trump and his family, he is leaving behind a large, energized, radicalized, fascist movement ungrounded by reality that is filled with true believers. There is no reason to believe this will dissipate. It may shift and change, as the Moral Majority became the Christian Coalition became the Tea Party became Trumpism, but the same people with the same, or worse, beliefs will remain. Much more likely is that the next aspiring authoritarian will simply pick them up like a $100 bill forgotten on a sidewalk...or an AR-15 left on a playground.

The Media

"If we do not have the capacity to distinguish what's true from what's false, then by definition the marketplace of ideas doesn't work. And by definition our democracy doesn't work."

Barack Obama

The final gasps of the Trump Administration after the election were all rooted in creating the narrative that the election was rigged, and widespread voter fraud was prevalent. Never mind the contradiction that somehow Democrats were able to rig the presidential election, but lost seats in the House and only took the Senate because of Vice President Harris' tiebreaker vote and the narrow wins in the Georgia special elections. The "firehose of falsehood" method of propaganda doesn't need to be consistent. It simply needs to create doubt. Which is exactly what it achieved here: 70% of Republicans came away from 2020 with the belief that the election was neither free nor fair.[124]

Fox News attempted to keep a toe-hold on reality when their elections desk first called Arizona for Biden, then the election five days later.[125] They began cutting off press conferences filled with lies and innuendo.[126] Some *Fox* hosts began pushing back on the unreality being created by the White House and its surrogates.[127] The White House was furious, and there were signs that the Trump faithful had begun to turn on the network.[128] After the election, it became clear that the network had paid a heavy price in ratings for even the most feeble attempts at reality, and quickly moved to provide less factual content, and more galaxy-brain editorial content.[129]

This may signal a new paradigm, and resultant shift, in both commercial and social right-wing media. Many die-hard Trump voters were enraged at this seeming betrayal by the network they trusted.[130] If *Fox News* viewership begins to collapse as a result of being told the truth, *Fox* will eventually decide that lies are far more profitable, and that truths that do not benefit Trump, the GOP, or its base being told by any part of the organization are money losers. It's not hard to figure out what decision they will make.

There are already marketplace alternatives that are less grounded in reality, such as *OAN* and *Newsmax*. People gravitate towards what they want to hear, and shy away from what they do not. Karl Rove, Steve Bannon, and other conservative operatives have clearly stated their goal of creating their own reality for their base. The base, for their part, has clearly shown that they would rather consume falsehoods, agitprop, conspiracies, and innuendo that reinforce their world view rather than gain a clearer understanding of what is actually happening. Conspiracy theories online are rapidly picked up by unscrupulous conservative media outlets, which amplify them, uncritically treat them as fact, and turn them into gospel for Republican politicians.

After four years of Trump, most media outlets still haven't figured out how to cover a fascist movement and an attempted autocratic breakthrough. When Trump's lawyers attempted to prevent Pennsylvania from seating electors in the hopes of throwing the Presidential decision to the House, it was an attempt to overturn a lawful election and create a system where Democrats would never win the White House again. Most media refused to call it an attempted coup, in part because it was so unlikely to succeed. They didn't want to sound extreme or alarmist.

However, legally and logically this makes no sense. If someone were to stick their finger in their jacket pocket, pretend it was a gun, walk into a bank, and demand all the money, it is still an attempted bank robbery regardless of whether the gun was real or the robbery doomed to failure from the start. They individual would also still be going to jail. Regardless, right-wing media will continue to grow more unhinged as it gives its audience what it wants. Centrist media will be unlikely to call the next autocratic attempt out explicitly for what it is. Nor will they be willing to discuss the chilling and dangerous historical roots of the ideology driving the movement that backs the next aspiring autocrat. There will be the assumption that the U.S. has rejected autocracy for good, and that the next Republican president cannot be an autocrat or a fascist because he sounds a little more like a politician. Or, they will simply treat Trump's next run as the new normal.

In this regard, the mainstream media has learned nothing from the last four years.

The Republican Party

"I cannot recognize the verdict of guilty. It was my misfortune to become entangled in these atrocities. But these misdeeds did not happen according to my wishes... At that time obedience was demanded, just as in the future it will also be demanded of the subordinate."

Adolph Eichmann, on following orders at his war crimes trial in 1961

"What he said was always the same, expressed in the same words. The longer one listened to him, the more obvious it became that his inability to speak was closely connected with an inability to think, namely, to think from the standpoint of somebody else. No communication was possible with him, not because he lied but because

261

he was surrounded by the most reliable of all safeguards against the words and the presence of others, and hence against reality as such."

Hannah Arendt, on Eichmann's performance at trial

The GOP became the party of Trump because it's what the base wanted. Most were unwilling to contradict Trump's claims of massive voter fraud and a rigged election.[131] They refused to acknowledge Biden as the winner, even after the election had been called by all the major news outlets, and congratulatory calls from foreign allies like the U.K., France, and Germany rolled in. Trump, for his part, was furious that the party didn't go "all in" on stealing the election with Electoral College shenanigans at the state legislature level.[132] Overall, it sent a message that while the GOP wouldn't organizationally make blatant and sudden attempts at autocratic breakthrough, they were more than willing to entertain them.

A few GOP leaders like Senator Marco Rubio (R-FL) called for a bigger tent and a more populist economic message after the 2020 Election.[133] The former is not particularly credible. Trump won in 2016 with just the base, and he came very close again in 2020. If not for narrow losses in Arizona, Georgia and Wisconsin, Trump would have had a second consecutive term. The real lesson of the 2020 Election for the GOP is that you can win with the base as long as you broadcast the more fascist bits with a dog whistle, rather than a bullhorn.

The GOP goes into the 2020s in exactly the position authoritarians would want to be in. The courts are stacked in their favor. Senate elections are stacked heavily in their favor. They control about 40 percent of state legislatures permanently via gerrymandering. They have near permanent control of the Senate. They have a media battlespace that keeps the base fearful, angry, and energized. The Biden Administration is likely to be nothing more than what the military calls an "operational pause" for Republicans. This means that they're not continuing to advance, but they are building forces, spares, fuel, and munitions for the next offensive. Right-wing parties in Europe have shown that it is not just possible, but relatively easy to turn democracy into autocracy through completely legal means on the second try.

Trump illustrated that such attempts in the U.S. can eventually succeed, given time. He showed that courts can be filled with partisans and ideologues. So can government positions, many of which function as watchdogs or checks against corrupt administrations. Norms can be broken, and there are no real consequences for a corrupt administration that breaks laws and democracy itself. A lack of dedication to democracy and democratic processes is an advantage that they have no intention of surrendering. It's also unlikely that the next autocrat will be nearly as incompetent as Trump. If he had handled COVID-19 just poorly (instead of disastrously), he likely would have won the 2020 Election. Even a small shift towards competence will probably be enough to ensure the next one succeeds where Trump did not.

It requires almost no effort for Republicans to win in the long run. They just need to keep doing what they're doing now. The courts, non-proportional representation, voter suppression and gerrymandering will do the rest. Conversely, for Democrats to prevent this, they will have to mount a Herculean effort that requires several miracles along the way to even have a chance of succeeding. The odds eventually catch up with everyone. In the long run, the house always wins, and the GOP holds all the Trump cards. They will continue down the path carved out by Trump and his followers. Fifty-seven percent of Republicans and Republican leading independents want the GOP to follow Trump's lead, even after the assault on the Capitol.[134] Nearly seven in ten Republicans believe Trump is better in touch with the GOP base than Republicans in Congress.[135] After decades of telling themselves that power is worth any price, and that they are on the side of God, Republicans cannot ignore what their base demands.

In the end, Republican leadership will inevitably turn their brains off, just follow orders, and hope that justice never finds them.

The Courts

> *"In the opinion of the court, the legislation and histories of the times, and the language used in the Declaration of Independence, show, that neither the class of persons who had been imported as slaves, nor their descendants, whether they had become free or not, were then acknowledged as a part of the people, nor intended to be included in the general words used in that memorable instrument... They had for more than a century before been regarded as beings of an inferior order, and altogether unfit to associate with the white race, either in social or political relations; and so far inferior, that they had no rights which the white man was bound to respect; and that the negro might justly and lawfully be reduced to slavery for his benefit."*

> Chief Justice William B. Taney's Opinion in *Dred Scott v. Sanford*

Only days after the election, Associate Justice Samuel Alito delivered a scathing speech to the Federalist Society. It was remarkable for how political it was, and that it clearly signaled that he was ready to rule on issues based on ideology rather than the facts of the case.[136] His tone was angry and aggrieved, seeing religious conservatives as the clear victims of women and LGBTQ people. He also railed against government officials who attempted to limit the spread of COVID-19 by limiting assemblies of people, including that of churches. Four other members of the Court belong to the Federalist Society as well: Kavanaugh, Coney-Barrett, Gorsuch, and Thomas.

Looking forward, it seems clear that we are headed to the end of *Roe v. Wade*; the court appears poised to whittle it down to a right that people have in theory, but not in practice. It will rule that most gun laws are unconstitutional, ushering in a bizarre era of open and concealed carry permissiveness. A religious right to discriminate will make most civil rights laws a moot point, given it was religion that was behind the discrimination that spurred the passage of the Civil Rights Act and the Voting Rights Act.

Prisoners, LGBTQ people, women and racial minorities will all suffer as the courts set much higher bars for proving discrimination, even when not religiously motivated, that are nearly impossible to meet. Efforts to disenfranchise voters by Republicans will become ever more blatant. Police will be further empowered to use violence and "hunches" to harass, intimidate and kill Black people. State laws that criminalize protests and allow the murder of peaceful protesters are likely to be upheld.[137] Religious employers, now exempt from labor laws under the ministerial exception, will grow more and more blatant in their abuses. Corporate interests will prosper, while employees will have fewer and fewer rights and protections in practice.

By the time the next autocrat comes to power, U.S. law will have shifted sufficiently to allow passage of laws mirroring those in Poland, Hungary, and Russia. The U.S. legal system is poised to grant expansive new powers to the executive branch the next time a conservative holds the White House. Laws against discussing LGBTQ issues, bans on health care for trans youth, laws against insulting religion, bans on recognizing transgender identities, and undermining marriage equality are all where this is going. Unions will continue their decline as the courts empower employers and government to bust them. Legal precedent will continue to evolve during Biden's time as president, mostly in directions that make suppressing minorities easier and protecting democracy harder.

By the time the next Republican assumes control of the White House, it will be much easier to retain permanent control as a result of the court's rulings on voting rights. At the same time, much of the culture war may already have been won at the state level via bills targeting women's health, LGBTQ people, worker's rights, and voting. The GOP will just finish the job at the federal level with the court's pre-approved case-law blessing. It's also likely that conservative Supreme Court decisions will contribute to the implosion of the Union, just as the Dred Scott decision made the Civil War inevitable.

The End of America Is Coming

"It is possible to commit no mistakes and still lose. That is not a weakness; that is life."

Jean Luc Picard

In 2019, at the International Society of Political Psychology's annual meeting in Lisbon, esteemed political psychologist Dr. Shawn Rosenberg made a shocking statement to the organization during his remarks: Democracy is devouring itself and is doomed. This set off ripples through the room and the academic community. But the facts that he observed were inescapable.

Right-wing populists are ascendant. The traditional influences that had kept the "whackadoodles" in check have been either undermined as authority figures or co-opted by the right-wing populists themselves. This includes the courts, the Republican Party, journalists, scientists, and government administrators. Rational political and policy discourse has become impossible under a deluge of misinformation and conspiracy theories engulfing the GOP base and the American public as a whole. Bereft of direction by experts and reliable information, people making political decisions on their own will inexorably drift to the simplistic solutions offered by the far-right world-wide: authoritarianism, xenophobia, homophobia, and racism. Right-wing populists no longer see intrinsic value in democracy, only in winning the war.[138] Rosenberg concluded, "In well-established democracies like the United States, democratic governance will continue its inexorable decline and will eventually fail."[139]

Rosenberg's analysis broadly confirms the trajectory seen in this book. Someday, probably in 2024, maybe in 2028, the U.S. will elect its next aspiring autocrat that has tapped into the Trumpist brand of fascism while the GOP provides cover for his actions. Maybe Trump comes back. Maybe it's Cotton. Maybe Hawley. Maybe Carlson. Maybe one of Trump's offspring. Maybe someone we don't see coming. But GOP presidential candidates for the foreseeable future will be cut from the same cloth as Trump and pander to his base. It doesn't really matter who: The GOP has a blueprint for building the autocracy they want, the votes to start the project, the judges to uphold voter suppression and disenfranchisement, and the anti-democratic party with which to finish it.

Whoever comes along will be more likely to succeed, even as they tear democracy down in broad daylight. Right-wing media sources will ensure the base is 100 percent on board, while traditional media will be even more flummoxed than they were under Trump, given that this new guy looks and sounds not just vaguely sane, but presidential in some conventional sense. The results will be the

265

same as any other culturally conservative authoritarian government; but this time it will be quieter, more organized, and less messy. He will use the ultra-conservative judiciary he's given, the compliant GOP-controlled Senate, and his attorney general to capture the remaining referees, quickly and quietly sideline anyone who can impede his progress, and then tilt the field so heavily that losing becomes a virtual impossibility.

It's likely to happen quickly after another Republican comes to power. Orbán was only out of power for eight years between 2002 and 2010. When he came back into office in 2010 it only took two years to rig the game so thoroughly that the Fidesz party could never lose again. Thus, once the country has gone that far, there's really only two likely paths.

The first is the road taken by most countries that fall into competitive authoritarianism: initial protests, followed by a slow descent into "boring and stable" life where meaningless elections are still held, political change is impossible, and almost everyone accepts this is just the way it is and nothing really can be done.[140] The Russian maxim, "Today is an average day; worse than yesterday, but better than tomorrow," captures this descent into hopeless apathy. Or, from Georgian autocrat Eduard Shevardnadze's perspective on what happens after rigged or stolen elections: "They will make a fuss for a few days, and then they will calm down and life will go on as usual."[141]

Since the end of the Cold War, there have been only a handful of nations that have escaped competitive autocracy, and none of them are as far down the road as we will be. This represents an event horizon for American democracy: Once we get that deep into the gravity well of autocracy, all the energy and matter in the universe isn't enough to escape.

The alternative is to stop trying to violate the metaphorical laws of physics and start thinking *sideways*. Masha Gessen, a Russian expatriot, published their rules for surviving autocracy immediately after the 2016 election.[142] The first three can be summed up as: "believe the autocrat, don't be taken in by small signs of normalcy, and your institutions will not save you." We have failed at all three. Democrats were not willing to call Trump an autocrat or his movement fascist, even when he and his cabal told us who they were and what they intended to do. Democratic leadership still isn't willing to call out the GOP and the Trumpist base for what they really are. Like the proverbial slowly boiled frog, Americans got used to the lying, graft, incompetence and destruction of norms to the point where killing over 235,000 Americans only cost him a couple of points in the polls. Our institutions were never going to save us, and now they have been so subverted that they are more likely to doom us, consigning us to perpetual single party rule instead.

Thus, if we reach a point where we cannot hope to effect change at the federal level, stop pouring money and effort into it. A Kabuki dance of performative democracy, in a country that clearly isn't one anymore, actively serves the interests of the autocrat and his party by providing a veneer of legitimacy. Much like the laws of thermodynamics, politics in competitive authoritarianism are governed by three rules:

There is a game.

You can't win.

You can't break even.

The first three will be true for Democrats at the federal level in a competitive autocracy. There is an additional, informal fourth rule: you can't quit the game. But in politics, unlike thermodynamics, you can effectively quit the game when it's been rigged, and the consequences of continuing to play (and inevitably losing) are your people being brutalized and humiliated. The trick is to make state-level Democratic politicians and the public see this clearly.

Going back to the black hole analogy, nothing can escape one once it goes past the event horizon. But, over time, black holes lose mass as particles near the event horizon are ripped apart. The "positive" particles are imbued with energy to become Hawking radiation, and the negative particles end up on the wrong side of the horizon. Over time, black holes emitting this radiation bleed off their mass in the form of energy and "evaporate." The metaphorical lesson here is that the only way not to get sucked into the black hole forever is to tear yourself apart and allow the negative part to be pulled in. Similarly, the only way not to be sucked down into an autocratic state from which there is no escape is to split and sacrifice the negative parts to the pull which they helped create.

Republicans quit playing the democracy game long ago. It works to their advantage when they're playing Calvinball, and Democrats are still playing by the Marquess of Queensberry rules. Democratic governors and legislatures need to recognize that they have the power to pick up their ball and go home.

This isn't to say secession, but there is a modern history of autonomous zones for marginalized groups that do not recognize the legitimacy of the government claiming sovereignty over them. Usually, the governments are autocratic and would do horrible things to the people of these regions if they were able. Examples of this include the autonomous Kurdish regions in Iraq, and the Republic of Taiwan. Even Scotland looks like it is leaving the U.K. over some of the same issues separating red and blue states.[143] Neither the Kurds nor Taiwanese formally claim to be separate nations, in order to stave off invasion and civil war, but at the same time, the governments of Iraq and the People's Republic of China hold no functional power there.

This may be the only way for places like California, Oregon and Washington to prevent the brutal crackdown on protesters and degradation of civil rights that would come with a fascist autocrat taking permanent control or federal attempts to override state sovereignty. We could see red states attempting to extradite and imprison doctors who perform abortions in blue states, leading to another Dred Scott-like decision at the Supreme Court. Trump and the GOP made it clear that it was acceptable for their autocrat to harm or kill people living in blue states, unless their governors bend the knee and kiss the ring.[144] They also made it clear they were willing to go along with violent insurrectionists attempting to overthrow the democratically elected government of the U.S. An autocratic and Machiavellian White House, and by extension its federal government, has little interest in stopping paramilitary groups which terrorize Democratic politicians who don't "respect" the leader.

In a strange way, the U.S. has been in almost exactly this position before. As Ronald Brownstein pointed out in *The Atlantic*:

> "These same flammable ingredients were present in the 1850s, when a rising majority found it impossible to impose its agenda because of all the structural obstacles laid down by the retreating minority. As the decade proceeded, it became more and more clear that the newly formed Republican Party, dedicated to barring the spread of slavery to the territories, constituted an emerging national majority. It was centered on the northern states, which by 1860 would represent 60 percent of America's population, including 70 percent of its white population. In their writings and speeches, southerners were acutely conscious of their status as a national minority. Yet for decades they successfully maneuvered to block restrictions on slavery through their powerful position in the Senate and their influence over pro-slavery Democratic presidents. That allowed them not only to suppress most legislative threats, but also to establish a friendly majority on the Supreme Court. In the 1857 Dred Scott decision, the Supreme Court, with seven of its nine justices appointed by earlier pro-South Democratic presidents, declared

that Congress could not prohibit slavery in the territories. As the Princeton University historian Sean Wilentz recently told me, 'what Dred Scott did, in effect, was to declare the platform of the Republican Party unconstitutional.'"[145]

The difference being that the modern Democratic position is in many ways even worse than the position of Republicans in the 1850's. The gap between rural and urban populations has widened, making representation even more disproportional. The Electoral College math favored Republicans over Democrats in 1860. Today, the Electoral College gives great advantage to the party representing white Southerners. Republicans have lost the popular vote in 7 out of the last 8 elections, yet 15 out of the last 19 Supreme Court justices have been appointed by them. Five out of six of the conservative justices on the court today were appointed by Republicans who lost the popular vote but ended up winning the Electoral College.[146] By 2030, 30% of the population will control 70% of Senate seats, most of which are deep red. In 1860, it was the majority of the country that was gaining the political upper hand: today it is the shrinking minority that is about to seize permanent power.

Thus, there are really only two options on the table for the U.S. if we fail the next time around, and elections cease to matter. Either there is a separation of states from a federal government which they have little in common with culturally, religiously, or economically; or an acceptance of life in a Trumpist/GOP/white evangelical autocratic state while continuing to pretend it's a democracy in which change can happen.

The hard part will be making Democratic politicians and the public understand the options: do we want to be more like Taiwan, or do we want to be like the competitive authoritarian states of Russia, Hungary, and Turkey? Because once the authoritarian has broken the system enough that change through elections becomes effectively impossible, that's all there is. One or the other. There isn't a third option. Once you pass the democracy event horizon, there is no longer an electoral or legal way to prevent the latter—or recover from it.

Democrats, LGBTQ people, women, immigrants, Blacks and people of color, and everyone else who doesn't want to live in a corrupt, fascist autocracy need to accept that the U.S. is unlikely to survive a second autocratic attempt. There will no longer be a way to win "playing by the rules." They need to start thinking, even now, about how to quit an unwinnable game. If we do not quit, millions of people will needlessly spend their lives in fear, oppression, and misery at the hands of a racist, homophobic, xenophobic, Christian nationalist, fascist minority. Whatever norms are served by continuing to play the game, pretending that the U.S. is still a democracy at that point is not worth the human cost.

Conclusion

> *"Ernest Hemingway once wrote, The World is a fine place, and worth fighting for."' I agree with the second part."*

William Somerset, Se7en

While most Americans wanted to take a deep breath and assume that the worst was behind them after Biden won the White House, the analyses of this book do not support this outlook. Other than four years of breathing space, nothing fundamentally changed. The same forces that put Trump in place in 2016 have only grown stronger, and the GOP has seen clearly that embracing a fascist movement, complete with conspiracies, was a very plausible path to long-term power. The math driving the institutional advantages of the GOP say these will continue to grow, and the GOP will shape the law to exploit these to the maximum extent practical to ensure permanent minoritarian rule.

Anti-democratic seizure of power is the only option for the GOP to remain relevant, and both their base and their donors are well aware of this. Republican leaders know that they must appease the thing they created. As Winston Churchill observed of such people, "Each one hopes that if he feeds the crocodile enough, the crocodile will eat him last. All of them hope that the storm will pass before their turn comes to be devoured." The Republican plan to rule as a minority via anti-democratic means is a strategic necessity from their standpoint. The Party cannot continue to exist as it is constructed, and serve their base, without it.

Right-wing media monocultures aren't going anywhere. Neither is the base, who are essentially the same people who started the last Civil War. Facebook makes money hand over fist catering to right-wing paranoia and conspiracy theories. The U.S. system of government prevents Democrats from taking steps to reverse the march towards competitive authoritarianism. Even when Democrats have the opportunity to prevent a further slide into autocracy, they refuse to do it, insisting on playing by rules that the GOP clearly no longer cares about. GOP dominated legislatures and courts are laying the groundwork for a final plunge into authoritarianism so abrupt and shocking that nothing can be done, much as Orbán destroyed Hungary's institutions less than two years after Fidesz returned to power.

It's a Republic, if we can keep it. But the odds are against it in the long run, and it's probably only a matter of time before we succumb to the inevitable. The bills to stop gerrymandering and restore voting rights represent the event horizon for democracy in the United States. If they are not passed within the next few years, the collective experiment will fail, and we will be left with only dissolution or hopeless descent into permanent American fascism.

Acknowledgments

I'd like to thank the people who made this book possible in a myriad of ways.

Doing a book of this length and depth on a zero budget requires a lot of help from friends who believed in the project. Drea Leed has served as an unofficial editor for both of my books now. Mara Glubka was willing to spend who knows how many hours helping me turn various images and diagrams into something that shows up well in print. Andrey Kaunov graciously agreed to help with the cover based on a mutual friend. Trystan Cotten, the owner of the publishing company, was the first person to believe in me enough to agree to publish this work, which has been five years in the making.

Brody Levesque has been my friend and confidante over the last four years. His background knowledge of Washington, DC, and how the White House works were invaluable, as was his encouragement to keep going on the project and introduction to Andrey. Dr. Rachel Bitecofer's encouragement and recognition of me as someone trying to break into the field buoyed my spirits. Jennifer Reitman at DAME Magazine gave me a venue to publish my thoughts as things developed, and much of the material I wrote for her ended up here in one form or another.

I'd also like to thank the giants in their fields who entertained my questions and helped provide data. Dr. Emmanuel Saez was gracious enough to permit me to use one of his figures, and even provided me with the most up to date data and diagram. Dr. Jason Stanley was kind enough to look at an early draft of Chapter 9 and let me know that I wasn't completely out in left field. Sarah Posner's work was hugely influential, and she, too, agreed to serve as something akin to a peer reviewer. Despite the time zone differences, Dr. Anna Lührmann always got back to me both quickly and thoughtfully, and was eager to see V-Dem's work put to use.

Doctors Robert P. George, Paul Djupe, and Ryan Burge were all kind enough to correspond with me and help provide cross-tabs on their survey work. Burge, in particular, went the extra mile, not only giving me permission to use his work, but providing print-friendly versions of his diagrams and providing links for citation. Dr. Raj Chetty was extremely helpful in granting permission to re-print some of his work, as were Doctors Steven Levitsky and Daniel Ziblatt.

Last, but not least, my long-suffering spouse Janis, who has put up with me talking about this stuff at dinner for almost five years now. I believe no one is happier than her that this book is finally done. Thank you for not smothering me in my sleep, because goodness knows I deserve it after what I've put you through with this door-stop sized tome.

My colleagues John Yurchak and Robert Button also provided a sanity check early in the compilation process.

Author

Brynn Tannehill is a graduate of the United States Naval Academy and Air Force Institute of Technology, with advanced degrees in Computer Science and Operations Research. As a Naval Aviator, she did four deployments to locations in Kosovo, the Middle East, and North Atlantic. After leaving active duty, Mrs. Tannehill continued working in defense research, while moonlighting as an activist and writer of LGBTQ civil rights and social policy. Currently, she works as a senior analyst at a well-known defense think-tank in the Washington, D.C. area, where she lives with her wife and three children.

Endnotes

Preface

1. McCammon, Sarah. "What Does Trump's Promise Of A Nation 'Under One God' Really Mean?" *NPR*, 18 Sept. 2016, https://www.npr.org/2016/09/18/494367803/what-does-trumps-promise-of-a-nation-under-one-god-really-mean.

2. Gessen, Masha. "Autocracy: Rules for Survival." *The New York Review of Books*, https://www.nybooks.com/daily/2016/11/10/trump-election-autocracy-rules-for-survival/. Accessed 21 Nov. 2020.

Chapter 1

1. Kertscher, Tom. "Fact-Check: They Signed the Declaration of Independence—but Nearly Three-Quarters Also Owned Slaves." *Chicago Sun-Times*, 10 Sept. 2019, https://chicago.suntimes.com/2019/9/10/20859458/fact-check-declaration-independence-slaves-trumbull-painting-arlen-parsa.

2. Bogus, Carl. "Opinion | Was Slavery a Factor in the Second Amendment? (Published 2018)." *NYTimes*, 24 May 2018, https://www.nytimes.com/2018/05/24/opinion/second-amendment-slavery-james-madison.html.

3. *Dred Scott v. Sanford* is now considered one of the worst, if not the worst, Supreme Court decisions in US history. Given the composition of the Supreme Court, and it how it has been stacked to favor the south, corporations, and religions, and dark money, and is willing to make decisions completely out of step with US opinion, it seems likely that the Roberts Court will challenge this record. *Citizens United* is already widely reviled.

4. Buchanan is widely regarded as one of the worst Presidents in US history. Presidential historians generally put Trump near the bottom as well.

5. To put this in context, if the US sustained a similar per capita death toll today, it would mean approximately 7 million people killed and another 5 million wounded.

6. Kolchin, Peter (1993). American Slavery, 1619–1877. New York: Hill & Wang. ISBN 978-0-8090-2568-8.

7. Rae, Noel. *The Great Stain: Witnessing American Slavery*. The Overlook Press, 2018.

8. Report on Slavery and Racism in the History of the Southern Baptist Theological Seminary http://www.sbts.edu/wp-content/uploads/2018/12/Racism-and-the-Legacy-of-Slavery-Report-v3.pdf

9. Jones, R. P. (2020). *White too long: The legacy of white supremacy in American Christianity*. New York, NY, NY: Simon & Schuster. p. 5

10. Ibid. p. 8

11. https://uselectionatlas.org/RESULTS/state.php?year=1860&fips=24&f=1&off=0&elect=0

12. Jones, R. P. (2020). *White too long: The legacy of white supremacy in American Christianity*. New York, NY, NY: Simon & Schuster. p. 36

13. Frederick, D. (2003). *Narrative of the life of Frederick Douglass*. New York, NY: Scholastic.

14. Serwer, Adam. "The Supreme Court Is Headed Back to the 19th Century." The Atlantic, Atlantic Media Company, 4 Sept. 2018, www.theatlantic.com/ideas/archive/2018/09/redemption-court/566963/.

15. Jones, R. P. (2020). *White too long: The legacy of white supremacy in American Christianity*. New York, NY, NY: Simon & Schuster. p. 27

16. Pruitt, S. (2020, January 21). How the 1876 Election Tested the Constitution and Ef-

fectively Ended Reconstruction. Retrieved September 20, 2020, from https://www.history.com/news/reconstruction-1876-election-rutherford-hayes

17. Levitsky, S., Ziblatt, D. (2018). *How democracies die* (pp. 111). New York: Crown.

18. Levitsky, S., Ziblatt, D. (2018). *How democracies die* (pp. 91-92). New York: Crown.

19. Keele, L., Cubbison, W., and White, I. (2021). "Suppressing Black Votes: A Historical Case Study of Voting Restrictions in Louisiana." *American Political Science Review*, 5 March 2021, https://www.cambridge.org/core/journals/american-political-science-review/article/suppressing-black-votes-a-historical-case-study-of-voting-restrictions-in-louisiana/662970B089BC99495ADC2F6E3CBF61FD

20. Brockell, Gillian. "A White Mob Unleashed the Worst Election Day Violence in U.S. History in Florida a Century Ago." *The Washington Post*, 2 Nov. 2020, https://www.washingtonpost.com/history/2020/11/02/ocoee-florida-election-day-massacre/.

21. Serwer, Adam. "The Supreme Court Is Headed Back to the 19th Century." *The Atlantic*, 4 Sept. 2018, https://www.theatlantic.com/politics/archive/2018/09/redemption-court/566963/.

22. Democrats won the west in 1880, 1912 (when Theodore Roosevelt split the Republican vote) and 1916 as World War One raged on (without the United States). They managed a split it in 1896 and 1900.

23. Cleveland's win was achieved thanks to his anti-corruption campaign, as New York governer, against a Republican unpopular within his own party.

24. Saez, Emmanuel, and Gabriel Zucman. "Wealth Inequality in the United States since 1913: Evidence from Capitalized Income Tax Data." *The Quarterly Journal of Economics*, vol. 131, no. 2, May 2016, pp. 519–578., doi:10.3386/w20625.

25. The Democratic party did not allow Black people to be delegates at its convention until 1924. Jackson, Brooks. "Blacks and the Democratic Party." *FactCheck.org*, 16 May 2011, www.factcheck.org/2008/04/blacks-and-the-democratic-party/.

26. Ample literature exists on the movement of Black voters from the Republican Party to the Democratic Party: Weiss, *Farewell to the Party of Lincoln*; Donald J. Lisio, *Hoover, Blacks & Lily-Whites: A Study of Southern Strategies* (Chapel Hill: University of North Carolina Press, 1985); Richard Sherman, *The Republican Party and Black America from McKinley to Hoover, 1896–1933* (Charlottesville: University of Virginia Press, 1973): 134–144.

27. John Hope Franklin and Alfred A. Moss, Jr., *From Slavery to Freedom: A History of African Americans*, 8th ed. (New York: Knopf, 2000): 421.

28. Bump, Philip. "When Did Black Americans Start Voting so Heavily Democratic?" *The Washington Post*, WP Company, 7 July 2015, www.washingtonpost.com/news/the-fix/wp/2015/07/07/when-did-black-americans-start-voting-so-heavily-democratic/?utm_term=.2183767615eb.

29. If this sounds familiar, it should. Modern republicans accuse virtually any efforts to protect LGBT people a form of fascism or totalitarianism.

30. Lemmon, Sarah M. "The Ideology of the 'Dixiecrat' Movement." *Social Forces*, vol. 30, no. 2, Dec. 1951, pp. 162–171., doi: 10.2307/2571628.

31. O'Donnell, Michael. "When Eisenhower and Warren Squared Off Over Civil Rights." *The Atlantic*, Atlantic Media Company, 17 Apr. 2018, www.theatlantic.com/magazine/archive/2018/04/commander-v-chief/554045/.

32. Serwer, Adam. "Why Don't We Remember Ike as a Civil Rights Hero?" *MSNBC*, NBCUniversal News Group, 18 May 2014, www.msnbc.com/msnbc/why-dont-we-

ike-civil-rights.

33. The dominant issues for voters outside the south in 1960 was the cold war, Sputnik, fear of Soviet technological superiority.

34. "1960 Democratic Party Platform." The American Presidency Project, *University of California Santa Barbara*, 11 July 1960, www.presidency.ucsb.edu/documents/1960-democratic-party-platform.

35. Frank, Jeffrey. "When Martin Luther King Jr. and Richard Nixon Were Friends." *The Daily Beast*, The Daily Beast Company, 21 Jan. 2013, www.thedailybeast.com/when-martin-luther-king-jr-and-richard-nixon-were-friends.

36. Harris Wofford and Sergeant Shriver

37. Levingston, Steven. "John F. Kennedy, Martin Luther King Call Changed History." Time, Time Warner Communications, 20 June 2017, time.com/4817240/martin-luther-king-john-kennedy-phone-call/.

38. Middleton, Russell (March 1962). "The Civil Rights Issue And Presidential Voting Among Southern Negroes And Whites. Social Forces. 40 (3): 209–215. doi:10.2307/2573630. JSTOR 2573630

Chapter 2

1. Enten, H. J. (2013, August 28). Were Republicans really the party of civil rights in the 1960s? | Harry J Enten. Retrieved March 7, 2019, from https://www.theguardian.com/commentisfree/2013/aug/28/republicans-party-of-civil-rights

2. "The Long Goodbye." The Economist, The Economist Newspaper, 11 Nov. 2010, www.economist.com/united-states/2010/11/11/the-long-goodbye.

3. Senator Doug Jones (D-AL) is an outlier, having narrowly beaten Republican Roy Moore in a special election after Roy Moore was credibly accused during the campaign by multiple women of trolling high schools for underage girls to date when he was a 30-something year old district attorney. Not every Republican is committing statutory rape.

4. THURMOND BREAK IS MADE OFFICIAL; He Will Work as Republican for Goldwater Election." *The New York Times*, *The New York Times*, 17 Sept. 1964, www.nytimes.com/1964/09/17/archives/thurmond-break-is-made-official-he-will-work-as-republican-for.html.

5. Jackson, Brooks. "Blacks and the Democratic Party." *FactCheck.org*, 16 May 2011, www.factcheck.org/2008/04/blacks-and-the-democratic-party/.

6. Zimmerman, Jonathan. "Trump and Republicans Are Following the Goldwater Model with QAnon. That Didn't End Well." *USA TODAY*, https://www.usatoday.com/story/opinion/2020/08/21/trump-republicans-qanon-goldwater-john-birch-society-column/5616711002/. Accessed 21 Nov. 2020.

7. "Nixon Opposes G.O.P. Birchers But Says Fringe Group Will Pass (Published 1964)." *NYTimes*, 16 July 1964, https://www.nytimes.com/1964/07/16/archives/nixon-opposes-gop-birchers-but-says-fringe-group-will-pass.html.

8. Churchwell, Sarah. "Can American Democracy Survive Donald Trump?" *The Guardian*, 21 Nov. 2020, http://www.theguardian.com/books/2020/nov/21/can-american-democracy-survive-donald-trump.

9. Robin, Corey (2011). *The Reactionary Mind: Conservatism from Edmund Burke to Sarah Palin*. New York: Oxford University Press. p. 50. ISBN 978-0-19-979393-8.

10. Phillips, K. (2015). *The emerging Republican majority*. Princeton, NJ: Princeton University Press.

11. Hacker, J. S., and Pierson, P. (2020*). Let them eat Tweets: How the right rules in an age of extreme inequality.* New York, NY, NY: Liveright Publishing Corporation, a division of W. W. Norton & Company. p. 112

12. Rosow, Jerome M., "The Problem of the Blue Collar Worker," Department of Labor, April 16, 1970, 4-9

13. Harwood, John. "From Taxes to Health Care to NAFTA, President Trump Has Forgotten His 'Forgotten People.'" *CNBC*, 5 Dec. 2017, https://www.cnbc.com/2017/12/05/president-trump-has-forgotten-his-forgotten-people.html.

14. Virginia is becoming more solidly Democratic in state level elections as the DC suburbs spill into Northern Virginia. However, Republican gerrymandering

15. Black, E., and Black, M. (2004). *The Rise of Southern Republicans.* Cambridge, MA: Belknap Press.

16. This started in the 1970s.

17. Miller, R. M. (1956). A Note on the Relationship between the Protestant Churches and the Revived Ku Klux Klan. *The Journal of Southern History*, 22(3), 355. doi:10.2307/2954550

18. Ibid. p. 7

19. Ibid p. 146

20. Jones, R. P. (2020*). White too long: The legacy of white supremacy in American Christianity.* New York, NY, NY: Simon & Schuster. p. 28

21. Ibid. p. 32-33

22. Freeman, C. W. (2007). "Never Had I Been So Blind": W. A. Criswell's "Change" on Racial Segregation. The Journal of Southern Religion, X, 1-12. Retrieved March 7, 2019, from http://jsr.fsu.edu/Volume10/Freeman.pdf

23. Jones, R. (April 17, 1960). Is Segregation Scriptural? Bob Jones University. Retrieved March 7, 2019 from https://docs.google.com/file/d/0B6A7PtfmRgT7Q1kzZEVX-UThMLWc/edit

24. On Renouncing The Doctrine Of The "Curse Of Ham" As A Justification For Racism. (n.d.). Retrieved March 7, 2019, from http://www.sbc.net/resolutions/2287/on-renouncing-the-doctrine-of-the-curse-of-ham-as-a-justification-for-racism

25. Edwards, S. (2016, June 15). Southern Baptist Convention Votes to Discourage Display of Confederate Flag at Member Churches . Retrieved March 7, 2019, from https://jezebel.com/southern-baptist-convention-votes-to-discourage-display-1782025002

26. Jones, R. P. (2020*). White too long: The legacy of white supremacy in American Christianity.* New York, NY, NY: Simon & Schuster. p. 44

27. Love the sinner. (2015, October 22). Retrieved March 7, 2019, from https://www.economist.com/united-states/2015/10/22/love-the-sinner.

28. In 1968 the Supreme Court issued a *per curiam* decision in *Newman v. Piggie Park Enterprises* that a religious objection to integration did not exempt a business owner from the CRA requirement to serve customers equally regardless of race. Today, the religious right isn't directly challenging this precedent, but they are arguing that the case only applies to protections on the basis of race, not sex, sexual orientation, or gender identity, and thus religious freedom and the First Amendment gives them a unique right to ignore civil rights laws.

29. 1971 *Coit v. Green* decision.

30. Balmer, R., Lowry, R., Shafer, J., & Greenfield, J. (2014, May 27). The Real Origins of the Religious Right. Retrieved March 7, 2019, from https://www.politico.com/maga-

zine/story/2014/05/religious-right-real-origins-107133?o=1

31. Duffy, Michael. "Breaking News, Analysis, Politics, Blogs, News Photos, Video, Tech Reviews - TIME.Com." *TIME.Com*, 15 May 2007, http://content.time.com/time/nation/article/0,8599,1621300,00.html.

32. Weyrich founded both ALEC and the Heritage Foundation at the age of 31 in 1973.

33. Ladd, C. (2017, May 22). Pastors, Not Politicians, Turned Dixie Republican. Retrieved March 8, 2019, from https://www.forbes.com/sites/chrisladd/2017/03/27/pastors-not-politicians-turned-dixie-republican/#73f1e65f695f

34. Allen, B. (2012, November 06). Evangelicals and abortion: Chicken or egg? – Baptist News Global. Retrieved March 8, 2019, from https://baptistnews.com/article/evangelicals-and-abortion-chicken-or-egg/#.XIJxVChKiUk . The SBC denomination supported access to abortion in 1971 (SBC Resolution on Abortion, 1971. http://www.sbc.net/resolutions/13/resolution-on-abortion) and did not adopt a firm pro-life stance until 1980. SBC Resolution on Abortion, 1980. (http://www.sbc.net/resolutions/19/resolution-on-abortion)

35. Williams, D. K. (2010). GOD'S OWN PARTY: The making of the Christian right. Pp. 221 OXFORD: OXFORD UNIV Press UK. p. 166

36. Balmer, R. (2014, May 23). Jimmy Carter's evangelical downfall: Reagan, religion and the 1980 presidential election. Retrieved March 8, 2019, from https://www.salon.com/2014/05/25/jimmy_carters_evangelical_downfall_reagan_religion_and_the_1980_presidential_election/

37. Naftali, Tim. "Ronald Reagan's Long-Hidden Racist Conversation With Richard Nixon." *The Atlantic*, 30 July 2019, https://www.theatlantic.com/ideas/archive/2019/07/ronald-reagans-racist-conversation-richard-nixon/595102/.

38. Lucks, Daniel. "Op-Ed: Donald Trump, a True Reagan Republican." *Los Angeles Times*, 19 July 2020, https://www.latimes.com/opinion/story/2020-07-19/ronald-reagans-racism-cleared-the-way-for-trump.

39. FitzGerald, F. (2017). *The Evangelicals: The struggle to shape America.* New York, NY, NY: Simon & Schuster. p. 304

40. Harley, R. M. (1980, June 25). THE EVANGELICAL VOTE AND THE PRESIDENCY. Retrieved March 8, 2019, from https://www.csmonitor.com/1980/0625/062555.html

41. Carter's life post presidency has been dedicated to charity and building peace processes. The irony is not lost on the author. It can be observed that if one wants to know what the moral and ethical thing to do in any given situation is, look at the position of the Southern Baptist Convention on the issue, and then do the exact opposite.

42. Johnson, S. D., & Tamney, J. B. (1982). The Christian Right and the 1980 Presidential Election. *Journal for the Scientific Study of Religion*, 21(2), 123. doi:10.2307/1385498

43. Reinhard, David (1983). *The Republican Right since 1945.* Lexington, KY: Univ Press of Kentucky. p. 245. ISBN 978-0813114842.

44. Eagan, M. (2018, February 05). Race, not abortion, was the founding issue of the religious right - The Boston Globe. Retrieved March 8, 2019, from https://www.bostonglobe.com/opinion/2018/02/05/race-not-abortion-was-founding-issue-religious-right/A5rnmClvuAU7EaThaNLAnK/story.html

45. Balmer, R., Lowry, R., Shafer, J., & Greenfield, J. (2014, May 27). The Real Origins of the Religious Right. Retrieved March 7, 2019, from https://www.politico.com/magazine/story/2014/05/religious-right-real-origins-107133?o=1

46. Ibid.

47. Ladd, C. (2017, May 22). Pastors, Not Politicians, Turned Dixie Republican. Retrieved March 8, 2019, from https://www.forbes.com/sites/chrisladd/2017/03/27/pastors-not-politicians-turned-dixie-republican/#73f1e65f695f

48. Brooks, K. J. (2020, June 12). Redlining's legacy: Maps are gone, but the problem hasn't disappeared. Retrieved September 18, 2020, from https://www.cbsnews.com/news/redlining-what-is-history-mike-bloomberg-comments/

49. Posner, S. (2020). *Unholy: Why white evangelicals worship at the altar of Donald Trump.* Pp. 159 New York, NY: Random House.

50. Fitzgerald, F. (2017). *The Evangelicals: The struggle to shape America.* pp. 321. New York, NY, NY: Simon & Schuster.

51. Posner, S. (2020). *Unholy: Why white evangelicals worship at the altar of Donald Trump.* Pp. xvi New York, NY: Random House.

52. Falwell, J. (1980) Listen America Broadcast. Retrieved from https://wwnorton.com/college/history/archive/resources/documents/ch36_02.htm on September 5, 2020.

53. Blumenthal, M. (2007, May 16). Agent of Intolerance. Retrieved September 05, 2020, from https://www.thenation.com/article/archive/agent-intolerance/

54. Tolchin, M. (1984, March 21). AMENDMENT DRIVE ON SCHOOL PRAYER LOSES SENATE VOTE. *New York Times.* Retrieved September 05, 2020, from https://www.nytimes.com/1984/03/21/us/amendment-drive-on-school-prayer-loses-senate-vote.html

55. Fitzgerald, F. (2017). *The Evangelicals: The struggle to shape America.* pp. 327. New York, NY, NY: Simon & Schuster.

56. Fitzgerald, F. (2017). *The Evangelicals: The struggle to shape America.* pp. 327. New York, NY, NY: Simon & Schuster. p. 324

57. Williams, D. K. (2010). GOD'S OWN PARTY: The making of the Christian right. Pp. 214 OXFORD: OXFORD UNIV Press UK.

58. Brumfield-Hessen, E. (2020, June 10). Millions of Americans Believe Trump Is Fighting Literal Demons. Retrieved September 06, 2020, from https://foreignpolicy.com/2020/06/10/trump-evangelicals-charismatics-paula-white-demons/

59. Williams, D. K. (2010). GOD'S OWN PARTY: The making of the Christian right. Pp. 221 OXFORD: OXFORD UNIV Press UK.

60. Baker, P. (2018, December 04). Bush Made Willie Horton an Issue in 1988, and the Racial Scars Are Still Fresh. Retrieved September 18, 2020, from https://www.nytimes.com/2018/12/03/us/politics/bush-willie-horton.html

61. Ortved, J. (2007, July 5). The Simpsons Family Values: How the Cartoon Took Over TV. Retrieved September 06, 2020, from https://www.vanityfair.com/news/2007/08/simpsons200708

62. Lopez, G. (2018, September 27). We need to talk about Brett Kavanaugh and alcohol. Retrieved September 06, 2020, from https://www.vox.com/policy-and-politics/2018/9/27/17906838/brett-kavanaugh-alcohol-sexual-assault-allegations

63. Fitzgerald, F. (2017). *The Evangelicals: The struggle to shape America.* pp. 416. New York, NY, NY: Simon & Schuster.

64. Coates, T. (2015, August 27). It Was No Compliment to Call Bill Clinton 'The First Black President'. Retrieved September 06, 2020, from https://www.theatlantic.com/notes/2015/08/toni-morrison-wasnt-giving-bill-clinton-a-compliment/402517/

65. Chozick, A. (2016, November 05). Hillary Clinton and the Return of the (Unbaked) Cookies. Retrieved September 06, 2020, from https://www.nytimes.com/2016/11/06/us/politics/hillary-clinton-cookies.html

66. Coppins, M. (2018, October 17). The Man Who Broke Politics. Retrieved September 06, 2020, from https://www.theatlantic.com/magazine/archive/2018/11/newt-gingrich-says-youre-welcome/570832/

67. Levitsky, S., Ziblatt, D. (2018). *How democracies die* (pp. 148). New York: Crown.

68. Nelson, J. (1994, July 28). GOP Moderates Warn of Religious Right Takeover: Politics: Conservatives are outflanking mainstream Republicans, leaving national party at risk, senators say. Retrieved September 06, 2020, from https://www.latimes.com/archives/la-xpm-1994-07-28-mn-20881-story.html

69. Ingraham, C. (2019, April 26). This astonishing chart shows how moderate Republicans are an endangered species. Retrieved September 23, 2020, from https://www.washingtonpost.com/news/wonk/wp/2015/06/02/this-astonishing-chart-shows-how-republicans-are-an-endangered-species/

70. Fitzgerald, F. (2017). *The Evangelicals: The struggle to shape America.* pp. 423. New York, NY, NY: Simon & Schuster. p. 332

71. Rozell, M. J., Wilcox, C. (1995). God at the grass roots: The Christian right in the 1994 elections. Lanham, MD: Rowman Littlefield. p.255

72. Cannon, Lou (2001). Ronald Reagan: The Presidential Portfolio. Public Affairs. p. 279 https://archive.org/details/ronaldreaganpres00cann

73. Waldron, T. W. (2018, October 23). Christian Coalition unveils social 'Contract with the American Family'. Retrieved September 06, 2020, from https://www.baltimoresun.com/news/bs-xpm-1995-05-18-1995138040-story.html

74. Brownstein, R. (1995, May 18). GOP Leaders Embrace Christian Coalition Plan : Congress: Conservative group's 10-point agenda includes abortion restrictions, elimination of Education Department. Retrieved September 06, 2020, from https://www.latimes.com/archives/la-xpm-1995-05-18-mn-3259-story.html

75. Fitzgerald, F. (2017). *The Evangelicals: The struggle to shape America.* pp. 423. New York, NY, NY: Simon & Schuster.

76. Williams, D. K. (2010). GOD'S OWN PARTY: The making of the Christian right. Pp. 242 OXFORD: OXFORD UNIV Press UK.

77. Lussenhop, J. (2016, April 18). Clinton crime bill: Why is it so controversial? Retrieved September 18, 2020, from https://www.bbc.com/news/world-us-canada-36020717

78. Adejumo, V. (2019, February 09). These numbers prove African-Americans still haven't recovered from the financial crisis. Retrieved September 18, 2020, from https://www.marketwatch.com/story/these-numbers-prove-african-americans-still-havent-recovered-from-the-financial-crisis-2019-02-06

79. President Clinton: Scandals and Investigations, continued https://www.pollingreport.com/scandal2.htm

Chapter 3

1. Leibovich, M. (2015, July 27). Should We Fear the Political 'Crazies'? Retrieved September 07, 2020, from https://www.nytimes.com/2015/08/02/magazine/should-we-fear-the-political-crazies.html

2. Williams, D. K. (2010). GOD'S OWN PARTY: The making of the Christian right. Pp. 248 OXFORD: OXFORD UNIV Press UK.

3. Mitchell, Alison. "CAMPAIGN 2000: McCAIN ON TAXES; Entering Fray on Re-

publicans' Issue of Choice, the Senator Pitches His Tax Proposal." *NYTimes*, 12 Jan. 2000, https://www.nytimes.com/2000/01/12/us/campaign-2000-mccain-taxes-entering-fray-republicans-issue-choice-senator.html.

4. Steinhauer, J. (2007, October 19). Confronting Ghosts of 2000 in South Carolina. Retrieved September 07, 2020, from https://www.nytimes.com/2007/10/19/us/politics/19mccain.html

5. Levitsky, S., Ziblatt, D. (2018). *How democracies die* (pp. 151). New York: Crown.

6. The Quiet Revolution: The President's Faith-Based and Community Initiative: A Seven-Year Progress Report Letter From President Bush. (2008, January 29). Retrieved September 07, 2020, from https://georgewbush-whitehouse.archives.gov/government/fbci/qr_summary.html

7. Toner, R. (2001, March 19). Conservatives Savor Their Role As Insiders at the White House. Retrieved September 07, 2020, from https://www.nytimes.com/2001/03/19/us/conservatives-savor-their-role-as-insiders-at-the-white-house.html

8. Hacker, J., & Pierson, P. (2005). Abandoning the Middle: The Bush Tax Cuts and the Limits of Democratic Control. Perspectives on Politics, 3(1), 33-53. Retrieved September 30, 2020, from http://www.jstor.org/stable/3688109

9. Lee, C. E. (2010, October 03). Rev. Franklin Graham: Islam 'evil'. Retrieved September 07, 2020, from https://www.politico.com/blogs/politico-now/2010/10/rev-franklin-graham-islam-evil-029683

10. Pew Research. (2020, May 30). War Concerns Grow, But Support Remains Steadfast. Retrieved September 07, 2020, from https://www.pewresearch.org/politics/2003/04/03/war-concerns-grow-but-support-remains-steadfast/

11. *Lawrence et al. v. Texas*, 539 U.S. 558 (2003): https://www.oyez.org/cases/2002/02-102

12. Coontz, S. (2004). The world historical transformation of marriage. *Journal of Marriage and Family*, 66(4), 974-979. doi:10.1111/j.0022-2445.2004.00067.x

13. Pew Research. (2020, May 30). Growing Support for Gay Marriage: Changed Minds and Changing Demographics. Retrieved September 07, 2020, from https://www.pewresearch.org/politics/2013/03/20/growing-support-for-gay-marriage-changed-minds-and-changing-demographics/

14. Bush stated, in December 2003 it was a matter for the states to consider

15. FDCH E-Media. (2004, January 20). Text of President Bush's 2004 State of the Union Address. Retrieved September 07, 2020, from https://www.washingtonpost.com/wp-srv/politics/transcripts/bushtext_012004.html

16. Wallsten, Hamburger, and Riccardi, "Bush Rewarded Black Pastors' Faith;" Kuo, p.212 *Los Angeles Times*, Jan 18, 2005 https://www.latimes.com/archives/la-xpm-2005-jan-18-na-faith18-story.html

17. Posner, S. (2020). *Unholy: Why white evangelicals worship at the altar of Donald Trump*. New York, NY: Random House.

18. Twitter, C. M. (2018, June 19). Russians and the American right started plotting in 1995. We have the notes from the first meeting. Retrieved September 07, 2020, from https://archive.thinkprogress.org/history-of-christian-fundamentalists-in-russia-and-the-us-a6bdd326841d/

19. Weyrich, P. (May 15, 2001). "Conferences Aim to Strengthen US-Russia Relations," Weyrich Free Congress Foundation (archived) https://web.archive.org/web/20061130054627/http://www.freecongress.org/commentaries/2001/010515PWfcc.asp

20. Weyrich, P.M., (October 22, 2001). "Our Old Enemy May Become Our Newest Friend," Free Congress Foundation (archived) https://web.archive.org/web/20061130055526/http://www.freecongress.org/commentaries/2001/011022PWfcc.asp

21. Posner, S. (2020). *Unholy: Why white evangelicals worship at the altar of Donald Trump.* P. 190. New York, NY: Random House.

22. Jeremy, H. (2014, May 08). Scott Lively stirring Russia's pot: A timeline. Retrieved September 07, 2020, from https://www.glaad.org/blog/scott-lively-stirring-russias-pot-timeline

23. Mufson, Steven. "Bush Saw Putin's 'Soul.' Obama Wants to Appeal to His Brain." *The Washington Post*, 1 Dec. 2015, https://www.washingtonpost.com/business/economy/bush-saw-putins-soul-obama-wants-to-appeal-to-his-brain/2015/12/01/264f-0c7c-984b-11e5-8917-653b65c809eb_story.html.

24. Albright, M. (2019). *FASCISM: A warning.* P. 159 New York, NY: WILLIAM COLLINS.

25. Van Look, Paul & Felicia Stewart. (1998). "EmergencyContraception." In Robert A. Hatcher et al., Eds, *Contraceptive Technology* — 17th Revised Edition. New York: Ardent Media.

26. Thomma, S. (2005, March 20). How GOP base flexed its political muscle. Retrieved September 07, 2020, from https://www.seattletimes.com/nation-world/how-gop-base-flexed-its-political-muscle/

27. Fitzgerald, F. (2017). *The Evangelicals: The struggle to shape America.* pp. 519-520. New York, NY, NY: Simon & Schuster.

28. Newport, F. (2017, June 07). The Terri Schiavo Case in Review. Retrieved September 07, 2020, from https://news.gallup.com/poll/15475/terri-schiavo-case-review.aspx

29. Gilgoff, D. (2008). *The Jesus machine: How James Dobson, Focus on the Family, and evangelical America are winning the culture war.* P. New York, NY: St. Martin's Griffin.

30. Kelly, C., Vogue, A. (2020, June 30). How John Roberts left the door open to more state limits on abortion. Retrieved September 07, 2020, from https://www.cnn.com/2020/06/29/politics/supreme-court-abortion-roberts-footnote/index.html

31. Greenhouse, L. (2008, April 29). In a 6-to-3 Vote, Justices Uphold a Voter ID Law. Retrieved September 07, 2020, from https://www.nytimes.com/2008/04/29/washington/29scotus.html

32. New, V. R., II. (2020, June 16). How a Pivotal Voting Rights Act Case Broke America. Retrieved September 07, 2020, from https://www.theatlantic.com/politics/archive/2018/07/how-shelby-county-broke-america/564707/

33. Pierce, C. P. (2020, August 21). Only Republicans Could Get Fewer Votes and Claim a 'Mandate' to Govern. Retrieved September 07, 2020, from https://www.esquire.com/news-politics/politics/a25226646/wisconsin-gerrymandering-republicans-mandate/

34. Wines, Michael. "Freed by Court Ruling, Republicans Step Up Effort to Patrol Voting." *NYTimes*, 18 May 2020, https://www.nytimes.com/2020/05/18/us/Voting-republicans-trump.html.

35. Fitzgerald, F. (2017). *The Evangelicals: The struggle to shape America.* pp. 571-572. New York, NY, NY: Simon & Schuster.

36. Bradley-Hagerty, B. (2008, March 31). Black Liberation Theology, in its Founder's Words. Retrieved September 08, 2020, from https://www.npr.org/templates/story/story.php?storyId=89236116

37. Hart, B. (2018, May 05). McCain Regrets His Palin Pick for the Wrong Reasons.

Retrieved September 12, 2020, from https://nymag.com/intelligencer/2018/05/mc-cain-regrets-palin-pick-wrong-reasons.html

38. Goldberg, Jeffrey. "Why Obama Fears for Our Democracy." *The Atlantic*, 16 Nov. 2020, https://www.theatlantic.com/ideas/archive/2020/11/why-obama-fears-for-our-democracy/617087/.

39. Chapman, S. (2008, October 27). Obama's message of unity is on the money. Retrieved September 12, 2020, from https://www.startribune.com/obama-s-message-of-unity-is-on-the-money/33251269/

40. Chafets, Z. (2010, May 23). 'Rush Limbaugh'. Retrieved September 12, 2020, from https://www.nytimes.com/2010/05/24/books/excerpt-rush-limbaugh.html

41. Kessler, G. (2018, August 15). When did Mitch McConnell say he wanted to make Obama a one-term president? Retrieved September 12, 2020, from https://www.washingtonpost.com/news/fact-checker/wp/2017/01/11/when-did-mitch-mcconnell-say-he-wanted-to-make-obama-a-one-term-president/

42. Kranish, Michael. "In His New Memoir, Barack Obama Writes of Hope, Despair and Life at the Center of a Divided Nation." *The Washington Post*, 13 Nov. 2020, https://www.washingtonpost.com/politics/obama-book-biden-trump-palin/2020/11/13/36c4828a-25b8-11eb-8599-406466ad1b8e_story.html.

43. Daley, D. (2016). Ratf**ked: Why Your Vote Doesn't Count. New York, NY: Liveright Publishing Corporation, a division of W.W. Norton Company. p. xxii

44. Robertson, L. (2013, September 16). Obamacare Myths. Retrieved September 12, 2020, from https://www.factcheck.org/2013/09/obamacare-myths/

45. Maxwell, A. (2009, March 30). Americans weigh in on Obama's automaker bailout plan. Retrieved September 12, 2020, from https://www.cnn.com/2009/POLITICS/03/30/auto.ireporters/index.html

46. Lane, S. (2018, May 24). Trump signs Dodd-Frank rollback. Retrieved September 12, 2020, from https://thehill.com/policy/finance/389212-trump-signs-dodd-frank-rollback

47. Volsky, I. (2010, May 24). Tony Perkins: 'If You Want A Military That Just Does Parades,' Allow Gays To Openly Serve. Retrieved September 12, 2020, from https://archive.thinkprogress.org/tony-perkins-if-you-want-a-military-that-just-does-parades-allow-gays-to-openly-serve-8ed9c5221f6/

48. Hertel-Fernandez, A., Tervo, C., Skocpol, T. (2018, September 26). How the Koch brothers built the most powerful rightwing group you've never heard of. Retrieved September 12, 2020, from https://www.theguardian.com/us-news/2018/sep/26/koch-brothers-americans-for-prosperity-rightwing-political-group

49. Hacker, J. S., & Pierson, P. (2020*). Let them eat Tweets: How the right rules in an age of extreme inequality*. New York, NY, NY: Liveright Publishing Corporation, a division of W. W. Norton & Company. p. 105

50. Jones, R. P. (2010, October 5). Religion and the Tea Party in the 2010 Elections. Retrieved September 12, 2020, from https://www.prri.org/research/religion-tea-party-2010/

51. Montopoli, B. (2012, December 14). Tea Party Supporters: Who They Are and What They Believe. Retrieved September 12, 2020, from https://www.cbsnews.com/news/tea-party-supporters-who-they-are-and-what-they-believe/

52. Maxwell, A. (2016, July 07). How Southern racism found a home in the Tea Party. Retrieved September 12, 2020, from https://www.vox.com/2016/7/7/12118872/

southern-racism-tea-party-trump

53. PRRI. (2012, September 20). Beyond Guns and God: Understanding the Complexities of the White Working Class in America. Retrieved September 12, 2020, from https://www.prri.org/wp-content/uploads/2012/09/WWC-Report-For-Web-Final-1.pdf

54. Montopoli, B. (2012, December 14). Tea Party Supporters: Who They Are and What They Believe. Retrieved September 12, 2020, from https://www.cbsnews.com/news/tea-party-supporters-who-they-are-and-what-they-believe/

55. PRRI. (2012, September 20). Beyond Guns and God: Understanding the Complexities of the White Working Class in America. Retrieved September 12, 2020, from https://www.prri.org/wp-content/uploads/2012/09/WWC-Report-For-Web-Final-1.pdf

56. Holden, J., Yan, L. (2008, September 30). Media conservatives baselessly blame Community Reinvestment Act for foreclosure spike. Retrieved September 12, 2020, from https://www.mediamatters.org/laura-ingraham/media-conservatives-baselessly-blame-community-reinvestment-act-foreclosure-spike

57. PRRI. (2012, September 20). Beyond Guns and God: Understanding the Complexities of the White Working Class in America. Retrieved September 12, 2020, from https://www.prri.org/wp-content/uploads/2012/09/WWC-Report-For-Web-Final-1.pdf

58. Cox, D., Navarro-Rivera, J., Jones, R. P. (2014, September 23). Economic Insecurity, Rising Inequality, and Doubts about the Future. Retrieved September 12, 2020, from: https://www.prri.org/research/survey-economic-insecurity-rising-inequality-and-doubts-about-the-future-findings-from-the-2014-american-values-survey/

59. McDaniel, J., McElwee, S. (2016, February 10). There's powerful evidence that racial attitudes drive Tea Party support. Retrieved September 12, 2020, from https://www.vox.com/2016/2/10/10943196/trump-racial-resentment-vs-economic-anxiety

60. Shabad, R. (2016, February 02). Tea Party stands alone on immigration, education, environment. Retrieved September 12, 2020, from https://thehill.com/blogs/ballot-box/polls/209911-tea-party-stands-alone-on-key-issues-poll-finds

61. Campbell, D. E.; Putnam, R. (2011, August 17). Crashing the Tea Party. Retrieved September 12, 2020, from https://www.nytimes.com/2011/08/17/opinion/crashing-the-tea-party.html?hp

62. Ibid.

63. Pew Research. (2011, February 23). Growing Support for Gay Marriage: Changed Minds and Changing Demographics. Retrieved September 07, 2020, from https://www.pewresearch.org/politics/2013/03/20/growing-support-for-gay-marriage-changed-minds-and-changing-demographics/

64. Maxwell, A. (2016, July 07). How Southern racism found a home in the Tea Party. Retrieved September 12, 2020, from https://www.vox.com/2016/7/7/12118872/southern-racism-tea-party-trump

65. Fish Montopoli, B. (2012, December 14). Tea Party Supporters: Who They Are and What They Believe. Retrieved September 12, 2020, from https://www.cbsnews.com/news/tea-party-supporters-who-they-are-and-what-they-believe/er, M. (2015, February 25). Poll: 54 percent of Republicans say that, "deep down," Obama is a Muslim. Retrieved September 08, 2020, from https://www.vox.com/2015/2/25/8108005/obama-muslim-poll

66. Zorn, E. (2019, June 02). Polls reveal sobering extent of nation's fact crisis. Retrieved September 08, 2020, from https://www.chicagotribune.com/columns/eric-zorn/ct-polling-ignorance-facts-trump-zorn-perspec-0106-md-20170105-column.html

67. Gangitano, A. (2016, May 10). Poll: Two-Thirds of Trump Backers Think Obama Is Muslim. Retrieved September 08, 2020, from https://www.rollcall.com/2016/05/10/poll-two-thirds-of-trump-backers-think-obama-is-muslim/
68. McCrummen, S. (2016, October 01). 'Finally. Someone who thinks like me.' Retrieved September 13, 2020, from https://www.washingtonpost.com/national/finally-some-one-who-thinks-like-me/2016/10/01/c9b6f334-7f68-11e6-9070-5c4905bf40dc_story.html
69. Cesca, B. (2013, July 30). The Top 9 Glenn Beck Conspiracy Theories. Retrieved September 12, 2020, from https://www.huffpost.com/entry/the-top-9-glenn-beck-cons_b_3361097
70. Gervais, B. T., & Morris, I. L. (2018, September 07). Analysis | How the tea party paved the way for Donald Trump. Retrieved September 23, 2020, from https://www.washingtonpost.com/news/monkey-cage/wp/2018/09/07/how-the-tea-party-paved-the-way-for-donald-trump/
71. Elliott, R. D. (2017, July 31). It's Just a Jump to the Right: The Tea Party's Influence on Conserv... Retrieved September 23, 2020, from https://journals.openedition.org/ejas/12212
72. Dionne, E. (2019, April 22). Mission accomplished: The tea party shutdown. Retrieved September 12, 2020, from https://www.washingtonpost.com/blogs/post-partisan/wp/2013/10/01/mission-accomplished-the-tea-party-shutdown/
73. Levitsky, S., Ziblatt, D. (2018). *How democracies die* (pp. 23-24). New York: Crown.
74. Franke-Ruta, G. (2019, November 06). What You Need to Read in the RNC Election-Autopsy Report. Retrieved September 12, 2020, from https://www.theatlantic.com/politics/archive/2013/03/what-you-need-to-read-in-the-rnc-election-autopsy-report/274112/
75. Spiering, C.,; Johnston, D. (2013, January 25). Full text: Bobby Jindal's dynamite speech to the Republican National Committee in Charlotte. Retrieved September 12, 2020, from https://www.washingtonexaminer.com/full-text-bobby-jindals-dyna-mite-speech-to-the-republican-national-committee-in-charlotte
76. Helderman, Rosalind. "As Republican Convention Emphasizes Diversity, Racial Incidents Intrude." *The Washington Post*, 29 Aug. 2012, https://www.washingtonpost.com/politics/2012/08/29/b9023a52-f1ec-11e1-892d-bc92fee603a7_story.html.
77. Jones, R. P. (2020). White too long: The legacy of white supremacy in American Christianity. New York, NY, NY: Simon & Schuster. p. 12
78. Hagan, J. (2020, September 10). "I'll Never Question 1938 in Germany Again": An Ex-Republican Strategist Surveys the Wreckage of Trump's GOP. Retrieved September 13, 2020, from https://www.vanityfair.com/news/2020/09/ex-republican-strate-gist-surveys-the-wreckage-of-trumps-gop?utm_source=facebook
79. Chait, J. (2018, February 15). Bobby 'Stop Being the Stupid Party' Jindal Now Says GOP Isn't Stupid Enough. Retrieved September 12, 2020, from https://nymag.com/intelligencer/2018/02/bobby-stop-being-the-stupid-party-jindal-is-now-pro-stupid.html
80. Gessen, Masha. "Opinion | In Praise of Hypocrisy (Published 2017)." *NY-Times*, 18 Feb. 2017, https://www.nytimes.com/2017/02/18/opinion/sunday/in-praise-of-hypocrisy.html.
81. Chasmar, Jessica (June 16, 2015). "Donald Trump changed political parties at least five times: report". The Washington Times. Retrieved October 5, 2015.

82. Harris, A. (2019, May 30). The Central Park Five: 'We Were Just Baby Boys'. Retrieved September 12, 2020, from https://www.nytimes.com/2019/05/30/arts/television/when-they-see-us.html

83. Kelly, M. (2020, January 26). Some in South Jersey have a message for Trump: Pay your old Atlantic City casino bills. Retrieved September 12, 2020, from https://www.northjersey.com/story/news/columnists/mike-kelly/2020/01/24/donald-trump-still-owes-money-to-contractors-who-built-taj-mahal-atlantic-city/4547037002/

84. Kendzior, S. (2020). Hiding in plain sight: The invention of Donald Trump and the erosion of America. New York, NY, NY: Flatiron Books.

85. Taylor, K. (2018, August 25). Porn star Stormy Daniels is taking a Victory lap after Michael Cohen's guilty plea. Here's a timeline of Trump's many marriages and rumored affairs. Retrieved September 12, 2020, from https://www.businessinsider.com/trump-melania-stormy-daniels-affairs-marriages-timeline-2018-3

86. Tani, M. (2016, January 17). Trump on God: 'I don't like to have to ask for forgiveness'. Retrieved September 12, 2020, from https://www.businessinsider.com/trump-on-god-i-dont-like-to-have-to-ask-for-forgiveness-2016-1

87. *Washington Post*. (2016, September 26). Fact Check: Has Trump declared bankruptcy four or six times? Retrieved September 12, 2020, from https://www.washingtonpost.com/politics/2016/live-updates/general-election/real-time-fact-checking-and-analysis-of-the-first-presidential-debate/fact-check-has-trump-declared-bankruptcy-four-or-six-times/

88. Confessore, Nicholas. "$2 Billion Worth of Free Media for Donald Trump (Published 2016)." *NYTimes*, 15 Mar. 2016, https://www.nytimes.com/2016/03/16/upshot/measuring-donald-trumps-mammoth-advantage-in-free-media.html.

89. DeVega, C. (2019, May 10). Historian Christopher Browning on the Trump regime: We're "close to the point of no return". Retrieved September 12, 2020, from https://www.salon.com/2018/10/18/historian-christopher-browning-on-the-trump-regime-were-close-to-the-point-of-no-return/

90. Hannity-Donald Trump-Obama's Birth Certificate; YouTube Video. https://www.youtube.com/watch?v=O5oGtWDNAls Retrieved on September 9, 2020

91. Pfeiffer, Dan. "President Obama's Long Form Birth Certificate." *Whitehouse.Gov*, 27 Apr. 2011, https://obamawhitehouse.archives.gov/blog/2011/04/27/president-obamas-long-form-birth-certificate.

92. Kolbert, E., Konnikova, M. (2017, February 20). Why Facts Don't Change Our Minds. Retrieved September 12, 2020, from https://www.newyorker.com/magazine/2017/02/27/why-facts-dont-change-our-minds

93. Schwartz, I. (2015, June 16). Trump: Mexico Not Sending Us Their Best; Criminals, Drug Dealers And Rapists Are Crossing Border. Retrieved September 12, 2020, from https://www.realclearpolitics.com/video/2015/06/16/trump_mexico_not_sending_us_their_best_criminals_drug_dealers_and_rapists_are_crossing_border.html

94. "Chasing the Dragon" is a metaphor for smoking opium and seeking yet another drug high.

95. McCrummen, S. (2016, October 01). 'Finally. Someone who thinks like me.' Retrieved September 13, 2020, from https://www.washingtonpost.com/national/finally-someone-who-thinks-like-me/2016/10/01/c9b6f334-7f68-11e6-9070-5c4905bf40dc_story.html

96. Seipel, Brooke. "Trump: 'We Are Going to Say Merry Christmas Again.'" *TheHill*, 14

Dec. 2016, https://thehill.com/blogs/in-the-know/in-the-know/310311-trump-fulfills-merry-christmas-campaign-promise-at-wisconsin.

97. Beauchamp, Z. (2019, January 08). "He's not hurting the people he needs to be": A Trump voter says the quiet part out loud. Retrieved September 13, 2020, from https://www.vox.com/policy-and-politics/2019/1/8/18173678/trump-shut-down-voter-florida?fbclid=IwAR21Q_HFCzr_OI-H5I_GtnCdIakKtTdQcxjusxzo_rxm3u2j2q41bFbvMBM

98. Hesse, Monica. "Perspective | 'Make Liberals Cry Again' Became the Battle Hymn of the Republicans under Trump." *The Washington Post*, 5 Nov. 2020, https://www.washingtonpost.com/lifestyle/style/trump-republican-liberal-tears-make-america-cry-again/2020/11/04/2342f0de-1eb0-11eb-90dd-abd0f7086a91_story.html.

99. "Michael Moore: People Will Vote for Donald Trump as a Giant 'F**k You' — and He'll Win." *Salon.Com*, 26 Oct. 2016, https://www.salon.com/2016/10/26/michael-moore-people-will-vote-for-donald-trump-as-a-giant-fk-you-and-hell-win/.

100. Bruenig, E. (2016, February 24). How Ted Cruz Lost the Evangelical Vote. Retrieved September 12, 2020, from https://newrepublic.com/article/130422/ted-cruz-lost-evangelical-vote

101. Rubin, J. (2016, June 22). Opinion | Trump met with evangelical Christians and all he got was a lousy list. Retrieved September 12, 2020, from https://www.washingtonpost.com/blogs/right-turn/wp/2016/06/22/trump-met-with-evangelical-christians-and-all-he-got-was-a-lousy-list/

102. Bassett, L. (2016, May 11). Trump Says He'll Appoint Anti-Abortion Supreme Court Justices. Retrieved September 12, 2020, from https://www.huffpost.com/entry/donald-trump-abortion-supreme-court_n_5733400be4b0bc9cb048aef2

103. Corrales, J. (2016, June 22). Donald Trump Asks for Evangelicals' Support and Questions Hillary Clinton's Faith. Retrieved September 12, 2020, from https://www.nytimes.com/2016/06/22/us/politics/donald-trump-asks-for-evangelicals-support-and-questions-hillary-clintons-faith.html

104. Gabriel, T., & Luo, M. (2016, June 25). A Born-Again Donald Trump? Believe It, Evangelical Leader Says. Retrieved September 12, 2020, from https://www.nytimes.com/2016/06/26/us/politics/a-born-again-donald-trump-believe-it-evangelical-leader-says.html

105. Grant, T. (2016, June 22). Who flipped to join Trump's evangelical advisory board? (COMMENTARY). Retrieved September 12, 2020, from https://religionnews.com/2016/06/22/who-flipped-to-join-trumps-evangelical-advisory-board/

106. SPLC. (n.d.). Tony Perkins. Retrieved September 12, 2020, from https://www.splcenter.org/fighting-hate/extremist-files/individual/tony-perkins

107. Badash, D. (2016, July 11). Tony Perkins Successfully Introduces Plank Supporting Anti-LGBT Conversion Therapy Into GOP Platform. Retrieved September 12, 2020, from https://www.thenewcivilrightsmovement.com/2016/07/tony_perkins_successfully_introduces_plank_supporting_anti_lgbt_conversion_therapy_into_gop_platform/

108. Green, E. (2017, March 14). The Russell Moore Controversy Is About the Soul of the Southern Baptist Convention. Retrieved September 12, 2020, from https://www.theatlantic.com/politics/archive/2017/03/russell-moore-southern-baptist-convention/519540/

109. Helderman, R., & Parker, A. (2020, September 06). In new book, former Trump

lawyer Michael Cohen describes alleged episodes of racism and says president likes how Putin runs Russia. Retrieved September 13, 2020, from https://www.washingtonpost.com/politics/cohen-trump-book/2020/09/05/235aa10a-ef96-11ea-ab4e-581edb849379_story.html

110. "An Examination of the 2016 Electorate, Based on Validated Voters." *Pew Research Center - U.S. Politics & Policy*, 9 Aug. 2018, https://www.pewresearch.org/politics/2018/08/09/an-examination-of-the-2016-electorate-based-on-validated-voters/.

111. Gallup. (2020, August 17). Presidential Approval Ratings -- Donald Trump. Retrieved September 13, 2020, from https://news.gallup.com/poll/203198/presidential-approval-ratings-donald-trump.aspx

112. According to theorists such as Rachel Bitecofer

113. Schwalbe, M. C., Cohen, G. L., Ross, L. D. (2020). The objectivity illusion and voter polarization in the 2016 presidential election. Proceedings of the National Academy of Sciences, 117(35), 21218-21229. doi:10.1073/pnas.1912301117

114. Bartels, L. M. (2020). Ethnic antagonism erodes Republicans' commitment to democracy. *Proceedings of the National Academy of Sciences*. doi:10.1073/pnas.2007747117

115. Mus, Publius. "The Flight 93 Election - Claremont Review of Books." *Claremont Review of Books*, https://claremontreviewofbooks.com/digital/the-flight-93-election/. Accessed 10 Mar. 2020.

116. Green, J. (2018). *Devil's bargain: Steve Bannon, Donald Trump, and the nationalist uprising.* New York, NY: Penguin Books. p. 8

117. Hacker, J. S., & Pierson, P. (2015). *Confronting Asymmetric Polarization.* In N. Persily (Author), *Solutions to Political Polarization in America* (pp. 59-72). New York, NY: Cambridge University Press.

118. Chinoy, Sahil. "Opinion | What Happened to America's Political Center of Gravity?" *The New York Times The New York Times*, 26 June 2019, https://www.nytimes.com/interactive/2019/06/26/opinion/sunday/republican-platform-far-right.html.

119. Hagan, J. (2020, September 10). "I'll Never Question 1938 in Germany Again": An Ex-Republican Strategist Surveys the Wreckage of Trump's GOP. Retrieved September 13, 2020, from https://www.vanityfair.com/news/2020/09/ex-republican-strategist-surveys-the-wreckage-of-trumps-gop?utm_source=facebook

Chapter 4

1. Jost, J. T., Linden, S. V., Panagopoulos, C., Hardin, C. D. (2018). Ideological asymmetries in conformity, desire for shared reality, and the spread of misinformation. Current Opinion in Psychology, 23, 77-83. doi:10.1016/j.copsyc.2018.01.003

2. Beer, T. (2020, September 03). Majority Of Republicans Believe The QAnon Conspiracy Theory Is Partly Or Mostly True, Survey Finds. Retrieved September 19, 2020, from https://www.forbes.com/sites/tommybeer/2020/09/02/majority-of-republicans-believe-the-qanon-conspiracy-theory-is-partly-or-mostly-true-survey-finds/

3. Tucker, D. R. (2017, July 31). How the Repeal of the Fairness Doctrine Gave Us Donald Trump. Retrieved March 1, 2020, from https://washingtonmonthly.com/2017/07/31/how-the-repeal-of-the-fairness-doctrine-gave-us-donald-trump/

4. Finkel, D. (1994, June 12). Dialing for Dittos. Retrieved September 19, 2020, from https://www.washingtonpost.com/lifestyle/style/dialing-for-dittos/2012/10/02/bc11e83e-0cac-11e2-bb5e-492c0d30bff6_story.html

5. Blake, Aaron. "The GOP Hates the 'Lamestream Media' Even More than You

Think." *The Washington Post*, 21 Oct. 2014, https://www.washingtonpost.com/news/the-fix/wp/2014/10/21/the-gop-hates-the-lamestream-media-even-more-than-you-think/.

6. Fisk, Robert. "*CNN* Journalist Jim Acosta Received Death Threats Reporting on Trump." *Share Your Thoughts and Debate the Big Issues*, 11 June 2019, https://www.independent.co.uk/news/world/americas/us-politics/jim-acosta-trump-cnn-fbi-enemy-people-book-death-threats-hope-hicks-a8953551.html.

7. Video, H. P. (2019, March 19). Rush Limbaugh Pushes Mosque Massacre Conspiracy Theory. Retrieved March 1, 2020, from https://www.huffpost.com/entry/rush-limbaugh-pushes-mosque-massacre-conspiracy-theory_n_5c913d0ee4b0a31de79ddc47

8. Silverstein, J. (2020, February 6). Rush Limbaugh now has a Presidential Medal of Freedom. Here are just 20 of the outrageous things he's said. Retrieved March 1, 2020, from https://www.cbsnews.com/news/rush-limbaugh-presidential-medal-of-freedom-state-of-the-union-outrageous-quotes/

9. THOMAS B. ROSENSTIEL Dec. 11, 199412. "It's Rush Night for GOP's Lawmakers-in-Waiting : Republicans: Congress' Incoming Conservatives Enjoy Red Meat, Apple Pie at Orientation Dinner. But Main Course at Love Feast Is Talk Show Host Limbaugh." *Los Angeles Times*, 11 Dec. 1994, https://www.latimes.com/archives/la-xpm-1994-12-11-mn-7794-story.html.

10. Hananoki, E., & Dimiero, B. (2012, March 15). FLASHBACK: When Rush Limbaugh's Hate Was Televised. Retrieved March 1, 2020, from https://www.mediamatters.org/rush-limbaugh/flashback-when-rush-limbaughs-hate-was-televised

11. Eviatar, D. (2015, June 29). Murdoch's *Fox News*. Retrieved March 1, 2020, from https://www.thenation.com/article/archive/murdochs-fox-news/

12. Nichols, T. (2017). *The Death of Expertise*. New York, NY: Oxford University Press. p. 153

13. Price, G. (2018, August 10). *Fox News's* audience is almost exclusively white, according to new report. Retrieved March 1, 2020, from https://www.newsweek.com/fox-news-white-audience-immigration-1067807

14. Martin, G. J., & Yurukoglu, A. (2017). Bias in Cable News: Persuasion and Polarization. American Economic Review, 107(9), 2565–2599. doi: 10.1257/aer.20160812

15. Schroeder, E., & Stone, D. F. (2015). *Fox News* and political knowledge. Journal of Public Economics, 126, 52–63. doi: 10.1016/j.jpubeco.2015.03.009

16. Arceneaux, K., Johnson, M., Lindstädt, R., & Wielen, R. J. (2015). The Influence of News Media on Political Elites: Investigating Strategic Responsiveness in Congress. American Journal of Political Science, 60(1), 5–29. doi: 10.1111/ajps.12171

17. Hacker, J. S., & Pierson, P. (2020*). Let them eat Tweets: How the right rules in an age of extreme inequality*. New York, NY, NY: Liveright Publishing Corporation, a division of W. W. Norton & Company. p. 98

18. Hacker, J. S., & Pierson, P. (2020*). Let them eat Tweets: How the right rules in an age of extreme inequality*. New York, NY, NY: Liveright Publishing Corporation, a division of W. W. Norton & Company. p. 98, 108

19. Gentzkow, M., & Shapiro, J. M. (2010). What Drives Media Slant? Evidence From U.S. Daily Newspapers. Econometrica, 78(1), 35–71. doi: 10.3982/ecta7195

20. Interactive Media Bias Chart. (2020, February 1). Retrieved March 1, 2020, from https://www.adfontesmedia.com/interactive-media-bias-chart/?v=402f03a963ba

21. Roose, K. (n.d.). Facebook's Top 10. Retrieved September 19, 2020, from https://

twitter.com/FacebooksTop10

22. Kelley, M. B. (2012, May 22). STUDY: Watching Only *Fox News* Makes You Less Informed Than Watching No News At All. Retrieved from https://www.businessinsider.com/study-watching-fox-news-makes-you-less-informed-than-watching-no-news-at-all-2012-5

23. Nagler, J., Guess, A., & Tucker, J. (2019, January 9). Analysis | Who was most likely to share fake news in 2016? Seniors. Retrieved March 1, 2020, from https://www.washingtonpost.com/news/monkey-cage/wp/2019/01/09/who-shared-fake-news-during-the-2016-election-campaign-youll-be-surprised/?fbclid=IwAR3SxQHuuXn-qhRzzExjB8-CbNbOL1u7btbcugL91lfN9g-nFftqz-K17p-o

24. Peck, R. (2019). *Fox populism: branding conservatism as working class.* Cambridge: Cambridge University Press.

25. Segers, G. (2019, October 24). 99 percent of Republican white evangelical Protestants oppose impeaching and removing Trump, new poll finds. Retrieved March 1, 2020, from https://www.cbsnews.com/news/99-of-white-evangelical-protestants-oppose-impeaching-and-removing-trump/

26. Staff, PRRI. "Trumpism After Trump? How *Fox News* Structures Republican Attitudes | PRRI." *PRRI*, https://www.prri.org/research/trumpism-after-trump-how-fox-news-structures-republican-attitudes/. Accessed 20 Nov. 2020.

27. "In U.S., Decline of Christianity Continues at Rapid Pace." *Pew Research Center's Religion & Public Life Project*, 17 Oct. 2019, https://www.pewforum.org/2019/10/17/in-u-s-decline-of-christianity-continues-at-rapid-pace/.

28. Staff, PRRI. "Trumpism After Trump? How *Fox News* Structures Republican Attitudes | PRRI." *PRRI*, https://www.prri.org/research/trumpism-after-trump-how-fox-news-structures-republican-attitudes/. Accessed 20 Nov. 2020.

29. Associated Press. (2020, February 24). Connecticut runners suing to stop transgender competitors wins on track. Retrieved from https://www.thewesterlysun.com/news/stonington/connecticut-runners-suing-to-stop-transgender-competitors-wins-on-track/article_189c9344-54bc-5879-a10c-bebd3c4ce859.html

30. Beer, Tommy. "Majority Of Republicans Believe The QAnon Conspiracy Theory Is Partly Or Mostly True, Survey Finds." *Forbes*, 2 Sept. 2020, https://www.forbes.com/sites/tommybeer/2020/09/02/majority-of-republicans-believe-the-qanon-conspiracy-theory-is-partly-or-mostly-true-survey-finds/.

31. Limpert, Ann. "Comet Ping Pong Has Been Getting a New Uptick in Pizzagate Messages | Washingtonian (DC)." *Washingtonian*, 12 May 2020, https://www.washingtonian.com/2020/05/11/comet-ping-pong-has-been-getting-a-new-uptick-in-pizzagate-messages/.

32. Cox, Kate. "FBI Says 'Extremists' Motivated by Pizzagate, QAnon Are Threats." *Ars Technica*, 1 Aug. 2019, https://arstechnica.com/tech-policy/2019/08/fbi-says-extremists-motivated-by-pizzagate-qanon-are-threats/.

33. Roberts, D. (2017, May 19). Donald Trump and the rise of tribal epistemology. Retrieved from https://www.vox.com/policy-and-politics/2017/3/22/14762030/donald-trump-tribal-epistemology

34. Hacker, J. S., & Pierson, P. (2020*). Let them eat Tweets: How the right rules in an age of extreme inequality.* New York, NY, NY: Liveright Publishing Corporation, a division of W. W. Norton & Company. p. 103

35. Jurkowitz, M., Mitchell, A., Shearer, E., & Walker, M. (2020, February 21). U.S. Media

Polarization and the 2020 Election: A Nation Divided. Retrieved from https://www.journalism.org/2020/01/24/u-s-media-polarization-and-the-2020-election-a-nation-divided/

36. Marcin, T. (2019, February 25). Trump voters trust Infowars as much as NYT, WaPo, poll shows. Retrieved September 19, 2020, from https://www.newsweek.com/trump-voters-trust-infowars-much-new-york-times-washington-post-poll-1331958

37. Jurkowitz, M., Mitchell, A., Shearer, E., Walker, M. (2020, August 28). U.S. Media Polarization and the 2020 Election: A Nation Divided. Retrieved September 17, 2020, from https://www.journalism.org/2020/01/24/u-s-media-polarization-and-the-2020-election-a-nation-divided/

38. Mitchell, Amy. "People Around World Want Unbiased News." *Pew Research Center's Global Attitudes Project*, 11 Jan. 2018, https://www.pewresearch.org/global/2018/01/11/publics-globally-want-unbiased-news-coverage-but-are-divided-on-whether-their-news-media-deliver/.

39. Based on ad fontes' interactive "Media Bias" chart 5.1. https://www.adfontesmedia.com/interactive-media-bias-chart/?v=402f03a963ba

40. Lewis, B. (2019, October 25). I watched *Fox News* every day for 44 months – here's what I learned. Retrieved from https://www.theguardian.com/media/2019/oct/25/fox-news-watching-what-i-learned

41. Coppins, S. by M. K. (2020, February 10). The Billion-Dollar Disinformation Campaign to Reelect the President. Retrieved from https://www.theatlantic.com/magazine/archive/2020/03/the-2020-disinformation-war/605530/?fbclid=IwAR017JG-SmUsMD8BmzE5zg5MSdcCVI9LXeQ5Haq5pSRrsuA6MqJlHo1aI31g

42. Robins-Early, N. (2020, September 17). 16 Straight Hours Inside The Alternate Reality Of Pro-Trump TV Channel *OAN*. Retrieved September 19, 2020, from https://www.huffpost.com/entry/oan-trump-news-network_n_5f5bbbf8c5b62874bc1cadd4

43. Bump, P. (2019, November 5). Analysis | Republicans have heard less about the impeachment probe - and are more likely to reject established details. Retrieved March 3, 2020, from https://www.washingtonpost.com/politics/2019/11/05/republicans-have-heard-less-about-impeachment-probe-and-are-more-likely-reject-established-details/

44. Bierbauer, Charles. "Trump White House Goes 300+ Days without a Press Briefing – Why That's Unprecedented." *The Conversation*, 24 Feb. 2020, http://theconversation.com/trump-white-house-goes-300-days-without-a-press-briefing-why-thats-unprecedented-130164.

45. Sisk, Richard. "The Drought Is Over: Pentagon Spokesman Holds 1st Formal Press Briefing." *Military.Com*, 20 Sept. 2019, https://www.military.com/daily-news/2019/09/20/drought-over-pentagon-spokesman-holds-1st-formal-press-briefing.html.

46. Gertz, M., Glover, J., Greenfield, J., & Glorioso, A. (2018, January 5). I've Studied the Trump-Fox Feedback Loop for Months. It's Crazier Than You Think. Retrieved from https://www.politico.com/magazine/story/2018/01/05/trump-media-feedback-loop-216248

47. Garber, M. (2020, September 16). Do You Speak Fox? Retrieved September 19, 2020, from https://www.theatlantic.com/culture/archive/2020/09/fox-news-trump-language-stelter-hoax/616309/

48. "Tamarian Language." *Memory Alpha*, https://memory-alpha.fandom.com/wiki/

Tamarian_language. Accessed 10 Nov. 2020.

49. Goldhill, O. (2017, April 22). Rhetoric scholars pinpoint why Trump's inarticulate speaking style is so persuasive. Retrieved September 19, 2020, from https://qz.com/965004/rhetoric-scholars-pinpoint-why-trumps-inarticulate-speaking-style-is-so-persuasive/

50. Bump, P. (2019, March 29). Analysis | A glossary of Trump's rhetorical shorthand. Retrieved September 19, 2020, from https://www.washingtonpost.com/news/politics/wp/2017/07/22/a-glossary-of-trumps-rhetorical-shorthand/

51. Coppins, M. K. (2017). What if the right-wing media wins? Retrieved from https://www.cjr.org/special_report/right-wing-media-breitbart-fox-bannon-carlson-hannity-coulter-trump.php

52. Kavanagh, Jennifer and Michael D. Rich, Truth Decay: An Initial Exploration of the Diminishing Role of Facts and Analysis in American Public Life. Santa Monica, CA: RAND Corporation, 2018. https://www.rand.org/pubs/research_reports/RR2314.html. Also available in print form.

53. Rosenthal, A. (2016, December 15). To Understand Trump, Learn Russian. Retrieved September 19, 2020, from https://www.nytimes.com/2016/12/15/opinion/to-understand-trump-learn-russian.html

54. The Economist Staff. (2007, January 12). Europe: From Estonia to Atlantis. Retrieved September 19, 2020, from https://www.economist.com/taxonomy/term/122?page=12

55. Kuzio, T. (2019, October 11). How Putin used propaganda to deftly turn Russians against Ukrainians. Retrieved September 19, 2020, from https://theconversation.com/how-putin-used-propaganda-to-deftly-turn-russians-against-ukrainians-81376

56. Elder, Miriam. "'Nothing Is True and Everything Is Possible,' by Peter Pomerantsev (Published 2014)." *NYTimes*, 25 Nov. 2014, https://www.nytimes.com/2014/11/30/books/review/nothing-is-true-and-everything-is-possible-by-peter-pomerantsev.html.

57. Snyder, T. (2019). *The road to unfreedom: Russia, Europe, America*. London, UK: Vintage. p. 161

58. Hern, A. (2018, February 06). Fake news sharing in US is a rightwing thing, says study. Retrieved September 19, 2020, from https://www.theguardian.com/technology/2018/feb/06/sharing-fake-news-us-rightwing-study-trump-university-of-oxford

59. Toler, Aric. "The Kremlin's Shifting, Self-Contradicting Narratives on MH17 - Bellingcat." *Bellingcat*, 5 Jan. 2018, https://www.bellingcat.com/news/uk-and-europe/2018/01/05/kremlins-shifting-self-contradicting-narratives-mh17/.

60. Snyder, T. (2019). *The road to unfreedom: Russia, Europe, America*. London, UK: Vintage. p. 181-182

61. Snyder, T. (2019). *The road to unfreedom: Russia, Europe, America*. London, UK: Vintage. p. 195

62. Wright, Eric. "Trump Says Putin Is 'Not Going to Go into Ukraine,' despite Crimea." *CNN*, 31 July 2016, https://www.cnn.com/2016/07/31/politics/donald-trump-russia-ukraine-crimea-putin/index.html.

63. Gessen, M. (2020). *Surviving Autocracy*. New York, NY: Riverhead Books. p. 134

64. Sinderbrand, Rebecca. "How Kellyanne Conway Ushered in the Era of 'Alternative Facts.'" *The Washington Post*, 22 Jan. 2017, https://www.washingtonpost.com/news/the-fix/wp/2017/01/22/how-kellyanne-conway-ushered-in-the-era-of-alternative-

facts/.

65. Gessen, M. (2020). *Surviving Autocracy*. New York, NY: Riverhead Books. p. 105

66. Julia Ainsley, Carol. "Vindman's Brother Files Whistleblower Complaint Alleging White House Retaliation." *NBC News*, 26 Aug. 2020, https://www.nbcnews.com/politics/white-house/vindman-s-brother-files-whistleblower-complaint-alleging-white-house-retaliation-n1238273.

67. Edkins, B. (2016, December 20). Americans Believe They Can Detect Fake News. Studies Show They Can't. Retrieved September 19, 2020, from https://www.forbes.com/sites/brettedkins/2016/12/20/americans-believe-they-can-detect-fake-news-studies-show-they-cant/

68. Barthell, M., Mitchell, A., Holcomb, J. (2020, August 27). Many Americans Believe Fake News Is Sowing Confusion. Retrieved September 19, 2020, from https://www.journalism.org/2016/12/15/many-americans-believe-fake-news-is-sowing-confusion/?utm_source=Pew+Research+Center

69. Fischer, S. (2018, June 26). 92 percent of Republicans think media intentionally reports fake news. Retrieved September 19, 2020, from https://www.axios.com/trump-effect-92-percent-republicans-media-fake-news-9c1bbf70-0054-41dd-b506-0869bb-10f08c.html

70. Fessler, D. M., Pisor, A. C., Holbrook, C. (2017). Political Orientation Predicts Credulity Regarding Putative Hazards. Psychological Science, 28(5), 651-660. doi:10.1177/0956797617692108

71. Nyhan, B., & Reifler, J. (2010). When Corrections Fail: The Persistence of Political Misperceptions. Political Behavior, 32(2), 303-330. doi:10.1007/s11109-010-9112-2

72. Merlan, Anna. *The Conspiracy Singularity Has Arrived*. 24 Feb. 2020, https://www.vice.com/en/article/v7gz53/the-conspiracy-singularity-has-arrived.

73. Cox, Kate. "Former Facebook Manager: 'We Took a Page from Big Tobacco's Playbook.'" *Ars Technica*, 24 Sept. 2020, https://arstechnica.com/tech-policy/2020/09/former-facebook-manager-we-took-a-page-from-big-tobaccos-playbook/.

74. Burton, T. I. (2018, October 30). The Bible says to welcome immigrants. So why don't white evangelicals? Retrieved September 19, 2020, from https://www.vox.com/2018/10/30/18035336/white-evangelicals-immigration-nationalism-christianity-refugee-honduras-migrant

75. Barthell, M., Mitchell, A., Holcomb, J. (2020, August 27). Many Americans Believe Fake News Is Sowing Confusion. Retrieved September 19, 2020, from https://www.journalism.org/2016/12/15/many-americans-believe-fake-news-is-sowing-confusion/?utm_source=Pew+Research+Center

76. Tannehill, B. (2020, February 24). The U.S. Is Headed for Single-Party Rule. Retrieved September 19, 2020, from https://www.damemagazine.com/2020/02/24/the-u-s-is-headed-for-single-party-rule/

77. Coppins, M. (2020, April 19). The Billion-Dollar Disinformation Campaign to Reelect the President. Retrieved September 19, 2020, from https://www.theatlantic.com/magazine/archive/2020/03/the-2020-disinformation-war/605530/?fbclid=IwAR-017JGSmUsMD8BmzE5zg5MSdcCVI9LXeQ5Haq5pSRrsuA6MqJlHo1aI31g

78. Milbank, Dana. "Opinion | In Trump's Mind, It's Always 'Really Sunny.' And That's Terrifying." *The Washington Post*, 27 Jan. 2017, https://www.washingtonpost.com/opinions/in-trumps-mind-its-always-really-sunny-and-thats-terrifying/2017/01/27/ff0a6278-e499-11e6-a547-5fb9411d332c_story.html.

79. Rizzo, S., Kessler, G. (2020, July 13). Analysis | President Trump has made more than 20,000 false or misleading claims. Retrieved September 19, 2020, from https://www.washingtonpost.com/politics/2020/07/13/president-trump-has-made-more-than-20000-false-or-misleading-claims/

80. Paletta, D., Dawsey, J., & Werner, E. (2019, April 28). In fundraising speech, Trump says he made up trade claim in meeting with Justin Trudeau. Retrieved September 19, 2020, from https://www.washingtonpost.com/news/post-politics/wp/2018/03/14/in-fundraising-speech-trump-says-he-made-up-facts-in-meeting-with-justin-trudeau/

81. Vosoughi, S., Roy, D., Aral, S. (2018). The spread of true and false news online. *Science,* 359(6380), 1146-1151. doi:10.1126/science.aap9559

82. Lewandowski, S., Ecker, U. K., &; Seifert, C. M. (2012, September 17). Misinformation and Its Correction: Continued Influence and Successful Debiasing - Stephan Lewandowsky, Ullrich K. H. Ecker, Colleen M. Seifert, Norbert Schwarz, John Cook, 2012. Retrieved September 19, 2020, from https://journals.sagepub.com/doi/full/10.1177/1529100612451018

83. Alviani, C. (2017, February 08). There's a name for Trump's technique to overwhelm the public with a stream of tiny lies. Retrieved September 19, 2020, from https://qz.com/905252/donald-trumps-lies-are-all-part-of-a-debate-tactic-called-the-gish-gallop/

84. Dewey, Caitlin. "What Was Fake on the Internet This Week: Why Do We Even Bother, Honestly?" *The Washington Post*, 30 Oct. 2015, https://www.washingtonpost.com/news/the-intersect/wp/2015/10/30/what-was-fake-on-the-internet-this-week-why-do-we-even-bother-honestly/.

85. Swire, B., Berinsky, A. J., Lewandowsky, S., & Ecker, U. K. H. (2017). Processing political misinformation: comprehending the Trump phenomenon. *Royal Society Open Science,* 4(3), 160802. doi: 10.1098/rsos.160802

86. Rupar, A. (2019, May 6). Why Facebook is turning to a conservative website for fact checking. Retrieved March 3, 2020, from https://www.vox.com/2019/5/2/18522758/facebook-fact-checking-partnership-daily-caller

87. Legum, J. (2020, March 3). The Daily Caller uses status as Facebook fact-checker to boost Trump . Retrieved from https://popular.info/p/the-daily-caller-uses-status-as-facebook

88. Timberg, C., Dwoskin, E., & Romm, T. (2020, June 29). Zuckerberg once wanted to sanction Trump. Then Facebook wrote rules that accommodated him. Retrieved September 19, 2020, from https://www.washingtonpost.com/technology/2020/06/28/facebook-zuckerberg-trump-hate/

89. Ortutay, B. (2020, January 09). Facebook again refuses to ban political ads, even false ones. Retrieved September 19, 2020, from https://apnews.com/90e5e81f501346f-8779cb2f8b8880d9c

90. Shearer, Elisa. "News Use Across Social Media Platforms 2017." *Pew Research Center's Journalism Project*, 7 Sept. 2017, https://www.journalism.org/2017/09/07/news-use-across-social-media-platforms-2017/.

91. Goldman, R. (2017, January 7). Russia's RT: The Network Implicated in U.S. Election Meddling. Retrieved from https://www.nytimes.com/2017/01/07/world/europe/russias-rt-the-network-implicated-in-us-election-meddling.html

92. Derysh, I. (2019, April 12). New data suggests Russians targeted Bernie Sanders voters to help elect Trump. Retrieved from https://www.salon.com/2019/04/12/new-

data-suggests-russians-targeted-bernie-sanders-voters-to-help-elect-trump/

93. Satariano, A. (2019, January 17). Facebook Identifies Russia-Linked Misinformation Campaign. Retrieved from https://www.nytimes.com/2019/01/17/business/facebook-misinformation-russia.html

94. Parks, M. (2019, April 24). FACT CHECK: Russian Interference Went Far Beyond 'Facebook Ads' Kushner Described. Retrieved from https://www.npr.org/2019/04/24/716374421/fact-check-russian-interference-went-far-beyond-facebook-ads-kushner-described

95. Abbruzzese, J. (2019, July 10). Conspiracy theory about slain DNC staffer was planted by Russian intelligence, report finds. Retrieved from https://www.nbcnews.com/tech/tech-news/conspiracy-theory-about-slain-dnc-staffer-was-planted-russian-intelligence-n1027826

96. Barrett, B. (2020, February 21). Russia Doesn't Want Bernie Sanders. It Wants Chaos. Retrieved from https://www.wired.com/story/bernie-sanders-russia-chaos-2020-election/

97. Paul, Christopher and Miriam Matthews, The Russian "Firehose of Falsehood" Propaganda Model: Why It Might Work and Options to Counter It, Santa Monica, Calif.: RAND Corporation, PE-198-OSD, 2016. As of February 04, 2020: https://www.rand.org/pubs/perspectives/PE198.html

98. Perlroth, N. (2019, November 21). A Former *Fox News* Executive Divides Americans Using Russian Tactics. Retrieved from https://www.nytimes.com/2019/11/21/technology/LaCorte-edition-news.html?fbclid=IwAR22PW6l7BCEJg6aku0K-MEghZ0WzZqegWbwX1b1iyoCcYRwta_nEJkwWWu8

99. Legum, J. (2019, October 28). Facebook allows prominent right-wing website to break the rules . Retrieved from https://popular.info/p/facebook-allows-prominent-right-wing

100. Rieger, J. M. (2020, February 7). Analysis | The 30 defenses Trump's allies have floated on Ukraine and impeachment. Retrieved from https://www.washingtonpost.com/politics/2019/11/18/defenses-trumps-allies-have-floated-ukraine-impeachment/

101. Smith, B. (2019, November 20). What's Really Happening At *The New York Times*? A Succession Fight. Retrieved from https://www.buzzfeednews.com/article/bensmith/new-york-times-editor

102. Rosen, Jay. "America's Press and the Asymmetric War for Truth." *The New York Review of Books*, https://www.nybooks.com/daily/2020/11/01/americas-press-and-the-asymmetric-war-for-truth/. Accessed 16 Nov. 2020.

103. Wright, Colin. "Okrent's Law." *Brain Lenses*, https://brainlenses.substack.com/p/okrents-law. Accessed 19 Dec. 2020.

104. Haynes, Suyin. "President Trump Said Revolutionary War Troops 'Took Over the Airports' in Fourth of July Speech." *Time*, 5 July 2019, https://time.com/5620936/donald-trump-revolutionary-war-airports/.

105. Rosenberg, M., Confessore, N., & Cadwalladr, C. (2018, March 17). How Trump Consultants Exploited the Facebook Data of Millions. Retrieved from https://www.nytimes.com/2018/03/17/us/politics/cambridge-analytica-trump-campaign.html

106. Green, J., & Issenberg, S. (2016, October 27). Inside the Trump Bunker, With Days to Go. Retrieved from https://www.bloomberg.com/news/articles/2016-10-27/inside-the-trump-bunker-with-12-days-to-go

107. https://www.washingtonpost.com/news/opinions/wp/2017/06/22/maybe-de-

mocracy-dies-in-broad-daylight/

108. DeVega, C. (2018, October 18). Historian Christopher Browning on the Trump regime: We're "close to the point of no return." Retrieved from https://www.salon.com/2018/10/18/historian-christopher-browning-on-the-trump-regime-were-close-to-the-point-of-no-return/?fbclid=IwAR2ndFWkfyk8YK2asbqzjBY-kopApzejIjNk-8fkMfrCBeaUNc_gQrUQAZzI

109. Walsh, J. (2020, February 07). Perspective | Joe Walsh: Challenging Trump for the GOP nomination taught me my party is a cult. Retrieved September 19, 2020, from https://www.washingtonpost.com/outlook/2020/02/06/joe-walsh-challenging-trump-gop-nomination-taught-me-my-party-is-cult/

110. Coppins, S. by M. K. (2020, February 10). The Billion-Dollar Disinformation Campaign to Reelect the President. Retrieved from https://www.theatlantic.com/magazine/archive/2020/03/the-2020-disinformation-war/605530/?fbclid=IwAR017JG-SmUsMD8BmzE5zg5MSdcCVI9LXeQ5Haq5pSRrsuA6MqJlHo1aI31g

Chapter 5

1. Nichols, T. (2017). *The Death of Expertise*. New York, NY: Oxford University Press.

2. Brandt AM. Inventing conflicts of interest: a history of tobacco industry tactics. Am J Public Health. 2012;102(1):63-71. doi:10.2105/AJPH.2011.300292

3. Campaign for Tobacco Free Kids. (2019, August 20). U.S. Racketeering Verdict: Timeline: United States v. Philip Morris USA Inc., et al. Retrieved September 19, 2020, from https://www.tobaccofreekids.org/what-we-do/industry-watch/doj/timeline

4. Dreisbach, T. (2019, June 17). Tobacco's 'Special Friend': What Internal Documents Say About Mitch McConnell. Retrieved September 19, 2020, from https://www.npr.org/2019/06/17/730496066/tobaccos-special-friend-what-internal-documents-say-about-mitch-mcconnell

5. Matthews, D. (2020, February 03). Rush Limbaugh denied health risks of smoking years before lung cancer diagnosis: 'I would like a medal for smoking cigars'. Retrieved September 19, 2020, from https://www.nydailynews.com/news/national/ny-rush-limbaugh-smoking-effects-cancer-diagnosis-20200203-4ma66mowazek-tovzh7hg2aynhq-story.html

6. Kennedy, M. (2020, February 03). Rush Limbaugh Says He Has Been Diagnosed With Advanced Lung Cancer. Retrieved September 19, 2020, from https://www.npr.org/2020/02/03/802388079/rush-limbaugh-says-he-has-been-diagnosed-with-advanced-lung-cancer

7. Roberts, D. (2020, February 05). New conservative climate plans are neither conservative nor climate plans. Retrieved September 19, 2020, from https://www.vox.com/energy-and-environment/2020/2/5/21121935/climate-change-republicans-conservatives

8. Zaleha, Bernard & Szasz, Andrew. (2015). Why Conservative Christians Don't Believe in Climate Change. Bulletin of the Atomic Scientists. 71. 19-30. 10.1177/0096340215599789.

9. Pew Research Center. (2019, December 31). Section 2: Views of Gay Men and Lesbians, Roots of Homosexuality, Personal Contact with Gays. Retrieved September 19, 2020, from https://www.pewresearch.org/politics/2013/06/06/section-2-views-of-gay-men-and-lesbians-roots-of-homosexuality-personal-contact-with-gays/

10. Tankersley, Jim. "It's Official: The Trump Tax Cuts Didn't Pay for Themselves in Year One (Published 2019)." *NYTimes*, 11 Jan. 2019, https://www.nytimes.

com/2019/01/11/business/trump-tax-cuts-revenue.html.

11. Kurtzman, L. (2020, September 15). Five Years After Abortion, Nearly All Women Say It Was the Right Decision, Study Finds. Retrieved September 19, 2020, from https://www.ucsf.edu/news/2020/01/416421/five-years-after-abortion-nearly-all-women-say-it-was-right-decision-study; Epstein, K. (2019, July 03). Medication abortions can't be 'reversed.' A law forcing doctors to say they can be is headed to court. Retrieved September 19, 2020, from https://www.washingtonpost.com/health/2019/07/02/medication-abortions-cant-be-reversed-law-forcing-doctors-say-they-can-be-is-headed-court/

12. Allen, A. (2019, April 17). Republicans reject Democratic attempts to tighten vaccine laws. Retrieved September 19, 2020, from https://www.politico.com/story/2019/04/16/republican-reject-democrat-vaccines-1361277

13. Krugman, P. (2019, June 22). Notes on Excessive Wealth Disorder. Retrieved September 19, 2020, from https://www.nytimes.com/2019/06/22/opinion/notes-on-excessive-wealth-disorder.html

14. Atkinson, K. (2018, July 12). House Republicans reject funding for gun violence research. Retrieved September 19, 2020, from https://www.axios.com/house-republicans-rejects-funding-for-gun-violence-research--748c5f1f-017f-4182-9e3d-07c835aed5d0.html

15. *BBC News*. (2019, August 05). America's gun culture in charts. Retrieved September 19, 2020, from https://www.bbc.com/news/world-us-canada-41488081

16. Zarracina, J. (2018, February 16). Guns Make Republicans Feel Safe. So America Can't Be. Retrieved September 19, 2020, from https://nymag.com/intelligencer/2018/02/the-gop-is-putting-political-correctness-above-public-safety.html

17. Sullivan, K. (2019, August 07). Mental illness isn't a major risk factor for gun violence, but here's what is. Retrieved September 19, 2020, from https://www.nbcnews.com/health/health-news/mental-illness-isn-t-major-risk-factor-gun-violence-here-n1039666

18. Whitten, S. (2019, August 09). No evidence that violent video games are causing mass shootings, despite politicians' claims. Retrieved September 19, 2020, from https://www.cnbc.com/2019/08/09/no-evidence-that-violent-video-games-are-causing-mass-shootings.html

19. Tenbarge, K. (2019, August 04). In a '*Fox Friends*' segment, Texas' Lieutenant Governor suggested violent video games and a lack of prayer in schools could be factors in the El Paso mass shooting. Retrieved September 19, 2020, from https://www.businessinsider.com/texas-lieutenant-govenor-dan-patrick-video-games-el-paso-shooting-2019-8

20. Aaron R. Brough, James E. B. Wilkie, Jingjing Ma, Mathew S. Isaac, David Gal, Is Eco-Friendly Unmanly? The Green-Feminine Stereotype and Its Effect on Sustainable Consumption, Journal of Consumer Research, Volume 43, Issue 4, December 2016, Pages 567–582, https://doi.org/10.1093/jcr/ucw044

21. Bort, R. (2019, March 01). No, Democrats Don't Want to 'Murder' or 'Execute' Babies. Retrieved September 19, 2020, from https://www.rollingstone.com/politics/politics-news/cpac-mike-pence-abortion-802060/

22. Welna, D. (2013, April 08). Some Gun Control Opponents Cite Fear Of Government Tyranny. Retrieved September 19, 2020, from https://www.npr.org/sections/itsallpolitics/2013/04/08/176350364/fears-of-government-tyranny-push-some-to-reject-

gun-control; Martinez, M. (2013, April 8). Communism Survivor Blasts Gun Control: "You Don't Know What Freedom Is." Retrieved September 19, 2020, from https://www.realclearpolitics.com/video/2013/04/08/communism_survivor_blasts_gun_control_you_dont_know_what_freedom_is.html

23. PRRI. (2012, September 20). Beyond Guns and God: Understanding the Complexities of the White Working Class in America. Retrieved September 12, 2020, from https://www.prri.org/wp-content/uploads/2012/09/WWC-Report-For-Web-Final-1.pdf

24. Bacon, P., Jr. (2018, September 11). Americans Are Shifting The Rest Of Their Identity To Match Their Politics. Retrieved September 19, 2020, from https://fivethirtyeight.com/features/americans-are-shifting-the-rest-of-their-identity-to-match-their-politics/

25. Appelbaum, Y. (2019, November 17). How America Ends. Retrieved September 19, 2020, from https://www.theatlantic.com/magazine/archive/2019/12/how-america-ends/600757/

26. Appelbaum, Y. (2019, November 17). How America Ends. Retrieved September 19, 2020, from https://www.theatlantic.com/magazine/archive/2019/12/how-america-ends/600757/

27. Eco, U. (1995, June 22). Ur-Fascism. Retrieved September 19, 2020, from https://www.nybooks.com/articles/1995/06/22/ur-fascism/

28. Mason, L., & Wronski, J. (2018). One Tribe to Bind Them All: How Our Social Group Attachments Strengthen Partisanship. Political Psychology, 39, 257-277. doi:10.1111/pops.12485

29. Lührmann, Anna, Nils Düpont, Masaaki Higashijima, Yaman Berker Kavasoglu, Kyle L. Marquardt, Michael Bernhard, Holger Döring, Allen Hicken, Melis Laebens, Sta□an I. Lindberg, Juraj Medzihorsky, Anja Neundorf, Ora John Reuter, Saskia Ruth–Lovell, Keith R. Weghorst, Nina Wiesehomeier, JosephWright, Nazifa Alizada, Paul Bederke, Lisa Gastaldi, Sandra Grahn, Garry Hindle, Nina Ilchenko, Johannes von Römer, Daniel Pemstein, and Brigitte Seim. 2020. "Varieties of Party Identity and Organization (V–Party) Dataset V1." Varieties of Democracy (V-Dem) Project, https://www.v-dem.net/en/data/data/v-party-dataset

30. Roberts, D. (2017, March 22). Donald Trump and the rise of tribal epistemology. Retrieved September 19, 2020, from https://www.vox.com/policy-and-politics/2017/3/22/14762030/donald-trump-tribal-epistemology

31. Bump, P. (2019, April 26). Jim Inhofe's snowball has disproven climate change once and for all. Retrieved September 19, 2020, from https://www.washingtonpost.com/news/the-fix/wp/2015/02/26/jim-inhofes-snowball-has-disproven-climate-change-once-and-for-all/

32. Ganzach, Y., Hanoch, Y., & Choma, B. L. (2019). Attitudes Toward Presidential Candidates in the 2012 and 2016 American Elections: Cognitive Ability and Support for Trump. Social Psychological and Personality Science, 10(7), 924–934. https://doi.org/10.1177/1948550618800494

33. Nichols, T. M. (2019). *The death of expertise: The campaign against established knowledge and why it matters.* New York, NY: Oxford University Press. p. 5

34. Suls, R. (2020, August 28). Educational divide in vote preferences on track to be wider than in recent elections. Retrieved September 19, 2020, from https://www.pewresearch.org/fact-tank/2016/09/15/educational-divide-in-vote-preferences-on-track-to-be-wider-than-in-recent-elections/

35. Kurtzleben, D. (2020, January 09). Richest Republicans View Health Care Far Differently Than Poorest, *NPR* Poll Finds. Retrieved September 19, 2020, from https://www.npr.org/2020/01/09/789127994/npr-poll-finds-sizable-income-gap-on-republicans-views-of-health-coverage

36. Parker, K. (2019, August 19). Views of Higher Education Divided by Party. Retrieved September 19, 2020, from https://www.pewsocialtrends.org/essay/the-growing-partisan-divide-in-views-of-higher-education/

37. Politico Staff. (2012, September 15). Rick Santorum Values Voter Summit speech transcript (full text). Retrieved September 19, 2020, from https://www.politico.com/story/2012/09/rick-santorum-values-voter-summit-speech-transcript-full-text-081256

38. Molloy, P. (2019, September 19). PragerU relies on a veneer of respectability to obscure its propagandist mission. Retrieved September 19, 2020, from https://www.mediamatters.org/dennis-prager/prageru-relies-veneer-respectability-obscure-its-propagandist-mission

39. Musto, J. (2019, November 26). Dennis Prager: Why sending your child to college is like playing 'Russian roulette'. Retrieved September 19, 2020, from https://www.foxnews.com/media/dennis-prager-education-first-amendment-no-safe-spaces-free-speech

40. The Economist Daily Chart. (2020, January 9). Are left-wing American professors indoctrinating their students? Retrieved September 23, 2020, from https://www.economist.com/graphic-detail/2020/01/09/are-left-wing-american-professors-indoctrinating-their-students

41. Tyson, Charlie and Naomi Oreskes. 2020. "The American University, the Politics of Professors and the Narrative of 'Liberal Bias'." Social Epistemology Review and Reply Collective 9 (8): 14-32. https://wp.me/p1Bfg0-5gq.

42. Strauss, Valerie. "Texas GOP Rejects 'Critical Thinking' Skills. Really." *The Washington Post*, 9 July 2012, https://www.washingtonpost.com/blogs/answer-sheet/post/texas-gop-rejects-critical-thinking-skills-really/2012/07/08/gJQAHNpFXW_blog.html.

43. Zhang, S. (2019, January 14). Trump's Most Trusted Adviser Is His Own Gut. Retrieved September 19, 2020, from https://www.theatlantic.com/politics/archive/2019/01/trump-follows-his-gut/580084/

44. Reich, R. (2018, January 07). Robert Reich: Trump may be dumb, but he has plenty of emotional intelligence. Retrieved September 19, 2020, from https://www.newsweek.com/robert-reich-trump-may-be-dumb-he-has-plenty-emotional-intelligence-773200

45. Graham, D. A. (2018, January 05). The President Who Doesn't Read. Retrieved September 19, 2020, from https://www.theatlantic.com/politics/archive/2018/01/americas-first-post-text-president/549794/

46. Mark, M. (2019, November 19). The anonymous White House official says in their new book that Trump aides had to dumb down his briefings to one key point repeated over and over. Retrieved September 19, 2020, from https://www.businessinsider.com/anonymous-white-house-book-trump-briefings-2019-11

47. Applebaum, A. (2019, May 10). Opinion | Trump has the attention span of a gnat. It's destroying our foreign policy. Retrieved September 19, 2020, from https://www.washingtonpost.com/opinions/global-opinions/trump-has-the-attention-span-of-a-gnat-its-destroying-our-foreign-policy/2019/05/10/c5b30620-733e-11e9-9f06-5fc2ee80027a_story.html

48. Schwartz, I. (2015, June 18). Donald Trump: Eventually 50 percent Of Americans Are Not Going To Be Able to Carry The Other 50 percent. Retrieved September 19, 2020, from https://www.realclearpolitics.com/video/2015/06/18/donald_trump_eventually_50_of_americans_are_not_going_to_be_able_to_carry_the_other_50.html; Hale, T. (2015, November 25). Rush Limbaugh is a hypocrite when it comes to Trump. Retrieved September 19, 2020, from https://thehill.com/blogs/pundits-blog/presidential-campaign/261258-when-it-comes-to-trump-rush-limbaugh-is-a-hypocrite

49. Morin, R. (2018, September 04). 'Idiot,' 'Dope,' 'Moron': How Trump's aides have insulted the boss. Retrieved September 19, 2020, from https://www.politico.com/story/2018/09/04/trumps-insults-idiot-woodward-806455; Riotta, C. (2018, September 04). James Mattis said Trump has 'understanding of a fifth or sixth grader,' new book claims. Retrieved September 19, 2020, from https://www.independent.co.uk/news/world/americas/donald-trump-bob-woodward-new-book-fear-robert-mueller-white-house-a8523066.html

50. Collins, Eliza. "Trump: I Consult Myself on Foreign Policy." POLITICO, 16 Mar. 2016, https://www.politico.com/blogs/2016-gop-primary-live-updates-and-results/2016/03/trump-foreign-policy-adviser-220853.

51. Gass, Nick. "Trump: 'The Experts Are Terrible.'" POLITICO, 4 Apr. 2016, https://www.politico.com/blogs/2016-gop-primary-live-updates-and-results/2016/04/donald-trump-foreign-policy-experts-221528.

52. Lewis, M. (2019). Fifth Risk: Undoing Democracy. New York, NY: W.W. Norton & Company. p. 19

53. Smith, David. "Chris Christie Dropped as Head of Trump's White House Transition Team." The Guardian, 11 Nov. 2016, http://www.theguardian.com/us-news/2016/nov/11/chris-christie-dropped-trump-transition-team.; Berkowitz, Bonnie. "Laws and Customs Guide Presidential Transitions — but Some Go off the Rails Anyway." The Washington Post, 1 Dec. 2020, https://www.washingtonpost.com/graphics/2020/politics/abnormal-transitions-of-power-timeline/.

54. Lewis, M. (2019). Fifth Risk: Undoing Democracy. New York, NY: W.W. Norton & Company. p. 39

55. Thrush, Glenn. "Trump and Staff Rethink Tactics After Stumbles (Published 2017)." NYTimes, 6 Feb. 2017, https://www.nytimes.com/2017/02/05/us/politics/trump-white-house-aides-strategy.html.

56. Victoria Knight, Kaiser. "Obama Team Left Pandemic Playbook for Trump Administration, Officials Confirm." PBS NewsHour, 15 May 2020, https://www.pbs.org/newshour/nation/obama-team-left-pandemic-playbook-for-trump-administration-officials-confirm.

57. Friedersdorf, C. (2019, October 04). You Can't Drain the Swamp and Also Defend the President. Retrieved September 19, 2020, from https://www.theatlantic.com/ideas/archive/2019/10/trump-making-swamp-worse/599344/

58. Gross, T. (2018, May 17). How Trump's 'War' On The 'Deep State' Is Leading To The Dismantling Of Government. Retrieved September 19, 2020, from https://www.npr.org/2018/05/17/611922875/how-trump-s-war-on-the-deep-state-is-leading-to-the-dismantling-of-government

59. Packer, G. (2020, May 11). The President Is Winning His War on American Institutions. Retrieved September 20, 2020, from https://www.theatlantic.com/magazine/archive/2020/04/how-to-destroy-a-government/606793/

60. Lewis, M. (2019). *Fifth Risk: Undoing Democracy*. New York, NY: W.W. Norton & Company. p. 39
61. Jacobs, M. (2016, December 12). Trump is appointing people who hate the agencies they will lead. Retrieved September 19, 2020, from https://www.cnn.com/2016/12/10/opinions/government-is-the-problem-jacobs/index.html
62. Filkins, D., Yaffa, J., Coll, S. (2017, October 6). Rex Tillerson at the Breaking Point. Retrieved September 19, 2020, from https://www.newyorker.com/magazine/2017/10/16/rex-tillerson-at-the-breaking-point
63. Buncombe, A. (2017, January 19). Donald Trump's energy secretary didn't know his department oversaw the US nuclear stockpiles. Retrieved September 19, 2020, from https://www.independent.co.uk/news/world/americas/rick-perry-enerhy-secretary-donald-trump-nominee-senate-hearing-not-know-nuclear-weapon-stockpile-arsenal-a7535876.html
64. Lewis, M. (2019). *Fifth Risk: Undoing Democracy*. New York, NY: W.W. Norton & Company. p. 43-44
65. Phillips, A. (2019, April 29). Betsy DeVos just gave a master class in what not to do in a confirmation hearing. Retrieved September 19, 2020, from https://www.washingtonpost.com/news/the-fix/wp/2017/01/18/betsy-devos-demonstrates-exactly-how-you-dont-want-your-confirmation-hearing-to-go/
66. Gass, N. (2015, November 06). Ben Carson's 15 most controversial quotes. Retrieved September 19, 2020, from https://www.politico.com/story/2015/10/ben-carson-controversial-quotes-214614
67. Gee, A. (2017, May 25). Ben Carson, tasked with helping the poor, believes poverty is 'a state of mind'. Retrieved September 19, 2020, from https://www.theguardian.com/us-news/2017/may/25/ben-carson-poverty-state-of-mind
68. Analysis by Chris Cillizza, *CNN*. "Ben Carson's 'Oreo' Screw-up Is the Most Predictable Thing Ever." *CNN*, 22 May 2019, https://www.cnn.com/2019/05/22/politics/donald-trump-ben-carson-oreo-hud/index.html.
69. Rochabrun, Eric. "5 Trump Cabinet Members Who've Made False Statements to Congress." *ProPublica*, 2 Mar. 2017, https://www.propublica.org/article/five-trump-cabinet-members-made-false-statements-to-congress?token=sYB-NO6t1202JOb6ILFkA_eTWzPmpol3N.
70. Gessen, M. (2020). *Surviving Autocracy*. New York, NY: Riverhead Books. p. 20
71. Zielinski, S. (2010, February 01). When the Soviet Union Chose the Wrong Side on Genetics and Evolution. Retrieved September 19, 2020, from https://www.smithsonianmag.com/science-nature/when-the-soviet-union-chose-the-wrong-side-on-genetics-and-evolution-23179035/
72. Thomas Childers Thomas Childers, author of is the recently. "Perspective | Five Myths about Nazis." *The Washington Post*, 20 Oct. 2017, https://www.washingtonpost.com/outlook/five-myths/five-myths-about-nazis/2017/10/20/f4463dea-b2b5-11e7-9e58-e6288544af98_story.html.
73. Nichols, T. M. (2019). The death of expertise: The campaign against established knowledge and why it matters. New York, NY: Oxford University Press. p. XII
74. Kasperkevic, Jana. "Poll: 30 percent of GOP Voters Support Bombing Agrabah, the City from Aladdin." *The Guardian*, 18 Dec. 2015, http://www.theguardian.com/us-news/2015/dec/18/republican-voters-bomb-agrabah-disney-aladdin-donald-trump.

75. Fisk, Robert. "Most Americans Say 'Arabic Numerals' Should Not Be Taught in School." *Share Your Thoughts and Debate the Big Issues*, 17 May 2019, https://www.independent.co.uk/news/arabic-numerals-survey-prejudice-bias-survey-research-civic-science-a8918256.html.

76. Nichols, T. M. (2019). The death of expertise: The campaign against established knowledge and why it matters. New York, NY: Oxford University Press. p. 110

77. Alter/Kenosha, Charlotte. "How Conspiracy Theories Are Shaping the 2020 Election—and Shaking the Foundation of American Democracy." *Time*, 10 Sept. 2020, https://time.com/5887437/conspiracy-theories-2020-election/.

78. Toosi, N. (2019, December 17). Pompeo Gets Low Marks From Employees Who Know Him Best. Retrieved September 19, 2020, from https://www.politico.com/news/agenda/2019/12/17/government-morale-pompeo-state-086218

79. Wilson, R. (2019, October 21). Diplomats describe all-time low in morale at State under Trump. Retrieved September 19, 2020, from https://thehill.com/homenews/administration/466538-diplomats-describe-all-time-low-in-morale-at-state-under-trump

80. Perrigo, B. (2017, November 09). U.S. Has Lost 60 percent Of Ambassadors Under Trump. Retrieved September 19, 2020, from https://time.com/5016774/trump-ambassadors-state-department-lost-60-percent-afsa-barbara-stephenson/

81. Boggioni, T. (2020, February 17). 'Morale is at a low point' under Bill Barr as career attorneys flee Justice Dept: Ex-federal prosecutor. Retrieved September 19, 2020, from https://www.rawstory.com/2020/02/morale-is-at-a-low-point-under-bill-barr-as-career-attorneys-flee-justice-dept-ex-federal-prosecutor/

82. Clark, D., Kosnar, M., Gregorian, D., & Winter, T. (2020, February 12). All four Roger Stone prosecutors resign from case after DOJ backpedals on sentencing recommendation. Retrieved September 19, 2020, from https://www.nbcnews.com/politics/politics-news/doj-backpedalling-sentencing-recommendation-trump-ally-roger-stone-n1134961

83. Gessen, M. (2020). *Surviving Autocracy*. New York, NY: Riverhead Books. p. 181

84. LaFrance, A. (2017, March 16). Scientists Brace for a Lost Generation in American Research. Retrieved September 19, 2020, from https://www.theatlantic.com/science/archive/2017/03/trump-budget-cuts-science/519825/?utm_campaign=the-atlantic

85. "How Trump Damaged Science." *Nature*, 5 Oct. 2020, https://www.nature.com/articles/d41586-020-02800-9.

86. Fisk, Robert. "Trump Passes Executive Order That Could Destroy a Future Biden Administration." *The Independent*, 23 Oct. 2020, https://www.independent.co.uk/voices/trump-executive-order-civil-service-biden-election-schedule-f-b1255692.html.

87. Rogers, Katie. "Trump Administration Signals Formal Withdrawal From W.H.O." *NYTimes*, 2 Sept. 2020, https://www.nytimes.com/2020/07/07/us/politics/coronavirus-trump-who.html.

88. Keith Johnson, Colum. "Trump Rushes to Kill Off Iran Nuclear Deal Before Election." *Foreign Policy*, 12 June 2020, https://foreignpolicy.com/2020/06/12/trump-rushes-to-kill-off-iran-nuclear-deal-before-election/.

89. Bacon, Rep. "Divided We Fall: The United States Needs International Partners Now More Than Ever - War on the Rocks." *War on the Rocks*, 12 June 2020, https://warontherocks.com/2020/06/divided-we-fall-the-united-states-needs-internation-

al-partners-now-more-than-ever/.

90. Illing, S. (2019, February 22). It is absolutely time to panic about climate change. Retrieved September 19, 2020, from https://www.vox.com/energy-and-environment/2019/2/22/18188562/climate-change-david-wallace-wells-the-uninhabitable-earth

91. Levy, K., & Johns, D. (2019, December 13). Perspective | How Trump's war on science is borrowing from the tobacco industry playbook. Retrieved September 19, 2020, from https://www.washingtonpost.com/outlook/2019/12/13/how-trumps-war-science-is-borrowing-tobacco-industry-playbook/

92. "How Trump Damaged Science." *Nature*, 5 Oct. 2020, https://www.nature.com/articles/d41586-020-02800-9.

93. Browne, Ryan. "Member of Pentagon Advisory Board Resigns in Protest at Recent Purge." *CNN*, 7 Dec. 2020, https://www.cnn.com/2020/12/07/politics/pentagon-advisory-board-resignation/index.html.; Press, 11. "Kellyanne Conway on the Air Force Academy Board of Visitors." *Military.Com*, 11 Dec. 2020, https://www.military.com/daily-news/2020/12/11/kellyanne-conway-air-force-academy-board-of-visitors.html.

94. Lewis, M. (2019). Fifth Risk: Undoing Democracy. New York, NY: W.W. Norton & Company. p. 75

95. Walcott, J. (2019, February 05). Donald Trump Rejects Intelligence Briefing Facts. Retrieved September 20, 2020, from https://time.com/5518947/donald-trump-intelligence-briefings-national-security/

96. Diamond, D. (2020, March 08). Trump's mismanagement helped fuel coronavirus crisis. Retrieved September 20, 2020, from https://www.politico.com/news/2020/03/07/trump-coronavirus-management-style-123465

97. Tracy, Abigail. "How Trump Gutted Obama's Pandemic-Preparedness Systems." *Vanity Fair*, 1 May 2020, https://www.vanityfair.com/news/2020/05/trump-obama-coronavirus-pandemic-response.

98. Victoria Knight, Kaiser. "Obama Team Left Pandemic Playbook for Trump Administration, Officials Confirm." *PBS NewsHour*, 15 May 2020, https://www.pbs.org/newshour/nation/obama-team-left-pandemic-playbook-for-trump-administration-officials-confirm.

99. Zeballos-Roig, J. (2020, February 9). Here's why the 2020 election-year economy is shaping up perfectly for Trump | Markets Insider. Retrieved September 20, 2020, from https://markets.businessinsider.com/news/stocks/why-economy-trump-biggest-strengths-campaign-election-jobs-unemployment-2020-2-1028886799

100. Long, H. (2019, December 28). Trump's stock market rally is very good, but still lags Obama and Clinton. Retrieved September 20, 2020, from https://www.washingtonpost.com/business/2019/12/28/trumps-stock-market-rally-is-very-good-still-lags-obama-clinton/

101. Lee, T. (2016, July 19). Donald Trump can't admit when he's made a mistake. That's a bad trait for a president. Retrieved September 20, 2020, from https://www.vox.com/2016/7/19/12226316/trump-never-admit-mistakes

102. Danner, C. (2020, March 07). Trump Says Coronavirus Testing Is As 'Perfect' As His Ukraine Call. Retrieved September 20, 2020, from https://nymag.com/intelligencer/2020/03/trump-coronavirus-testing-as-perfect-as-ukraine-call.html

103. Nakamura, D. (2020, March 07). 'Maybe I have a natural ability': Trump plays medi-

cal expert on coronavirus by second-guessing the professionals. Retrieved September 20, 2020, from https://www.washingtonpost.com/politics/maybe-i-have-a-natural-ability-trump-plays-medical-expert-on-coronavirus-by-second-guessing-the-professionals/2020/03/06/3ee0574c-5ffb-11ea-9055-5fa12981bbbf_story.html

104. Sullivan, B. K. (2020, March 05). Trump Assurances Aside, Warmer Weather May Not Slow Coronavirus. Retrieved September 20, 2020, from https://www.bloomberg.com/news/articles/2020-03-05/trump-assurances-aside-warmer-weather-may-not-slow-coronavirus

105. Brockell, G. (2020, March 08). Trump 'didn't know people died from the flu.' It killed his grandfather. Retrieved September 20, 2020, from https://www.washingtonpost.com/history/2020/03/07/flu-trump-grandfather-death-coronavirus/

106. Pengelly, M., & Holpuch, A. (2020, March 01). Coronavirus: Pence defends Trump Jr claim Democrats want 'millions' to die. Retrieved September 20, 2020, from https://www.theguardian.com/world/2020/mar/01/coronavirus-mike-pence-donald-trump-jr-democrats-millions-die

107. Lancaster, G. (2017, December 17). The nomination of Alex Azar says a lot about our broken health care system. Retrieved September 20, 2020, from https://thehill.com/opinion/healthcare/365342-the-nomination-of-alex-azar-says-a-lot-about-our-broken-health-care-system

108. Gonsalves, G., Crawford, F. (2020, March 03). How Mike Pence Made Indiana's HIV Outbreak Worse. Retrieved September 20, 2020, from https://www.politico.com/news/magazine/2020/03/02/how-mike-pence-made-indianas-hiv-outbreak-worse-118648

109. Gittleson, B., & Cathey, L. (2020, February 27). Trump, Pence try to manage coronavirus response amid new fears it could spread. Retrieved September 20, 2020, from https://abcnews.go.com/Politics/trump-pence-manage-coronavirus-response-amid-fears-spread/story?id=69255477

110. White House. (2020, March 6). Remarks by President Trump at Signing of the Coronavirus Preparedness and Response Supplemental Appropriations Act, 2020. Retrieved September 20, 2020, from https://www.whitehouse.gov/briefings-statements/remarks-president-trump-signing-coronavirus-preparedness-response-supplemental-appropriations-act-2020/

111. Cancryn, A., Diamond, D. (2020, February 14). Escaping the coronavirus 'petri dish': Doctor, lawmakers seek evacuations from quarantined cruise. Retrieved September 20, 2020, from https://www.politico.com/news/2020/02/14/escaping-the-coronavirus-petri-dish-doctor-lawmakers-seek-evacuations-from-quarantined-cruise-115143

112. Stobbe, M. (2020, March 8). Official: White House didn't want to tell seniors not to fly. Retrieved September 20, 2020, from https://abcnews.go.com/Health/wireStory/official-white-house-seniors-fly-69462660

113. Ward, A. (2020, February 27). Closed schools and empty stadiums: How countries are trying to stop coronavirus's spread. Retrieved September 20, 2020, from https://www.vox.com/2020/2/27/21155864/coronavirus-italy-saudi-arabia-south-korea-japan-military

114. King, R. (2020, July 06). Fauci says U.S. 'still knee-deep in the first wave' of COVID-19 as daily cases top 50K. Retrieved September 20, 2020, from https://www.fiercehealthcare.com/hospitals/fauci-clarifies-u-s-not-midst-new-COVID-19-wave-as-daily-cases-top-50k

115. New York Times Staff. (2020, March 08). In U.S., Cases of Coronavirus Cross 500, and Deaths Rise to 22. Retrieved September 20, 2020, from https://www.nytimes.com/2020/03/08/world/coronavirus-news.html

116. Prayias, G. (2020, February 24). Overhyped Coronavirus Weaponized Against Trump. Retrieved September 20, 2020, from https://www.rushlimbaugh.com/daily/2020/02/24/overhyped-coronavirus-weaponized-against-trump/

117. Gettys, T. (2020, February 26). Trump stokes coronavirus conspiracy theory involving Rod Rosenstein's sister. Retrieved September 20, 2020, from https://www.rawstory.com/2020/02/trump-stokes-coronavirus-conspiracy-theory-involving-rod-rosensteins-sister/

118. Media Matters Staff. (2020, March 4). *Fox News* guest calls the CDC a "highly politicized organization" because of "how they've acted on gun control." Retrieved September 20, 2020, from https://www.mediamatters.org/laura-ingraham/fox-news-guest-calls-cdc-highly-politicized-organization-because-how-theyve-acted

119. Okun, E. (2020, February 25). Kudlow breaks with CDC on coronavirus: 'We have contained this'. Retrieved September 20, 2020, from https://www.politico.com/news/2020/02/25/kudlow-white-house-coronavirus-117402

120. Keith, T., & Romo, V. (2020, March 05). Trump's Gut Collides With Science On Coronavirus Messaging. Retrieved September 20, 2020, from https://www.npr.org/2020/03/05/812519679/trumps-gut-collides-with-science-on-coronavirus-messaging

121. Rupar, A. (2020, March 05). "This is just my hunch": Trump goes on *Fox News* and spreads misinformation about the coronavirus. Retrieved September 20, 2020, fromhttps://www.vox.com/2020/3/5/21166031/trump-hannity-coronavirus-who-death-rate

122. Folley, Aris. "Trump: Biden Will 'Listen to the Scientists' If Elected." *The Hill*, 19 Oct. 2020, https://thehill.com/homenews/521638-trump-biden-will-listen-to-the-scientists-if-elected.

123. Staff, Media. "Laura Ingraham Attacks Joe Biden for Promising to Listen to Health Experts on COVID-19." *Media Matters for America*, 29 Oct. 2020, https://www.mediamatters.org/fox-news/laura-ingraham-attacks-joe-biden-promising-listen-health-experts-COVID-19.

124. Sullivan, B. K. (2020, March 05). Trump Assurances Aside, Warmer Weather May Not Slow Coronavirus. Retrieved September 20, 2020, from https://www.bloomberg.com/news/articles/2020-03-05/trump-assurances-aside-warmer-weather-may-not-slow-coronavirus

125. Centers for Disease Control. (2018, May 11). 1918 Pandemic Influenza: Three Waves. Retrieved September 20, 2020, from https://www.cdc.gov/flu/pandemic-resources/1918-commemoration/three-waves.htm

126. Owermohle, S. (2020, March 03). 'You don't want to go to war with a president'. Retrieved September 20, 2020, from https://www.politico.com/news/2020/03/03/anthony-fauci-trump-coronavirus-crisis-118961

127. Centers for Disease Control. (2020, January 21). First Travel-related Case of 2019 Novel Coronavirus Detected in United States. Retrieved September 20, 2020, from https://www.cdc.gov/media/releases/2020/p0121-novel-coronavirus-travel-case.html

128. Vergano, D. (2020, February 28). New York Is Making Its Own Coronavirus Test

After The CDC's Tests Failed. Retrieved September 20, 2020, from https://www.buzzfeednews.com/article/danvergano/coronavirus-test-new-york-cdc

129. Rabin, R. C., & Thomas, K. (2020, March 04). Coronavirus Testing Offered With Just a Doctor's Approval, C.D.C. Says. Retrieved September 20, 2020, from https://www.nytimes.com/2020/03/04/health/coronavirus-test-demand.html

130. Liu, J., Liao, X., Qian, S., Yuan, J., Wang, F., Liu, Y....Zhang, Z. (2020). Community Transmission of Severe Acute Respiratory Syndrome Coronavirus 2, Shenzhen, China, 2020. Emerging Infectious Diseases, 26(6), 1320-1323. https://dx.doi.org/10.3201/eid2606.200239.

131. Diamond, D. (2020, March 08). Trump's mismanagement helped fuel coronavirus crisis. Retrieved September 20, 2020, from https://www.politico.com/news/2020/03/07/trump-coronavirus-management-style-123465

132. Bump, P. (2020, July 24). Analysis | Trump is right that with lower testing, we record fewer cases. That's already happening. Retrieved September 20, 2020, from https://www.washingtonpost.com/politics/2020/07/23/trumps-right-that-with-less-testing-we-record-fewer-cases-fact-thats-already-happening/

133. Werner, E., Bernstein, L., Sun, L. H., Berger, M., & Brice-Sadler, M. (2020, February 26). Spread of coronavirus in U.S. appears inevitable, health officials warn, as Trump defends response. Retrieved September 20, 2020, from https://www.washingtonpost.com/world/asia_pacific/coronavirus-china-live-updates/2020/02/25/f4045570-5758-11ea-9000-f3cffee23036_story.html

134. Lovelace, B., Jr. (2020, February 22). Hospitals across the US prepare for coronavirus outbreak to become global pandemic. Retrieved September 20, 2020, from https://www.cnbc.com/2020/02/19/hospitals-across-the-us-prepare-for-coronavirus-outbreak-to-become-global-pandemic.html

135. Zhang, S., Diao, M., Yu, W., Pei, L., Lin, Z., Chen, D. (2020). Estimation of the reproductive number of novel coronavirus (COVID-19) and the probable outbreak size on the Diamond Princess cruise ship: A data-driven analysis. International Journal of Infectious Diseases, 93, 201-204. doi:10.1016/j.ijid.2020.02.033; Kelley, A. (2020, April 03). Harvard scientist: Coronavirus pandemic likely will infect 40-70 percent of world this year. Retrieved September 20, 2020, from https://thehill.com/changing-america/well-being/prevention-cures/482794-officials-say-the-cdc-is-preparing-for

136. Zoellner, D. (2020, March 07). Expert warns of 96 million possible coronavirus infections in US with up to half a million dead. Retrieved September 20, 2020, from https://www.independent.co.uk/news/world/americas/coronavirus-dr-james-lawler-warning-us-hospitals-infection-a9385031.html

137. Kenen, J. (2020, March 05). Trump's coronavirus musings put scientists on edge. Retrieved September 20, 2020, from https://www.politico.com/news/2020/03/05/trump-coronavirus-scientists-on-edge-122121

138. JASON DEAREN, MIKE. "White House Puts 'Politicals' at CDC to Try to Control Info." *Associated Press*, 16 Oct. 2020, https://apnews.com/article/election-2020-virus-outbreak-pandemics-public-health-new-york-e321f4c9098b4db4dd6b1e-da76a5179e.

139. Glasser, S. (2020, April 9). How Did the U.S. End Up with Nurses Wearing Garbage Bags? Retrieved September 20, 2020, from https://www.newyorker.com/news/letter-from-trumps-washington/the-coronavirus-and-how-the-united-states-ended-up-with-nurses-wearing-garbage-bags

140. Malcom, K., Raftery, I., & Farmer, M. (2020, March 06). The ominous days leading up to the coronavirus outbreak in the Seattle area. Retrieved September 20, 2020, from https://www.kuow.org/stories/the-days-leading-up-to-the-outbreak-at-life-care-center-in-kirkland

141. Schneider, H. (2020, April 29). Much of U.S. economy still plugging along despite coronavirus pain. Retrieved September 20, 2020, from https://www.reuters.com/article/us-health-coronavirus-usa-gdp-insight/much-of-u-s-economy-still-plugging-along-despite-coronavirus-pain-idUSKCN22B0DZ

142. Wright, J. (2020, March 03). Perspective | Four disastrous mistakes that leaders make during epidemics. Retrieved September 20, 2020, from https://www.washingtonpost.com/outlook/2020/03/03/four-disastrous-mistakes-that-leaders-make-during-epidemics/?utm_campaign=wp_opinions

143. Goldberg, Michelle. "Opinion | Trump's Calamitous Coronavirus Response." NYTimes, 6 Mar. 2020, https://www.nytimes.com/2020/03/06/opinion/trump-coronavirus-us.html.

144. Weixel, Nathaniel. "Stanford Faculty Condemn Scott Atlas for 'View of COVID-19 That Contradicts Medical Science.'" The Hill, 20 Nov. 2020, https://thehill.com/policy/healthcare/526900-stanford-faculty-condemn-scott-atlas-for-view-of-COVID-19-that-contradicts.

145. Hamilton, Lawrence C., Joel Hartter, and Kei Saito. 2015. "Trust in Scientists on Climate Change and Vaccines." Sage Open 5: 3: 1–13. https://doi.org/10.1177/2158244015602752.

146. Evanega, S., Lynas, M., Adams, J., & Smolenyak, K. (2020). Coronavirus misinformation: Quantifying sources and themes in the COVID-19 'infodemic' (Preprint). doi:10.2196/preprints.25143

147. Spangler, Todd. "After Twitter Banned Donald Trump, Election Misinformation Online Plunged Dramatically." Variety, 17 Jan. 2021, https://variety.com/2021/digital/news/twitter-ban-trump-election-misinformation-research-1234887030/.

148. Staff, PRRI. "Trumpism After Trump? How Fox News Structures Republican Attitudes | PRRI." PRRI, https://www.prri.org/research/trumpism-after-trump-how-fox-news-structures-republican-attitudes/. Accessed 20 Nov. 2020.

149. Diamond, D. (2020, March 08). Trump's mismanagement helped fuel coronavirus crisis. Retrieved September 20, 2020, from https://www.politico.com/news/2020/03/07/trump-coronavirus-management-style-123465

150. Jurkowitz, Mark. "Republicans Who Rely Most on Trump for COVID-19 News See the Outbreak Differently from Those Who Don't." Pew Research Center, 12 Oct. 2020, https://www.pewresearch.org/fact-tank/2020/10/12/republicans-who-rely-most-on-trump-for-COVID-19-news-see-the-outbreak-differently-from-those-who-dont/.

151. Heath, B. (2020, March 06). Americans divided on party lines over risk from coronavirus: Reuters/Ipsos poll. Retrieved September 20, 2020, from https://www.reuters.com/article/us-health-coronavirus-usa-polarization/americans-divided-on-party-lines-over-risk-from-coronavirus-reuters-ipsos-poll-idUSKBN20T2O3

152. Johnson, CK., Fingerhut, H., Deshpande, P., "Counties with Worst Virus Surges Overwhelmingly Voted Trump." Associated Press, 5 Nov. 2020, https://apnews.com/article/counties-worst-virus-surges-voted-trump-d671a483534024b5486715da6edb6ebf.

153. Gollwitzer, A., Martel, C., Brady, W.J. *et al.* Partisan differences in physical distancing are linked to health outcomes during the COVID-19 pandemic. *Nat Hum Behav* **4**, 1186–1197 (2020). https://doi.org/10.1038/s41562-020-00977-7

154. Centers for Disease Control. (2020, August 18). COVID-19 Hospitalization and Death by Age. Retrieved September 20, 2020, from https://www.cdc.gov/coronavirus/2019-ncov/COVID-19-data/investigations-discovery/hospitalization-death-by-age.html

155. Saba, J. (2017, April 04). *Fox* Scandals May Weaken Murdochs' TV Future. Retrieved September 20, 2020, from https://www.nytimes.com/2017/04/04/business/dealbook/fox-scandals-may-weaken-murdochs-tv-future.html

156. Snouwaert, J. (2020, April 15). 2 medical experts estimate 90 percent of coronavirus deaths in the US could have been avoided if everyone started social distancing on March 2. Retrieved September 20, 2020, from https://www.businessinsider.com/coronavirus-deaths-us-could-avoided-by-social-distancing-sooner-experts-2020-4

157. Sullivan, P. (2020, August 31). Trump retweets conspiracy theory questioning COVID-19 death toll. Retrieved September 20, 2020, from https://thehill.com/policy/healthcare/514430-trump-retweets-conspiracy-theory-questioning-COVID-19-death-toll

158. Bump, P. (2020, August 24). Analysis | What does it mean that most Republicans see the coronavirus death toll as acceptable? Retrieved September 20, 2020, from https://www.washingtonpost.com/politics/2020/08/24/what-does-it-mean-that-most-republicans-see-coronavirus-death-toll-acceptable/

159. Gross, T. (2020, April 30). How The CARES Act Became A Tax-Break Bonanza For The Rich, Explained. Retrieved September 20, 2020, from https://www.npr.org/2020/04/30/848321204/how-the-cares-act-became-a-tax-break-bonanza-for-the-rich-explained

160. Romm, T., Bogage, J., Sun, L. H. (2020, September 17). Newly revealed USPS documents show an agency struggling to manage Trump, Amazon and the pandemic. Retrieved September 20, 2020, from https://www.washingtonpost.com/us-policy/2020/09/17/usps-trump-coronavirus-amazon-foia/

161. Eban, K. (2020, July 30). How Jared Kushner's Secret Testing Plan "Went Poof Into Thin Air." Retrieved September 20, 2020, from https://www.vanityfair.com/news/2020/07/how-jared-kushners-secret-testing-plan-went-poof-into-thin-air

162. Eban, K. (2020, September 17). "That's Their Problem": How Jared Kushner Let the Markets Decide America's COVID-19 Fate. Retrieved September 20, 2020, from https://www.vanityfair.com/news/2020/09/jared-kushner-let-the-markets-decide-COVID-19-fate

163. Parker, A., Dawsey, J., & Abutleb, Y. (2020, September 17). Ten days: After an early coronavirus warning, Trump is distracted as he downplays threat. Retrieved September 20, 2020, from https://www.washingtonpost.com/politics/trump-woodward-coronavirus-downplay-ten-days/2020/09/16/6529318c-f69e-11ea-a275-1a2c-2d36e1f1_story.html

164. Baragona, J. (2020, September 10). Lou Dobbs Ignores Woodward Tapes: Trump Had a 'Great Day!' Retrieved September 20, 2020, from https://www.thedailybeast.com/lou-dobbs-ignores-woodward-tapes-declares-that-trump-had-a-great-day

165. Kaplan, T. (2020, September 10). Joe Concha blasts media's claim that Trump 'misled' the public following Woodward book revelations. Retrieved September 20, 2020, from

https://www.foxnews.com/media/joe-concha-blasts-medias-woodward-book-revelations

166. Goldberg, J. (2020, September 03). Trump: Americans Who Died in War Are 'Losers' and 'Suckers'. Retrieved September 20, 2020, from https://www.theatlantic.com/politics/archive/2020/09/trump-americans-who-died-at-war-are-losers-and-suckers/615997/

167. Baragona, J. (2020, September 04). *Fox News* Bashes Anonymous Sourcing of Trump Army 'Losers' Story, Then Uses Anonymous Sources to Dispute It. Retrieved September 20, 2020, from https://www.thedailybeast.com/fox-ridicules-anonymous-sourcing-of-trump-military-losers-report-then-uses-anonymous-sources-to-dispute-it

168. Friedersdorf, C. (2020, April 27). The Implications of 'Trump Derangement Syndrome'. Retrieved September 20, 2020, from https://www.theatlantic.com/ideas/archive/2020/04/the-implications-of-trump-derangement-syndrome/610705/

169. Forrest, A. (2020, September 18). Trump said coronavirus was good because he didn't have shake hands with 'disgusting people', claims ex-White House aide. Retrieved September 20, 2020, from https://www.independent.co.uk/news/world/americas/us-politics/trump-coronavirus-good-thing-shake-hands-disgusting-people-olivia-troye-b480406.html

170. DeVega, C. (2018, May 15). Historian Timothy Snyder on Trump's war on democracy: He is deliberately "hurting white people." Retrieved September 20, 2020, from https://www.salon.com/2018/05/09/timothy-snyder-on-trumps-campaign-against-democracy-he-is-deliberately-hurting-white-people/

171. Bote, Joshua. "Half of Trump Supporters Believe in QAnon Conspiracy Theory's Baseless Claims, Poll Finds." *USA TODAY*, https://www.usatoday.com/story/news/politics/2020/10/22/qanon-poll-finds-half-trump-supporters-believe-baseless-claims/3725567001/. Accessed 16 Nov. 2020.

Chapter 6

1. Troy, Gil. "What Is the Least Credible History Book in Print?" *Departments*, https://historynewsnetwork.org/article/147149. Accessed 10 Apr. 2020.

2. Yudkin, D. A. (2019, August 21). Hidden Tribes: A Study of America's Polarized Landscape. https://doi.org/10.31234/osf.io/xz25v

3. Hawkins, S., Yudkin, D., Juan-Torres, M., Dixon, T. (2018). *Hidden Tribes: A Study of America's Polarized Landscape* (pp. 1-159, Rep.). New York, NY: More in Common.

4. Jones, R. P. (2020). *White too long: The legacy of white supremacy in American Christianity*. New York, NY, NY: Simon & Schuster. p. 175

5. Ibid. p. 177

6. Adam Meyerson, "Conscience of a Cultural Conservative. Paul M. Weyrich on the Politics of Character in Russia and America," *Policy Review* 59 (Winter 1992).

7. Blumenthal, Max. "Justice Sunday Preachers." *The Nation*, 26 Apr. 2005, https://www.thenation.com/article/archive/justice-sunday-preachers/.

8. Pew Research. (2019, May 14). Changing Attitudes on Same-Sex Marriage. Retrieved from https://www.pewforum.org/fact-sheet/changing-attitudes-on-gay-marriage/

9. Pew Research. (2015, May 11). Religion in America: U.S. Religious Data, Demographics and Statistics. Retrieved from https://www.pewforum.org/religious-landscape-study/

10. Edsall, T. B. (2019, July 3). Trump Needs His Base to Burn With Anger. Retrieved March 1, 2020, from https://www.nytimes.com/2019/07/03/opinion/trump-republican-base.html

11. "An Examination of the 2016 Electorate, Based on Validated Voters." *Pew Research Center - U.S. Politics & Policy*, 9 Aug. 2018, https://www.pewresearch.org/politics/2018/08/09/an-examination-of-the-2016-electorate-based-on-validated-voters/.

12. The non-white data was back calculated from the Pew data above.

13. Steinhauer, J. (2007, October 19). Confronting Ghosts of 2000 in South Carolina. Retrieved from https://www.nytimes.com/2007/10/19/us/politics/19mccain.html

14. Luo, M. (2008, June 9). McCain Extends His Outreach, but Evangelicals Are Still Wary. Retrieved from https://www.nytimes.com/2008/06/09/us/politics/09mccain.html

15. Maxwell, A. (2016, July 7). How Southern racism found a home in the Tea Party. Retrieved from https://www.vox.com/2016/7/7/12118872/southern-racism-tea-party-trump

16. Cillizza, C. (2015, January 28). Mitt Romney still has a Mormon problem. Retrieved from https://www.washingtonpost.com/news/the-fix/wp/2015/01/28/mitt-romney-still-has-a-mormon-problem

17. Edsall, T. B. (2019, July 3). Trump Needs His Base to Burn With Anger. Retrieved March 1, 2020, from https://www.nytimes.com/2019/07/03/opinion/trump-republican-base.html

18. McCammon, S. (2016, June 22). Inside Trump's Closed-Door Meeting, Held To Reassure 'The Evangelicals'. Retrieved from https://www.npr.org/2016/06/21/483018976/inside-trumps-closed-door-meeting-held-to-reassures-the-evangelicals

19. "Trump Inauguration: President Vows to End 'American Carnage.'" *BBC News*, 21 Jan. 2017, https://www.bbc.com/news/world-us-canada-38688507.

20. Green, E. (2016, August 2). Trump Wants to Make Churches the New Super PACs. Retrieved from https://www.theatlantic.com/politics/archive/2016/08/how-trump-is-trying-to-put-more-money-in-politics/493823/

21. Stewart, K. (2019, January 1). Why Trump Reigns as King Cyrus. Retrieved from https://www.nytimes.com/2018/12/31/opinion/trump-evangelicals-cyrus-king.html

22. Kuruvilla, C. (2019, April 26). Trump Has Changed White Evangelicals' Views On Morality In One Major Way. Retrieved from https://www.huffpost.com/entry/white-evangelicals-trump-morality_n_5cc20d6de4b031dc07efb940

23. Bailey, S. P. (2016, November 9). White evangelicals voted overwhelmingly for Donald Trump, exit polls show. Retrieved from https://www.washingtonpost.com/news/acts-of-faith/wp/2016/11/09/exit-polls-show-white-evangelicals-voted-overwhelmingly-for-donald-trump/

24. Zhao, C. (2019, July 23). Nearly three-quarters of white Evangelicals approve of Donald Trump. Retrieved from https://www.newsweek.com/nearly-three-quarters-white-evangelicals-approve-donald-trump-1450610

25. Maxwell, A. (2019, July 26). What we get wrong about the Southern strategy. Retrieved from: https://beta.washingtonpost.com/outlook/2019/07/26/what-we-get-wrong-about-southern-strategy/#click=https://t.co/emBy1i8Fnb

26. Serwer, A. (2019, January 3). The Cruelty Is the Point. Retrieved from https://www.theatlantic.com/ideas/archive/2018/10/the-cruelty-is-the-point/572104/

27. U.S. Census Bureau. (2017, January 7). New Census Bureau Report Analyzes U.S. Population Projections. Retrieved from https://www.census.gov/newsroom/press-re-

leases/2015/cb15-tps16.html

28. McCarthy, J. (2019, August 5). U.S. Support for Gay Marriage Stable, at 63 percent. Retrieved from https://news.gallup.com/poll/257705/support-gay-marriage-stable.aspx

29. Jones, R. P., & Cox, D. (2017, September 6). America's Changing Religious Identity: Findings from the 2016 American Values Atlas. Retrieved from https://www.prri.org/wp-content/uploads/2017/09/PRRI-Religion-Report.pdf

30. Renaud, M. (2017, January 19). Myths Debunked: Why Did White Evangelical Christians Vote for Trump?: The University of Chicago Divinity School. Retrieved from https://divinity.uchicago.edu/sightings/myths-debunked-why-did-white-evangelical-christians-vote-trump

31. French, D. (2019, June 27). Why Evangelicals Support Trump Out of Fear, Not Faith. Retrieved from https://time.com/5615617/why-evangelicals-support-trump/

32. Riess, J. (2018, July 2). Why white evangelicals voted for Trump: Fear, power and nostalgia. Retrieved from https://religionnews.com/2018/07/02/why-white-evangelicals-voted-for-trump-fear-power-and-nostalgia/

33. Fea, J. (2018, September 4). Evangelical Fear Elected Trump. Retrieved from https://www.theatlantic.com/ideas/archive/2018/06/a-history-of-evangelical-fear/563558/

34. Ibid.

35. Barthélemy, Hélène. "Christian Right Tips to Fight Transgender Rights: Separate the T from the LGB." *Southern Poverty Law Center*, 23 Oct. 2017, https://www.splcenter.org/hatewatch/2017/10/23/christian-right-tips-fight-transgender-rights-separate-t-lgb.

36. Jost, J. T., West, T. V., Gosling, S. D. (2009). Personality and ideology as determinants of candidate preferences and "Obama conversion" in the 2008 U.S. presidential election. Du Bois Review, 6, 103–124.

37. Jones, R. P. (2020). *White too long: The legacy of white supremacy in American Christianity*. New York, NY, NY: Simon & Schuster. p. 56

38. Shelton, J. E., & Emerson, M. O. (2012). *Blacks and Whites in Christian America: How racial discrimination shapes religious convictions*. New York, NY: New York University Press.

39. Vandermaas-Peeler, A., Cox, D., Najle, M., Fisch-Friedman, M., Griffin, R., & Jones, R. P. (2019, October 29). Partisan Polarization Dominates Trump Era: Findings from the 2018 American Values Survey. Retrieved from https://www.prri.org/research/partisan-polarization-dominates-trump-era-findings-from-the-2018-american-values-survey/

40. Adorno, T., Frenkel-Brunswick, E., Levinson, D., Sanford, R. (1950). The authoritarian personality. New York, NY: Harper.

41. Altemeyer, B. (1981). Right-wing authoritarianism. Winnipeg, Canada: University of Manitoba Press.

42. Feldman, S., & Stenner, K. (1997). Perceived threat and authoritarianism. Political Psychology, 18, 741-770. doi:10.1111/0162-895X.00077

43. Pettigrew, T. F. (2017). Social psychological perspectives on Trump supporters. *Journal of Social and Political Psychology*, 5(1), 107–116. doi: 10.5964/jspp.v5i1.750

44. Keersmaecker, J. D., & Roets, A. (2019). Is there an ideological asymmetry in the moral approval of spreading misinformation by politicians? *Personality and Individual Differences*, 143, 165–169. doi: 10.1016/j.paid.2019.02.003

45. Levin, S.; Federico, C. M.; Sidanius, J.; Rabinowitz, J. L. (2002). "Social Dominance Ori-

entation and Intergroup Bias: The Legitimation of Favoritism for High-Status Groups." *Personality and Social Psychology Bulletin.* 28 (2): 144–57. doi:10.1177/0146167202282002

46. Duriez, B., & Hiel, A. V. (2002). The march of modern fascism. A comparison of social dominance orientation and authoritarianism. *Personality and Individual Differences,* 32(7), 1199–1213. doi: 10.1016/s0191-8869(01)00086-1

47. Sidanius, Jim; Pratto, Felicia; Bobo, Lawrence (1994). "Social dominance orientation and the political psychology of gender: A case of invariance?." *Journal of Personality and Social Psychology.* 67 (6): 998–1011. doi:10.1037/0022-3514.67.6.998

48. Pew Research. (2017, December 14). How Americans Feel About Different Religious Groups. Retrieved from https://www.pewforum.org/2017/02/15/americans-express-increasingly-warm-feelings-toward-religious-groups/; Pew Research. (2015, September 25). Hispanic Catholics echo Pope Francis' call to embrace immigrants. Retrieved from https://www.pewresearch.org/fact-tank/2015/09/25/catholics-especially-hispanics-echo-popes-call-to-embrace-immigrants/

49. Whitley, B. E., & Ægisdottir, S. (2000). The Gender Belief System, Authoritarianism, Social Dominance Orientation, and Heterosexuals' Attitudes Toward Lesbians and Gay Men. *Sex Roles,* 42(11/12), 947–967. Retrieved from https://link.springer.com/content/pdf/10.1023/A:1007026016001.pdf

50. Aune, K. (2008). Evangelical Christianity and Women's Changing Lives. *European Journal of Womens Studies,* 15(3), 277–294. doi: 10.1177/1350506808091508

51. Cowgill, C. M., Rios, K., Simpson, A. (2017). Generous heathens? Reputational concerns and atheists' behavior toward Christians in economic games. *Journal of Experimental Social Psychology,* 73, 169-179. doi:10.1016/j.jesp.2017.06.015

52. Bartels, L. M. (2020). Ethnic antagonism erodes Republicans' commitment to democracy. Proceedings of the National Academy of Sciences, 117(37), 22752-22759. doi:10.1073/pnas.2007747117

53. Buntin, J. (2019, April). Evangelical Voters' Power Isn't Eroding in the Age of Trump. It's Adjusting. Retrieved from https://www.governing.com/topics/politics/gov-government-religion-church-state-evangelicals.html

54. One study found that "the racial and ethnic isolation of whites at the zip-code level is one of the strongest predictors of Trump support." Yudkin, D. A. (2019, August 21). Hidden Tribes: A Study of America's Polarized Landscape. https://doi.org/10.31234/osf.io/xz25v

55. Ibid.

56. Silver, N. (2016, May 3). The Mythology Of Trump's 'Working Class' Support. Retrieved from https://fivethirtyeight.com/features/the-mythology-of-trumps-working-class-support/

57. Graham, K. C. (2008, September 24). The Pope is Not a Biblical Literalist. Retrieved from http://religiondispatches.org/the-pope-is-not-a-biblical-literalist/

58. Pew Research. (2017, September 7). America's Changing Religious Landscape. Retrieved from https://www.pewforum.org/2015/05/12/americas-changing-religious-landscape/

59. Saad, L. (2019, April 23). Record Few Americans Believe Bible Is Literal Word of God. Retrieved from https://news.gallup.com/poll/210704/record-few-americans-believe-bible-literal-word-god.aspx

60. Stokes, B. (2017, February 1). Faith has few strong links to national identity. Retrieved from https://www.pewresearch.org/global/2017/02/01/faith-few-strong-links-to-

national-identity/

61. Jenkins, J. (2019, March 25). 'Nones' now as big as evangelicals, Catholics in the US. Retrieved from https://religionnews.com/2019/03/21/nones-now-as-big-as-evangelicals-catholics-in-the-us/

62. Vandermaas-Peeler, A., Cox, D., Najle, M., Fisch-Friedman, M., Griffin, R., & Jones, R. P.(2018, October 29). Partisan Polarization Dominates Trump Era: Findings from the 2018 American Values Survey. Retrieved from https://www.prri.org/research/partisan-polarization-dominates-trump-era-findings-from-the-2018-american-values-survey/

63. Murphy, C. (2016). The most and least educated U.S. religious groups. [online] Pew Research Center. Available at: https://www.pewresearch.org/fact-tank/2016/11/04/the-most-and-least-educated-u-s-religious-groups/ [Accessed 23 Sep. 2019].

64. Bronstein, M. V., Pennycook, G., Bear, A., Rand, D. G., & Cannon, T. D. (2019). Belief in Fake News is Associated with Delusionality, Dogmatism, Religious Fundamentalism, and Reduced Analytic Thinking. Journal of Applied Research in Memory and Cognition, 8(1), 108–117. doi: 10.1016/j.jarmac.2018.09.005

65. Vandermaas-Peeler, A., Cox, D., Fisch-Friedman, M., Griffin, R., & Jones, R. P. (2018, July 17). American Democracy in Crisis: The Challenges of Voter Knowledge, Participation, and Polarization. Retrieved from https://www.prri.org/research/american-democracy-in-crisis-voters-midterms-trump-election-2018/

66. Vandermaas-Peeler, A., Cox, D., Fisch-Friedman, M., Griffin, R., & Jones, R. P. (2018, July 17). American Democracy in Crisis: The Challenges of Voter Knowledge, Participation, and Polarization. Retrieved from https://www.prri.org/research/american-democracy-in-crisis-voters-midterms-trump-election-2018/

67. Wong, J. (2018, June 19). This is why white evangelicals still support Donald Trump. (It's not economic anxiety.). Retrieved from https://beta.washingtonpost.com/news/monkey-cage/wp/2018/06/19/white-evangelicals-still-support-donald-trump-because-theyre-more-conservative-than-other-evangelicals-this-is-why/?noredirect=on; Klein, L. K. (2019, February 12). Southern Baptist Convention report on sex abuse shines a light on evangelical culture. Retrieved from https://www.nbcnews.com/think/opinion/southern-baptist-convention-report-sex-abuse-shines-light-evangelical-culture-ncna970756

68. Klein, L. K. (2019, February 12). Southern Baptist Convention report on sex abuse shines a light on evangelical culture. Retrieved from https://www.nbcnews.com/think/opinion/southern-baptist-convention-report-sex-abuse-shines-light-evangelical-culture-ncna970756

69. Cox, D., Lienesch, R., & Jones, R. P. (2017, June 21). Who Sees Discrimination? Attitudes about Sexual Orientation, Gender Identity, Race, and Immigration Status: Findings from PRRI's American Values Atlas. Retrieved from https://www.prri.org/research/americans-views-discrimination-immigrants-blacks-lgbt-sex-marriage-immigration-reform/

70. Jones, Robert P., Daniel Cox, Betsy Cooper, and Rachel Lienesch. "Anxiety, Nostalgia, and Mistrust: Findings from the 2015 American Values Survey." PRRI. 2015. http://www.prri.org/research/survey-anxiety-nostalgia-and-mistrust-findings-from-the-2015-american-values-survey/.

71. Jones, Robert P., and Daniel Cox. "Attitudes on Child and Family Wellbeing: National and Southeast/Southwest Perspectives." PRRI. 2017. https://www.prri.org/

research/poll-child-welfare-poverty-race-relations-government-trust-policy/.

72. Vandermaas-Peeler, A., Cox, D., Najle, M., Fisch-Friedman, M., Griffin, R., & Jones, R. P. (2018, October 29). Partisan Polarization Dominates Trump Era: Findings from the 2018 American Values Survey. Retrieved from https://www.prri.org/research/partisan-polarization-dominates-trump-era-findings-from-the-2018-american-values-survey/

73. Quinnipiac University. (2019, July 30). QU Poll Release Detail. Retrieved from https://poll.qu.edu/national/release-detail?ReleaseID=3636

74. Vandermaas-Peeler, A., Cox, D., Najle, M., Fisch-Friedman, M., Griffin, R., & Jones, R. P.(2018, October 29). Partisan Polarization Dominates Trump Era: Findings from the 2018 American Values Survey. Retrieved from https://www.prri.org/research/partisan-polarization-dominates-trump-era-findings-from-the-2018-american-values-survey/

75. Jones, Robert P., and Daniel Cox. "Deep Divide between Black and White Americans in Views of Criminal Justice System." PRRI. 2015. http://www.prri.org/research/divide-white-black-americans-criminal-justice-system/.

76. Balko, R. (2018, September 18). There's overwhelming evidence that the criminal-justice system is racist. Here's the proof. Retrieved from https://www.washingtonpost.com/news/opinions/wp/2018/09/18/theres-overwhelming-evidence-that-the-criminal-justice-system-is-racist-heres-the-proof/

77. Jones, Robert P., Daniel Cox, Betsy Cooper, and Rachel Lienesch. "Anxiety, Nostalgia, and Mistrust: Findings from the 2015 American Values Survey." PRRI. 2015. http://www.prri.org/research/survey-anxiety-nostalgia-and-mistrust-findings-from-the-2015-american-values-survey/.

78. Jones, Robert P., Daniel Cox, Betsy Cooper, and Rachel Lienesch. "Anxiety, Nostalgia, and Mistrust: Findings from the 2015 American Values Survey." PRRI. 2015. http://www.prri.org/research/survey-anxiety-nostalgia-and-mistrust-findings-from-the-2015-american-values-survey/.

79. Vandermaas-Peeler, A., Cox, D., Najle, M., Fisch-Friedman, M., Griffin, R., & Jones, R. P. (2018, October 29). Partisan Polarization Dominates Trump Era: Findings from the 2018 American Values Survey. Retrieved from https://www.prri.org/research/partisan-polarization-dominates-trump-era-findings-from-the-2018-american-values-survey/

80. Jones, R. P. (2020). *White too long: The legacy of white supremacy in American Christianity.* New York, NY, NY: Simon & Schuster. p. 160

81. Beauchamp, Zack. "'Ethnic Outbidding': The Academic Theory That Helps Explain Trump's Anti-Muslim Rhetoric." *Vox*, 10 Dec. 2015, https://www.vox.com/world/2015/12/10/9881876/trump-muslims-ethnic-outbidding.

82. Karp, A. (2018, June). Estimating Global Civilian Held Firearms Numbers. Study conducted for the Government of Australia Retrieved from http://www.smallarmssurvey.org/fileadmin/docs/T-Briefing-Papers/SAS-BP-Civilian-Firearms-Numbers.pdf

83. Montanaro, D. (2019, August 10). Americans Largely Support Gun Restrictions To 'Do Something' About Gun Violence. Retrieved from https://www.npr.org/2019/08/10/749792493/americans-largely-support-gun-restrictions-to-do-something-about-gun-violence

84. Scott, E. (2019, September 4). Why Ted Cruz was making a biblical case for gun rights after the Odessa shooting. Retrieved from https://www.washingtonpost.com/

politics/2019/09/04/why-ted-cruz-was-making-biblical-case-gun-rights-after-odessa-shooting/

85. Griswold, E. (2019, April 23). God, Guns, and Country: The Evangelical Fight Over Firearms. Retrieved from https://www.newyorker.com/news/on-religion/god-guns-and-country-the-evangelical-fight-over-firearms

86. Withrow, B. (2018, April 29). Does Jesus Want Gun-Toting Christians? Retrieved from https://www.thedailybeast.com/does-jesus-want-gun-toting-christians

87. Parker, K., Horowitz, J. M., Igielnik, R., Oliphant, J. B., & Brown, A. (2018, September 18). Guns in America: Attitudes and Experiences of Americans. Retrieved from https://www.pewsocialtrends.org/2017/06/22/americas-complex-relationship-with-guns/

88. Riess, J. (2019, September 3). Which religions support gun control in the US? Retrieved from https://religionnews.com/2019/08/29/which-religions-support-gun-control-in-the-us/

89. Parker, K., Horowitz, J. M., Igielnik, R., Oliphant, J. B., & Brown, A. (2018, September 18). Guns in America: Attitudes and Experiences of Americans. Retrieved from https://www.pewsocialtrends.org/2017/06/22/americas-complex-relationship-with-guns/

90. Vegter, A., Kelley, M. (2020). The Protestant Ethic and the Spirit of Gun Ownership. *Journal for the Scientific Study of Religion*, 59(3), 526-540. doi:10.1111/jssr.12672

91. Shepard, S. (2019, August 7). Poll: Most Republicans support assault weapons ban, despite Trump saying 'no appetite'. Retrieved from https://www.politico.com/story/2019/08/07/poll-most-voters-support-assault-weapons-ban-1452586

92. Shellnutt, K. (2017, November 8). Packing in the Pews: The Connection Between God and Guns. Retrieved from https://www.christianitytoday.com/news/2017/november/god-gun-control-white-evangelicals-texas-church-shooting.html

93. Quinnipiac University. (2019, August 29). QU Poll Release Detail. Retrieved from https://poll.qu.edu/national/release-detail?ReleaseID=3639

94. Wan, W., & Bever, L. (2019, August 5). Are video games or mental illness causing America's mass shootings? No, research shows. Retrieved from https://www.washingtonpost.com/health/2019/08/05/is-mental-illness-causing-americas-mass-shootings-no-research-shows/

95. Wise, J. (2019, September 3). Evangelical leader suggests teaching evolution contributes to mass shootings. Retrieved from https://thehill.com/homenews/media/459763-evangelical-leader-suggests-teaching-evolution-contributes-to-mass-shootings

96. Rocha, A. (2019, August 4). Lt. Gov. Dan Patrick blames video games, lack of prayer in schools for El Paso shooting. Retrieved from https://cbsaustin.com/news/local/lt-gov-dan-patrick-blames-video-games-lack-of-prayer-in-schools-for-el-paso-shooting

97. "Religious Right Joins the NRA in Gun Control Battle." *Salon.Com*, 23 Jan. 2013, https://www.salon.com/2013/01/23/religious_right_joins_the_nra_in_gun_control_battle/.

98. Why Do Jehovah's Witnesses Maintain Political Neutrality? (n.d.) Retrieved from https://www.jw.org/en/jehovahs-witnesses/faq/political-neutrality/

99. Former Attorney General Jeff Sessions broadly hinted to an Evangelical Legal Group that he would like to help them overturn *Lawrence*. https://www.justice.gov/

opa/speech/attorney-general-jeff-sessions-delivers-remarks-alliance-defending-free-doms-summit

100. Knueven, T. (2015, April 14). Outlawed by Supreme Court, sodomy laws still on the books: Scripps Howard Foundation Wire. Retrieved from http://www.shfwire.com/ outlawed-supreme-court-sodomy-laws-still-books/

101. Vandermaas-Peeler, A., Cox, D., Fisch-Friedman, M., Griffin, R., & Jones, R. P. (2018, May 1). Emerging Consensus on LGBT Issues: Findings From the 2017 American Values Atlas. Retrieved from https://www.prri.org/research/emerging-consensus-on-lgbt-issues-findings-from-the-2017-american-values-atlas/

102. Smith, S. (2019, March 13). Most evangelicals favor LGBT nondiscrimination protections: poll. Retrieved from https://www.christianpost.com/news/most-evangelicals-favor-lgbt-nondiscrimination-protections-poll.html

103. Piacenza, J. (2018, June 5). Christians, White Evangelicals Have Contrasting Views On Issues in Cake Case. Retrieved from https://morningconsult.com/2018/06/04/ christians-white-evangelicals-have-contrasting-views-issues-cake-case/

104. Pew Research. (2018, September 24). More Support for Gun Rights, Gay Marriage than in 2008 or 2004. Retrieved from https://www.people-press.org/2012/04/25/ more-support-for-gun-rights-gay-marriage-than-in-2008-or-2004/

105. Lienesch, R., Cox, D., & Jones, R. P. (2017, June 21). Who Sees Discrimination? Attitudes about Sexual Orientation, Gender Identity, Race, and Immigration Status: Findings from PRRI's American Values Atlas. Retrieved from https://www.prri.org/ research/americans-views-discrimination-immigrants-blacks-lgbt-sex-marriage-im-migration-reform/

106. Ziblatt, D. (2017). *Conservative parties and the birth of democracy*. Cambridge, United Kingdom, NY: Cambridge University Press.

107. Wallace-Wells, D. (2018, October 10). UN Says Climate Genocide Is Coming. It's Actually Worse Than That. Retrieved from http://nymag.com/intelligencer/2018/10/ un-says-climate-genocide-coming-but-its-worse-than-that.html

108. Fischetti, M. (2015, March 2). Climate Change Hastened Syria's Civil War. Retrieved from https://www.scientificamerican.com/article/climate-change-hastened-the-syri-an-war/

109. Carrington, D. (2017, July 10). Earth's sixth mass extinction event under way, scientists warn. Retrieved from https://www.theguardian.com/environment/2017/ jul/10/earths-sixth-mass-extinction-event-already-underway-scientists-warn

110. Watts, J. (2019, July 24). 'No doubt left' about scientific consensus on global warming, say experts. Retrieved from https://www.theguardian.com/science/2019/jul/24/sci-entific-consensus-on-humans-causing-global-warming-passes-99

111. Pew Research. (2015, October 22). How Religion Impacts Americans' Views on Climate Change and Energy Issues. Retrieved from https://www.pewresearch.org/ science/2015/10/22/religion-and-views-on-climate-and-energy-issues/

112. Jones, Robert P., Daniel Cox, and Juhem Navarro-Rivera. "Believers, Sympathizers, & Skeptics: Why Americans Are Conflicted about Climate Change, Environmental Policy, and Science." PRRI. 2014. http://www.prri.org/research/believers-sympathiz-ers-skeptics-americans-conflicted-climate-change-environmental-policy-science/.

113. Jones, Robert P., Daniel Cox, and Juhem Navarro-Rivera. "Believers, Sympathizers, & Skeptics: Why Americans Are Conflicted about Climate Change, Environmental Policy, and Science." PRRI. 2014. http://www.prri.org/research/believers-sympathiz-

ers-skeptics-americans-conflicted-climate-change-environmental-policy-science/.

114. Cornwall Alliance. (2018, October 19). An Evangelical Declaration on Global Warming. Retrieved from https://cornwallalliance.org/2009/05/evangelical-declaration-on-global-warming/

115. Brough, Aaron R., W., James E. B., M., Isaac, S., M., & David. (2016, August 4). Is Eco-Friendly Unmanly? The Green-Feminine Stereotype and Its Effect on Sustainable Consumption. Retrieved from https://academic.oup.com/jcr/article/43/4/567/2630509

116. Mooney, M. J. (2019, August 22). Trump's Apostle. Retrieved from https://www.texasmonthly.com/articles/donald-trump-defender-dallas-pastor-robert-jeffress/

117. Moritz-Rabson, D. (2019, September 23). Democrats believe "great human right is the right to kill your own babies through abortion," pastor says on *Fox News*. Retrieved from https://www.newsweek.com/pastor-says-fox-news-democrats-believe-great-human-right-right-kill-your-own-babies-through-1460713

118. Mantyla, K. (2019, September 24). Robert Jeffress: Climate Change Is an 'Imaginary Crisis' That God Won't Let Happen. Retrieved from https://www.rightwingwatch.org/post/robert-jeffress-climate-change-is-an-imaginary-crisis-that-god-wont-let-happen/

119. Cooper, B., Cox, D., Lienesch, R., & Jones, R. P. (2016, March 29). How Americans View Immigrants, and What They... Retrieved from https://www.prri.org/research/poll-immigration-reform-views-on-immigrants/

120. Cox, D. (2018, June 26). Growing Divide on Immigration and America's Moral Leadership. Retrieved from https://www.prri.org/research/growing-divide-on-immigration-and-americas-moral-leadership/

121. Hartig, H. (2018, May 24). GOP views of accepting refugees to US turn more negative as admissions plummet. Retrieved from https://www.pewresearch.org/fact-tank/2018/05/24/republicans-turn-more-negative-toward-refugees-as-number-admitted-to-u-s-plummets/

122. Tyson, A. (2019, January 19). 74 percent favor legal status for those brought to US illegally as children. Retrieved from https://www.pewresearch.org/fact-tank/2018/01/19/public-backs-legal-status-for-immigrants-brought-to-u-s-illegally-as-children-but-not-a-bigger-border-wall/

123. Boorstein, M., & Zauzmer, J. (2018, June 18). Why many white evangelicals are not protesting family separations on the U.S. border. Retrieved from https://beta.washingtonpost.com/news/acts-of-faith/wp/2018/06/18/why-many-white-evangelical-christians-are-not-protesting-family-separations-on-the-u-s-border/

124. Christina Jewett and Shefali Luthra, Kaiser. "Immigrant Toddlers Ordered to Appear in Court Alone." *The Texas Tribune*, 28 June 2018, https://www.texastribune.org/2018/06/27/immigrant-toddlers-ordered-appear-court-alone/.

125. Pew Research. (2017, December 14). Many Americans Hear About Politics at Church. Retrieved from https://www.pewforum.org/2016/08/08/many-americans-hear-politics-from-the-pulpit/

126. Hananoki, E. (2019, June 8). Right-wing media have repeatedly used fears of a supposed immigrant "invasion" to raise money. Retrieved from https://www.mediamatters.org/immigration/right-wing-media-have-repeatedly-used-fears-supposed-immigrant-invasion-raise-money

127. Wong, J. (2018, June 19). This is why white evangelicals still support Donald Trump.

(It's not economic anxiety.). Retrieved from https://beta.washingtonpost.com/news/ monkey-cage/wp/2018/06/19/white-evangelicals-still-support-donald-trump-be- cause-theyre-more-conservative-than-other-evangelicals-this-is-why/?noredirect=on

128. Mervosh, S. (2018, June 26). 'Why Do You Hate Us?' He Asked. 'Because You're Mexicans,' She Replied. Retrieved from https://www.nytimes.com/2018/06/25/us/ video-diatribe-mexicans.html

129. Buncombe Washington DC @AndrewBuncombe, A. (2018, November 2). Outrage as Trump releases 'racist dog-whistle' midterms advert. Retrieved from https://www. independent.co.uk/news/world/americas/us-politics/midterms-2018/trump-rac- ist-commercial-new-ad-willie-horton-midterm-election-luis-bracamontes-cara- van-a8612676.html

130. Smietana, B. (2017, August 23). 2016 Election Exposes Evangelical Divides. Re- trieved from https://lifewayresearch.com/2016/10/14/2016-election-exposes-evan- gelical-divide/

131. Gessen, M. (2019, July 10). Mike Pompeo's Faith-Based Attempt to Narrowly Rede- fine Human Rights. Retrieved from https://www.newyorker.com/news/our-colum- nists/mike-pompeos-faith-based-attempt-to-narrowly-redefine-human-rights

132. Michaelson, J. (2019, April 9). Trump Lets Foster Agency Turn Away Catholics and Jews. Retrieved from https://www.thedailybeast.com/trump-administration-lets-mir- acle-hill-foster-agency-turn-away-catholics-and-jews

133. Paton, C. (2019, May 23). White Evangelicals are the most Islamophobic Amer- icans, poll shows. Retrieved from https://www.newsweek.com/white-evangeli- cals-are-most-islamophobic-americans-poll-shows-1433592

134. Pew Research. (2017, July 26). U.S. Muslims Concerned About Their Place in Soci- ety, but Continue to Believe in the American Dream. Retrieved from https://www. pewforum.org/2017/07/26/findings-from-pew-research-centers-2017-survey-of-us- muslims/

135. Cooper, B., Cox, D., Lienesch, R., & Jones, R. P. (2015, November 17). Anxiety, Nostalgia, and Mistrust: Findings from the 2015 American Values Survey. Retrieved from https://www.prri.org/research/survey-anxiety-nostalgia-and-mistrust-find- ings-from-the-2015-american-values-survey/#.VpevaPkrJD8

136. Rogers, K., & Fandos, N. (2019, July 14). Trump Tells Congresswomen to 'Go Back' to the Countries They Came From. Retrieved from https://www.nytimes. com/2019/07/14/us/politics/trump-twitter-squad-congress.html

137. Smith, G. A. (2017, February 27). Most white evangelicals approve of Trump refugee policy, express concerns about extremism. Retrieved from https://www.pewresearch. org/fact-tank/2017/02/27/most-white-evangelicals-approve-of-trump-travel-prohi- bition-and-express-concerns-about-extremism/

138. Manchester, J. (2018, August 3). Morning Consult Editor: White Evangelicals' sup- port of religious freedom depends on business owner's religion. Retrieved from https://thehill.com/hilltv/what-americas-thinking/400281-pollster-white-evangeli- cals-support-of-religious-freedom?page=16

139. Green, E. (2017, March 10). White Evangelicals Believe They Face More Discrim- ination Than Muslims. Retrieved from https://www.theatlantic.com/politics/ar- chive/2017/03/perceptions-discrimination-muslims-christians/519135/

140. Stroop, C. (2019, March 26). America's Islamophobia Is Forged at the Pulpit. Retrieved from https://foreignpolicy.com/2019/03/26/americas-islamopho-

bia-is-forged-in-the-pulpit/
141. Abdelfatah, R. (2019, June 20). 'Throughline' Traces Evangelicals' History On The Abortion Issue. Retrieved from https://www.npr.org/2019/06/20/734303135/throughline-traces-evangelicals-history-on-the-abortion-issue; Chepkemoi, J. (2017, October 25). US States by Population of Catholics. Retrieved from https://www.worldatlas.com/articles/us-states-by-population-of-catholics.html
142. Chepkemoi, J. (2017, October 25). US States by Population of Catholics. Retrieved from https://www.worldatlas.com/articles/us-states-by-population-of-catholics.html
143. Gordon, M., & Hurt, A. (2019, June 5). Early Abortion Bans: Which States Have Passed Them? Retrieved from https://www.npr.org/sections/health-shots/2019/06/05/729753903/early-abortion-bans-which-states-have-passed-them
144. Boorman, G. (2019, September 19). Is Abortion Really Necessary For Treating Ectopic Pregnancies? Retrieved from https://thefederalist.com/2019/09/09/is-abortion-really-necessary-for-treating-ectopic-pregnancies/
145. Gallup, Inc. (2019, July 25). Abortion. Retrieved from https://news.gallup.com/poll/1576/abortion.aspx
146. Pew Research. (2019, August 29). U.S. Public Continues to Favor Legal Abortion, Oppose Overturning Roe v. Wade. Retrieved from https://www.people-press.org/2019/08/29/u-s-public-continues-to-favor-legal-abortion-oppose-overturning-roe-v-wade/
147. Vandermaas-Peeler, A., Cox, D., Najile, M., Fisch-Friedman, M., Griffin, R., & Jones, R. O. P. (2018, October 3). Partisanship Trumps Gender: Sexual Harassment, Woman Candidates, Access to Contraception, and Key Issues in 2018 Midterms. Retrieved from https://www.prri.org/research/abortion-reproductive-health-midterms-trump-kavanaugh/
148. Marist University Polls. (2019, June 7). NPR/PBS NewsHour/Marist Poll Results & Analysis. Retrieved from http://maristpoll.marist.edu/npr-pbs-newshour-marist-poll-results-analysis-5/#sthash.tzineqvU.dpbs
149. PRRI Staff. (2019, August 13). The State of Abortion and Contraception Attitudes in All 50 States. Retrieved from https://www.prri.org/research/legal-in-most-cases-the-impact-of-the-abortion-debate-in-2019-america/
150. Burge, Ryan. "Partisanship Rules Everything – Abortion in 2020." *Religion in Public*, 16 Dec. 2020, https://religioninpublic.blog/2020/12/16/partisanship-rules-everything-abortion-in-2020/.
151. Guyot, K., & Sawhill, I. V. (2019, July 29). Reducing access to contraception won't reduce the abortion rate. Retrieved from https://www.brookings.edu/blog/up-front/2019/07/29/reducing-access-to-contraception-wont-reduce-the-abortion-rate/
152. Robert P. Jones, Natalie Jackson, Maxine Najle, Oyindamola Bola, and Daniel Greenberg. "The State of Abortion and Contraception Attitudes in All 50 States" PRRI (March 26, 2019). [prr.org/research/legal-in-most-cases-the-impact-of-the-abortion-debate-in-2019-america]
153. Robert P. Jones, PhD, Daniel Cox, PhD, Rob Griffin, PhD, Maxine Najle, PhD, Molly Fisch-Friedman, and Alex Vandermaas-Peeler. "Partisanship Trumps Gender: Sexual Harassment, Woman Candidates, Access to Contraception, and Key Issues in 2018 Midterms." PRRI. 2018. https://www.prri.org/research/abortion-reproductive-health-midterms-trump-kavanaugh.

154. Robert P. Jones, Natalie Jackson, Maxine Najle, Oyindamola Bola, and Daniel Greenberg. "The State of Abortion and Contraception Attitudes in All 50 States" PRRI (March 26, 2019). [prr.org/research/legal-in-most-cases-the-impact-of-the-abortion-debate-in-2019-america]

155. Gordon, M., & Hurt, A. (2019, June 5). Early Abortion Bans: Which States Have Passed Them? Retrieved from https://www.npr.org/sections/health-shots/2019/06/05/729753903/early-abortion-bans-which-states-have-passed-them

156. Vinett, K. (2019). Trump and Jeffrey Epstein Once Hosted a Party for "28 Girls" at Mar-a-Lago. [online] Vice. Available at: https://www.vice.com/en_us/article/ywy7zj/trump-and-jeffrey-epstein-once-partied-with-28-women-at-mar-a-lago [Accessed 23 Sep. 2019].

157. Scott, E. (2019). More white evangelicals believe Stormy Daniels, and that could have some long-term implications. [online] The Washington Post. Available at: https://www.washingtonpost.com/news/the-fix/wp/2018/03/27/more-white-evangelicals-believe-stormy-daniels-and-that-could-have-some-long-term-implications/ [Accessed 23 Sep. 2019].

158. Hudak, J. (2019). Alabama reminds America to have a little faith in American voters. [online] Brookings. Available at: https://www.brookings.edu/blog/fix-gov/2017/12/13/alabama-reminds-america-to-have-a-little-faith-in-american-voters/ [Accessed 23 Sep. 2019].

159. Post Staff (2017). Exit poll results: How different groups voted in Alabama. [online] The Washington Post. Available at: https://www.washingtonpost.com/graphics/2017/politics/alabama-exit-polls/ [Accessed 23 Sep. 2019].

160. The Hill. (2018). Evangelical voters driving support for Kavanaugh's confirmation, says pollster. [online] Available at: https://thehill.com/hilltv/what-americas-thinking/408588-evangelical-voters-driving-support-for-kavanaughs-confirmation [Accessed 23 Sep. 2019].

161. Burton, T. (2018). Poll: 48 percent of white evangelicals would support Kavanaugh even if the allegations against him were true. [online] Vox. Available at: https://www.vox.com/policy-and-politics/2018/9/27/17910016/brett-kavanaugh-christine-blasey-ford-white-evangelicals-poll-support [Accessed 23 Sep. 2019].

162. Barnes, R. and Guskin, E. (2018). More Americans disapprove of Kavanaugh's confirmation than support it, new poll shows. [online] The Washington Post. Available at: https://www.washingtonpost.com/politics/more-americans-disapprove-of-kavanaughs-confirmation-than-support-it-new-poll-shows/2018/10/12/18dbf872-cd93-11e8-a3e6-44daa3d35ede_story.html [Accessed 23 Sep. 2019].

163. Bacon Jr., P. (2018). Republicans Rescued Kavanaugh's Nomination By Making It About #MeToo. [online] FiveThirtyEight. Available at: https://fivethirtyeight.com/features/republicans-rescued-kavanaughs-nomination-by-making-it-about-metoo/ [Accessed 23 Sep. 2019].

164. Vandermaas-Peeler, A., Cox, D., Najle, M., Fisch-Friedman, M., Griffin, R., & Jones, R. P. (2018, October 29). Partisan Polarization Dominates Trump Era: Findings from the 2018 American Values Survey. Retrieved from https://www.prri.org/research/partisan-polarization-dominates-trump-era-findings-from-the-2018-american-values-survey/

165. Meckler, L. (2018). Betsy DeVos releases sexual assault rules she hails as balancing rights of victims, accused. [online] The Washington Post. Available at: https://www.

washingtonpost.com/local/education/betsy-devos-releases-sexual-assault-rules-she-hails-as-balancing-rights-of-victims-accused/2018/11/16/4aa136d4-e962-11e8-a939-9469f1166f9d_story.html [Accessed 23 Sep. 2019].

166. Stratford, Michael. "DeVos Urges Career Staff to 'Be the Resistance' as Biden Takes Over." *POLITICO*, 15 Dec. 2020, https://www.politico.com/news/2020/12/15/betsy-devos-biden-education-department-445900.

167. Lucado, A. (2019). How the female body became the scapegoat for white evangelicals. [online] *The Washington Post*. Available at: https://www.washingtonpost.com/religion/2019/08/29/how-female-body-became-scapegoat-white-evangelicals/ [Accessed 23 Sep. 2019].

168. Levin, J. (2013, December 19). The Real Story of Linda Taylor, America's Original Welfare Queen. Retrieved from http://www.slate.com/articles/news_and_politics/history/2013/12/linda_taylor_welfare_queen_ronald_reagan_made_her_a_notorious_american_villain.html

169. "The Racism at the Heart of the Reagan Presidency." *Salon.Com*, 12 Jan. 2014, https://www.salon.com/2014/01/11/the_racism_at_the_heart_of_the_reagan_presidency/.

170. Zauzmer, J. (2017, August 03). Christians are more than twice as likely to blame a person's poverty on lack of effort. Retrieved from https://www.washingtonpost.com/news/acts-of-faith/wp/2017/08/03/christians-are-more-than-twice-as-likely-to-blame-a-persons-poverty-on-lack-of-effort/?utm_term=.009827d34d74

171. Smietana, B. (2018, July 31). Prosperity Gospel Taught to 4 in 10 Evangelical Churchgoers. Retrieved from https://www.christianitytoday.com/news/2018/july/prosperity-gospel-survey-churchgoers-prosper-tithe-blessing.html

172. Duin, J. (2017, November 14). She led Trump to Christ: The rise of the televangelist who advises the White House. Retrieved from https://www.washingtonpost.com/lifestyle/magazine/she-led-trump-to-christ-the-rise-of-the-televangelist-who-advises-the-white-house/2017/11/13/1dc3a830-bb1a-11e7-be94-fabb0f1e9ffb_story.html

173. Gilgoff, D. (2008). *The Jesus machine: How James Dobson, Focus on the Family, and evangelical America are winning the culture war*. New York, NY: St. Martin's Griffin.

174. Fitzgerald, F. (2017). *The Evangelicals: The struggle to shape America*. pp. 321. New York, NY, NY: Simon & Schuster.

175. Silver, N. (2016, May 03). The Mythology Of Trump's 'Working Class' Support. Retrieved from https://fivethirtyeight.com/features/the-mythology-of-trumps-working-class-support/

176. McCarthy, N. (2019). The Men And Women Most Admired In The U.S. In 2019 [Infographic]. [online] Forbes.com. Available at: https://www.forbes.com/sites/niallmccarthy/2019/07/24/the-men-and-women-most-admired-in-the-us-in-2019-infographic/#112e817d2ff0 [Accessed 23 Sep. 2019].

177. Jones, Robert P., Daniel Cox, Betsy Cooper, and Rachel Lienesch. "Majority of Americans Oppose Transgender Bathroom Restrictions." PRRI. 2017. http://www.prri.org/research/lgbt-transgender-bathroom-discrimination-religious-liberty/

178. https://www.nytimes.com/2019/01/07/us/florida-government-shutdown-marianna.html

179. https://www.theatlantic.com/ideas/archive/2018/10/the-cruelty-is-the-point/572104/

180. Smith, W. C. (2016, July 14). Is Media Bias Real? Retrieved from https://billygraham. org/decision-magazine/july-august-2016/is-media-bias-real/

181. Yudkin, D. A. (2019, August 21). Hidden Tribes: A Study of America's Polarized Landscape. https://doi.org/10.31234/osf.io/xz25v

182. Graham, D. A. (2019, June 12). Some Real News About Fake News. Retrieved from https://www.theatlantic.com/ideas/archive/2019/06/fake-news-republicans-democrats/591211/

183. Jenkins, J. (2020, September 18). Head of Federal Election Commission calls separation of church and state a 'fallacy' and 2020 election a 'spiritual war'. Retrieved September 23, 2020, from https://religionnews.com/2020/09/17/head-of-federal-election-commission-calls-separation-of-church-and-state-a-fallacy-and-2020-election-a-spiritual-war/

184. Shenon, P. (2019, October 20). 'A threat to democracy': William Barr's speech on religious freedom alarms liberal Catholics. Retrieved September 23, 2020, from https://www.theguardian.com/us-news/2019/oct/19/william-barr-attorney-general-catholic-conservative-speech

185. O'Toole, Fintan. "Democracy's Afterlife." *The New York Review of Books*, https://www.nybooks.com/articles/2020/12/03/democracys-afterlife/. Accessed 21 Nov. 2020.

186. Congressional Prayer Caucus Foundation. (n.d.). Retrieved from https://cpcfoundation.com/about/mission/

187. Burton, T. I. (2018, January 25). Understanding the fake historian behind America's religious right. Retrieved from https://www.vox.com/identities/2018/1/25/16919362/understanding-the-fake-historian-behind-americas-religious-right

188. National Legal Foundation: About. (n.d.). Retrieved from https://nationallegalfoundation.org/about/

189. Clarkson, F. (2018, December 18). Ringing in a Christian Nationalist 2019 With an Even Larger Legislative Playbook - Rewire.News - Religion Dispatches. Retrieved from https://rewire.news/religion-dispatches/2018/12/18/ringing-in-a-christian-nationalist-2019-with-an-even-larger-legislative-playbook/

190. Clarkson, F. (2018, April 27). "Project Blitz" Seeks to Do for Christian Nationalism What ALEC Does for Big Business - Rewire.News - Religion Dispatches. Retrieved from https://rewire.news/religion-dispatches/2018/04/27/project-blitz-seeks-christian-nationalism-alec-big-business/

191. Taylor, D. (2018, June 4). Project Blitz: the legislative assault by Christian nationalists to reshape America. Retrieved from https://www.theguardian.com/world/2018/jun/04/project-blitz-the-legislative-assault-by-christian-nationalists-to-reshape-america

192. Clarkson, F. (2018, April 27). "Project Blitz" Seeks to Do for Christian Nationalism What ALEC Does for Big Business - Rewire.News - Religion Dispatches. Retrieved from https://rewire.news/religion-dispatches/2018/04/27/project-blitz-seeks-christian-nationalism-alec-big-business/

193. CPFC. (2016). Report and Analysis on Religious Freedom Measures Impacting Prayer and Faith in America (2017 Version). Retrieved from https://drive.google.com/file/d/0BwfCh32HsC3UYmV0NUp5cXZjT28/view

194. The Republic of Gilead was the name of the dystopian Christo-fascist theocratic regime that took over America in Margaret Atwood's book *A Handmaid's Tale*

195. CPFC. (2018, December 18). Report and Analysis on Religious Freedom Measures Impacting Prayer and Faith in America Legislation Proclamations (2018-19 Version). Retrieved from https://rewire.news/wp-content/uploads/2018/12/Report-and-Analysis-on-Religious-Freedom-Measures-Impacting-Prayer-and-Faith_2018-2019.pdf

196. Sokol, S. (2019, March 29). Project Blitz Wants To Bring Bible Class To A Public School Near You. Retrieved from https://www.au.org/blogs/wall-of-separation/project-blitz-wants-to-bring-bible-class-to-a-public-school-near-you

197. Gessen, M. (2016, November 10). Autocracy: Rules for Survival. Retrieved from https://www.nybooks.com/daily/2016/11/10/trump-election-autocracy-rules-for-survival/

198. Pew Research. (2019, July 23). Which religious groups know what about religion? Retrieved from https://www.pewforum.org/2019/07/23/which-religious-groups-know-what-about-religion/

199. Burge, Ryan. "Retired Evangelicals Care A Lot about Immigration, Less about Gay Marriage." *Religion in Public*, 10 Sept. 2018, https://religioninpublic.blog/2018/09/10/retired-evangelicals-care-a-lot-about-immigration-less-about-gay-marriage/.

200. Cox, D., & Thomson-DeVeaux, A. (2019, September 18). The Christian Right Is Helping Drive Liberals Away From Religion. Retrieved from https://fivethirtyeight.com/features/the-christian-right-is-helping-drive-liberals-away-from-religion/

201. Winston, Kimberly. "The History behind the Christian Flags Spotted at the Pro-Trump U.S. Capitol 'Coup.'" *Religion Unplugged*, 7 Jan. 2021, https://religionunplugged.com/news/2021/1/6/some-history-behind-the-christian-flags-at-the-pro-trump-capitol-coup.

Chapter 7

1. Chetty, R., Grusky, D., Hell, M., Hendren, N., Manduca, R., & Narang, J. (2016). The Fading American Dream: Trends in Absolute Income Mobility Since 1940. Science. doi:10.3386/w22910

2. DeSilver, Drew. "The Many Ways to Measure Economic Inequality." *Pew Research Center*, 22 Sept. 2015, https://www.pewresearch.org/fact-tank/2015/09/22/the-many-ways-to-measure-economic-inequality/.

3. Hassett, K. A., & Mathur, A. (2012, June). *A New Measure of Consumption Inequality*. American Enterprise Institute. Retrieved October 21, 2020, from https://www.aei.org/wp-content/uploads/2012/06/-a-new-measure-of-consumption-inequality_142931647663.pdf

4. Ingraham, Christopher. "For the First Time in History, U.S. Billionaires Paid a Lower Tax Rate than the Working Class Last Year." *The Washington Post*, 8 Oct. 2019, https://www.washingtonpost.com/business/2019/10/08/first-time-history-us-billionaires-paid-lower-tax-rate-than-working-class-last-year/.

5. Piketty, T., & Saez, E. (2003). Income Inequality in the United States, 1913-1998 (series updated to 2018 available). *The Quarterly Journal of Economics*, CXVIII(1). doi:10.3386/w8467

6. Stiglitz, J. (2013). *Price of Inequality*. New York, NY: Wiley. p. 31

7. Kochhar, Rakesh. "How U.S. Wealth Inequality Has Changed since Great Recession." *Pew Research Center*, 1 Nov. 2017, https://www.pewresearch.org/fact-tank/2017/11/01/how-wealth-inequality-has-changed-in-the-u-s-since-the-great-

recession-by-race-ethnicity-and-income/.

8. "The World Factbook — Central Intelligence Agency." *Central Intelligence Agency*, https://www.cia.gov/library/publications/the-world-factbook/rankorder/2172rank.html. Accessed 21 Oct. 2020.

9. Wesley, E., Peterson, F., (2017) Is Economic Inequality Really a Problem? A Review of the Arguments. University of Nebraska Social Sciences December 2017 DOI: 10.3390/socsci6040147

10. Wilkinson, R., & Pickett, K. (2009). *The spirit level: Why more equal societies almost always do better.* London: Allen Lane. p. 18

11. Miles Corak (2013), "Inequality from Generation to Generation: The United States in Comparison," in Robert Rycroft (editor), *The Economics of Inequality, Poverty, and Discrimination in the 21st Century,* ABC-CLIO.

12. Raj Chetty & David Grusky & Maximilian Hell & Nathaniel Hendren & Robert Manduca & Jimmy Narang, 2017. "The fading American dream: Trends in absolute income mobility since 1940," *Science*, vol 356(6336), pages 398-406.

13. Nicholas W Papageorge, Kevin Thom, Genes, Education, and Labor Market Outcomes: Evidence from the Health and Retirement Study, *Journal of the European Economic Association*, Volume 18, Issue 3, June 2020, Pages 1351–1399, https://doi.org/10.1093/jeea/jvz072

14. Stiglitz, J. (2013). *Price of Inequality.* New York, NY: Wiley. p. 24

15. McCarthy, Niall. Where the World's Millennials Work The Longest Hours. *Forbes Magazine*. Retrieved December 31, 2018 from https://www.forbes.com/sites/niallmccarthy/2016/05/26/where-the-worlds-millennials-work-the-longest-hours-infographic/#6499dfec3b9a

16. O'Donnell, Jayne. "U.S. Deaths from Alcohol, Drugs and Suicide Hit Highest Level since Record-Keeping Began." *USA Today*, Gannett Satellite Information Network, 5 Mar. 2019, www.usatoday.com/story/news/health/2019/03/05/suicide-alcohol-drug-deaths-centers-disease-control-well-being-trust/3033124002/?fbclid=IwAR2uzjHeGLUK_seFv96G7PRBgGwNlD_aRhS61e2WA4uZVP_n6yXo0VemY-Mo

17. Escobari, Marcela. "The Economy Is Growing and Leaving Low-Wage Workers Behind." *Brookings*, 19 Dec. 2019, https://www.brookings.edu/blog/education-plus-development/2019/12/19/the-economy-is-growing-and-leaving-low-wage-workers-behind/.

18. Worstall, Tim. "Ludicrous Economic Numbers: 40 percent Of Americans Make Less Than The 1968 Minimum Wage." *Forbes*, 7 Feb. 2016, https://www.forbes.com/sites/timworstall/2016/02/07/ludicrous-economic-numbers-40-of-americans-make-less-than-the-1968-minimum-wage/.

19. Kirsch, Noah. "Members Of The Forbes 400 Hold More Wealth Than All U.S. Black Families Combined, Study Finds." *Forbes*, 14 Jan. 2019, https://www.forbes.com/sites/noahkirsch/2019/01/14/members-of-forbes-400-hold-more-wealth-than-all-us-black-families-combined-study-finds/.

20. Kirsch, Noah. "The 3 Richest Americans Hold More Wealth Than Bottom 50 percent Of The Country, Study Finds." *Forbes*, 9 Nov. 2017, https://www.forbes.com/sites/noahkirsch/2017/11/09/the-3-richest-americans-hold-more-wealth-than-bottom-50-of-country-study-finds/.

21. Woods, Hiatt. "How Billionaires Got $637 Billion Richer during the Coronavirus

Pandemic." *Business Insider*, 3 Aug. 2020, https://www.businessinsider.com/billion-aires-net-worth-increases-coronavirus-pandemic-2020-7.

22. Carmichael, Sarah. Millennials Are Actually Workaholics, According to Research. Harvard Business Review. Retrieved on December 31, 2018 from https://hbr.org/2016/08/millennials-are-actually-workaholics-according-to-research; Chetty, R., Grusky, D., Hell, M., Hendren, N., Manduca, R., & Narang, J. (2016). The Fading American Dream: Trends in Absolute Income Mobility Since 1940. Science. doi:10.3386/w22910

23. Alvaredo, F., Garbinti, B., & Piketty, T. (2017). On the Share of Inheritance in Aggregate Wealth: Europe and the USA, 1900-2010. *Economica*, 84(334), 239-260. doi:10.1111/ecca.12233

24. McCammond, A. and Swan, J. (2019). Scoop: More Trump schedules leaked as enraged officials launch internal hunt. *Axios*. Available at: https://www.axios.com/trump-schedule-leaks-4840f751-e663-49c0-b288-2dd39bde9c79.html [Accessed 5 Mar. 2019]

25. Harwell, D., Brittain, A. and O'Connell, J. (2019). Trump family's elaborate lifestyle is a 'logistical nightmare' — at taxpayer expense. [online] *Washington Post*. Available at: https://www.washingtonpost.com/business/economy/trump-familys-elaborate-life-style-a-logistical-nightmare--at-taxpayer-expense/2017/02/16/763cce8e-f2ce-11e6-a9b0-ecee7ce475fc_story.html?utm_term=.7c7e0441b41c [Accessed 5 Mar. 2019].

26. Jake Tapper, Anchor and Chief. "Former White House Chief of Staff Tells Friends That Trump 'Is the Most Flawed Person' He's Ever Met." *CNN*, 16 Oct. 2020, https://www.cnn.com/2020/10/16/politics/donald-trump-criticism-from-former-administration-officials/index.html.

27. Nichols, T. (2017). *The Death of Expertise*. New York, NY: Oxford University Press. p. 33

28. The Peter principle is a concept in management developed by Laurence J. Peter, which observes that people in a hierarchy tend to rise to their "level of incompetence." In other words, an employee is promoted based on their success in previous jobs until they reach a level at which they are no longer competent, as skills in one job do not necessarily translate to another.

29. Hacker, J. S., & Pierson, P. (2020*). Let them eat Tweets: How the right rules in an age of extreme inequality*. New York, NY, NY: Liveright Publishing Corporation, a division of W. W. Norton & Company.

30. Gilens, M., & Page, B. I. (2014). Testing Theories of American Politics: Elites, Interest Groups, and Average Citizens. *Perspectives on Politics*, 12(03), 564-581. doi:10.1017/s1537592714001595

31. Brenan, Megan. "More Still Disapprove Than Approve of 2017 Tax Cuts." *Gallup*, 10 Oct. 2018, https://news.gallup.com/poll/243611/disapprove-approve-2017-tax-cuts.aspx.

32. Schlozman, D. (2015). *When movements anchor parties: Electoral alignments in American history*. Princeton, NJ: Princeton University Press.

33. Stiglitz, J. (2013). *Price of Inequality*. New York, NY: Wiley. p. 59

34. Dyal JW, Grant MP, Broadwater K, et al. COVID-19 Among Workers in Meat and Poultry Processing Facilities — 19 States, April 2020. MMWR Morb Mortal Wkly Rep 2020;69:557–561. DOI: http://dx.doi.org/10.15585/mmwr.mm6918e3external icon.

35. Kauffman, Clark. "Lawsuit: Tyson Managers Bet Money on How Many Workers

Would Contract COVID-19 - Iowa Capital Dispatch." *Iowa Capital Dispatch*, 18 Nov. 2020, https://iowacapitaldispatch.com/2020/11/18/lawsuit-tyson-managers-bet-money-on-how-many-workers-would-contract-COVID-19/.

36. *EPIC SYSTEMS CORP. v. LEWIS* No. 16–285, 823 F. 3d 1147, and No. 16–300, 834 F. 3d 975, reversed and remanded; No. 16–307, 808 F. 3d 1013, affirmed.

37. Krieckhaus, J., Son, B., Bellinger, N., & Wells, J. (2013). Economic Inequality and Democratic Support. *The Journal of Politics, 76*(1), 139-151. doi:10.1017/s0022381613001229

38. Foa, R. S., & Mounk, Y. (2017). The Signs of Deconsolidation. *Journal of Democracy*, 28(1), 5-15. doi:10.1353/jod.2017.0000

39. Howe, P. (2017). Eroding Norms and Democratic Deconsolidation. *Journal of Democracy*, 28(4), 15-29. doi:10.1353/jod.2017.0061

40. Goering, Laurie. "Growing Wealth Inequality 'Dangerous' Threat to Democracy: Experts." *Reuters*, https://www.reuters.com/article/us-democracy-wealth-inequality-idUSKCN0XC1Q2. Accessed 21 Oct. 2020.

41. Grigoli, F. et al. (December 16, 2016) Inequality and Growth: A Heterogeneous Approach. *International Monetary Fund.*

42. Kurz, Christopher, Geng Li, and Daniel J. Vine (2018). "Are Millennials Different?," Finance and Economics Discussion Series 2018-080. Washington: *Board of Governors of the Federal Reserve System*, https://doi.org/10.17016/FEDS.2018.080.

43. Bartlett, B. (2007). "Starve the Beast" Origins and Development of a Budgetary Metaphor. *The Independent Review*, XII(1), 5-26. Retrieved March 12, 2019, from http://www.independent.org/pdf/tir/tir_12_01_01_bartlett.pdf ISSN 1086–1653

44. Kochhar, R., Fry, R., Kochhar, R., & Fry, R. (2014, December 12). Wealth inequality has widened along racial, ethnic lines since end of Great Recession. Retrieved March 11, 2019, from http://www.pewresearch.org/fact-tank/2014/12/12/racial-wealth-gaps-great-recession/

45. Ingraham, Christopher. "Analysis | The Top Tax Rate Has Been Cut Six Times since 1980 — Usually with Democrats' Help." *The Washington Post*, 27 Feb. 2019, https://www.washingtonpost.com/us-policy/2019/02/27/top-tax-rate-has-been-cut-six-times-since-usually-with-democrats-help/.

46. Fung, A. (2020, September 08). It's The Gap, Stupid. Retrieved September 23, 2020, from http://bostonreview.net/class-inequality/archon-fung-its-gap-stupid

47. Page, B. I., Seawright, J., & Lacombe, M. J. (2019). *Billionaires and stealth politics*. Chicago, IL: The University of Chicago Press. 82

48. Manjoo, Farhad. "Silicon Valley's Politics: Liberal, With One Big Exception." *NY-Times*, 6 Sept. 2017, https://www.nytimes.com/2017/09/06/technology/silicon-valley-politics.html.

49. Hope, D., Limberg, J. (2020, December). The Economic Consequences of Major Tax Cuts for the Rich [Scholarly project]. In International Inequities Institute. Retrieved December 19, 2020, from http://eprints.lse.ac.uk/107919/1/Hope_economic_consequences_of_major_tax_cuts_published.pdf

50. Denning, S. (2019, February 26). Why A 70 percent Marginal Tax Rate Won't Fix Inequality. Retrieved from https://www.forbes.com/sites/stephaniedenning/2019/02/25/why-a-70-marginal-tax-rate-wont-fix-inequality/

51. Sheffield, M. (2019, January 24). Poll: Majority of voters support $15 minimum wage. Retrieved from https://thehill.com/hilltv/what-americas-thinking/426780-poll-a-majority-of-voters-want-a-15-minimum-wage

52. Gramlich, J., & Gramlich, J. (2017, May 26). Few Americans support cuts to most government programs. Retrieved from http://www.pewresearch.org/fact-tank/2017/05/26/few-americans-support-cuts-to-most-government-programs-inc-luding-medicaid/

53. Kelly, E. (2018, August 23). *Fox News* poll: Voters like Obamacare more than GOP tax cuts. Retrieved from https://www.usatoday.com/story/news/politics/onpoli-tics/2018/08/23/fox-news-poll-obamacare-gop-tax-cuts/1074570002/

54. Gallup, Inc. (2018, August 30). Labor Union Approval Steady at 15-Year High. Retrieved from https://news.gallup.com/poll/241679/labor-union-approval-steady-year-high.aspx

55. Trabandt, Mathias; Uhlig, Harald (2011). "The Laffer Curve Revisited". Journal of Monetary Economics. 58 (4): 305–27. doi:10.1016/j.jmoneco.2011.07.003

56. Hacker, J., & Pierson, P. (2005). Abandoning the Middle: The Bush Tax Cuts and the Limits of Democratic Control. *Perspectives on Politics*, 3(1), 33-53. Retrieved September 29, 2020, from http://www.jstor.org/stable/3688109

57. Hacker, J. S., & Pierson, P. (2020). *Let them eat Tweets: How the right rules in an age of extreme inequality.* p. 4 New York, NY, NY: Liveright Publishing Corporation, a division of W. W. Norton & Company.

58. Hacker, J. S., & Pierson, P. (2020). *Let them eat Tweets: How the right rules in an age of extreme inequality.* New York, NY, NY: Liveright Publishing Corporation, a division of W. W. Norton & Company. p. 65

59. Stiglitz, J. (2013). *Price of Inequality.* New York, NY: Wiley. p. 336-355

60. Svrluga, Susan. "Justice Department Sues Yale, Alleging Discrimination against White and Asian Applicants." *The Washington Post*, 9 Oct. 2020, https://www.wash-ingtonpost.com/education/2020/10/08/yale-lawsuit-admissions/.

61. Stiglitz, J. (2013). *Price of Inequality.* New York, NY: Wiley. p. 38

62. Gramlich, J., & Gramlich, J. (2017, May 26). Few Americans support cuts to most government programs. Retrieved from http://www.pewresearch.org/fact-tank/2017/05/26/few-americans-support-cuts-to-most-government-programs-inc-luding-medicaid/

63. Times, The. "Political Divisions in 2016 and Beyond." *Democracy Fund Voter Study Group*, https://www.voterstudygroup.org/publication/political-divi-sions-in-2016-and-beyond. Accessed 10 Feb. 2020.

64. "Nixon and the Southern Strategy." *NYTimes*, 12 Apr. 1970, https://www.nytimes.com/1970/04/12/archives/nixon-and-the-southern-strategy-what-was-clothed-has-been-stripped.html.

65. *Fox Business News*, Retrieved February 26, 2019 https://www.facebook.com/FoxBusi-ness/videos/vb.12795435237/10153878971005238/?type=2&theater

66. Lewis, A. R., & Djupe, P. A. (2016, March 10). Americans May Be Too Religious To Embrace Socialism. Retrieved from https://fivethirtyeight.com/features/ameri-cans-may-be-too-religious-to-embrace-socialism/

67. Hacker, J. S., & Pierson, P. (2020). Let them eat Tweets: How the right rules in an age of extreme inequality. New York, NY, NY: Liveright Publishing Corporation, a divi-sion of W. W. Norton & Company.

68. "Opinion | Democrats, Here's How to Lose in 2022. And Deserve It." *NYTimes*, 21 Jan. 2021, https://www.nytimes.com/2021/01/21/opinion/biden-inaugura-tion-democrats.html.

69. Stiglitz, J. (2013). *Price of Inequality*. New York, NY: Wiley. p. 37
70. Rent seeking occurs when business activities funnel money away from the poor and give it to the rich, producing nothing tangible in return.
71. White, Gillian. "Workers Wages Aren't Rising Even Though They're More Productive." *The Atlantic*, 25 Feb. 2015, https://www.theatlantic.com/business/archive/2015/02/why-the-gap-between-worker-pay-and-productivity-is-so-problematic/385931/.
72. Stiglitz, J. (2013). *Price of Inequality*. New York, NY: Wiley. p. 33
73. Scheidel, W. (2018). *The great leveler violence and the history of inequality from the Stone Age to the twenty-first century*. Princeton, NJ: Princeton University Press.
74. Alberta, T. (2020). *American carnage: On the front lines of the Republican Civil War and the rise of President Trump*. New York, NY: Harper Paperbacks. P. 504

Chapter 8

1. PBS Frontline. (n.d.). A 1978 Speech By Gingrich | The Long March Of Newt Gingrich | FRONTLINE. Retrieved September 20, 2020, from https://www.pbs.org/wgbh/pages/frontline/newt/newt78speech.html
2. Berman, S. (2018). A Discussion of Steven Levitsky and Daniel Ziblatt's How Democracies Die. Perspectives on Politics, 16(4), 1092-1094. doi:10.1017/s1537592718002852
3. Silver, Nate. "Race and the 2008 Election, Revisited." FiveThirtyEight, 24 Apr. 2009, https://fivethirtyeight.com/features/race-and-2008-election-revisited/.
4. Daley, David. "How the GOP Made Your Vote Useless." *The Daily Beast*, 7 Oct. 2017, https://www.thedailybeast.com/how-gop-gerrymandering-made-your-democratic-vote-useless.
5. Newkirk, Vann. "How Redistricting Became a Technological Arms Race." The Atlantic, 28 Oct. 2017, https://www.theatlantic.com/politics/archive/2017/10/gerrymandering-technology-redmap-2020/543888/.
6. Hacker, J. S., & Pierson, P. (2020). *Let them eat Tweets: How the right rules in an age of extreme inequality*. New York, NY, NY: Liveright Publishing Corporation, a division of W. W. Norton & Company. p. 174
7. Liptak, Adam. "Supreme Court Bars Challenges to Partisan Gerrymandering." NYTimes, 27 June 2019, https://www.nytimes.com/2019/06/27/us/politics/supreme-court-gerrymandering.html.
8. Lockhart, P. R. "How *Shelby County v. Holder* Upended Voting Rights in America." Vox, 25 June 2019, https://www.vox.com/policy-and-politics/2019/6/25/18701277/shelby-county-v-holder-anniversary-voting-rights-suppression-congress.
9. Stern, Mark. "Trump Judge Argues Voters Can't Sue States Over Voting Rights." *Slate*, 4 Feb. 2020, https://slate.com/news-and-politics/2020/02/trump-judge-voters-sue-voting-rights-act.html.
10. Lieb, D. Election Shows How Gerrymandering Is Difficult to Overcome. US News, 8 Nov 2018, https://www.usnews.com/news/politics/articles/2018-11-17/midterm-elections-reveal-effects-of-gerrymandered-districts
11. de Vogue, Ariane. "Supreme Court Hands Democrats a Win in Virginia Racial Gerrymander Case." *CNN*, 17 June 2019, https://www.cnn.com/2019/06/17/politics/supreme-court-racial-virginia-gerrymandering-case/index.html.
12. Parks, Miles. "Redistricting Guru's Hard Drives Could Mean Legal, Political Woes For GOP." *NPR*, 6 June 2019, https://www.npr.org/2019/06/06/730260511/redistricting-gurus-hard-drives-could-mean-legal-political-woes-for-gop.

13. Chang, Alvin. "The Man Who Rigged America's Election Maps." *Vox*, 17 Oct. 2019, https://www.vox.com/videos/2019/10/17/20917852/gerrymander-hofeller-election-map.

14. Ralph Hise, David. "We Drew Congressional Maps for Partisan Advantage. That Was the Point." *The Atlantic*, 25 Mar. 2019, https://www.theatlantic.com/ideas/archive/2019/03/ralph-hise-and-david-lewis-nc-gerrymandering/585619/.

15. Domonoske, Camila. "Supreme Court Declines Republican Bid To Revive North Carolina Voter ID Law." *NPR*, 15 May 2017, https://www.npr.org/sections/thetwo-way/2017/05/15/528457693/supreme-court-declines-republican-bid-to-revive-north-carolina-voter-id-law.

16. Wang, Hansi. "Deceased GOP Strategist's Daughter Makes Files Public That Republicans Wanted Sealed." *NPR*, 5 Jan. 2020, https://www.npr.org/2020/01/05/785672201/deceased-gop-strategists-daughter-makes-files-public-that-republicans-wanted-sea.

17. Behrmann, Savannah. "'Extreme Partisan Gerrymandering': North Carolina Judges Rule Legislative Maps Violate State Constitution." *USA TODAY*, https://www.usatoday.com/story/news/politics/2019/09/03/north-carolina-judges-toss-maps-partisan-gerrymandering/2204294001/. Accessed 19 Dec. 2020.

18. Berman, Ari. "GOP Senators Representing a Minority of Americans Are Preventing a Fair Impeachment Trial." Mother Jones, 22 Jan. 2020, https://www.motherjones.com/politics/2020/01/gop-senators-representing-a-minority-of-americans-are-preventing-a-fair-impeachment-trial/.

19. Hacker, J. S., & Pierson, P. (2020*). Let them eat Tweets: How the right rules in an age of extreme inequality*. New York, NY, NY: Liveright Publishing Corporation, a division of W. W. Norton & Company. p. 187

20. The thing about the stupid "We're a republic, not a democracy!" comments is that republics are supposed to have indirect **representation** for voters — and under no reasonable national parameterization can you call what the Senate is doing today "representation."

21. Jones, Jeffrey. "Conservatives Greatly Outnumber Liberals in 19 U.S. States." Gallup, 22 Feb. 2019, https://news.gallup.com/poll/247016/conservatives-greatly-outnumber-liberals-states.aspx.

22. Klein, Ezra. "Nate Silver on Why 2020 Isn't 2016." *Vox*, 30 Oct. 2020, https://www.vox.com/21538214/nate-silver-538-2020-forecast-2016-trump-biden-election-podcast.

23. LoGiurato, Brett. "Here's How Americans Really Feel About Gun Control." *Business Insider*, 14 Dec. 2013, https://www.businessinsider.com/gun-control-polls-sandy-hook-shooting-anniversary-2013-12.

24. Silver, Nate. "The Senate's Rural Skew Makes It Very Hard For Democrats To Win The Supreme Court." *FiveThirtyEight*, 20 Sept. 2020, https://fivethirtyeight.com/features/the-senates-rural-skew-makes-it-very-hard-for-democrats-to-win-the-supreme-court/.

25. Brownstein, Ronald. "Why the 2020s Could Be as Dangerous as the 1850s." *The Atlantic*, 30 Oct. 2020, https://www.theatlantic.com/politics/archive/2020/10/biden-2020-trump-election/616912/.

26. MacGillis, Alec. "Go Midwest, Young Hipster." NYTimes, 22 Oct. 2016, https://www.nytimes.com/2016/10/23/opinion/campaign-stops/go-midwest-young-hip-

ster.html.; Wasserman, David. "The Congressional Map Has A Record-Setting Bias Against Democrats." FiveThirtyEight, 7 Aug. 2017, https://fivethirtyeight.com/features/the-congressional-map-is-historically-biased-toward-the-gop/.

27. Bui, Quoctrung. "The States That College Graduates Are Most Likely to Leave." NYTimes, 22 Nov. 2016, https://www.nytimes.com/2016/11/22/upshot/the-states-that-college-graduates-are-most-likely-to-leave.html.

28. Harris, Adam. "America Is Divided by Education." The Atlantic, 7 Nov. 2018, https://www.theatlantic.com/education/archive/2018/11/education-gap-explains-american-politics/575113/.

29. "College Graduates Continue to Shift toward the Democratic Party." Pew Research Center - U.S. Politics & Policy, 20 Mar. 2018, https://www.pewresearch.org/politics/wp-content/uploads/sites/4/2018/03/2_6.png.

30. "Trump Has a Growing Suburban Voter Problem." Fortune, https://fortune.com/2019/11/06/suburban-voters-trump-losing-election-results-2019/. Accessed 20 Sept. 2020.

31. Millhiser, Ian. "The Astounding Advantage the Electoral College Gives to Republicans, in One Chart." Vox, 17 Sept. 2019, https://www.vox.com/policy-and-politics/2019/9/17/20868790/republicans-lose-popular-vote-win-electoral-college.

32. Collin, Katy. "The Electoral College Badly Distorts the Vote. And It's Going to Get Worse." *The Washington Post*, 17 Nov. 2016, https://www.washingtonpost.com/news/monkey-cage/wp/2016/11/17/the-electoral-college-badly-distorts-the-vote-and-its-going-to-get-worse/.

33. Prokop, Andrew. "Why the Electoral College Is the Absolute Worst, Explained." Vox, 7 Nov. 2016, https://www.vox.com/policy-and-politics/2016/11/7/12315574/electoral-college-explained-presidential-elections-2016.

34. al-Gharbi, Musa. "Reality Check: Demographic Trends Won't Save the Democrats." MarketWatch, 26 Mar. 2020, https://www.marketwatch.com/story/reality-check-demographic-trends-wont-save-the-democrats-2017-03-06.

35. "Political Polarization in the American Public." Pew Research Center - U.S. Politics & Policy, 12 June 2014, https://www.pewresearch.org/politics/2014/06/12/political-polarization-in-the-american-public/.

36. Freedlander, David. "An Unsettling New Theory: There Is No Swing Voter." POLITICO, 6 Feb. 2020, https://www.politico.com/news/magazine/2020/02/06/rachel-bitecofer-profile-election-forecasting-new-theory-108944.

37. Marcotte, Amanda."Republicans Freak out over HR1: They Don't Want America to Have Fair Elections." Salon.Com, 8 Mar. 2019, https://www.salon.com/2019/03/08/republicans-freak-out-over-hr1-they-dont-want-america-to-have-fair-elections/.

38. See Anderson, Carol. "The Five Ways Republicans Will Crack down on Voting Rights in 2020." The Guardian, 13 Nov. 2019, http://www.theguardian.com/us-news/2019/nov/13/voter-suppression-2020-democracy-america. and Coppins, McKay. "The Billion-Dollar Disinformation Campaign to Reelect the President." The Atlantic, 6 Feb. 2020, https://www.theatlantic.com/magazine/archive/2020/03/the-2020-disinformation-war/605530/.

39. "Paul Weyrich - 'I Don't Want Everybody to Vote' (Goo Goo)." YouTube, 8 June 2007, https://www.youtube.com/watch?v=8GBAsFwPglw.

40. Domonoske, Camila. "Supreme Court Declines Republican Bid To Revive North Carolina Voter ID Law." NPR, 15 May 2017, https://www.npr.org/sections/thet-

wo-way/2017/05/15/528457693/supreme-court-declines-republican-bid-to-revive-north-carolina-voter-id-law.

41. Knight, Frederick. "Georgia Election Fight Shows That Black Voter Suppression, a Southern Tradition, Still Flourishes." PBS NewsHour, 28 Oct. 2018, https://www.pbs.org/newshour/politics/georgia-election-fight-shows-that-black-voter-suppression-a-southern-tradition-still-flourishes.

42. Pope, Devin. "There Are Stark Racial Disparities in Voting Times. Here's How to Fix Them." *The Washington Post*, 27 Dec. 2019, https://www.washingtonpost.com/opinions/there-are-stark-racial-disparities-in-voting-times-heres-how-to-fix-them/2019/12/16/5fb4948a-1c5b-11ea-b4c1-fd0d91b60d9e_story.html.

43. McCarthy, Tom. "Alarm over Voter Purges as 17m Americans Removed from Rolls in Two Years." The Guardian, 1 Aug. 2019, http://www.theguardian.com/us-news/2019/aug/01/voter-purges-us-elections-brennan-center-report.

44. The Economist/YouGov Poll. November 8 - 10, 2020 - 1500 U.S. Registered Voters. https://docs.cdn.yougov.com/9j7sr0my95/econTabReport.pdf

45. Bentele, K., & O'Brien, E. (2013). Jim Crow 2.0? Why States Consider and Adopt Restrictive Voter Access Policies. *Perspectives on Politics, 11*(4), 1088-1116. doi:10.1017/S1537592713002843

46. Rubin, Jennifer. "The Demographic Change Fueling the Angst of Trump's Base." *The Washington Post*, 6 Sept. 2017, https://www.washingtonpost.com/blogs/right-turn/wp/2017/09/06/the-demographic-change-fueling-the-angst-of-trumps-base/.

47. Edsall, Thomas. "Trump Needs His Base to Burn With Anger." NYTimes, 3 July 2019, https://www.nytimes.com/2019/07/03/opinion/trump-republican-base.html.

48. Golshan, Tara. "How Republicans are trying to strip power from Democratic governors-elect." Vox, 4 Dec. 2018, https://www.vox.com/policy-and-politics/2018/12/4/18123784/gop-legislature-wisconsin-michigan-power-grab-lame-duck.

49. Dionne, E. J. "Are Republicans Abandoning Democracy?" The Washington Post, 10 Dec. 2018, https://www.washingtonpost.com/opinions/are-republicans-abandoning-democracy/2018/12/09/8ad0b278-fa62-11e8-8c9a-860ce2a8148f_story.html.

50. Stern, Mark. "Despite a Court Ruling, Most of Florida's Ex-Felons Will Still Face a 'Poll Tax.'" *Slate*, 21 Oct. 2019, https://slate.com/news-and-politics/2019/10/florida-voting-rights-felons-poll-tax-injunction.html.

51. Simonds, Dave. "Republican State Legislatures Are Overturning Ballot Initiatives." The Economist, 20 Apr. 2019, https://www.economist.com/united-states/2019/04/20/republican-state-legislatures-are-overturning-ballot-initiatives.

52. Gardiner, Andrew. "Revamp of Arizona Panel That Guards against Gerrymandering Is One Step from Ballot." The Arizona Republic, https://www.azcentral.com/story/news/politics/arizona/2018/05/02/arizona-house-passes-republican-plan-overhaul-redistricting-commission/574421002/. Accessed 20 Sept. 2020.

53. Daugherty, Owen. "Michigan Governor Signs Bill Making Ballot Drives Harder." TheHill, 29 Dec. 2018, https://thehill.com/homenews/state-watch/423164-michigan-governor-signs-bill-making-ballot-drives-harder.

54. Cooper, Cox, Lienesch and Jones. "Anxiety, Nostalgia, and Mistrust: Findings from the 2015 American Values Survey | PRRI." PRRI, https://www.prri.org/research/survey-anxiety-nostalgia-and-mistrust-findings-from-the-2015-american-values-survey/. Accessed 20 Sept. 2020.

55. French, Sally. "Raising Fast-Food Hourly Wages to $15 Would Raise Prices by 4 percent, Study Finds." *MarketWatch*, 22 Oct. 2020, https://www.marketwatch.com/story/raising-fast-food-hourly-wages-to-15-would-raise-prices-by-4-study-finds-2015-07-28.

56. Pettigrew, Thomas F. "Social Psychological Perspectives on Trump Supporters." Journal of Social and Political Psychology, 3 Feb. 2017, https://jspp.psychopen.eu/article/view/750/html.

57. Jacobs, Tom. "A New Study Confirms (Again) That Race, Not Economics, Drove Former Democrats to Trump." Pacific Standard, 29 Apr. 2019, https://psmag.com/news/new-study-confirms-again-that-race-not-economics-drove-former-democrats-to-trump.

58. Bacon, Perry. "The Republican Party Has Changed Dramatically Since George H.W. Bush Ran It." FiveThirtyEight, 1 Dec. 2018, https://fivethirtyeight.com/features/the-republican-party-has-changed-dramatically-since-george-h-w-bush-ran-it/.

59. "Voteview: Parties at a Glance." https://voteview.com/parties. Accessed 20 Sept. 2020.

60. "Congressional Elections Decided by 10 Percent or Less" Ballotpedia, 9 Apr. 2019, https://ballotpedia.org/Congressional_elections_decided_by_10_percent_or_less,_2018.

61. Civiqs Poll. "Donald Trump: Job Approval," https://civiqs.com/results/approve_president_trump, accessed 20 Sep 2020

Chapter 9

1. Wise, J. (2020, February 06). Collins admits comments about Trump learning a lesson are 'aspirational'. Retrieved September 20, 2020, from https://thehill.com/homenews/senate/481782-collins-admits-comments-about-trump-learning-a-lesson-are-aspirational

2. Oprysko, Caitlin. "Trump Announces a Blitz of Pardons and Commutations." POLITICO, 18 Feb. 2020, https://www.politico.com/news/2020/02/18/trump-commutes-sentence-of-rod-blagojevich-115807.

3. Naylor, Brian. "Former FBI Official Andrew McCabe Won't Face Charges." *NPR*, 14 Feb. 2020, https://www.npr.org/2020/02/14/806052193/former-fbi-official-andrew-mccabe-wont-face-charges.

4. Fisk, Robert. "Trump Asked Aides 'Can We Just Get Rid of the Judges?', Book Claims." Share Your Thoughts and Debate the Big Issues, 8 Nov. 2019, https://www.independent.co.uk/news/world/americas/us-politics/trump-federal-judges-rant-white-house-official-book-anonymous-a9194871.html.

5. Mueller, Eleanor. "Trump Executive Order Strips Protections for Key Federal Workers, Drawing Backlash." *POLITICO*, 22 Oct. 2020, https://www.politico.com/news/2020/10/22/trump-order-strips-worker-protections-431359.

6. Fandos, Nicholas. "White House Declares War on Impeachment Inquiry, Claiming Effort to Undo Trump's Election." NYTimes, 24 Oct. 2019, https://www.nytimes.com/2019/10/08/us/politics/sondland-trump-ukraine-impeach.html.

7. "10 Ways America Has Come to Resemble a Banana Republic." Salon.Com, 11 Sept. 2013, https://www.salon.com/2013/09/11/10_ways_america_has_come_to_resemble_a_banana_republic/.

8. Fisk, Robert. "Trump Is Eligible to Serve Third Term, Senior Republican Says without Providing Evidence." Share Your Thoughts and Debate the Big Issues, 13 Dec. 2019,

https://www.independent.co.uk/news/world/americas/us-politics/trump-2024-election-third-term-mike-huckabee-impeachment-inquiry-a9244761.html.

9. Fisk, Robert. "After Trump's Behavior This Week, Experts Worry 2020 Could Be Our Last Free Election." Share Your Thoughts and Debate the Big Issues, 14 Feb. 2020, https://www.independent.co.uk/voices/trump-2020-election-roger-stone-tweets-barr-giuliani-ukraine-a9336601.html.

10. Cameron, M. (2018). Making Sense of Competitive Authoritarianism: Lessons from the Andes. Latin American Politics and Society, 60(2), 1-22. doi:10.1017/lap.2018.3

11. Snyder, T. (2019). *The road to unfreedom: Russia, Europe, America*. London, UK: Vintage. p. 45

12. Erlanger, Steven. "What Should Europe Do About Viktor Orbán and 'Illiberal Democracy'?" *NYTimes*, 23 Dec. 2019, https://www.nytimes.com/2019/12/23/world/europe/tusk-Orbán-migration-eu.html.

13. Bump, Philip. "Analysis | *Fox News* Begins and Ends Its Super Bowl Coverage the Same Way: Getting Trump's Back." *The Washington Post*, 3 Feb. 2020, https://www.washingtonpost.com/politics/2020/02/03/fox-news-begins-ends-its-super-bowl-coverage-same-way-getting-trumps-back/.

14. "Trump's 2,000 Conflicts of Interest (and Counting)" CREW, 23 Mar. 2020, https://www.citizensforethics.org/2000-trump-conflicts-of-interest-counting/. Also, Willis, Jay. "How Donald Trump's Kids Have Profited Off Their Dad's Presidency." GQ, 6 June 2012, https://www.gq.com/story/trump-kids-profit-presidency.

15. Bernstein, Richard. "Thailand's Playboy King Isn't Playing around." Vox, 24 Jan. 2020, https://www.vox.com/2020/1/24/21075149/king-thailand-maha-vajiralong-korn-facebook-video-tattoos.

16. Gessen, M. (2020). Surviving Autocracy. New York, NY: Riverhead Books. p. 9

17. Oaks, D. (Feb 1992) The Divinely Inspired Constitution. *Ensign Magazine* https://www.churchofjesuschrist.org/study/ensign/1992/02/the-divinely-inspired-constitution?lang=eng. Accessed 24 Oct. 2020.

18. Snyder, T. (2019). *The road to unfreedom: Russia, Europe, America*. London, UK: Vintage. p. 7

19. Paxton, R. (1998). The Five Stages of Fascism. *The Journal of Modern History*, 70(1), 1-23. doi:10.1086/235001

20. Churchwell, Sarah. "American Fascism: It Has Happened Here." *The New York Review of Books*, https://www.nybooks.com/daily/2020/06/22/american-fascism-it-has-happened-here/. Accessed 26 Sept. 2020.

21. Churchwell, Sarah. "The Return of American Fascism." *New Statesman*, 2 Sept. 2020, https://www.newstatesman.com/international/places/2020/09/return-american-fascism.

22. Soucy, Robert. "Fascism: Definition, Characteristics, & History." Encyclopedia Britannica, https://www.britannica.com/topic/fascism. Accessed 23 Sept. 2020.

23. "Life for Women and the Family in Nazi Germany." BBC Bitesize, https://www.bbc.co.uk/bitesize/guides/zxb8msg/revision/1. Accessed 23 Sept. 2020.

24. "Persecution of Homosexuals in the Third Reich." United States Holocaust Memorial Museum, https://encyclopedia.ushmm.org/content/en/article/persecution-of-homosexuals-in-the-third-reich. Accessed 23 Sept. 2020.

25. Snyder, T. (2019). The road to unfreedom: Russia, Europe, America. London, UK: Vintage. p. 53

26. Woolf, Jake. "President Obama's Infamous Mom Jeans Are Actually Cool Now." *GQ*, https://www.gq.com/story/president-obamas-mom-jeans-are-actually-cool-now. Accessed 10 Oct. 2020.

27. Dicker, Ron. "Tomi Lahren Ticks Off Twitter With Oddly Sexist Dig At Biden's Mask-Wearing." *HuffPost*, 6 Oct. 2020, https://www.huffpost.com/entry/tomi-lahren-twitter-joe-biden-purse_n_5f7c7454c5b6e5aba0d0534c.

28. Hohmann, James. "Analysis | The Daily 202: Trump Faces Historic Gender Gap Heading into First Debate." *The Washington Post*, 29 Sept. 2020, https://www.washingtonpost.com/politics/2020/09/29/daily-202-trump-faces-historic-gender-gap-heading-into-first-debate/.

29. Gjelten, Tom. "For Evangelicals, A Year Of Reckoning On Sexual Sin And Support For Donald Trump." *NPR*, 24 Dec. 2018, https://www.npr.org/2018/12/24/678390550/for-evangelicals-a-year-of-reckoning-on-sexual-sin-and-support-for-donald-trump.

30. Stanton, Glenn. *Marriage on Trial: The Case Against Same-Sex Marriage and Parenting:* Stanton, Glenn T., Maier, Dr. Bill: 9780830832743: Amazon.Com: Books. https://www.amazon.com/Marriage-Trial-Against-Same-Sex-Parenting/dp/0830832742. Accessed 24 Sept. 2020.

31. Gander, Kashmira. "First White House Bible Study Group in a Century Led by Anti-Gay, Anti-Catholic, Anti-Women Pastor." Newsweek, 11 Apr. 2018, https://www.newsweek.com/white-house-bible-group-led-pastor-anti-gay-anti-women-anti-catholic-881860.

32. Amanda L. Martens, Evelyn Stratmoen & Donald A. Saucier (2018) To Preserve, Protect, and Defend: Masculine Honor Beliefs and Perceptions of the 2016 Presidential Candidates, Basic and Applied Social Psychology, 40:5, 308-319, DOI: 10.1080/01973533.2018.1500288

33. DiMuccio, Eric. "Analysis | How Donald Trump Appeals to Men Secretly Insecure about Their Manhood." *The Washington Post*, 29 Nov. 2018, https://www.washingtonpost.com/news/monkey-cage/wp/2018/11/29/how-donald-trump-appeals-to-men-secretly-insecure-about-their-manhood/.

34. Persio, Sofia. "Anti-Trans Group Admits Bathroom Predator Myth Is Made Up." PinkNews - Gay News, Reviews and Comment from the World's Most Read Lesbian, Gay, Bisexual, and Trans News Service, 7 Dec. 2018, https://www.pinknews.co.uk/2018/12/07/anti-trans-group-bathroom-predator-myth/; Ring, Trudy. "James Dobson: Be a Man, Shoot a Transgender Woman in the Bathroom." Advocate.Com, 1 June 2016, http://www.advocate.com/transgender/2016/6/01/james-dobson-be-man-shoot-transgender-woman-bathroom.

35. Fries, Kenny. "The Nazis' First Victims Were the Disabled." *New York Times*, 13 Sept. 2017, https://www.nytimes.com/2017/09/13/opinion/nazis-holocaust-disabled.html.

36. "Black Triangle (Badge) - Wikipedia." Wikimedia Foundation, Inc., 14 Sept. 2012, https://en.wikipedia.org/wiki/Black_triangle_(badge).

37. O'Mathúna, Dónal. "Human Dignity in the Nazi Era: Implications for Contemporary Bioethics." PubMed Central (PMC), 1 Jan. 2006, https://www.ncbi.nlm.nih.gov/pmc/articles/PMC1484488/.

38. Stanley, Jason. (2018) How Fascism Works. Random House, New York, NY. p. 179

39. Dunn, Amina. "Partisans are divided over the fairness of the U.S. economy – and why people are rich or poor." Pew Research Center, 4 Oct. 2018, https://www.pewre-

search.org/fact-tank/2018/10/04/partisans-are-divided-over-the-fairness-of-the-u-s-economy-and-why-people-are-rich-or-poor/.

40. "Donald Trump Mocks Reporter with Disability – Video." The Guardian, 26 Nov. 2015, http://www.theguardian.com/us-news/video/2015/nov/26/donald-trump-appears-to-mock-disabled-reporter-video.

41. "Public Opinion on Single-Payer, National Health Plans, and Expanding Access to Medicare Coverage." KFF, 27 May 2020, https://www.kff.org/slideshow/public-opinion-on-single-payer-national-health-plans-and-expanding-access-to-medicare-coverage/.

42. HOPE YEN, RICARDO. "AP FACT CHECK: Trump's Dubious Claims on Health Care, Court." *Associated Press*, 28 Sept. 2020, https://apnews.com/article/election-2020-race-and-ethnicity-ap-fact-check-virus-outbreak-voting-fraud-and-irregularities-5dd4ed156b8b8f9c36cd1812ed1b317c.

43. "Trump's Election Year Budget Proposal Slashes Medicaid, Other Social Safety Nets." *NBC News*, 10 Feb. 2020, https://www.nbcnews.com/politics/donald-trump/trump-s-election-year-budget-proposal-slashes-medicaid-other-social-n1134081.

44. https://www.washingtonpost.com/business/2019/09/10/trump-pushing-major-crackdown-homeless-camps-california-with-aides-discussing-moving-residents-government-backed-facilities/

45. "Trump's Election Year Budget Proposal Slashes Medicaid, Other Social Safety Nets." *NBC News*, 10 Feb. 2020, https://www.nbcnews.com/politics/donald-trump/trump-s-election-year-budget-proposal-slashes-medicaid-other-social-n1134081; Dwyer, Colin. "U.S. Announces Its Withdrawal From U.N. Human Rights Council." *NPR*, 19 June 2018, https://www.npr.org/2018/06/19/621435225/u-s-announces-its-withdrawal-from-u-n-s-human-rights-council.

46. Gessen, Masha. "Mike Pompeo's Faith-Based Attempt to Narrowly Redefine Human Rights." The New Yorker, https://www.newyorker.com/news/our-columnists/mike-pompeos-faith-based-attempt-to-narrowly-redefine-human-rights. Accessed 24 Sept. 2020.

47. Fox, Ben.. "At Least 138 Sent from US to El Salvador Were Killed." San Diego Union-Tribune, 5 Feb. 2020, https://www.sandiegouniontribune.com/news/nation-world/story/2020-02-04/report-at-least-138-sent-from-us-to-el-salvador-were-killed.

48. Aguilera, Jasmine. "Here's Everything To Know About The Status of Family Separation, Which Isn't Nearly Over." Time, 25 Oct. 2019, https://time.com/5678313/trump-administration-family-separation-lawsuits/

49. Jameel, Robert. "Inside the Cell Where a Sick 16-Year-Old Boy Died in Border Patrol Care." ProPublica, 5 Dec. 2019, https://www.propublica.org/article/inside-the-cell-where-a-sick-16-year-old-boy-died-in-border-patrol-care?token=XgFT9qOh9SrXdo-ACBzMzWe_PuorElToO.

50. Serwer, Adam. "The Cruelty Is the Point." The Atlantic, 3 Oct. 2018, https://www.theatlantic.com/ideas/archive/2018/10/the-cruelty-is-the-point/572104/.

51. Krieg, Gregory. "Donald Trump Reveals When America Was 'Great.'" *CNN*, 26 Mar. 2016, https://www.cnn.com/2016/03/26/politics/donald-trump-when-america-was-great/index.html.

52. *"Engel v. Vitale-Wikipedia."* Wikimedia Foundation, Inc., 28 Nov. 2018, https://en.wikipedia.org/wiki/Engel_v._Vitale.

53. The Supreme Court, in this case, held that the Fourteenth Amendment requires states to license and recognize same-sex marriage.

54. "Redlining-Wikipedia." Wikimedia Foundation, Inc., 1 Apr. 2019, https://en.wikipedia.org/wiki/Redlining.

55. Moyers, Bill. "WHAT A REAL PRESIDENT WAS LIKE." *The Washington Post*, 13 Nov. 1988, https://www.washingtonpost.com/archive/opinions/1988/11/13/what-a-real-president-was-like/d483c1be-d0da-43b7-bde6-04e10106ff6c/.

56. Katznelson, Ira. "What America Taught the Nazis." The Atlantic, 3 Oct. 2017, https://www.theatlantic.com/magazine/archive/2017/11/what-america-taught-the-nazis/540630/.

57. Hooghe, Marc & Dassonneville, Ruth. (2018). Explaining the Trump Vote: The Effect of Racist Resentment and Anti-Immigrant Sentiments. PS: Political Science & Politics. 1-7. 10.1017/S1049096518000367.

58. Jones, R. P. (2017). *The end of White Christian America*. New York, NY: Simon Schuster.

59. Mutz, D. C. (2018). Status threat, not economic hardship, explains the 2016 presidential vote. *Proceedings of the National Academy of Sciences*, 115(19). doi:10.1073/pnas.1718155115

60. Pettigrew, T. F. (2017). Social psychological perspectives on Trump supporters. *Journal of Social and Political Psychology*, 5(1), 107-116. doi:10.5964/jspp.v5i1.750

61. *Newman v. Piggie Park Enterprises, Inc.*, 390 U.S. 400 (1968) https://supreme.justia.com/cases/federal/us/390/400/

62. Carney, Jordain. "GOP Senator Blocks Vote on House-Passed Violence Against Women Act." *The Hill*, 20 Nov. 2019, https://thehill.com/homenews/senate/471386-gop-senator-blocks-vote-on-house-passed-violence-against-women-act.

63. Carney, Jordain. "GOP Senator Blocks Vote on House-Passed Violence Against Women Act." *The Hill*, 20 Nov. 2019, https://thehill.com/homenews/senate/471386-gop-senator-blocks-vote-on-house-passed-violence-against-women-act.

64. Hagle, Courtney. "How *Fox News* Pushed the White Supremacist 'Great Replacement' Theory." *Media Matters for America*, 5 Aug. 2019, https://www.mediamatters.org/tucker-carlson/how-fox-news-pushed-white-supremacist-great-replacement-theory.

65. Gentile, E. (2004). Fascism, totalitarianism and political religion: Definitions and critical reflections on criticism of an interpretation. Totalitarian Movements and Political Religions, 5(3), 326-375. doi:10.1080/14690760042000312177

66. Margolis, M. F. (2019). Who Wants to Make America Great Again? Understanding Evangelical Support for Donald Trump. *Politics and Religion*, 13(1), 89-118. doi:10.1017/s1755048319000208

67. Jacoby, Susan. "Opinion | The White House Is Tearing Down the Wall Between Church and State." *NYTimes*, 5 July 2018, https://www.nytimes.com/2018/07/05/opinion/sunday/church-state-supreme-court-religion.html.

68. Wallace, A. F. (1966). Religion; an anthropological view. New York, NY: Random House. p. 30

69. Jacobs, Ben. "Donald Trump Calls Pope Francis 'Disgraceful' for Questioning His Faith." *The Guardian*, 18 Feb. 2016, http://www.theguardian.com/us-news/2016/feb/18/donald-trump-pope-francis-christian-wall-mexico-border.

70. Staff, Media. *"Fox News'* Pastor Robert Jeffress Says Liberal Churches 'Deserve to Die.'" *Media Matters for America,* 22 Feb. 2020, https://www.mediamatters.org/robert-jeffress/fox-news-pastor-robert-jeffress-says-liberal-churches-deserve-die.
71. Taylor, David. "Project Blitz: The Legislative Assault by Christian Nationalists to Reshape America." *The Guardian,* 4 June 2018, http://www.theguardian.com/world/2018/jun/04/project-blitz-the-legislative-assault-by-christian-nationalists-to-reshape-america.
72. Burleigh, Nina. "Does God Believe in Trump? White Evangelicals Are Sticking with Their 'Prince of Lies.'" *Newsweek,* 5 Oct. 2017, https://www.newsweek.com/2017/10/13/donald-trump-white-evangelicals-support-god-677587.html.
73. Bailey, Sarah. "Trump Promised to Destroy the Johnson Amendment. Congress Is Targeting It Now." *The Washington Post,* 30 June 2017, https://www.washingtonpost.com/news/acts-of-faith/wp/2017/06/30/trump-promised-to-destroy-the-johnson-amendment-congress-is-targeting-it-now/; Press, Associated. "S.C. Group Can Reject Gays and Jews as Foster Parents, Admin Says." *NBC News,* 24 Jan. 2019, https://www.nbcnews.com/feature/nbc-out/s-c-group-can-reject-gays-jews-foster-parents-trump-n962306.
74. Sherwood, Harriet. "'Toxic Christianity': The Evangelicals Creating Champions for Trump." *The Guardian,* 21 Oct. 2018, http://www.theguardian.com/us-news/2018/oct/21/evangelical-christians-trump-liberty-university-jerry-falwell.
75. Gerson, Michael. "Opinion | White Evangelical Protestants Are Fully Disrobed. And It Is an Embarrassing Sight." *The Washington Post,* 28 Oct. 2019, https://www.washingtonpost.com/opinions/evangelicals-have-been-reshaped-into-the-image-of-trump-himself/2019/10/28/f37f5154-f9c0-11e9-ac8c-8eced29ca6ef_story.html.
76. Stoehr, John. "For White Evangelicals, It's Not About Fear." *The Editorial Board,* 15 Aug. 2020, https://stoehr.substack.com/p/for-white-evangelicals-its-not-about.
77. Kilgore, Ed. "Christian Conservative Politics Are Driving Liberals Out of the Pews." *Intelligencer,* 18 Sept. 2019, https://nymag.com/intelligencer/2019/09/christian-right-politics-closing-church-door-to-liberals.html.
78. Diavolo, Lucy. "Nazis Destroyed This Amazing LGBTQ Library in Germany." *Teen Vogue,* https://www.teenvogue.com/story/lgbtq-institute-in-germany-was-burned-down-by-nazis. Accessed 26 Sept. 2020.
79. Foer, Franklin. "Viktor Orbán's War on Intellect." *The Atlantic,* 9 May 2019, https://www.theatlantic.com/magazine/archive/2019/06/george-soros-viktor-Orbán-ceu/588070/.
80. Suls, Rob. "Educational Divide in Vote Preferences on Track to Be Wider than in Recent Elections." *Pew Research Center,* 15 Sept. 2016, https://www.pewresearch.org/fact-tank/2016/09/15/educational-divide-in-vote-preferences-on-track-to-be-wider-than-in-recent-elections/.
81. Wasserman, David. "The Key To The GOP Race: The Diploma Divide." *FiveThirtyEight,* 21 Dec. 2015, https://fivethirtyeight.com/features/the-key-to-the-gop-race-the-diploma-divide/.
82. "A Policy Expert Explains How Anti-Intellectualism Gave Rise to Donald Trump." *The World from PRX,* 2 Aug. 2016, https://www.pri.org/stories/2016-08-02/policy-expert-explains-how-anti-intellectualism-gave-rise-donald-trump.
83. Hafner, Josh. "Donald Trump Loves the 'Poorly Educated' — and They Love Him." *USA TODAY,* https://www.usatoday.com/story/news/politics/onpoli-

tics/2016/02/24/donald-trump-nevada-poorly-educated/80860078/. Accessed 26 Sept. 2020.

84. Collins, Eliza. "Trump: I Consult Myself on Foreign Policy." *POLITICO*, 16 Mar. 2016, https://www.politico.com/blogs/2016-gop-primary-live-updates-and-results/2016/03/trump-foreign-policy-adviser-220853.

85. Shafer, Jack. "Donald Trump Talks Like a Third-Grader." *POLITICO Magazine*, 13 Aug. 2015, https://www.politico.com/magazine/story/2015/08/donald-trump-talks-like-a-third-grader-121340.html.

86. Eco, Umberto. "Ur-Fascism." *The New York Review of Books*, https://www.nybooks.com/articles/1995/06/22/ur-fascism/. Accessed 26 Sept. 2020.

87. Parker, Kim. "Views of Higher Education Divided by Party." *Pew Research Center's Social & Demographic Trends Project*, 19 Aug. 2020, https://www.pewsocialtrends.org/essay/the-growing-partisan-divide-in-views-of-higher-education/.

88. Davies, William. "The Free Speech Panic: How the Right Concocted a Crisis." *The Guardian*, 26 July 2018, http://www.theguardian.com/news/2018/jul/26/the-free-speech-panic-censorship-how-the-right-concocted-a-crisis.

89. Hohman, Harrison. "The Stifling Hypocrisy of Turning Point | The Stanford Daily." *The Stanford Daily*, 25 May 2018, https://www.stanforddaily.com/2018/05/25/the-stifling-hypocrisy-of-turning-point/.; "Professor Watchlist." *Professor Watchlist*, https://professorwatchlist.org. Accessed 26 Sept. 2020.

90. Svrluga, Susan. "Trump Signs Executive Order on Free Speech on College Campuses." *The Washington Post*, 21 Mar. 2019, https://www.washingtonpost.com/education/2019/03/21/trump-expected-sign-executive-order-free-speech/.

91. Gessen, M. (2020). *Surviving Autocracy*. New York, NY: Riverhead Books. p. 87-88

92. Gauchat, G. (2012). Politicization of Science in the Public Sphere. *American Sociological Review*, 77(2), 167-187. doi:10.1177/0003122412438225

93. "A Former GOP Congressman Believes Climate Change Is Real. Can He Convince His Party?" *NBC News*, 30 Sept. 2018, https://www.nbcnews.com/news/us-news/bob-inglis-republican-believer-climate-change-out-convert-his-party-n912066.

94. Plumer, Brad. "Science Under Attack: How Trump Is Sidelining Researchers and Their Work." *NYTimes*, 28 Dec. 2019, https://www.nytimes.com/2019/12/28/climate/trump-administration-war-on-science.html.; Sun, Lena. "CDC Gets List of Forbidden Words: Fetus, Transgender, Diversity." *The Washington Post*, 15 Dec. 2017, https://www.washingtonpost.com/national/health-science/cdc-gets-list-of-forbidden-words-fetus-transgender-diversity/2017/12/15/f503837a-e1cf-11e7-89e8-edec16379010_story.html.

95. Baldasty, Jerry. "Fake News and Misinformation: Why Teaching Critical Thinking Is Crucial for Democracy." *Office of the Provost*, 23 Apr. 2018, https://www.washington.edu/provost/2018/04/23/fake-news-and-misinformation-why-teaching-critical-thinking-is-crucial-for-democracy/.

96. Baker, Peter. "'Use That Word!': Trump Embraces the 'Nationalist' Label." *NYTimes*, 23 Oct. 2018, https://www.nytimes.com/2018/10/23/us/politics/nationalist-president-trump.html.

97. Oprysko, Caitlin. "Trump Pushes Aggressive 'America First' Message to World Leaders." *POLITICO*, 24 Sept. 2019, https://politi.co/2mooUya.

98. Fredericks, B. "White House Tweets Photo of Trump Hugging Old Glory for Flag Day." *New York Post*, 14 June 2019, https://nypost.com/2019/06/14/white-house-

tweets-photo-of-trump-hugging-old-glory-for-flag-day/.

99. Axelrod, Tal. "A Look at the Military Hardware in Trump's Fourth of July Celebration." *The Hill*, 4 July 2019, https://thehill.com/policy/defense/451684-a-look-at-the-military-hardware-in-trumps-fourth-of-july-celebration.

100. Lamothe, Dan. "Trump's July 4 Celebration Will Cost Millions — and It Will Take a While to Know How Much." *The Washington Post*, 3 July 2019, https://www.washingtonpost.com/politics/trumps-july-4-celebration-will-cost-millions--and-it-will-take-a-while-to-know-how-much/2019/07/03/77ea1006-9dae-11e9-9ed4-c9089972ad5a_story.html.

101. McCammon, Sarah. "What Does Trump's Promise Of A Nation 'Under One God' Really Mean?" *NPR*, 18 Sept. 2016, https://www.npr.org/2016/09/18/494367803/what-does-trumps-promise-of-a-nation-under-one-god-really-mean.

102. Baron, R. "Germany's Unity Myth." *Red Baron's Blog*, 3 Oct. 2015, https://mhoefert.blogspot.com/2015/10/germany-unity-myth.html.

103. Kurtz, Judy. "Trump Doubles down on 'Parasite' Criticism: 'I like to See Things That We Do Get Honored.'" *The Hill*, 21 Feb. 2020, https://thehill.com/blogs/in-the-know/in-the-know/484112-trump-doubles-down-on-parasite-criticism-i-like-to-see-things.

104. "Trump Referred to Haiti and African Nations as 'Shithole' Countries." *NBC News*, 12 Jan. 2018, https://www.nbcnews.com/politics/white-house/trump-referred-haiti-african-countries-shithole-nations-n836946.

105. Tharoor, Ishaan. "Analysis | Trump Scapegoats Almost a Quarter of Africa's Population." *The Washington Post*, 5 Feb. 2020, https://www.washingtonpost.com/world/2020/02/05/trump-scapegoats-almost-quarter-africas-population/.

106. Baker, Peter. "Once Trump Talked About 'American Carnage.' Now He Says Critics Should Leave." *NYTimes*, 16 July 2019, https://www.nytimes.com/2019/07/16/us/politics/trump-america-criticism.html.

107. Zimmer, Ben. "How the 'U-S-A' Chant Became a Political Weapon." *The Atlantic*, 8 Feb. 2019, https://www.theatlantic.com/ideas/archive/2019/02/republicans-and-democrats-chant-usa-at-state-of-union/582325/.

108. Affairs, Current. "The West According to Ben Shapiro □ Current Affairs." *Current Affairs*, 24 June 2019, https://www.currentaffairs.org/2019/06/the-west-according-to-ben-shapiro.

109. Green, Emma. "Imagining Post-Trump Nationalism." *The Atlantic*, 30 June 2019, https://www.theatlantic.com/politics/archive/2019/06/first-things-nationalism-trump/592996/.

110. Clifton, Derrick. "How the Trump Administration's '1776 Report' Warps the History of Racism and Slavery." *NBC News*, 20 Jan. 2021, https://www.nbcnews.com/news/nbcblk/how-trump-administration-s-1776-report-warps-history-racism-slavery-n1254926.

111. Colson, Thomas. "RANKED: How Patriotic 19 World-Leading Economies Are." *Business Insider*, 23 Nov. 2016, https://www.businessinsider.com/yougov-19-most-patriotic-countries-in-the-world-2016-11.

112. Thorsett, Laura. "U.S. Is among World's Greatest Countries, Say Most Americans." *Pew Research Center*, 30 June 2017, https://www.pewresearch.org/fact-tank/2017/06/30/most-americans-say-the-u-s-is-among-the-greatest-countries-in-the-world/.

113. Merelli, Annalisa. "The US Has a Lot of Money, but It Does Not Look like a Developed Country." *Quartz*, 10 Mar. 2017, https://qz.com/879092/the-us-doesnt-look-like-a-developed-country/.

114. Mathur, Aparna. "The U.S. Does Poorly On Yet Another Metric of Economic Mobility." *Forbes*, 16 July 2018, https://www.forbes.com/sites/aparnamathur/2018/07/16/the-u-s-does-poorly-on-yet-another-metric-of-economic-mobility/.

115. Coaston, Jane. "Adolf Hitler Was Not a Socialist." *Vox*, 27 Mar. 2019, https://www.vox.com/2019/3/27/18283879/nazism-socialism-hitler-gop-brooks-gohmert.

116. Bel, G. (2010). Against the mainstream: Nazi privatization in 1930s Germany1. *The Economic History Review*, 63(1), 34-55. doi:10.1111/j.1468-0289.2009.00473.x

117. Tankersley, Jim. "Trump Administration Scaling Back Rules Meant to Stop Corporate Inversions." *NYTimes*, 31 Oct. 2019, https://www.nytimes.com/2019/10/31/business/trump-treasury-corporate-inversions.html.; Bergengruen, V. (2016, December 1). Here are 4 government programs Trump's team wants to privatize. Retrieved September 26, 2020, from https://www.mcclatchydc.com/news/politics-government/white-house/article118284043.html; Drucker, Jesse. "How Big Companies Won New Tax Breaks From the Trump Administration." *NYTimes*, 30 Dec. 2019, https://www.nytimes.com/2019/12/30/business/trump-tax-cuts-beat-gilti.html.

118. Spaid, Jacob. "In Corporations We Trust: Ongoing Deregulation and Government Protections." *The Harvard Law School Forum on Corporate Governance*, 6 Feb. 2019, https://corpgov.law.harvard.edu/2019/02/06/in-corporations-we-trust-ongoing-deregulation-and-government-protections/.; Eggerton, John. "FCC Prepares to Defend Broadcast Ownership Deregulation." *Broadcasting+Cable*, 10 June 2019, https://www.nexttv.com/news/fcc-prepares-to-defend-broadcast-ownership-deregulation.

119. Setty, Ganesh. "US Lost More Tax Revenue than Any Other Developed Country in 2018 Due to Trump Tax Cuts, New Report Says." *CNBC*, 5 Dec. 2019, https://www.cnbc.com/2019/12/05/us-tax-revenue-dropped-sharply-due-to-trump-tax-cuts-report.html.; Lartey, Jamiles. "Corporate Penalties Dropped as Much as 94 percent under Trump, Study Says." *The Guardian*, 25 July 2018, http://www.theguardian.com/us-news/2018/jul/25/trump-corporate-penalties-drop-public-citizen-study.

120. Pound, Jesse. "These 91 Companies Paid No Federal Taxes in 2018." *CNBC*, 16 Dec. 2019, https://www.cnbc.com/2019/12/16/these-91-fortune-500-companies-didnt-pay-federal-taxes-in-2018.html.; Matt Egan, *CNN*. "Stock Buybacks Exploded after the Tax Cuts. Now They're Slowing down." *CNN*, 22 Aug. 2019, https://www.cnn.com/2019/08/22/investing/stock-buybacks-drop-tax-cuts/index.html.

121. Leonhardt, David. "Opinion | The Rich Really Do Pay Lower Taxes Than You." *The Rich Really Do Pay Lower Taxes Than You - The New York Times*, 6 Oct. 2019, https://www.nytimes.com/interactive/2019/10/06/opinion/income-tax-rate-wealthy.html.

122. Rosalsky, Greg. "Is the American Tax System Regressive?" *NPR*, 29 Oct. 2019, https://www.npr.org/sections/money/2019/10/29/774091313/is-the-american-tax-system-regressive

123. Palmer, Amanda. "Amazon Wants to Question Trump after Losing $10 Billion Pentagon Cloud Contract." *CNBC*, 10 Feb. 2020, https://www.cnbc.com/2020/02/10/amazon-wants-to-depose-president-trump-over-jedi-cloud-contract-loss.html.

124. Feuer, Will. "Trump Told Mattis to 'Screw Amazon' out of $10 Billion Pentagon

Cloud Contract, Insider Account Claims." *CNBC*, 26 Oct. 2019, https://www.cnbc.com/2019/10/26/trump-mattis-screw-amazon-10-billion-pentagon-cloud-contract-jedi.html.

125. Tabuchi, Hiroko. "Justice Dept. Investigates California Emissions Pact That Embarrassed Trump." *NYTimes*, 6 Sept. 2019, https://www.nytimes.com/2019/09/06/climate/automakers-california-emissions-antitrust.html.

126. Liptak, Adam. "Supreme Court Ruling Delivers a Sharp Blow to Labor Unions." *NYTimes*, 27 June 2018, https://www.nytimes.com/2018/06/27/us/politics/supreme-court-unions-organized-labor.html.

127. Rein, Lisa. "Trump Takes Aim at Federal Bureaucracy with New Executive Orders Rolling Back Civil-Service Protections." *The Washington Post*, 25 May 2018, https://www.washingtonpost.com/politics/trump-takes-aim-at-federal-bureaucracy-with-new-executive-orders-altering-civil-service-protections/2018/05/25/3ed8bf84-6055-11e8-9ee3-49d6d4814c4c_story.html.; Davidson, Joe. "Perspective | Trump Has Attacked Federal Unions. Now, for the First Time, He's Trying to Bust One." *The Washington Post*, 18 Jan. 2020, https://www.washingtonpost.com/politics/trump-has-attacked-federal-unions-now-for-the-first-time-hes-trying-to-bust-one/2020/01/17/3426d8ea-3971-11ea-a01d-b7cc8ec1a85d_story.html.; Papenfuss, Mary. "Trump Gives Defense Department Power To Abolish Bargaining For Civilian Unions." *HuffPost*, 21 Feb. 2020, https://www.huffpost.com/entry/collective-bargaining-union-trump-defense-department_n_5e4f5f21c5b6b82aa650a857.

128. Mueller, Eleanor. "Trump Executive Order Strips Protections for Key Federal Workers, Drawing Backlash." *POLITICO*, 22 Oct. 2020, https://www.politico.com/news/2020/10/22/trump-order-strips-worker-protections-431359.

129. Rhinehart, Lynn. "Under Trump the NLRB Has Gone Completely Rogue." *The Nation*, 7 Apr. 2020, https://www.thenation.com/article/politics/nlrb-workers-rights-trump/.

130. Wiessner, Daniel. "U.S. Makes It Harder to Sue Corporations over Franchise Wage Law Violations." *Reuters*, https://www.reuters.com/article/us-usa-labor-idUSKBN1ZC1LU. Accessed 27 Sept. 2020.

131. Thomsen, Jacqueline. "Supreme Court Rules in Favor of Businesses Seeking to Block Class-Action Lawsuits." *TheHill*, 24 Apr. 2019, https://thehill.com/regulation/court-battles/440395-supreme-court-rules-in-favor-of-businesses-seeking-to-block-class.

132. "SCOTUS Rules on *Our Lady of Guadalupe School v. Morrissey-Berru*, Law School Faculty React." *Penn Law*, 8 July 2020, https://www.law.upenn.edu/live/news/10220-scotus-rules-on-our-lady-of-guadalupe-school-v.

133. ACLU. (2016, May 5). New Report Reveals 1 in 6 U.S. Hospital Beds Are in Catholic Facilities That Prohibit Essential Health Care for Women. Retrieved September 27, 2020, from https://www.aclu.org/press-releases/new-report-reveals-1-6-us-hospital-beds-are-catholic-facilities-prohibit-essential

134. "Statistics About Non-Public Education in the United States." *U.S. Department of Education*, 1 Mar. 2017, https://www2.ed.gov/about/offices/list/oii/nonpublic/statistics.html.

135. Zeballos-Roig, Joseph. "The House Just Passed a Bill Designed to Strengthen Worker Rights. Here's an Astounding Chart Showing How the Death of the Union Worsened Economic Inequality. | Markets Insider." *Markets.Businessinsider.Com*, 15

Jan. 2020, https://markets.businessinsider.com/news/stocks/how-economic-inequality-has-worsened-with-death-of-american-union-2020-1-1028820308.

136. Fung, Archon. "It's The Gap, Stupid." *Boston Review*, 1 Sept. 2017, http://bostonreview.net/class-inequality/archon-fung-its-gap-stupid.

137. Pongsudhirak, Thitinan. "Thailand's Urban-Rural Split | Thitinan Pongsudhirak." *The Guardian*, 8 Nov. 2009, http://www.theguardian.com/commentisfree/2009/nov/08/thailand-rural-urban-split.

138. Pesek, William. "Thailand Just Can't Quit Populism." *Nikkei Asian Review*, 17 Jan. 2019, https://asia.nikkei.com/Opinion/Thailand-just-can-t-quit-populism.

139. "Hammer and Sickle Symbol." *Ancient Symbols*, https://www.ancient-symbols.com/symbols-directory/hammer_sickle.html. Accessed 27 Sept. 2020.

140. Grier, P. (2018, December 26). The deep roots of America's rural-urban political divide. Retrieved September 27, 2020, from https://www.csmonitor.com/USA/Politics/2018/1226/The-deep-roots-of-America-s-rural-urban-political-divide

141. Lowe, Josh. "Why Brussels Is Not a #hellhole." *Newsweek*, 28 Jan. 2016, https://www.newsweek.com/trump-brussels-hellhole-420451.

142. Babwin, Aamer. "In Chicago, Trump Calls the City an Embarrassment to the US." *Associated Press*, 28 Oct. 2019, https://apnews.com/article/e1e156deb2004bd49ee40bf9af4c73ec.

143. Goodyear, Dana. "Trump's Potty Obsession, and the Streets of San Francisco." *The New Yorker*, https://www.newyorker.com/news/california-chronicles/trumps-potty-obsession-and-the-streets-of-san-francisco. Accessed 27 Sept. 2020.

144. Kranish, Michael. "Trump Says Baltimore Is 'Worse than Honduras' in Terms of Violent Crime." *The Washington Post*, 31 July 2019, https://www.washingtonpost.com/politics/trump-says-baltimore-is-worse-than-honduras-in-terms-of-violent-crime/2019/07/30/5f56572a-b320-11e9-8f6c-7828e68cb15f_story.html.

145. Fausset, Richard. "Donald Trump's Description of Black America Is Offending Those Living in It." *NYTimes*, 24 Aug. 2016, https://www.nytimes.com/2016/08/25/us/politics/donald-trump-black-voters.html.

146. Goldmacher, Shane. "'This American Carnage Stops Right Here.'" *POLITICO*, 20 Jan. 2017, https://www.politico.eu/article/this-american-carnage-stops-right-here/.

147. Gramlich, John. "Voters' Perceptions of Crime Continue to Conflict with Reality." *Pew Research Center*, 16 Nov. 2016, https://www.pewresearch.org/fact-tank/2016/11/16/voters-perceptions-of-crime-continue-to-conflict-with-reality/.

148. Gramlich, John. "5 Facts about Crime in the U.S." *Pew Research Center*, 17 Oct. 2019, https://www.pewresearch.org/fact-tank/2019/10/17/facts-about-crime-in-the-u-s/.

149. Mills, Robert. "What Are Much Maligned 'San Francisco Values'? Prioritizing the Welfare of Families and Children." *San Francisco Chronicle*, 21 Dec. 2018, https://www.sfchronicle.com/opinion/article/What-are-much-maligned-San-Francisco-13482664.php.

150. Rubin, Jennifer. "Opinion | Trump Exploited the Cultural Divide, Not Economic Unfairness." *The Washington Post*, 19 June 2017, https://www.washingtonpost.com/blogs/right-turn/wp/2017/06/19/trump-exploited-the-cultural-divide-not-economic-unfairness/.

151. "Why Conservatives See Rural America as the 'Real' America." *The Week*, 24 Apr.

2014, https://theweek.com/articles/447585/why-conservatives-rural-america-re-al-america.

152. Zimmer, Ben. "Pete Buttigieg's Coded Use of 'American Heartland.'" *The Atlantic*, 30 Jan. 2020, https://www.theatlantic.com/culture/archive/2020/01/pete-butti-giegs-coded-use-of-american-heartland/605788/.

153. Olorunnipa, Toluse. "'This Is What I'm Fighting': Trump Tries to Cast U.S. Cities as Filthy and Crime-Ridden in Attempt to Sway 2020 Voters." *The Washington Post*, 2 July 2019, https://www.washingtonpost.com/politics/this-is-what-im-fighting-trump-tries-to-cast-us-cities-as-filthy-and-crime-ridden-in-attempt-to-sway-2020-voters/2019/07/02/089463ca-9cda-11e9-b27f-ed2942f73d70_story.html.

154. Eco, Umberto. "Ur-Fascism." *The New York Review of Books*, https://www.nybooks.com/articles/1995/06/22/ur-fascism/. Accessed 27 Sept. 2020.

155. Bump, Philip. "Analysis | A Brief History of Trump's Empty Rhetoric on Uniting the Country." *The Washington Post*, 5 Feb. 2019, https://www.washingtonpost.com/politics/2019/02/05/brief-history-trumps-empty-rhetoric-uniting-country/.

156. https://www.washingtonpost.com/politics/2019/03/22/trump-said-hes-bring-ing-america-together-majority-americans-disagree/

157. Benen, Steve. "Trump Says He's 'the Only One' Who Can Protect the U.S." *MSN-BC*, 12 Oct. 2016, http://www.msnbc.com/rachel-maddow-show/trump-says-hes-the-only-one-who-can-protect-the-us.

158. Boot, Max. "Opinion | Trump Doesn't Seem to Grasp That Blue Staters Are Real Americans Too." *The Washington Post*, 17 Feb. 2020, https://www.washingtonpost.com/opinions/2020/02/17/blue-state-residents-are-real-americans-too-regard-less-trumps-messaging/.

159. Friedman, Uri. "What Is a Populist?" *The Atlantic*, 27 Feb. 2017, https://www.theatlantic.com/international/archive/2017/02/what-is-populist-trump/516525/.

160. Sanders, Sam. "Trump Champions The 'Silent Majority,' But What Does That Mean In 2016?" *NPR*, 22 Jan. 2016, https://www.npr.org/2016/01/22/463884201/trump-champions-the-silent-majority-but-what-does-that-mean-in-2016.

161. Zauzmer, Julie. "'He Gets It': Evangelicals Aren't Turned off by Trump's First Term." *The Washington Post*, 11 Aug. 2019, https://www.washingtonpost.com/politics/evangelicals-arent-turned-off-by-trumps-first-term--theyre-delighted-by-it/2019/08/11/3911bc88-a990-11e9-a3a6-ab670962db05_story.html.

162. Müller, Jan-Werner. "Trump, Erdoğan, Farage: The Attractions of Populism for Politicians, the Dangers for Democracy." *The Guardian*, 2 Sept. 2016, http://www.theguardian.com/books/2016/sep/02/trump-erdogan-farage-the-attrac-tions-of-populism-for-politicians-the-dangers-for-democracy.

163. Mascaro, Lisa. "Free Traders No More? GOP Warms up to Trump's Use of Tariffs." *Associated Press*, 8 June 2019, https://apnews.com/article/5f6abe7ce-5c248b891f55d08e7476742.

164. Steve Israel, opinion. "Why Republicans Should Think Twice about Increasing Presidential Power." *The Hill*, 14 Aug. 2019, https://thehill.com/opinion/white-house/457325-why-republicans-should-think-twice-about-increasing-presidential-power.

165. Hansler, Jennifer. "Ben Carson Leads Trump Cabinet in Prayer." *CNN*, 20 Dec. 2017, https://www.cnn.com/2017/12/20/politics/ben-carson-prayer-cabi-net-meeting/index.html.

166. Twitter, Anthony. "Republicans Scrap Party Platform. What That Means..." *BBC News*, 20 Aug. 2027, https://www.bbc.com/news/election-us-2020-53914829.

167. "The National Archives Learning Curve | The Great War | Making Peace | Reaction to the Treaty of Versailles | Background." *The Great War | Making Peace | Reaction to the Treaty of Versailles | Background*, https://www.nationalarchives.gov.uk/education/greatwar/g5/cs2/background.htm. Accessed 27 Sept. 2020.

168. Associated Press. "Judge Dismisses Professor's Lawsuit over Transgender Pronoun Dispute." *NBC News*, 18 Feb. 2020, https://www.nbcnews.com/feature/nbc-out/judge-dismisses-professor-s-lawsuit-over-transgender-pronoun-dispute-n1137976.

169. Epps, Garrett. "Justice Kennedy's 'Masterpiece' Ruling." *The Atlantic*, 4 June 2018, https://www.theatlantic.com/ideas/archive/2018/06/the-court-slices-a-narrow-ruling-out-of-masterpiece-cakeshop/561986/.

170. Kobin, Billy. "Court Rejects Kentucky's Attempt to Shirk Legal Fees in Kim Davis Gay Marriage Case." *USA TODAY*, https://www.usatoday.com/story/news/nation/2019/08/23/kim-davis-same-sex-marriage-suit-court-rules-kentucky-must-pay-fees/2101785001/. Accessed 27 Sept. 2020.

171. Mass Resistance. *Analysis: MA Voters Pass Trans Law by Large Margin!* https://www.massresistance.org/docs/gen3/18d/NoTo3/election-analysis.html. Accessed 27 Sept. 2020.

172. Kyle Mantyla | April 17, 2019. "E.W. Jackson: Pete Buttigieg Wants to Turn America Into a 'Homocracy' | Right Wing Watch." *Right Wing Watch*, 17 Apr. 2019, https://www.rightwingwatch.org/post/e-w-jackson-pete-buttigieg-wants-to-turn-america-into-a-homocracy/.

173. Hahl, O., Kim, M., & Sivan, E. (2017). The Authentic Appeal of the Lying Demagogue: Proclaiming the Deeper Truth About Political Illigitimacy. *American Sociological Review*, 83(1), 1-33. doi:10.31235/osf.io/tkpn5

174. Stracqualursi, Veronica. "Kelly Says Undocumented Immigrants 'Don't Have the Skills' to Assimilate into US Society." *CNN*, 11 May 2018, https://www.cnn.com/2018/05/11/politics/john-kelly-immigration-education/index.html.

175. Analysis by Chris Cillizza, *CNN*. "The 29 Most Cringe-Worthy Lines from Donald Trump's Hyper-Political Speech to the Boy Scouts." *CNN*, 25 July 2017, https://www.cnn.com/2017/07/25/politics/donald-trump-boy-scouts-speech/index.html.

176. Perrett, Connor. "Trump Suggests He Would 'Negotiate' a 3rd Term as President Because He Is 'Probably Entitled' to It." *Business Insider*, 13 Sept. 2020, https://www.businessinsider.com/trump-negotiate-third-term-in-office-2020-9.

177. Scott, Eugene. "Analysis | Trump's Most Insulting — and Violent — Language Is Often Reserved for Immigrants." *The Washington Post*, 2 Oct. 2019, https://www.washingtonpost.com/politics/2019/10/02/trumps-most-insulting-violent-language-is-often-reserved-immigrants/.

178. "Tony Norman: The Protocols of the Elders of Zion 2.0: The Rise of QAnon." *Pittsburgh Post-Gazette*, 27 Sept. 2020, https://www.post-gazette.com/opinion/tony-norman/2020/08/25/QAnon-conspiracy-theory-Elders-Zion-blood-libel-cannibalism-pedophile-Democrats-Trump/stories/202008250020.

179. Roberts, David. "Why Conspiracy Theories Flourish on the Right." *Vox*, 10 Dec. 2015, https://www.vox.com/2015/12/10/9886222/conspiracy-theories-right-wing.

180. Olorunnipa, Toluse. "Trump Embarks on Expansive Search for Disloyal-

ty as Administration-Wide Purge Escalates." *The Washington Post*, 22 Feb. 2020, https://www.washingtonpost.com/politics/were-cleaning-it-out-trump-em-barks-on-expansive-search-for-disloyalty-as-administration-wide-purge-esca-lates/2020/02/21/870e6c56-54c1-11ea-b119-4faabac6674f_story.html.

181. Cook, Nancy. "'Everything Becomes a Conspiracy Theory': Trump Leans into Spu-rious Claims for Impeachment Defense." *POLITICO*, 15 Oct. 2019, https://www.politico.com/news/2019/10/15/trump-conspiracy-impeachment-defense-046284.

182. Gambino, Lauren. "'Thank You for the Blessing': Cabinet Takes Turns Lavish-ing Trump with Praise." *The Guardian*, 12 June 2017, http://www.theguardian.com/us-news/2017/jun/12/donald-trump-first-cabinet-meeting-praise.; Collins, Betsy. "Trump's Top Trade Adviser 'Hunting' for Anonymous Op-Ed Author." *CNN*, 21 Feb. 2020, https://www.cnn.com/2020/02/21/politics/peter-navarro-anony-mous-hunt/index.html.

183. Bump, Philip. "Analysis | More than 8 in 10 Trump Voters Think Biden's Win Is Not Legitimate." *The Washington Post*, 11 Nov. 2020, https://www.washingtonpost.com/politics/2020/11/11/more-than-8-in-10-trump-voters-think-bidens-win-is-not-legitimate/.

184. Merlan, Anna. *The Conspiracy Singularity Has Arrived.* 24 Feb. 2020, https://www.vice.com/en_us/article/v7gz53/the-conspiracy-singularity-has-arrived.

185. Moyer, Melinda. "People Drawn to Conspiracy Theories Share a Cluster of Psy-chological Features." *Scientific American*, 1 Mar. 2019, https://www.scientificamer-ican.com/article/people-drawn-to-conspiracy-theories-share-a-cluster-of-psycho-logical-features/.

186. Mast, Nina. "Flashback: How *Fox News* Promoted Trump's Birtherism." *Media Mat-ters for America*, 16 Sept. 2016, https://www.mediamatters.org/sean-hannity/flash-back-how-fox-news-promoted-trumps-birtherism.

187. Coaston, Jane. "Seth Rich's Parents Are Taking Their Fight against *Fox News* to Court." *Vox*, 23 Mar. 2018, https://www.vox.com/2018/3/23/17129414/seth-rich-fox-news-lawsuit-conspiracy-theories.

188. McIntire, Mike. "What Happens When QAnon Seeps From the Web to the Offline World." *NYTimes*, 1 Sept. 2020, https://www.nytimes.com/2020/02/09/us/poli-tics/qanon-trump-conspiracy-theory.html.

189. Pengelly, Martin. "Republican Who Floated Virus Conspiracy Says 'Common Sense Has Been My Guide.'" *The Guardian*, 11 Apr. 2020, http://www.theguardian.com/us-news/2020/apr/11/republican-tom-cotton-coronavirus-china.

190. Wemple, Erik. "Opinion | Why *Fox News* Has Gone Wobbly on Anti-Semi-tism." *The Washington Post*, 15 Nov. 2019, https://www.washingtonpost.com/opin-ions/2019/11/15/why-fox-news-has-gone-wobbly-anti-semitism/.

191. Kelley, Michael. "STUDY: Watching Only *Fox News* Makes You Less Informed Than Watching No News At All." *Business Insider*, 22 May 2012, https://www.busi-nessinsider.com/study-watching-fox-news-makes-you-less-informed-than-watch-ing-no-news-at-all-2012-5.

192. Budryk, Zack. "*Fox News* Leads Ratings in Day One of Impeachment Trial." *The Hill*, 23 Jan. 2020, https://thehill.com/homenews/media/479548-fox-leads-rat-ings-in-day-one-of-impeachment-trial.

193. Garber, Megan. "*Fox News* Covered the Impeachment Hearings in the Fox News-iest Way Possible." *The Atlantic*, 14 Nov. 2019, https://www.theatlantic.com/en-

tertainment/archive/2019/11/how-fox-news-covered-day-1-impeachment-hearings/602020/.

194. Rupar, Aaron. *"Fox News* Devised a Way to Cover the Impeachment Trial without Covering It at All." *Vox*, 23 Jan. 2020, https://www.vox.com/2020/1/23/21078346/fox-news-trump-impeachment-trial-coverage.

195. *"Fox News* Is Sharing an Impeachment Narrative 'Completely Untethered from Reality' with Viewers." *Salon.Com*, 25 Jan. 2020, https://www.salon.com/2020/01/25/fox-news-is-sharing-an-impeachment-narrative-completely-untethered-from-reality-with-viewers_partner/.

196. Haltiwanger, John. "Only 40 percent of Republicans Believe Trump Asked Ukraine to Investigate Biden, Even Though He Admitted That He Did." *Business Insider*, 2 Oct. 2019, https://www.businessinsider.com/only-40-percent-republicans-believe-trump-asked-ukraine-investigate-biden-2019-10.

197. White House. MEMORANDUM OF TELEPHONE CONVERSATION. https://www.whitehouse.gov/wp-content/uploads/2019/09/Unclassified09.2019.pdf. Accessed 27 Sept. 2020.

198. Kessler, Glenn. "Analysis | President Trump Has Made More than 20,000 False or Misleading Claims." *The Washington Post*, 13 July 2020, https://www.washingtonpost.com/politics/2020/07/13/president-trump-has-made-more-than-20000-false-or-misleading-claims/.

199. Hains, T. (2019, September 3). Joe Walsh vs. FBN's Stuart Varney: President Trump Has Never Lied, "He Exaggerates And Spins." Retrieved September 27, 2020, from https://www.realclearpolitics.com/video/2019/09/03/joe_walsh_vs_fbns_stuart_varney_president_trump_has_never_lied_he_exaggerates_and_spins.html

200. Yochai Benkler, Robert. "Study: Breitbart-Led Right-Wing Media Ecosystem Altered Broader Media Agenda." *Columbia Journalism Review*, https://www.cjr.org/analysis/breitbart-media-trump-harvard-study.php. Accessed 10 Nov. 2020.

201. Keith, Tamara. "President Trump's Description of What's 'Fake' Is Expanding." *NPR*, 2 Sept. 2018, https://www.npr.org/2018/09/02/643761979/president-trumps-description-of-whats-fake-is-expanding.

202. Smith, David. "'Enemy of the People': Trump's War on the Media Is a Page from Nixon's Playbook." *The Guardian*, 7 Sept. 2019, http://www.theguardian.com/us-news/2019/sep/07/donald-trump-war-on-the-media-oppo-research.

203. Snyder, T. (2019). The road to unfreedom: Russia, Europe, America. London, UK: Vintage. p. 8

204. "Top Voting Issues in 2016 Election." *Pew Research Center - U.S. Politics & Policy*, 7 July 2016, https://www.pewresearch.org/politics/2016/07/07/4-top-voting-issues-in-2016-election/.

205. Weigel, David. "Trump's 'LGBT Rights' Promises Were Tied to War on 'Radical Islam.'" *The Washington Post*, 26 July 2017, https://www.washingtonpost.com/news/powerpost/wp/2017/07/26/trumps-lgbt-supporters-defend-him-after-surprise-military-transgender-ban/.

206. Burns, Alexander. "Trump and G.O.P. Candidates Escalate Race and Fear as Election Ploys (Published 2018)." *NYTimes*, 22 Oct. 2018, https://www.nytimes.com/2018/10/22/us/politics/republicans-race-divisions-elections-caravan.html.

207. Snyder, T. (2019). The road to unfreedom: Russia, Europe, America. London, UK: Vintage. p. 160

208. Flynn, Meagan. "Police Blew up an Innocent Man's House in Search of an Armed Shoplifter. Too Bad, Court Rules." *The Washington Post*, 30 Oct. 2019, https://www.washingtonpost.com/nation/2019/10/30/police-blew-up-an-innocent-mans-house-search-an-armed-shoplifter-too-bad-court-rules/.

209. Michel, Casey. "How Militias Became the Private Police for White Supremacists." *POLITICO Magazine*, 17 Aug. 2017, https://www.politico.com/magazine/story/2017/08/17/white-supremacists-militias-private-police-215498.

210. Neuman, Scott. "No Joke: Trump Really Does Want To Buy Greenland." *NPR*, 19 Aug. 2019, https://www.npr.org/2019/08/19/752274659/no-joke-trump-really-does-want-to-buy-greenland.

211. Mitchell, Lincoln. "Commentary: Is the U.S. Still a Real Democracy?" *Reuters*, https://www.reuters.com/article/us-mitchell-democracy-commentary-idUSKCN-1N41YN. Accessed 27 Sept. 2020.

212. Acemoğlu, Daron. "Revisiting the Rise of Italian Fascism." *VOX, CEPR Policy Portal*, 28 Oct. 2020, https://voxeu.org/article/revisiting-rise-italian-fascism.

213. Bloomberg, Laurence. "Analysis | How Trump Runs Against Socialism Without a Socialist Opponent." *The Washington Post*, 24 Aug. 2020, https://www.washingtonpost.com/business/energy/how-trump-runs-against-socialism-without-a-socialist-opponent/2020/08/24/5e8ee016-e649-11ea-bf44-0d31c85838a5_story.html.

214. County, Mitch. *Trump's Florida Supporters Fear "Socialist" Society If Biden Is Elected.* 16 Nov. 2020, https://www.baynews9.com/fl/tampa/politics/2020/10/29/in-tampa--trump-supporters-fear--socialist--society-if-joe-biden-is-elected.

215. Graham, David. "The President Who Doesn't Read." *The Atlantic*, 5 Jan. 2018, https://www.theatlantic.com/politics/archive/2018/01/americas-first-post-text-president/549794/.

216. Gordon, Peter. "Theodor Adorno and the Crises of Liberalism." *The Nation*, 15 Dec. 2020, https://www.thenation.com/article/politics/adorno-aspects-new-right-wing-extremism/.

217. *Lochner v. New York*, Apr 19, 1905. The Supreme Court ruled that a state law regulating maximum working hours was unconstitutional. This decision triggered the erosion of many other laws regulating safe working conditions. https://www.oyez.org/cases/1900-1940/198us45

218. *Trinity Lutheran Church of Columbia, Inc. v. Comer*, 26 June 2017, https://www.oyez.org/cases/2016/15-577

219. Fitzsimons, Tim . "S.C. Group Can Reject Gays and Jews as Foster Parents, Admin Says." *NBC News*, 24 Jan. 2019, https://www.nbcnews.com/feature/nbc-out/s-c-group-can-reject-gays-jews-foster-parents-trump-n962306.

220. Derysh, Igot. "Trump Budget Would Cut Medicare, Medicaid and Social Security While Expanding Tax Cuts for the Rich." Salon, 10 Feb. 2020, https://www.salon.com/2020/02/10/trump-budget-would-cut-medicare-medicaid-and-social-security-while-expanding-tax-cuts-for-the-rich/.

221. Horsley, Scott. "From Jobs To Homeownership, Protests Put Spotlight On Racial Economic Divide." *NPR*, 1 June 2020, https://www.npr.org/2020/06/01/866794025/from-jobs-to-homeownership-protests-put-spotlight-on-economic-divide.

222. Ajilore, Olugbenga. "The United States Is Not Ready for a Recession, But It Can Be - Center for American Progress." Center for American Progress, 27 Sept. 2019, https://www.americanprogress.org/issues/economy/reports/2019/09/27/475075/

united-states-not-ready-recession-can/.

223. Ingraham, Christopher. "The Staggering Millennial Wealth Deficit, in One Chart." *The Washington Post*, 3 Dec. 2019, https://www.washingtonpost.com/business/2019/12/03/precariousness-modern-young-adulthood-one-chart/.

224. Waldman, Paul. "Opinion | Why Mitch McConnell Is Trying to Kill a Big Stimulus before the Election." *The Washington Post*, 21 Oct. 2020, https://www.washingtonpost.com/opinions/2020/10/21/why-mitch-mcconnell-is-trying-kill-big-stimulus-before-election/.

225. Egel, Naomi. "Analysis | The Trump Administration Approved the U.S. Use of Land Mines. That's a Step Back for Global Campaigns to Ban Their Deployment." *The Washington Post*, 11 Feb. 2020, https://www.washingtonpost.com/politics/2020/02/11/trump-administration-okd-us-use-landmines-thats-step-back-global-campaigns-ban-their-use/.

226. Millhiser, Ian. "The Head of ICE Says He Will Deport DREAMers If the Supreme Court Ends DACA." Vox, 25 Jan. 2020, https://www.vox.com/2020/1/25/21080610/daca-ice-supreme-court-john-roberts-matthew-albence-deport.

227. Taylor, David. "Project Blitz: The Legislative Assault by Christian Nationalists to Reshape America." *The Guardian*, 4 June 2018, http://www.theguardian.com/world/2018/jun/04/project-blitz-the-legislative-assault-by-christian-nationalists-to-reshape-america.

228. Duane, Marguerite. "Stop Denying Science. Birth Control Isn't Necessary For Women's Health." *The Federalist*, 2 Nov. 2017, https://thefederalist.com/2017/11/02/stop-denying-science-birth-control-isnt-necessary-womens-health/.

229. Baptiste, Nathalie. "Trump's Budget Is a $292 Billion Attack on Poor Americans." *Mother Jones*, 10 Feb. 2020, https://www.motherjones.com/politics/2020/02/trumps-budget-is-a-292-billion-attack-on-poor-americans/.

230. Reilly, Katie. "Donald Trump Is Promoting School Prayer to Rally His Base." *Time*, 16 Jan. 2020, https://time.com/5765829/trump-school-prayer-evangelicals/.

231. Liptak, Adam. "Supreme Court Invalidates Key Part of Voting Rights Act." *NYTimes*, 25 June 2013, https://www.nytimes.com/2013/06/26/us/supreme-court-ruling.html.

232. Walcott, John. "Why President Donald Trump Fired Joseph Maguire." Time, 21 Feb. 2020, https://time.com/5788479/trump-fires-maguire/.

233. Wise, Justin. "National Security Adviser: 'I Haven't Seen Any Intelligence' That Russia Is Trying to Help Trump." The Hill, 23 Feb. 2020, https://thehill.com/homenews/administration/484234-national-security-adviser-i-havent-seen-any-intelligence-that-russia.

234. *"Grimdark is a subgenre of speculative fiction with a tone, style, or setting that is particularly dystopian, amoral, or violent. The term is inspired by the tagline of the tabletop strategy game Warhammer 40,000: 'In the grim darkness of the far future there is only WAR.'"* "Grimdark - Wikipedia." Wikimedia Foundation, Inc., 31 Jan. 2015, https://en.wikipedia.org/wiki/Grimdark.

Chapter 10

1. Blake, A. (2020, August 21). Analysis | Five provocative nuggets from the Senate intel report on Trump and Russia. Retrieved September 26, 2020, from https://www.washingtonpost.com/politics/2020/08/21/provocative-details-senate-intel/

2. Stieb, Matt. "Trump Attitude Toward Ukraine Influenced by Putin and Orbán: Re-

port." *Intelligencer*, 22 Oct. 2019, https://nymag.com/intelligencer/2019/10/trump-attitude-on-ukraine-coached-by-putin-and-orbn-report.html.

3. Levitsky, S., Ziblatt, D. (2018). *How democracies die* (pp. 23-24). New York: Crown.

4. "Trump Suggests Delay to 2020 US Election." *BBC News*, 20 July 2025, https://www.bbc.com/news/world-us-canada-53597975.

5. Analysis by Chris Cillizza, *CNN*. "Analysis: Believe It or Not, Donald Trump Says He Should Get a Third Term." *CNN*, 18 Aug. 2020, https://www.cnn.com/2020/08/18/politics/donald-trump-third-term-2024/index.html.

6. Nelson, S. (2020, August 17). Trump jokes about running for third, fourth, fifth and sixth terms. Retrieved September 26, 2020, from https://nypost.com/2020/08/17/trump-jokes-about-running-for-third-fourth-fifth-and-sixth-terms/

7. Corasaniti, Nick. "Donald Trump Suggests 'Second Amendment People' Could Act Against Hillary Clinton (Published 2016)." *NYTimes*, 9 Aug. 2016, https://www.nytimes.com/2016/08/10/us/politics/donald-trump-hillary-clinton.html.

8. LeBlanc, Craig. "Trump Tweets 'Liberate' Michigan, Two Other States with Dem Governors." *The Detroit News*, https://www.detroitnews.com/story/news/politics/2020/04/17/trump-tweets-liberate-michigan-other-states-democratic-governors/5152037002/. Accessed 26 Sept. 2020.

9. Monitor, The. "Guns in Michigan Capitol: Defense of Liberty or Intimidation?" *The Christian Science Monitor*, 4 May 2020, https://www.csmonitor.com/USA/Politics/2020/0504/Guns-in-Michigan-Capitol-Defense-of-liberty-or-intimidation.

10. Mele, Christopher. "Man Faces Terrorism Charge After Threatening to Kill Michigan's Governor, Officials Say." *NYTimes*, 25 June 2020, https://www.nytimes.com/2020/05/15/us/virus-michigan-whitmer-threats.html.

11. Gray, Kathleen. "Kidnapping Plot Against Whitmer Becomes Part of Michigan Politics." *NYTimes*, 18 Oct. 2020, https://www.nytimes.com/2020/10/11/us/whitmer-kidnapping-plot-michigan.html.

12. Eggert, David. "Men Accused in Plot on Michigan Governor Attended Protests." *Associated Press*, 10 Oct. 2020, https://apnews.com/article/virus-outbreak-donald-trump-michigan-gretchen-whitmer-gun-politics-8aff3b8db-0c03a80946e054d602f70fe.

13. Blake, Aaron. "Donald Trump Claims None of Those 3 to 5 Million Illegal Votes Were Cast for Him. Zero." *The Washington Post*, 26 Jan. 2017, https://www.washingtonpost.com/news/the-fix/wp/2017/01/25/donald-trump-claims-none-of-those-3-to-5-million-illegal-votes-were-cast-for-him-zero/.

14. Viebeck, Elise. "Trump's Assault on Election Integrity Forces Question: What Would Happen If He Refused to Accept a Loss?" *The Washington Post*, 22 July 2020, https://www.washingtonpost.com/politics/trumps-assault-on-election-integrity-forces-question-what-would-happen-if-he-refused-to-accept-a-loss/2020/07/22/d2477150-caae-11ea-b0e3-d55bda07d66a_story.html.

15. Liptak, Kevin. "Trump Warns of 'Rigged Election' as He Uses Fear to Counter Biden's Convention Week." *CNN*, 17 Aug. 2020, https://www.cnn.com/2020/08/17/politics/donald-trump-campaign-swing/index.html.

16. Beckett, Lois. "Pelosi Vows to Protect USPS, Which Trump Is 'Openly Working to Destroy.'" *The Guardian*, 15 Aug. 2020, http://www.theguardian.com/business/2020/aug/15/nancy-pelosi-trump-usps-election-mail-in-ballots.

17. Rizzo, Salvador. "Analysis | Trump's Fusillade of Falsehoods on Mail Vot-

ing." *The Washington Post*, 11 Sept. 2020, https://www.washingtonpost.com/politics/2020/09/11/trumps-fusillade-falsehoods-mail-voting/.

18. Dale, Daniel. "Fact Check: Trump's Dishonest '911' Ad Fear-Mongers about Biden." *CNN*, 21 July 2020, https://www.cnn.com/2020/07/21/politics/fact-check-trump-ad-biden-police-911/index.html.

19. Lambert, Lisa. "Trailing in Election Polls, Trump Says Rival Biden Opposes God and Guns." *Reuters*, https://www.reuters.com/article/us-usa-election-trump-god-idUSKCN25237A. Accessed 26 Sept. 2020.

20. Olorunnipa, Toluse. "Trump Tries to Win over 'Suburban Housewives' with Repeal of Anti-Segregation Housing Rule." *The Washington Post*, 23 July 2020, https://www.washingtonpost.com/politics/trump-suburbs-biden-housing-suburban-house-wives/2020/07/23/2f269980-ccf5-11ea-bc6a-6841b28d9093_story.html.

21. Lemire | AP, Ellen. "Trump Downplays West Texas Energy Worries, Attacks Democrats." *The Washington Post*, 30 July 2020, https://www.washingtonpost.com/politics/trump-downplays-west-texas-energy-worries-attacks-democrats/2020/07/29/2b-f8efe6-d1fb-11ea-826b-cc394d824e35_story.html.

22. McEvoy, Jemima. "No More Christmas, Suburbs Under Siege: Trump Escalates Claims About A Biden Win." *Forbes*, 19 Oct. 2020, https://www.forbes.com/sites/jemimamcevoy/2020/10/19/no-more-christmas-suburbs-under-siege-trump-esca-lates-claims-about-a-biden-win/.

23. John, Arit. "From Birtherism to 'Treason': Trump's False Allegations against Obama." *Los Angeles Times*, 23 June 2020, https://www.latimes.com/politics/story/2020-06-23/trump-obamagate-birtherism-false-allegations.

24. Kessler, Glenn. "Analysis | A Quick Guide to Trump's False Claims about Ukraine and the Bidens." *The Washington Post*, 27 Sept. 2019, https://www.washingtonpost.com/politics/2019/09/27/quick-guide-trumps-false-claims-about-ukraine-bidens/.

25. Sonne, Paul. "Senate Republicans Advance Ukraine Probe Aimed at Biden despite Foreign Interference Concerns." *The Washington Post*, 5 Aug. 2020, https://www.washingtonpost.com/national-security/senate-republicans-advance-ukraine-probe-aimed-at-biden-despite-foreign-interference-concerns/2020/08/05/6eb3718e-d503-11ea-b9b2-1ea733b97910_story.html.

26. Gessen, M. (2020). Surviving Autocracy. New York, NY: Riverhead Books. p. 201

27. Caralle, Katelyn. "Donald Trump Says Joe Biden Is in Favor of 'Execution' of Newborns." *Daily Mail*, 6 Oct. 2020, https://www.dailymail.co.uk/news/article-8810511/Trump-tweets-furiously-east-wing-sick-bed-Biden-favor-execution-newborns.html.

28. Johnson, Jenna. "Trump on Rally Protester: 'Maybe He Should Have Been Roughed Up.'" *The Washington Post*, 22 Nov. 2015, https://www.washingtonpost.com/news/post-politics/wp/2015/11/22/black-activist-punched-at-donald-trump-rally-in-birmingham/.

29. Updated Apr. 13, 2017 5:51PM. "Trump: 'Knock the Crap Out' of Protesters, I'll Pay Legal Fees." *The Daily Beast*, 13 Apr. 2017, https://www.thedailybeast.com/cheats/2016/02/01/trump-i-ll-pay-for-protester-beatings.

30. Chappell, Bill. "'He Did Not Pray': Fallout Grows From Trump's Photo-Op At St. John's Church." *NPR*, 2 June 2020, https://www.npr.org/2020/06/02/867705160/he-did-not-pray-fallout-grows-from-trump-s-photo-op-at-st-john-s-church.

31. Bowman, Tom. "Trump Threatens To Send U.S. Military To States To End Violent Protests." *NPR*, 2 June 2020, https://www.npr.org/2020/06/02/867578071/trump-threatens-to-send-u-s-military-to-states-to-end-violent-protests.

32. "Proud Boys." *Anti-Defamation League*, https://www.adl.org/resources/backgrounders/proud-boys-0. Accessed 26 Sept. 2020.; "Three Percenters." *Anti-Defamation League*, https://www.adl.org/resources/backgrounders/three-percenters. Accessed 26 Sept. 2020.

33. https://www.portlandmercury.com/blogtown/2019/08/26/27039560/undercover-in-patriot-prayer-insights-from-a-vancouver-democrat-whos-been-working-against-the-far-right-group-from-the-inside

34. Belew, Kathleen. "Opinion | Why 'Stand Back and Stand By' Should Set Off Alarm Bells." *NYTimes*, 2 Oct. 2020, https://www.nytimes.com/2020/10/02/opinion/trump-proud-boys.html.

35. Richgels, Jeff. "4 File Federal Lawsuit against Facebook, Kyle Rittenhouse, Militia Groups in Wake of Kenosha Protest Shootings." *Madison.Com*, 24 Sept. 2020, https://madison.com/news/local/crime-and-courts/4-file-federal-lawsuit-against-facebook-kyle-rittenhouse-militia-groups-in-wake-of-kenosha-protest/article_646089ba-dbec-5972-9e8b-acc9ddac2559.html.

36. "Law Enforcement Thank and Offer Water to Kyle Rittenhouse, Later Charged with Protest Shooting." *The Washington Post*, https://www.washingtonpost.com/video/national/law-enforcement-thank-and-offer-water-to-kyle-rittenhouse-later-charged-with-protest-shooting/2020/08/27/5f80b4ec-2dc6-436c-b86d-3fa78226962e_video.html. Accessed 26 Sept. 2020.

37. Schwartz, Rafi. "Conservatives Want You to Believe Kyle Rittenhouse Is a Hero." *Mic*, 27 Aug. 2020, https://www.mic.com/p/kyle-rittenhouse-has-become-conservatives-latest-folk-hero-32451208.

38. Feldman, Kate. "Right-Wing Pundit Ann Coulter Praises Accused Kenosha Killer — 'I Want Him as My President.'" *New York Daily News*, 27 Aug. 2020, https://www.nydailynews.com/news/national/ny-ann-coulter-kenosha-gunman-rittenhouse-20200827-5cwmlr7gefgynn2sgvyekri5ou-story.html.

39. Roberts, Molly. "Opinion | Kyle Rittenhouse Is Trump's Type of Rule-Breaker." *The Washington Post*, 2 Sept. 2020, https://www.washingtonpost.com/opinions/2020/09/02/kyle-rittenhouse-trump-defense/.

40. Bogel-Burroughs, Nicholas. "Kyle Rittenhouse, Accused of Killing 2 in Kenosha, Freed on $2 Million Bail." *NYTimes*, 20 Nov. 2020, https://www.nytimes.com/2020/11/20/us/kyle-rittenhouse-bail-kenosha.html.

41. Kessler, Glenn. "Analysis | The 'Very Fine People' at Charlottesville: Who Were They?" *The Washington Post*, 8 May 2020, https://www.washingtonpost.com/politics/2020/05/08/very-fine-people-charlottesville-who-were-they-2/.

42. Taylor, Adam. "Analysis | From Tiananmen Square to Lafayette Square." *The Washington Post*, 4 June 2020, https://www.washingtonpost.com/world/2020/06/04/trump-tiananmen-square-protests-lafayette/.

43. Rummler, Orion. "Bolton Alleges Trump Encouraged Xi to Continue with Uighur Detainment Camps." *Axios*, 17 June 2020, https://www.axios.com/trump-uighur-muslim-bolton-73ebf1e2-9d34-4aaf-a9ba-17340d2847e4.html.

44. Godfrey, Elaine. "It Was Supposed to Be So Much Worse." *The Atlantic*, 9 Jan. 2021, https://www.theatlantic.com/politics/archive/2021/01/trump-rioters-want-

ed-more-violence-worse/617614/.

45. Lonas, Lexi. "Sasse Says Trump Was 'Delighted' and 'Excited' by Reports of Capitol Riot." *The Hill*, 8 Jan. 2021, https://thehill.com/homenews/senate/533403-sasse-says-trump-was-delighted-and-excited-by-reports-of-capitol-riot.

46. Beauchamp, Zack. "The Capitol Hill Mob Wanted to Intimidate Congress. It's Working." *Vox*, 13 Jan. 2021, https://www.vox.com/2021/1/13/22229052/capi-tol-hill-riot-intimidate-legislators.

47. Samuels, Brett. "Trump Ramps up Rhetoric on Media, Calls Press 'the Enemy of the People.'" *TheHill*, 5 Apr. 2019, https://thehill.com/homenews/administra-tion/437610-trump-calls-press-the-enemy-of-the-people.

48. Pearlstine, Norman. "Trump Wants to Toughen the Nation's Libel Laws. Here's Why He Isn't Likely to Succeed." *Los Angeles Times*, 8 Sept. 2018, https://www.latimes.com/nation/la-na-trump-libel-20180908-htmlstory.html.

49. Wemple, Erik. "Opinion | The Trump Campaign's Transparent Lawsuit against *CNN*." *The Washington Post*, 7 Mar. 2020, https://www.washingtonpost.com/opin-ions/2020/03/07/trump-campaigns-transparent-lawsuit-against-cnn/.

50. Power, Lis. "In 2019, 92 percent of Trump's Nationally Televised Interviews Have Been on *Fox News* or *Fox Business*." *Media Matters for America*, 10 May 2019, https://www.mediamatters.org/donald-trump/2019-92-trumps-nationally-televised-inter-views-have-been-fox-news-or-fox-business.

51. Bierbauer, Charles. "Trump White House Goes 300+ Days without a Press Briefing – Why That's Unprecedented." *The Conversation*, 24 Feb. 2020, http://theconver-sation.com/trump-white-house-goes-300-days-without-a-press-briefing-why-thats-unprecedented-130164.

52. Farhi, Paul. "OANN Threatened with Removal from White House Press Room af-ter Correspondent Chanel Rion Makes Unauthorized Appearances." *The Washington Post*, 1 Apr. 2020, https://www.washingtonpost.com/lifestyle/media/oann-is-boot-ed-from-white-house-press-room-after-correspondent-chanel-rion-makes-second-unauthorized-appearance/2020/04/01/ae27e19a-7439-11ea-85cb-8670579b863d_story.html.

53. Grynbaum, Michael. "White House Grants Press Credentials to a Pro-Trump Blog." *NYTimes*, 13 Feb. 2017, https://www.nytimes.com/2017/02/13/business/the-gateway-pundit-trump.html.

54. Gonzales, Richard. "White House Revokes Press Pass Of *CNN*'s Jim Acosta." *NPR*, 7 Nov. 2018, https://www.npr.org/2018/11/07/665497382/white-house-revokes-press-pass-of-cnns-jim-acosta.

55. Kovalev, Alexey. "A Warning to the American Media from a Russian Journalist Who Covers Putin." *Quartz*, 13 Jan. 2017, https://qz.com/884403/donald-trumps-press-conference-was-a-circus-but-vladimir-putins-is-way-worse-for-journalists/.

56. Lytvynenko, Jane. "RNC Video Showing Rioters In 'Biden's America' Is Actually Spain." *BuzzFeed News*, 27 Aug. 2020, https://www.buzzfeednews.com/article/jan-elytvynenko/rnc-protest-video-barcelona.

57. Perrett, Connor. "Florida's Governor Is Proposing a Law That Would Protect Drivers Who Kill or Injure People If They're Fleeing a 'Mob,' Following a Spate of Incidents of People Driving through Protest Crowds." *Insider*, 21 Sept. 2020, https://www.insider.com/desantis-proposes-law-to-protect-drivers-who-kill-peo-ple-2020-9.

58. Johnson, Eliana. "The Real Reason Bill Barr Is Defending Trump." *POLITICO*, 1 May 2019, https://politi.co/2J60TFn.

59. Brice-Saddler, Michael. "Analysis | While Bemoaning Mueller Probe, Trump Falsely Says the Constitution Gives Him 'the Right to Do Whatever I Want.'" *The Washington Post*, 23 July 2019, https://www.washingtonpost.com/politics/2019/07/23/trump-falsely-tells-auditorium-full-teens-constitution-gives-him-right-do-whatever-i-want/.

60. "White House Rally: Trump Holds First Public Event since COVID-19 Diagnosis." *BBC News*, 10 Oct. 2020, https://www.bbc.com/news/election-us-2020-54493575.

61. Baker, Sinéad. "Trump Aides 'Take Pride' in Violating Ethics Laws Because It Upsets the Media at No Cost to Them, Reports Say." *Business Insider*, 26 Aug. 2020, https://www.businessinsider.com/trump-aides-proud-to-violate-hatch-act-ethics-laws-reports-2020-8.

62. Levitsky, S., Ziblatt, D. (2018). *How democracies die* (pp. 102). New York: Crown.

63. Stewart, Emily. "Watch John McCain Defend Barack Obama against a Racist Voter in 2008." *Vox*, 26 Aug. 2018, https://www.vox.com/policy-and-politics/2018/8/25/17782572/john-mccain-barack-obama-statement-2008-video.

64. Nguyen, Tina. "Trump Is Still Pissed He Didn't Get an Invite to John McCain's Funeral." *Vanity Fair*, 20 Mar. 2019, https://www.vanityfair.com/news/2019/03/donald-trump-john-mccain-funeral.

65. "Statement by the President." *Whitehouse.Gov*, 9 Nov. 2016, https://obamawhitehouse.archives.gov/the-press-office/2016/11/09/statement-president.

66. Davis, Julie. "Trump Pardons Joe Arpaio, Who Became Face of Crackdown on Illegal Immigration." *NYTimes*, 26 Aug. 2017, https://www.nytimes.com/2017/08/25/us/politics/joe-arpaio-trump-pardon-sheriff-arizona.html.

67. Chappell, Bill. "Trump Pardons Michael Behenna, Former Soldier Convicted Of Killing Iraqi Prisoner." *NPR*, 7 May 2019, https://www.npr.org/2019/05/07/720967513/trump-pardons-former-soldier-convicted-of-killing-iraqi-prisoner.

68. Thomson-DeVeaux, Amelia. "Trump's Pardons Have Been Sparse and Self-Serving — And That's Without Even Pardoning His Kids." *FiveThirtyEight*, 10 Dec. 2020, https://fivethirtyeight.com/features/trumps-pardons-have-been-sparse-and-self-serving-and-thats-without-even-pardoning-his-kids/.

69. "Pardons Granted by President Donald Trump." *Email Icon*, 28 Aug. 2017, https://www.justice.gov/pardon/pardons-granted-president-donald-trump.

70. Eban, Katherine. "How Jared Kushner's Secret Testing Plan 'Went Poof Into Thin Air.'" *Vanity Fair*, 30 July 2020, https://www.vanityfair.com/news/2020/07/how-jared-kushners-secret-testing-plan-went-poof-into-thin-air.

71. Stefansky, Emma. "The State Department Is Reportedly Snubbing Ivanka's India Trip." *Vanity Fair*, 25 Nov. 2017, https://www.vanityfair.com/news/2017/11/rex-tillerson-state-department-snubbing-ivanka-trump-india-trip.

72. Naylor, Brian. "An Acting Government For The Trump Administration." *NPR*, 9 Apr. 2019, https://www.npr.org/2019/04/09/711094554/an-acting-government-for-the-trump-administration.

73. Lambert, Lisa. "Trump Nominates Acting EPA Head, an Ex-Coal Lobbyist, to Run Agency." *Reuters*, https://www.reuters.com/article/us-usa-trump-epa-idUSKCN1P324H. Accessed 26 Sept. 2020.

74. Hacker, J. S., & Pierson, P. (2020*). Let them eat Tweets: How the right rules in an age of extreme inequality*. New York, NY, NY: Liveright Publishing Corporation, a division of W. W. Norton & Company. p. 157

75. Edmondson, Catie. "DeJoy Earned Millions From Company With Financial Ties to Postal Service." *NYTimes*, 24 Aug. 2020, https://www.nytimes.com/2020/08/17/us/politics/dejoy-postal-service-mail-in-voting.html.

76. Lizza, Ryan. "How Trump Broke the Office of Government Ethics." *The New Yorker*, https://www.newyorker.com/news/ryan-lizza/how-trump-broke-the-office-of-government-ethics. Accessed 26 Sept. 2020.

77. Chait, Jonathan. "McConnell Admits the 'Rule' That Blocked Merrick Garland Is Not Actually a Rule." *Intelligencer*, 3 Apr. 2017, https://nymag.com/intelligencer/2017/04/mcconnell-rule-that-blocked-garland-not-actually-a-rule.html.

78. Everett, Burgess. "'We'Re Going to Fill It': Republicans Ready for Any Supreme Court Vacancy." *POLITICO*, 8 May 2020, https://www.politico.com/news/2020/05/08/republicans-ready-supreme-court-vacancy-243574.

79. Levitsky, S., Way, L.A. (2010). *Competitive Authoritarianism: Hybrid Regimes After the Cold War*. Cambridge University Press, New York, NY

80. "Historian Christopher Browning on the Trump Regime: We're 'Close to the Point of No Return.'" *Salon.Com*, 18 Oct. 2018, https://www.salon.com/2018/10/18/historian-christopher-browning-on-the-trump-regime-were-close-to-the-point-of-no-return/.

81. Pepinsky, Thomas. "Life in Authoritarian States Is Mostly Boring and Tolerable." *Vox*, 9 Jan. 2017, https://www.vox.com/the-big-idea/2017/1/9/14207302/authoritarian-states-boring-tolerable-fascism-trump.

82. Watkins, Eli. "Barr Authored Memo Last Year Ruling out Obstruction of Justice." *CNN*, 24 Mar. 2019, https://www.cnn.com/2019/03/24/politics/barr-memo-mueller/index.html.

83. Ellen Cranley, Michelle. "Here Are All the Sexual-Misconduct Allegations against Brett Kavanaugh." *Business Insider*, 27 Sept. 2018, https://www.businessinsider.com/brett-kavanaugh-sexual-assault-misconduct-allegations-2018-9.

84. Gramlich, John. "How Trump Compares with Other Recent Presidents in Appointing Federal Judges." *Pew Research Center*, 15 July 2020, https://www.pewresearch.org/fact-tank/2020/07/15/how-trump-compares-with-other-recent-presidents-in-appointing-federal-judges/.

85. Rogers, Ariane. "'Not Qualified' Rating and Accusation from American Bar Association Moves Trump Nominee to Tears." *CNN*, 30 Oct. 2019, https://www.cnn.com/2019/10/30/politics/american-bar-association-nominees-vandyke/index.html.

86. Kirby, Jen. "Trump's Purge of Inspectors General, Explained." *Vox*, 28 May 2020, https://www.vox.com/2020/5/28/21265799/inspectors-general-trump-linick-atkinson.

87. Fandos, Nicholas. "Republican Inquiry Finds No Evidence of Wrongdoing by Biden." *NYTimes*, 23 Sept. 2020, https://www.nytimes.com/2020/09/23/us/politics/biden-inquiry-republicans-johnson.html.

88. Konstantin Benyumov for Meduza.io, part. "How Russia's Independent Media Was Dismantled Piece by Piece." *The Guardian*, 25 May 2016, http://www.theguardian.com/world/2016/may/25/how-russia-independent-media-was-dismantled-piece-

by-piece.
89. Gessen, M. (2020). *Surviving Autocracy*. New York, NY: Riverhead Books. p. 119
90. Snyder, T. (2019). *The road to unfreedom: Russia, Europe, America*. London, UK: Vintage. p. 56
91. Chokshi, Niraj. "Eight U.S. States Have Policies Similar to Russia's Ban on Gay 'Propaganda.'" *The Washington Post*, 10 Feb. 2014, https://www.washingtonpost.com/blogs/govbeat/wp/2014/02/03/eight-u-s-states-have-policies-similar-to-russias-ban-on-gay-propaganda/.
92. "Hungary's Index Journalists Walk out over Sacking." *BBC News*, 24 July 2020, https://www.bbc.com/news/world-europe-53531948.
93. "Green Study Reveals Dangerous Media Concentration in Hungary: 78 Percent of News Media under Orbán's Control - Sven Giegold - Mitglied Der Grünen Fraktion Im Europaparlament." *Sven Giegold - Mitglied Der Grünen Fraktion Im Europaparlament*, 2 May 2019, https://sven-giegold.de/en/dangerous-media-concentration-in-hungary-78-percent-under-Orbáns-control/.
94. Gessen, M. (2020). *Surviving Autocracy*. New York, NY: Riverhead Books. p 119
95. Matthews, Dylan. "Sinclair Broadcast Group, the pro-Trump, Conservative Company Taking over Local News, Explained." *Vox*, 3 Apr. 2018, https://www.vox.com/2018/4/3/17180020/sinclair-broadcast-group-conservative-trump-david-smith-local-news-tv-affiliate.
96. Heilweil, Rebecca. "Right-Wing Media Thrives on Facebook. Whether It Rules Is More Complicated." *Vox*, 9 Sept. 2020, https://www.vox.com/recode/21419328/facebook-conservative-bias-right-wing-crowdtangle-election.
97. Roberts, William. "US Lawmakers Push for Release of Intelligence on Khashoggi Murder." *Al Jazeera*, +020203-03, https://www.aljazeera.com/news/2020/3/3/us-lawmakers-push-for-release-of-intelligence-on-khashoggi-murder.
98. "Trump Boasted He Protected MBS after Khashoggi Hit: Report." *Al Jazeera*, 20 Sept. 2010, https://www.aljazeera.com/news/2020/9/10/trump-boasted-he-protected-mbs-after-khashoggi-hit-report.
99. Leibovich, Mark. "How Lindsey Graham Went From Trump Skeptic to Trump Sidekick." *NYTimes*, 25 Feb. 2019, https://www.nytimes.com/2019/02/25/magazine/lindsey-graham-what-happened-trump.html.
100. John, Tara. "Marco Rubio Keeps Up Attacks on 'Con Artist' Trump." *Time*, 26 Feb. 2016, https://time.com/4238492/marco-rubio-donald-trump-a-con-artist/.
101. Mccaskill, Nolan. "Cruz: President Trump Would Nuke Denmark." *POLITICO*, 3 Feb. 2016, https://www.politico.com/story/2016/02/ted-cruz-donald-trump-denmark-218694.
102. Harrington, Rebecca. "All the Terrible Things Trump and Ted Cruz Said about Each Other before the President Decided He Was 'Beautiful Ted.'" *Business Insider*, 23 Oct. 2018, https://www.businessinsider.com/trump-cruz-feud-history-worst-attacks-2016-9.
103. Nowicki, Dan. "Here's a Blow-by-Blow Account of the Donald Trump vs. John McCain Feud." *The Arizona Republic*, https://www.azcentral.com/story/news/politics/azdc/2016/10/15/donald-trump-vs-john-mccain-feud/91960246/. Accessed 26 Sept. 2020.
104. Allen, Cooper. "Trump to Rubio: 'Don't Worry about It, Little Marco.'" *USA TODAY*, https://www.usatoday.com/story/news/politics/onpolitics/2016/03/03/

donald-trump-marco-rubio-fox-debate/81297752/. Accessed 26 Sept. 2020.

105. "Mark Meadows Is Donald Trump's Worst Chief of Staff—Which Is Really Saying Something." *Salon.Com*, 12 Aug. 2020, https://www.salon.com/2020/08/12/mark-meadows-is-donald-trumps-worst-chief-of-staff--which-is-really-saying-something/.

106. Zhou, Li. "11 Senate Republicans Voted to Block Trump's Border Wall Emergency Declaration." *Vox*, 25 Sept. 2019, https://www.vox.com/2019/9/25/20880248/senate-republicans-trump-border-wall.

107. "The Man Who Thinks Europe Has Been Invaded--*BBC News*." *BBC News*, https://www.bbc.co.uk/news/resources/idt-sh/Viktor_Orbán. Accessed 26 Sept. 2020.

108. Batory, A., "With the Final Votes Counted, Fidesz Has Secured a 'Super-Majority' in Hungary, but It Is Questionable How Fair the Election Really Was." *EUROPP*, 16 Apr. 2014, https://blogs.lse.ac.uk/europpblog/2014/04/16/with-the-final-votes-counted-fidesz-has-secured-a-super-majority-in-hungary-but-it-is-questionable-how-fair-the-election-really-was/.

109. https://www.reuters.com/article/us-usa-election-locations/southern-u-s-states-have-closed-1200-polling-places-in-recent-years-rights-group-idUSKCN1VV09J

110. Levine, Sam. "Voter Purges: Are Republicans Trying to Rig the 2020 Election?" *The Guardian*, 31 Dec. 2019, http://www.theguardian.com/us-news/2019/dec/31/voter-purges-republicans-2020-elections-trump.

111. Wise, Justin. "Georgia Accused of Wrongfully Purging Nearly 200,000 from Voter Rolls: Report." *The Hill*, 2 Sept. 2020, https://thehill.com/homenews/statewatch/514813-georgia-accused-of-wrongfully-purging-nearly-200000-from-voter-rolls.

112. Panetta, Grace. "How Black Americans Still Face Disproportionate Barriers to the Ballot Box in 2020." *Business Insider*, 18 Sept. 2020, https://www.businessinsider.com/why-black-americans-still-face-obstacles-to-voting-at-every-step-2020-6.

113. Rummler, Orion. "48 Senators Call on McConnell to Allow Vote on John Lewis Voting Rights Advancement Act." *Axios*, 22 July 2020, https://www.axios.com/john-lewis-voting-rights-senate-5fb8d35c-bac0-447c-a9ff-25603d96a901.html.

114. Kotch, Alex. "Republicans Make Big Advances Thanks to Citizens United." *The American Prospect*, 10 Sept. 2014, https://prospect.org/api/content/401bae4c-a3d7-58e5-925e-1559a09a6e1d/.

115. Adams, Kimberly. "How Campaigns Have Changed in the Decade since Citizens United - Marketplace." *Marketplace*, 21 Jan. 2020, https://www.marketplace.org/2020/01/21/how-campaigns-have-changed-since-citizens-united-2010/.

116. Tilman Klumpp & Hugo M. Mialon & Michael A. Williams, 2016. "The Business of American Democracy: Citizens United, Independent Spending, and Elections," Journal of Law and Economics, University of Chicago Press, vol. 59(1), pages 1-43.

117. Hacker, J. S., & Pierson, P. (2020*). Let them eat Tweets: How the right rules in an age of extreme inequality*. New York, NY, NY: Liveright Publishing Corporation, a division of W. W. Norton & Company. p. 185-186

118. https://www.washingtonpost.com/politics/2020/09/21/how-gop-is-trying-justify-its-supreme-court-reversal/

119. Anna Lührmann, Seraphine F. Maerz, Sandra Grahn, Nazifa Alizada, Lisa Gastaldi, Sebastian Hellmeier, Garry Hindle and Staffan I. Lindberg. 2020. Autocratization Surges – Resistance Grows. Democracy Report 2020. Varieties of Democracy Insti-

tute (V-Dem).

120 Borger, Julian. "Republicans Closely Resemble Autocratic Parties in Hungary and Turkey – Study." *The Guardian*, 26 Oct. 2020, http://www.theguardian.com/us-news/2020/oct/26/republican-party-autocratic-hungary-turkey-study-trump.

121. Lührmann, Anna, Nils Düpont, Masaaki Higashijima, Yaman Berker Kavasoglu, Kyle L. Marquardt, Michael Bernhard, Holger Döring, Allen Hicken, Melis Laebens, Sta□ an I. Lindberg, Juraj Medzihorsky, Anja Neundorf, Ora John Reuter, Saskia Ruth–Lovell, Keith R. Weghorst, Nina Wiesehomeier, JosephWright, Nazifa Alizada, Paul Bederke, Lisa Gastaldi, Sandra Grahn, Garry Hindle, Nina Ilchenko, Johannes von Römer, Daniel Pemstein, and Brigitte Seim. 2020. "Varieties of Party Identity and Organization (V–Party) Dataset V1." Varieties of Democracy (V-Dem) Project, https://www.v-dem.net/en/data/data/v-party-dataset

122. Lührmann, A., Medzihorsky, J., Hindle, G. (2020, October 26). V-Dem: Varieties of Democracy Project [Scholarly project]. In New Global Data on Political Parties: V-Party. Retrieved November 16, 2020, from https://www.v-dem.net/media/filer_public/b6/55/b6553f85-5c5d-45ec-be63-a48a2abe3f62/briefing_paper_9.pdf

123. Lührmann, A., & Lindberg, S. I. (2019). A third wave of autocratization is here: What is new about it? *Democratization*, 26(7), 1095-1113. doi:10.1080/13510347.2019.1582029

124. Bermeo, N. (2016). On Democratic Backsliding. *Journal of Democracy*, 27(1), 5-19. doi:10.1353/jod.2016.0012

125. *Twitter*, https://twitter.com/max_fisher/status/1326258226363555841. Accessed 15 Nov. 2020.

126. "Diseases like COVID-19 Are Deadlier in Non-Democracies." *The Economist*, 18 Feb. 2020, https://www.economist.com/graphic-detail/2020/02/18/diseases-like-COVID-19-are-deadlier-in-non-democracies.

127. Bermeo, N. (2016). On Democratic Backsliding. *Journal of Democracy*, 27(1), 5-19. doi:10.1353/jod.2016.0012

128. Ingraham, Christopher. "Analysis | The United States Is Backsliding into Autocracy under Trump, Scholars Warn." *The Washington Post*, 18 Sept. 2020, https://www.washingtonpost.com/business/2020/09/18/united-states-is-backsliding-into-autocracy-under-trump-scholars-warn/.

129. Paddock, Richard. "Democracy Fades in Malaysia as Old Order Returns to Power." *NYTimes*, 28 July 2020, https://www.nytimes.com/2020/05/22/world/asia/malaysia-politics-najib.html.

130 "Exit Poll Results and Analysis for the 2020 Presidential Election." *The Washington Post*, 10 Nov. 2020, https://www.washingtonpost.com/elections/interactive/2020/exit-polls/presidential-election-exit-polls/.

131. Milbank, Dana. "Opinion | Trump's Racist Appeals Powered a White Evangelical Tsunami." *The Washington Post*, 13 Nov. 2020, https://www.washingtonpost.com/opinions/2020/11/13/trumps-racist-appeals-powered-white-evangelical-tsunami/.

132. Hacker, J. S., & Pierson, P. (2020). *Let them eat Tweets: How the right rules in an age of extreme inequality*. New York, NY, NY: Liveright Publishing Corporation, a division of W. W. Norton & Company. p. 25

133. Guillermo O'Donnell and Phillippe C. Schmitter, *Transitions from Authoritarian Rule: Tentative Conclusions about Uncertain Democracies* (Baltimore: The Johns Hopkins UP, 1986), pp. 61-2.

134. "C3: Group Grievance | Fragile States Index." *Fragile States Index*, 1 May 2021, https://fragilestatesindex.org/indicators/c3/.

135. Aldhous, Peter. "This Scary Statistic Predicts Growing US Political Violence." *BuzzFeed News*, 24 Oct. 2020, https://www.buzzfeednews.com/article/peteraldhous/political-violence-inequality-us-election.

136. Turchin, P., Korotayev, A. (2020). The 2010 structural-demographic forecast for the 2010–2020 decade: A retrospective assessment. *Plos One*, 15(8). doi:10.1371/journal.pone.0237458

137. Center for Army Analysis (CAA), "Analyzing Complex Threats for Operations and Readiness," Fort Belvoir VA, September 2001.

Chapter 11

1. Seipel, Brooke. "Fireworks in London, Church Bells in Paris as Biden Win Celebrated Abroad." *The Hill*, 7 Nov. 2020, https://thehill.com/homenews/campaign/524962-fireworks-in-london-church-bells-in-paris-as-biden-win-celebrated-abroad.

2. Goldmacher, Shane. "Trump's Cash Crunch Limits His Options and Prompts Finger-Pointing." *NYTimes*, 2 Nov. 2020, https://www.nytimes.com/2020/10/22/us/politics/trump-campaign-money.html.

3. Mario Ariza, Anthony. "Ex-Trump Campaign Manager Brad Parscale Knocked to the Ground to End Standoff, Body Camera Footage Shows." *South Florida Sun-Sentinel*, 28 Sept. 2020, https://www.sun-sentinel.com/local/broward/fort-lauderdale/fl-ne-brad-parscale-suicide-attempt-saved-by-cop-friend-20200928-irc2wvhvczblhakhnsdnfeppme-story.html.

4. Date, S. V. "Win Or Lose, Trump's Top Campaign Aides Are Raking In The Cash." *HuffPost*, 6 May 2020, https://www.huffpost.com/entry/trump-consultants-rich-reelection-money_n_5eb1dae5c5b62b850f93abb3.

5. Scherer, Michael. "From 'Sleepy Joe' to a Destroyer of the 'American Way of Life,' Trump's Attacks on Biden Make a Dystopian Shift." *The Washington Post*, 18 July 2020, https://www.washingtonpost.com/politics/from-sleepy-joe-to-the-dystopian-candidate-how-trump-has-recast-his-attacks-on-biden/2020/07/18/5a6a3e36-c830-11ea-b037-f9711f89ee46_story.html.

6. Enten, Analysis. "New Polls Show Joe Biden Is Winning Suburbanites by a Historic Margin." *CNN*, 19 July 2020, https://www.cnn.com/2020/07/19/politics/joe-biden-donald-trump-suburban-voters-polling/index.html.

7. Analysis by Chris Cillizza, *CNN*. "Donald Trump's Answer on What He Would Do in a 2nd Term Is Literally Unintelligible." *CNN*, 28 Aug. 2020, https://www.cnn.com/2020/08/28/politics/donald-trump-2nd-term-new-york-times/index.html.

8. Liptak, Kevin. "A List of the Times Trump Has Said He Won't Accept the Election Results or Leave Office If He Loses." *CNN*, 24 Sept. 2020, https://www.cnn.com/2020/09/24/politics/trump-election-warnings-leaving-office/index.html.

9. Cohen, Marshall. "Trump Spreads New Lies about Foreign-Backed Voter Fraud, Stoking Fears of a 'Rigged Election' This November." *CNN*, 22 June 2020, https://www.cnn.com/2020/06/22/politics/trump-voter-fraud-lies-fact-check/index.html.

10. Crowley, Michael. "Trump Won't Commit to 'Peaceful' Post-Election Transfer of Power." *NYTimes*, 24 Sept. 2020, https://www.nytimes.com/2020/09/23/us/politics/trump-power-transfer-2020-election.html.

11. "Important Issues in the 2020 Election." *Pew Research Center - U.S. Politics & Policy*,

13 Aug. 2020, https://www.pewresearch.org/politics/2020/08/13/important-issues-in-the-2020-election/.

12. Bushwick, Sophie. "Mail-Sorting Machines Are Crucial for the U.S. Postal Service." *Scientific American*, 14 Sept. 2020, https://www.scientificamerican.com/article/mail-sorting-machines-are-crucial-for-the-u-s-postal-service/.

13. O'Donovan, Caroline. "The US Postal Service Said It Can't Track 300,000 Ballots Sent In The Mail, But That Doesn't Mean They're Lost." *BuzzFeed News*, 5 Nov. 2020, https://www.buzzfeednews.com/article/carolineodonovan/the-us-postal-service-said-it-cant-track-300000-ballots.

14. McCurdy, Jonna. "Postal Service Refuses Judge's Order to Quickly Sweep Facilities for Ballots." *UPI*, 3 Nov. 2020, https://www.upi.com/Top_News/US/2020/11/03/Postal-Service-refuses-judges-order-to-quickly-sweep-facilities-for-ballots/3791604430679/.

15. Clark, Dartunorro. "Fauci Calls Amy Coney Barrett Ceremony in Rose Garden 'Superspreader Event.'" *NBC News*, 9 Oct. 2020, https://www.nbcnews.com/politics/white-house/fauci-calls-amy-coney-barrett-ceremony-rose-garden-superspreader-event-n1242781.

16. Mandavilli, Apoorva. "White House Is Not Tracing Contacts for 'Super-Spreader' Rose Garden Event." *NYTimes*, 5 Oct. 2020, https://www.nytimes.com/2020/10/05/health/contact-tracing-white-house.html.

17. Bowden, Ebony "Swing State GOP Lawmakers Refused Early Vote Processing, Sowing Current Chaos." *New York Post*, 5 Nov. 2020, https://nypost.com/2020/11/05/swing-state-gop-lawmakers-refused-early-vote-processing-sewing-current-chaos/.

18. Bloomberg, Mark. "Analysis | What Is the 'Big Blue Shift' Scenario in U.S. Vote Counting?" *The Washington Post*, 30 Oct. 2020, https://www.washingtonpost.com/business/what-is-the-big-blue-shift-scenario-in-us-vote-counting/2020/10/30/17614e78-1ab4-11eb-8bda-814ca56e138b_story.html.

19. Copied, JOSH. "Another Republican Election Suit Strikes Out." *POLITICO*, 6 Nov. 2020, https://www.politico.com/news/2020/11/06/republican-election-lawsuit-nevada-434822.

20. Schulte, Gabriela. "Poll: Both Democrats and Republicans Believe There Is a Possibility of Rigged Election." *The Hill*, 30 Sept. 2020, https://thehill.com/hilltv/what-americas-thinking/518987-poll-bipartisan-agreement-on-the-possibility-of-a-rigged.

21. Ngangura, Tarisai. "Trump Wants to Steal the Election by Disenfranchising Thousands of Black Voters." *Vanity Fair*, 18 Nov. 2020, https://www.vanityfair.com/news/2020/11/trump-wants-to-steal-the-election-by-disenfranchising-thousands-of-black-voters.

22. Michael Martina, Karen. "Trump's Election Power Play: Persuade Republican Legislators to Do What U.S. Voters Did Not." *Reuters*, https://www.reuters.com/article/us-usa-election-trump-strategy-idUSKBN27Z30G. Accessed 20 Nov. 2020.

23. Corasaniti, Nick. "The Times Called Officials in Every State: No Evidence of Voter Fraud." *NYTimes*, 11 Nov. 2020, https://www.nytimes.com/2020/11/10/us/politics/voting-fraud.html.

24. Finchelstein, Federico. "Perspective | What the History of Coups Tells Us about Trump's Refusal to Concede." *The Washington Post*, 16 Nov. 2020, https://www.washingtonpost.com/outlook/2020/11/16/what-history-coups-tells-us-about-trumps-

refusal-concede/.

25. Richer, Colleen. "Trump, GOP Test out Rallying Cry: Count the 'Legal' Votes." *Associated Press*, 7 Nov. 2020, https://apnews.com/article/joe-biden-donald-trump-virus-outbreak-elections-electoral-college-0b26e5caa5180ed73a5ba5ef6fa57e17.

26. South Florida Sun Sentinel | Nov 09, 2020. "DeSantis' Outrageous Suggestion to Pennsylvania Legislature to Dismiss Popular Vote | Letters to the Editor." *South Florida Sun-Sentinel*, 9 Nov. 2020, https://www.sun-sentinel.com/opinion/letters/fl-op-letters-desantis-pennsylvania-legislature-20201109-rigfaik3mbd7na4kymmyuav7qy-story.html.

27. Gardner, Amy. "Ga. Secretary of State Says Fellow Republicans Are Pressuring Him to Find Ways to Exclude Ballots." *The Washington Post*, 16 Nov. 2020, https://www.washingtonpost.com/politics/brad-raffensperger-georgia-vote/2020/11/16/6b-6cb2f4-283e-11eb-8fa2-06e7cbb145c0_story.html.

28. *Twitter*, https://twitter.com/gop/status/1329490975266398210. Accessed 20 Nov. 2020.

29. Via y Rada, Nicole. "Republicans Who Have Broken with Trump to Congratulate Biden on His Win." *NBC News*, 12 Nov. 2020, https://www.nbcnews.com/politics/2020-election/republicans-who-have-broken-trump-congratulate-biden-his-win-n1247278.

30. "These Are the Foreign Leaders Who Have Congratulated President-Elect Joe Biden—before Donald Trump Has." *Fortune*, https://fortune.com/2020/11/07/foreign-leaders-congratulate-joe-biden-donald-trump/. Accessed 16 Nov. 2020.

31. Fisk, Robert. "Which World Leaders Are yet to Congratulate Biden?" *The Independent*, 12 Nov. 2020, https://www.independent.co.uk/news/world/americas/us-election-2020/biden-china-russia-brazil-north-korea-b1721781.html.

32. Demsas, Jerusalem. "A Majority of House Republicans Voted to Reject Results from Arizona and Pennsylvania." *Vox*, 7 Jan. 2021, https://www.vox.com/2021/1/7/22218225/house-republicans-senate-electoral-college-votes-storm-capitol-election-stop-the-steal-trump-biden.

33. RICCARDI, BOB. "GOP Leaders in 4 States Quash Dubious Trump Bid on Electors." *Associated Press*, 14 Nov. 2020, https://apnews.com/article/election-2020-joe-biden-donald-trump-legislature-pennsylvania-b199b2debc87fb-b20612a48835bc0dba.

34. Gabriel, Trip. "Could State Legislatures Pick Electors to Vote for Trump? Not Likely." *NYTimes*, 15 Nov. 2020, https://www.nytimes.com/article/electors-vote.html.

35. Packer, George. "A Political Obituary for Donald Trump." *The Atlantic*, 9 Dec. 2020, https://www.theatlantic.com/magazine/archive/2021/01/the-legacy-of-donald-trump/617255/.

36. Williams, Jordan. "18 States Join Texas Case Seeking to Overturn Biden Win." *The Hill*, 10 Dec. 2020, https://thehill.com/regulation/court-battles/529614-18-states-join-texas-case-seeing-to-overturn-biden-win.; Diaz, Daniella. "READ: Brief from 126 Republicans Supporting Texas Lawsuit in Supreme Court." *CNN*, 10 Dec. 2020, https://www.cnn.com/2020/12/10/politics/read-house-republicans-texas-supreme-court/index.html.

37. Lowry, Rich. "The Only Middle Finger Available | National Review." *National Review*, 26 Oct. 2020, https://www.nationalreview.com/2020/10/the-only-middle-finger-available/.

38. Walsh, Joe. "Republicans Will Enter 2021 With Control Over Most States' Governments. Here's Why That Matters For Redistricting." *Forbes*, 6 Nov. 2020, https://www.forbes.com/sites/joewalsh/2020/11/06/republicans-will-enter-2021-with-control-over-most-states-governments-heres-why-that-matters-for-redistricting/.

39. Rakich, Nathaniel. "Republicans Won Almost Every Election Where Redistricting Was At Stake." *FiveThirtyEight*, 18 Nov. 2020, https://fivethirtyeight.com/features/republicans-won-almost-every-election-where-redistricting-was-at-stake/.

40. Skelley, Geoffrey. "Republicans Are On Track To Take Back The House In 2022." *FiveThirtyEight*, 12 Nov. 2020, https://fivethirtyeight.com/features/republicans-2020-gains-in-the-house-set-them-up-well-for-2022/.

41. Altman, Howard. "26,000 National Guard Troops Came to DC and Protected the Inauguration without Incident. Now the Drawdown Begins." *Military Times*, 21 Jan. 2021, https://www.militarytimes.com/news/your-military/2021/01/21/26000-national-guard-troops-came-to-dc-to-protect-the-inauguration-now-the-drawdown-begins/.

42. Waldman, Paul. "Opinion | Ticket-Splitting Is for Fools." *The Washington Post*, 5 Nov. 2020, https://www.washingtonpost.com/opinions/2020/11/05/ticket-splitting-is-fools/.

43. Tackett, Michael. "Message of Election 2020: Trump Lost, but Trumpism Did Not." *Associated Press*, 8 Nov. 2020, https://apnews.com/article/election-2020-joe-biden-donald-trump-elections-aff4f036b6b1d5e6559a8b6438d730c7.

44. Allen, Jonathan. "Inside Trump's All-about-That-Base 2020 Strategy." *NBC News*, 8 Apr. 2019, https://www.nbcnews.com/politics/2020-election/inside-trump-s-all-about-base-2020-strategy-n991896.

45. O'Toole, Fintan. "Democracy's Afterlife." *The New York Review of Books*, https://www.nybooks.com/articles/2020/12/03/democracys-afterlife/. Accessed 21 Nov. 2020.

46. *PredictIt*. https://www.predictit.org/markets/detail/3698/Who-will-win-the-2020-US-presidential-election. Accessed 11 Aug. 2020.

47. Fisk, Robert. "Opinion: Trump Would Have Easily Won a Second Term If It Weren't for Covid-19." *The Independent*, 7 Nov. 2020, https://www.independent.co.uk/voices/trump-us-election-coronavirus-second-term-b1667035.html.

48. "Wasted Votes: Why National Polls Won't Predict Victory in 2020 – Third Way." *Third WayThird Way*, 6 May 2020, https://www.thirdway.org/memo/wasted-votes-why-national-polls-wont-predict-victory-in-2020.

49. https://fivethirtyeight.com/features/even-though-biden-won-republicans-enjoyed-the-largest-electoral-college-edge-in-70-years-will-that-last/

50. Brownstein, Ronald. "Why Republicans Still Can't Quit Trump." *The Atlantic*, 11 June 2020, https://www.theatlantic.com/politics/archive/2020/06/republicans-2024-nominee-will-be-trump-acolyte/612925/.

51. Phillips, Amber. "Analysis | Even If Trump Loses, the Takeaway for Some Top Republicans Is That Embracing Him Worked." *The Washington Post*, 5 Nov. 2020, https://www.washingtonpost.com/politics/2020/11/05/even-if-trump-loses-takeaway-some-top-republicans-is-that-embracing-him-worked/.

52. Lopez, German. "Survey: White Evangelicals Think Christians Face More Discrimination than Muslims." *Vox*, 10 Mar. 2017, https://www.vox.com/identities/2017/3/10/14881446/prri-survey-muslims-christians-discrimination.

53. Allen, Jonathan. "Tea Party Republicans Want to Fire John Boehner." *Vox*, 9 Sept. 2015, https://www.vox.com/2015/9/9/9288373/john-boehner-coup-meadows.

54. Fisk, Robert. "Republicans Are Congratulating Biden in Secret to Avoid Angering Trump." *The Independent*, 10 Nov. 2020, https://www.independent.co.uk/news/world/americas/us-election-2020/republicans-biden-trump-concede-b1720485.html.

55. Rosenberg, Matthew. "A QAnon Supporter Is Headed to Congress." *NYTimes*, 6 Nov. 2020, https://www.nytimes.com/2020/11/03/us/politics/qanon-candidates-marjorie-taylor-greene.html.

56. Eliza Relman, Dave. "How the GOP Learned to Love QAnon." *Business Insider*, 16 Oct. 2020, https://www.businessinsider.com/how-qanon-infiltrated-the-gop-2020-10.

57. Jones, Jeffrey. "U.S. Party Preferences Have Swung Sharply Toward Democrats." *Gallup*, 16 July 2020, https://news.gallup.com/poll/315734/party-preferences-swung-sharply-toward-democrats.aspx.

58. Moritz-Rabson, Daniel. "Ex-RNC Chair Michael Steele Blasts the GOP for Promoting Racism, Misogyny and Bad Behavior." *Newsweek*, 6 Nov. 2018, https://www.newsweek.com/former-rnc-chair-michael-steele-blasts-gop-1203028.

59. Bacon, Perry. "The Republican Party Has Changed Dramatically Since George H.W. Bush Ran It." *FiveThirtyEight*, 1 Dec. 2018, https://fivethirtyeight.com/features/the-republican-party-has-changed-dramatically-since-george-h-w-bush-ran-it/.

60. Durkee, Alison. "The GOP Won't Bother to Write a New Platform for 2020." *Vanity Fair*, 21 July 2016, https://www.vanityfair.com/news/2020/06/republican-party-keeping-2016-platform-2020.

61. Gallup. "Presidential Approval Ratings -- Donald Trump." *Gallup*, 16 Nov. 2016, https://news.gallup.com/poll/203198/presidential-approval-ratings-donald-trump.aspx.

62. Washington Post Opinion. "Opinion | Trump Looks down and out. But the 2024 GOP Field Is Forming." *The Washington Post*, 26 June 2020, https://www.washingtonpost.com/opinions/2020/06/26/trump-looks-down-out-2024-gop-field-is-forming/.

63. Hasan, Mehdi. "Sen. Josh Hawley Is Cast as a GOP Leader After Trump. But Like Trump, He's a Faux-Populist." *The Intercept*, 8 Nov. 2020, https://theintercept.com/2020/04/29/josh-hawley-republican-trump/.

64. McCarthy, Tom. "'His Hatred Is Infectious': Tucker Carlson, Trump's Heir Apparent and 2024 Candidate?" *The Guardian*, 12 July 2020, http://www.theguardian.com/media/2020/jul/12/tucker-carlson-trump-fox-news-republicans.

65. Impelli, Matthew. "Lincoln Project Founder Says *Fox News'* Tucker Carlson Is Frontrunner for 2024 GOP Nomination." *Newsweek*, 7 Nov. 2020, https://www.newsweek.com/lincoln-project-founder-says-fox-news-tucker-carlson-frontrunner-2024-gop-nomination-1545677.

66. Cotton, Tom. "Opinion | Tom Cotton: Send In the Troops." *NYTimes*, 3 June 2020, https://www.nytimes.com/2020/06/03/opinion/tom-cotton-protests-military.html.

67. Lee, Courtney. "Trump Considering a Move to Invoke Insurrection Act." *CNBC*, 1 June 2020, https://www.cnbc.com/2020/06/01/trump-considering-a-move-to-invoke-insurrection-act.html.

68. Doubek, James. "Federal Officers Use Unmarked Vehicles To Grab People In Port-

land, DHS Confirms." *Oregon Public Broadcasting*, 17 July 2020, https://www.npr.org/2020/07/17/892277592/federal-officers-use-unmarked-vehicles-to-grab-protesters-in-portland.

69. Phillips, Amber. "Analysis | Why Josh Hawley Is atop the List of GOP Lawmakers Getting Backlash over the Capitol Riots." *The Washington Post*, 11 Jan. 2021, https://www.washingtonpost.com/politics/2021/01/11/why-josh-hawley-is-top-list-gop-lawmakers-getting-backlash-over-capitol-riots/.

70. *Twitter*, https://twitter.com/gelliottmorris/status/1325146467938361345. Accessed 11 Nov. 2020.

71. "Text - H.R.1 - 116th Congress (2019-2020): For the People Act of 2019." *Congress.Gov*, 14 Mar. 2019, https://www.congress.gov/bill/116th-congress/house-bill/1/text.

72. "H.R.4 - 116th Congress (2019-2020): Voting Rights Advancement Act of 2019." *Congress.Gov*, 27 July 2020, https://www.congress.gov/bill/116th-congress/house-bill/4.

73. "Text - H.R.8363 - 116th Congress (2019-2020): Protecting Our Democracy Act." *Congress.Gov*, 23 Sept. 2020, https://www.congress.gov/bill/116th-congress/house-bill/8363/text.

74. "Text - H.R.2660 - 116th Congress (2019-2020): Election Security Act of 2019." *Congress.Gov*, 28 June 2019, https://www.congress.gov/bill/116th-congress/house-bill/2660/text. 72. Knutson, Jacob. "Where the 2020 Candidates Stand on Abolishing the Filibuster." Axios, 3 Nov. 2019, https://www.axios.com/filibuster-where-2020-candidates-stand-919c0b5b-16c0-4081-880e-abd9e4976e34.html.

75. Everett, Burgess. "Democrats Rebuff McConnell's Filibuster Demands." *POLITICO*, 21 Jan. 2021, https://www.politico.com/news/2021/01/21/democrats-mcconnell-filibuster-460967.

76. Jacobs, Shayna. "Acting U.S. Attorney in New York Expected to Advance Politically Sensitive Cases, Safeguard Office's Independence, Colleagues Say." *The Washington Post*, 22 June 2020, https://www.washingtonpost.com/national-security/audrey-strauss-us-attorney-new-york-geoffrey-berman-william-barr/2020/06/21/21f7d-7ba-b3fa-11ea-a8da-693df3d7674a_story.html.

77. Pete Williams, Tom. "'I Have Not Resigned': Manhattan U.S. Attorney Geoffrey Berman Fires Back at Barr, Who Says He's Leaving." *NBC News*, 20 June 2020, https://www.nbcnews.com/politics/justice-department/manhattan-u-s-attorney-geoffrey-berman-who-investigated-trump-associates-n1231628.

78. Mulraney, Frances. "Trump Insists He DIDN'T Fire Top U.S. Attorney in Manhattan." *Daily Mail*, 20 June 2020, https://www.dailymail.co.uk/news/article-8443311/Trump-FIRES-embattled-federal-prosecutor-Manhattan-Geoffrey-Berman.html.

79. *Twitter*, https://twitter.com/davidfrum/status/1274436572935487489. Accessed 8 Nov. 2020.

80. Merle, Renae. "Trump's Pick to Run Manhattan U.S. Attorney's Office Defended Prominent Wall Street Firms for Years." *The Washington Post*, 20 June 2020, https://www.washingtonpost.com/business/2020/06/20/trumps-pick-run-manhattan-us-attorneys-office-defended-prominent-wall-street-firms-years/.

81. Jacobs, Shayna. "Acting U.S. Attorney in New York Expected to Advance Politically Sensitive Cases, Safeguard Office's Independence, Colleagues Say." *The Washington Post*, 22 June 2020, https://www.washingtonpost.com/national-security/audrey-

strauss-us-attorney-new-york-geoffrey-berman-william-barr/2020/06/21/21f7d-7ba-b3fa-11ea-a8da-693df3d7674a_story.html.

82. Thompson, Derek. "Do Trump's Taxes Show He's a Failure, a Cheat, or a Criminal?" *The Atlantic*, 5 Oct. 2020, https://www.theatlantic.com/ideas/archive/2020/10/three-interpretations-of-trumps-tax-records/616570/.

83. Fernandez, Marisa. "All the Trump Associates Convicted or Sentenced in the Mueller Investigation." *Axios*, 15 Nov. 2019, https://www.axios.com/trump-associates-convicted-mueller-investigations-206295a1-5abc-4573-be25-4da19d9adcc9.html.

84. Mcgraw, Meridith. "Trump Asked China for Help Getting Reelected, Bolton Book Claims." *POLITICO*, 17 June 2020, https://www.politico.com/news/2020/06/17/john-bolton-book-trump-china-326563.

85. Mason, Jeff. "'Lock Her Up!' But No 'Send Her Back!' Chant at Trump Rally in Ohio." *Reuters*, https://www.reuters.com/article/us-usa-trump-idUSKCN1US02V. Accessed 11 Aug. 2020.

86. Pierson, Jacob. "The Republican 'Lock Her up!' Chants Were Disturbing. They Were Also Inevitable." *The Washington Post*, 22 July 2016, https://www.washingtonpost.com/posteverything/wp/2016/07/22/the-republican-lock-her-up-chants-were-disturbing-they-were-also-inevitable/.

87. Siegel, Paul. "The Projector in Chief." *Psychology Today*, 29 July 2018, https://www.psychologytoday.com/blog/freud-lives/201807/the-projector-in-chief.

88. Eric Bradner, Pamela. "FBI Clears Clinton -- Again." *CNN*, 6 Nov. 2016, https://www.cnn.com/2016/11/06/politics/comey-tells-congress-fbi-has-not-changed-conclusions/index.html.

89. https://www.justice.gov/file/1071991/download. Accessed 8 Nov. 2020.

90. Macias, Amanda. "Trump Accuses Barr of Double Standard for Saying It's Unlikely DOJ Will Prosecute Obama, Biden." *CNBC*, 18 May 2020, https://www.cnbc.com/2020/05/18/obama-biden-criminal-investigation-unlikely-attorney-general-barr-says.html.

91. RoyalScribe Community Wednesday January 11, 2017. "Comparing Presidential Administrations by Arrests and Convictions: A Warning for Trump Appointees." *Daily Kos*, 11 Jan. 2017, https://www.dailykos.com/story/2017/1/11/1619079/-Comparing-Presidential-Administrations-by-Arrests-and-Convictions-A-Warning-for-Trump-Appointees.

92. Whalen, Thomas. "From Jimmy Carter to Donald Trump in Four Short Decades." *The Conversation*, 10 Sept. 2015, http://theconversation.com/from-jimmy-carter-to-donald-trump-in-four-short-decades-46379.

93. Ibid.

94. Barrett, Devlin. "Notes Made by FBI Director Comey Say Trump Pressured Him to End Flynn Probe." *The Washington Post*, 16 May 2017, https://www.washingtonpost.com/world/national-security/notes-made-by-former-fbi-director-comey-say-trump-pressured-him-to-end-flynn-probe/2017/05/16/52351a38-3a80-11e7-9e48-c4f199710b69_story.html.

95. Fahrenthold, David. "Saudi-Funded Lobbyist Paid for 500 Rooms at Trump's Hotel after 2016 Election." *The Washington Post*, 5 Dec. 2018, https://www.washingtonpost.com/politics/saudi-funded-lobbyist-paid-for-500-rooms-at-trumps-hotel-after-2016-election/2018/12/05/29603a64-f417-11e8-bc79-68604ed88993_story.html.

96. Helmore, Edward. "Ivanka Trump Won China Trademarks Days before Her Father's Reversal on ZTE." *The Guardian*, 28 May 2018, http://www.theguardian.com/us-news/2018/may/28/ivanka-trump-won-china-trademarks-donald-trump-zte-reversal.

97. Gangitano, Alex. "281 Lobbyists Have Worked in Trump Administration: Report." *The Hill*, 15 Oct. 2019, https://thehill.com/business-a-lobbying/465865-281-lobbyists-have-worked-in-trump-administration-report.

98. 24, September. "President Trump's 3,400 Conflicts of Interest - CREW | Citizens for Responsibility and Ethics in Washington." *CREW | Citizens for Responsibility and Ethics in Washington*, 24 Sept. 2020, https://www.citizensforethics.org/reports-investigations/crew-reports/president-trumps-3400-conflicts-of-interest/.

99. Gersen, Jeannie. "Can the Constitution Reach Trump's Corruption?" *The New Yorker*, https://www.newyorker.com/news/our-columnists/can-the-constitution-reach-donald-trumps-corruption-emoluments. Accessed 11 Aug. 2020.

100. Malka, A., Lelkes, Y., Bakker, B., & Spivack, E. (2020). Who Is Open to Authoritarian Governance within Western Democracies? *Perspectives on Politics*, 1-20. doi:10.1017/S1537592720002091

101. Taschka, Sylvia. "From Nazism to Democracy: Lessons from Germany." *YES! Magazine*, 15 Jan. 2021, https://www.yesmagazine.org/democracy/2021/01/15/capitol-insurrection-nazi-germany.

102. Heer, Jeet. "Is Trump Authoritarian or Incompetent? Yes." *The New Republic*, 3 May 2017, https://newrepublic.com/article/142468/trump-authoritarian-incompetent-yes.

103. Drew, K. (2020, January 15). World's Trust in the U.S. Has Plummeted Under Trump's Leadership. Retrieved November 08, 2020, from https://www.usnews.com/news/best-countries/articles/2020-01-15/us-trustworthiness-rating-dives-in-2020-best-countries-report

104. Trump's agenda was wildly unpopular his first two years, then he lost the House. Obama's was popular, but Democrats never controlled the House and Senate in his second term.

105. Seligman, Lara. "White House Fires Pentagon Advisory Board Members, Installs Loyalists." *POLITICO*, 4 Dec. 2020, https://www.politico.com/news/2020/12/04/pentagon-fires-business-advisory-board-members-442892.

106. Nicole Gaouette, Kylie. "Trump Team Looks to Box in Biden on Foreign Policy by Lighting Too Many Fires to Put Out." *CNN*, 18 Nov. 2020, https://www.cnn.com/2020/11/17/politics/trump-biden-natsec-transition-fires/index.html.

107. Waldman, Paul. "Opinion | Republicans Have Declared War on Democracy Itself." *The Washington Post*, 10 Nov. 2020, https://www.washingtonpost.com/opinions/2020/11/10/republicans-have-declared-war-democracy-itself/.

108. "Tracking Voter Trust in the American Electoral System." *Morning Consult*, https://morningconsult.com/form/tracking-voter-trust-in-elections/. Accessed 16 Nov. 2020.

109. *RealClearPolitics - Election 2020 - General Election: Trump vs. Harris.* https://www.realclearpolitics.com/epolls/2020/president/us/general_election_trump_vs_harris-6252.html. Accessed 11 Sept. 2020.

110. Protess, Ben. "The War on Coronavirus Comes to Trump Properties." *NYTimes*, 23 Sept. 2020, https://www.nytimes.com/2020/03/20/business/trump-business-

es-coronavirus.html.

111. Alexander, Dan. "Donald Trump Has At Least $1 Billion In Debt, More Than Twice The Amount He Suggested." *Forbes*, 16 Oct. 2020, https://www.forbes.com/sites/danalexander/2020/10/16/donald-trump-has-at-least-1-billion-in-debt-more-than-twice-the-amount-he-suggested/.

112. Porter, Tom. "Deutsche Bank Plans to Cut Ties with Trump after the Election and Could Seize His Assets If He Can't Pay Back His Debts, Reuters Reports." *Business Insider*, 3 Nov. 2020, https://www.businessinsider.com/deutsche-bank-trump-ties-debts-after-election-reuters-2020-11.

113. Shehata, Samer. "The Real Reason Trump Is Terrified of Losing the Presidency: Fear of Prosecution | Samer S Shehata." *The Guardian*, 3 Nov. 2020, http://www.theguardian.com/commentisfree/2020/nov/03/donald-trump-fear-lose-election-prosecution.

114. Seddiq, Oma. "Trump Floats Idea of His Own News Network to Counter CNN." *POLITICO*, 3 Oct. 2019, https://www.politico.com/news/2019/10/03/trump-proposes-creating-own-news-network-025988.

115. Stelter, Brian. "'Hannity Has Said to Me More Than Once, "He's Crazy"': *Fox News* Staffers Feel Trapped in the Trump Cult." *Vanity Fair*, 20 Aug. 2020, https://www.vanityfair.com/news/2020/08/sean-hannity-fox-news-staffers-feel-trapped-in-trump-cult.

116. Rucker, Philip. "Trump Insists He'll Win, but Aides Say He Has No Real Plan to Overturn Results and Talks of 2024 Run." *The Washington Post*, 12 Nov. 2020, https://www.washingtonpost.com/politics/trump-election-results-strategy/2020/11/11/a32e2cba-244a-11eb-952e-0c475972cfc0_story.html.

117. Swan, Jonathan. "Sources: Trump Privately Discussing 2024 Run." *Axios*, 9 Nov. 2020, https://www.axios.com/trump-2024-presidential-run-4add0d86-02be-41f9-b2fd-5aaca96ce6ce.html.

118. Isenstadt, Alex. "4 More Years: Trump Freezes 2024 Presidential Field." *POLITICO*, 16 Nov. 2020, https://www.politico.com/news/2020/11/16/trump-2024-presidential-field-436864.

119. Peters, Jeremy. "Trump Lost the Race. But Republicans Know It's Still His Party." *NYTimes*, 9 Nov. 2020, https://www.nytimes.com/2020/11/09/us/politics/republican-party-trump.html.

120. Preliminary Data from Public Discourse and Ethics Survey (PDES) Wave 7. Fielded by Joshua Grubbs and run by YouGov. Used with permission.

121. McKee, Guian. "What 2020 Election Results Tell Us About America's Growing Urban-Rural Divide." *UVA Today*, 5 Nov. 2020, https://news.virginia.edu/content/what-2020-election-results-tell-us-about-americas-growing-urban-rural-divide.

122. "Commentary: Why Trump Made Gains among Minority Men against Biden." *Fortune*, https://fortune.com/2020/11/06/trump-support-black-latino-men-rappers/. Accessed 11 Oct. 2020.

123. Weaver, C., Fedor, L., & Manson, K., "Joe Biden's socialism problem with Latinos," *Financial Times*, https://www.ft.com/content/f5fd8720-3ecb-4f57-96f8-28029915dce7. Accessed 11 Oct. 2020.

124. "Tracking Voter Trust in the American Electoral System." *Morning Consult*, https://morningconsult.com/form/tracking-voter-trust-in-elections/. Accessed 11 Oct. 2020.

125. Ellison, Sarah. "The Long Love Affair between *Fox News* and Trump May Be over. Here's How It All Soured Last Week." *The Washington Post*, 9 Nov. 2020, https://www.washingtonpost.com/lifestyle/the-long-love-affair-between-fox-news-and-trump-may-be-over-heres-how-it-ended-last-week/2020/11/09/f4dddb5e-2095-11eb-90dd-abd0f7086a91_story.html.

126. Izadi, Elahe. "*Fox News* Cuts Away from Kayleigh McEnany News Conference after She Alleges Vote Fraud with No Evidence." *The Washington Post*, 9 Nov. 2020, https://www.washingtonpost.com/media/2020/11/09/fox-news-kayleigh-mcenany-cut-away-fraud/.

127. Fisk, Robert. "Hot Mic Catches *Fox News* Anchor Dismay at Trump Election Fraud Claims." *The Independent*, 9 Nov. 2020, https://www.independent.co.uk/news/world/americas/us-election-2020/us-election-fraud-fox-news-sandra-smith-b1719838.html.

128. News, Fox. "*Fox News* Created a Monster. And Now That Monster Wants Revenge." *The Daily Beast*, 10 Nov. 2020, https://www.thedailybeast.com/fox-news-created-a-monster-and-now-that-trump-worshipping-monster-wants-revenge.

129. Battaglio, Stephen. "Facing Ratings Pressure, *Fox News* Replaces News with Opinion at 7 p.M." *Los Angeles Times*, 11 Jan. 2021, https://www.latimes.com/entertainment-arts/business/story/2021-01-11/fox-news-changes-daytime-schedule-martha-maccallum-afternoon.

130. Keeley, Matt. "Pro-Trump 'Million MAGA March' Protesters Chant '*Fox News* Sucks' after Network Calls Election for Biden." *Newsweek*, 15 Nov. 2020, https://www.newsweek.com/pro-trump-million-maga-march-protesters-chant-fox-news-sucks-after-network-calls-election-biden-1547527.

131. Fandos, Nicholas. "Republicans Back Trump's Refusal to Concede, Declining to Recognize Biden." *NYTimes*, 10 Nov. 2020, https://www.nytimes.com/2020/11/09/us/politics/republicans-trump-concede-2020-election.html.

132. Prokop, Andrew. "The Many Obstacles to the 'GOP State Legislatures Steal the Election for Trump' Scenario." *Vox*, 13 Nov. 2020, https://www.vox.com/21562815/biden-trump-fraud-state-legislatures-electors.

133. Treene, Alayna. "Rubio Says the GOP Needs to Reset after 2020." *Axios*, 11 Nov. 2020, https://www.axios.com/rubio-gop-reset-trump-872340a7-4c75-4c2b-9261-9612c590ee14.html.

134. "The Republican Party After Trump." *Stand with the Facts Site Menu Donate Stand with the Facts*, 16 Jan. 2021, https://www.nprillinois.org/post/republican-party-after-trump.

135. Yokley, Eli. "Polling Shows Why Trump Will Retain His Bully Pulpit With the GOP Base Even After He Leaves Office - Morning Consult." *Morning Consult*, 24 Nov. 2020, https://morningconsult.com/2020/11/24/trump-gop-congress-2024-polling/.

136. Liptak, Adam. "In Unusually Political Speech, Alito Says Liberals Pose Threat to Liberties." *NYTimes*, 13 Nov. 2020, https://www.nytimes.com/2020/11/13/us/samuel-alito-religious-liberty-free-speech.html.

137. Ceballos, Ana. "How DeSantis Wants to Crack down on Protests: Expand 'Stand Your Ground.'" *Tampa Bay Times*, https://www.tampabay.com/news/florida-politics/2020/11/10/how-desantis-wants-to-crack-down-on-protests-expand-stand-your-ground/. Accessed 14 Nov. 2020.

138. Malka, Ariel & Lelkes, Yphtach & Bakker, Bert & Spivack, Eliyahu. (2020). Who is Open to Authoritarian Governance within Western Democracies?. 10.31234/osf.io/m8ze5.

139. White, Jeremy. "The Shocking Paper Predicting the End of Democracy." *POLITICO Magazine*, 8 Sept. 2019, https://politi.co/2zZ90hi.

140. Pepinsky, Thomas. "Life in Authoritarian States Is Mostly Boring and Tolerable." *Vox*, 9 Jan. 2017, https://www.vox.com/the-big-idea/2017/1/9/14207302/authoritarian-states-boring-tolerable-fascism-trump.

141. Levitsky, S., Way, L. A. (2013). *Competitive authoritarianism: Hybrid regimes after the Cold War*. Cambridge: Cambridge University Press.

142. Gessen, Masha. "Autocracy: Rules for Survival." *The New York Review of Books*,https://www.nybooks.com/daily/2016/11/10/trump-election-autocracy-rules-for-survival/. Accessed 11 Aug. 2020.

143. McDonald, Andrew. "Support for Scottish Independence at Highest Ever Level: Poll." *POLITICO*, 14 Oct. 2020, https://www.politico.eu/article/support-for-scotland-independence-uk-at-highest-ever-level-poll/.

144. Tannehill, Brynn. "Will Trump 2020 Break Apart the Nation? | Dame Magazine." *Dame Magazine*, 20 Apr. 2020, https://www.damemagazine.com/2020/04/20/will-trump-2020-break-apart-the-nation/.

145. Brownstein, Ronald. "Why the 2020s Could Be as Dangerous as the 1850s." *The Atlantic*, 30 Oct. 2020, https://www.theatlantic.com/politics/archive/2020/10/biden-2020-trump-election/616912/.

146. Millhiser, Ian. "The Danger the Supreme Court Poses to Democracy, in Just Two Numbers." *Vox*, 27 Oct. 2020, https://www.vox.com/2020/10/26/21534358/supreme-court-amy-coney-barrett-constitution-anti-democratic-electoral-college-senate.

Index

BOOKS PUBLISHED BY TRANSGRESS PRESS

Vicissitudes: Love Transforms
Kim Green

Tomorrow, or Forever
And Other Stories
Jack Kaulfus

Swimming Upstream: A Novel
Jacob Anderson-Minshall

Lou Sullivan
Daring To Be A Man Among Men
Brice D. Smith

Giving It Raw: Nearly 30 Years with AIDS
Francisco Ibañez-Carrasco

Life Beyond My Body
Transgender Journey to Manhood in China
Lei Ming

Below the Belt: Genital Talk by Men of Trans Experience
Edited by Trystan Theosophus cotton

Trunky (Transgender Junky)
A Memoir of Institutionalization and Southern Hospitality
Sam Peterson

Queer Rock Love: A Family Memoir
Paige Schilt

Love Always
Partners of Trans People on Intimacy, Challenge, and Resilience
Edited by Jordon Johnson and Becky Garrison

Now What?
A Handbook for Families with Transgender Children
Rex Butt

375

Trans Homo…Gasp! Gay FTM and Cis Men on Sex and Love
Edited by Avi Ben-Zeev and Pete Bailey

New Girl Blues…or Pinks
Mary Degroat Ross

Letters for My Sisters: Transitional Wisdom in Retrospect
Edited by Andrea James and Deanne Thornton

Manning Up: Transsexual Men on
Finding Brotherhood, Family and Themselves
Edited by Zander Keig and Mitch Kellaway

Hung Jury: Testimonies of Genital Surgery by Transsexual Men
Edited by Trystan Theosophus Cotten

Words of Fire!
Women Loving Women in Latin America
Antonia Amprino

The Wanderings of Chela Coatlicue
On Tour with Los Huerfanos
Ananda Esteva

Printed in Great Britain
by Amazon

21330436R00215